D0032468

Uncle John's

UNSTOPPABLE BATHROOM READER

By the Bathroom Readers' Institute

Bathroom Readers' Press
Ashland, Oregon

OUR "REGULAR" READERS RAVE!

"Thank you for helping me get an 'A' in my college speech class. We had to do an impromptu tribute speech and I chose *Uncle John's Bathroom Reader* for my subject. I actually made my professor laugh all through the speech."

—*CeCe R.*

"Several years ago, for Father's Day, we sent my Dad a gift certificate to a book store. He purchased a *Bathroom Reader*. We continued to send gift certificates; he continued to buy *Bathroom Readers*. When he passed away last year, my mom gave me his collection. He had 7. Since then, I've started buying more volumes. My son, Mitchell, even bought *Uncle John's Bathroom Reader For Kids Only* with his own money. Now three generations of my family enjoy your books."

—*Mark A.*

"I received an e-mail from your staff welcoming me to the BRI family. It said if I wanted to be flushed, I should tell you. Never—and I say never—flush me. Thanks to your books I keep my friends amazed with the info I know. I give you credit for teaching me more stuff then I learned in school."

—*Brendan*

"It's perfect for any occasion. When we needed a house warming gift, we got an *Uncle John's*. When we needed Christmas presents, we gave *Uncle John's*. We were invited to a birthday party for three men and needed gifts for all three. Not knowing what they liked or needed, we bought three *Bathroom Readers*! The response?... They can't stop talking about it. Thank you."

—*John J.*

"You're the best thing to happen to the reading room since indoor plumbing and store-bought tissue (them cornhusks can get mighty rough you know!) Keep up the good work and Go with the Flow!"

—*Rick B.*

UNCLE JOHN'S UNSTOPPABLE
BATHROOM READER®

For information, write
The Bathroom Readers' Institute,
P.O. Box 1117, Ashland, OR 97520
www.bathroomreader.com
541-488-4642

Cover design by Michael Brunsfeld,
San Rafael, CA (*brunsfeldo@comcast.net*)
BRI "technician" on back cover: Larry Kelp

Uncle John's
Unstoppable Bathroom Reader®
by The Bathroom Readers' Institute

ISBN: 1-59223-116-0

Printed in the United States of America

First Printing, October 2003
10 9 8 7 6 5 4 3 2

* * * * *

"What's the Number for 911 Again?," © 2001 by Leland H. Gregory. Visit
www.realwacky.com for actual, stupid 911 calls as well as to purchase his
audio CD, *Wacky 911*, and his previous book, *What's the Number for 911?*
Used by permission from the author and Andrews McMeel Publishing,
4520 Main St., Kansas City, MO 64111.

THANK YOU!

The Bathroom Readers' Institute sincerely thanks the people whose advice and assistance made this book possible.

Gordon Javna
John Dollison
Jay Newman
Jennifer
Jeff Altemus
Julia Papps
Thom Little
Jahnna Beecham
Sharilyn Hovind
Michael Brunsfeld
Brian Henry
Angela Kern
Lori Larson
Sam Javna
Sydney Stanley
Gideon Javna
Jim McCluskey
Alan Reder
Janet Spencer
Malcolm Hillgartner
Maggie McLaughlin
Amanda Wilson

Allen Orso
Mike Nicita
Georgine Liedell
JoAnn Padgett
Dylan Drake
Paul Stanley
Jenny Baldwin
Barb Porshe
Paula Leith
Chris Olsen
Raingirl Thering
Joyce Slayton
Steve Pitt
Lyne Brennanski
Jolly Jeff Cheek
Bruce Carlson
David Harp
Nate Hendley
Scarab Media
John Javna
Marley & Catie Pratt
Thomas Crapper

*   *   *

THE BRI HONOR ROLL
(Our most diligent contributors)

Steve Sutherland • Jim de Graff • Aaron Allermann • Nate Nathanson
Shari Mikaelsson • Richard Cranston II • Beth Scribble • Dean Bliss
David Crumpler • Max L. Israel • Sara Cole • Artemio Visaya
Richard Staples • *And a special thanks to* Eddie Deezen

CONTENTS

Because the BRI understands your reading needs, we've divided the contents by length as well as subject.

Short—a quick read

Medium—2 to 3 pages

Long—for those extended visits, when something a little more involved is required

*Extended—for those leg-numbing experiences

*   *   *

"No, I don't understand my husband's theory of relativity,
but I know my husband and I know he can be trusted."
—**Elsa Einstein**

INTRODUCTION

When we were kids, the end of summer meant the start of school, and that got us nervous and excited. For us here at the Bathroom Readers' Institute, the end of summer now means "Uh-oh! It's time to get the next *Bathroom Reader* into bookstores!" And you know what? We still get nervous and excited.

This year we decided to try something different. Instead of spending months and months on writing and researching as usual, we went to see Dr. Flipseater, the Mad Inventor. And he built us a contraption called the "Information Grinder."

Here's how it works: We shovel mountains of books, newspapers, and magazines into one end of the Information Grinder, flip the switch, and after a few minutes of buzzing and whirring, guess what comes out of the other end—this book.

...Well, that's not exactly how it happens. The *Bathroom Reader* is a result a lot of hard work by some wonderfully dedicated people, like John D., Jay, Julia, Jahnna, Jeff, Jennifer, Joyce, Jim—plus a few whose names don't begin with "J" (like Thom, Sharilyn, Malcolm, Maggie, Bryan, and Angie).

And the product, we hope, is a great book that will tickle you, our wonderfully dedicated readers.

It's hard for us to believe that we've been creating *Bathroom Readers* for *15 years*...but we have. The other day, when I was leaving a restaurant, the owner stopped me and pointed to my *Uncle John's Bathroom Reader* cap (available at *www.bathroomreader.com*...I'd mention the name of the restaurant, too—it might be good for a free meal—but I can't remember it).

"Hey, great hat," he said. I thanked him and told him about *www.bathroomreader.com*, because you can find some great hats there (black or tan).

Anyway, he told me that he had several *Bathroom Readers* and that he'd been reading them for years. Suddenly I felt good all over because it reminded me of why we keep making these books: we love doing it, and our readers love reading them. How do we know? You keep telling us.

> Dear BRI,
>
> I received my first *Bathroom Reader* as a graduation gift from college. I now have seven books (a pittance of your offering). You make bathroom time, brain time. Thanks.
>
> —Kara

Thanks to you, dear readers, we are—like the title says— *UNSTOPPABLE.*

A few notes:

• Readers looking for our Extended Sitting Section may turn to the back of the book, get upset that they can't find it and assume we omitted it. Not so. We only omitted the divider page, figuring, why waste a page? We'd rather give you more bathroom reading.

• We've included a bunch of articles about Canada. They're spread over the entire book, so you have to look for them...but they're worth it.

• For years we've wanted to do an article about the classic Beatles album *Sgt. Peppers Lonely Hearts Club Band.* But for some reason, we've never gotten around to it...until now. At the last minute one of our writers, Alan Reder, sent us his finished article, and we think it's worthy of the word "classic." We hope you like it, too.

• Check out our "BRI Honor Roll" on the Thank You page. It's our way of recognizing some loyal fans who've sent us great ideas. Thanks, team!

• The *Bathroom Reader* family keeps growing—there are more writers and more members of the Bathroom Readers' Institute than ever before. Sadly, though, we lost one member of our family this year: our good friend Marley J. Pratt, who taught us as no one else could to Go with the Flow. We miss you, Marley.

Well, that's it from Ashland, Oregon...until next year.

And as always,

Go with the Flow!

Uncle John and the BRI staff

YOU'RE MY INSPIRATION

*It's always interesting to find out where the architects of
pop culture get their ideas. These may surprise you.*

PRINCESS LEIA'S HAIR: According to *Star Wars* creator
George Lucas, "I was trying to create something different, so
I went with a kind of Southwestern Pancho Villa woman
look. The buns are basically from turn-of-the-century Mexico."

SCOOBY-DOO: Modeled after Bob Hope's movie persona, "in
which he played the coward for laughs before ending up the reluc-
tant hero."

"DOUBLE VISION": The title of Foreigner's 1978 hit song
came from a hockey injury. Frontman Lou Gramm was at a New
York Rangers game when the goalie was knocked in the head with
a stick. After the dazed player was taken off the ice, the arena
announcer reported that he was "suffering double vision."

ELLIE ARROWAY: The protagonist in Carl Sagan's novel *Contact* (played by Jodie Foster in the movie) was based on a real-life
SETI (Search for Extra-Terrestrial Intelligence) member Jill
Tarter, who "has logged more telescope hours in the search for
cosmic company than any other human on the planet."

CAPTAIN JACK SPARROW: Johnny Depp based his character
in *Pirates of the Caribbean* on a mix of Rolling Stones guitarist
Keith Richards and the amorous cartoon skunk, Pepe LePew.

THE EXORCIST: Both the novel and film were based on reports
of an actual exorcism performed on a 14-year-old boy in Maryland
in 1949, the last official case of exorcism in the United States.

"ME AND BOBBY MCGEE": Songwriter Kris Kristofferson got
his inspiration from a scene in Fellini's movie *La Strada*. When
Anthony Quinn realizes that Giulietta Masina is dead, "he suddenly realized he was free but he was also the loneliest son of a
bitch in the world. It showed the two sides of freedom—that freedom is just another word for nothing left to lose."

FUN WITH NAMES

We've always been fascinated by strange (real) names. Lucky for us there doesn't seem to be a shortage of them.

PEOPLE

Derek Tuba, band teacher in Winnipeg, Ontario

Milo Shocker, electrician in Oak Creek, Wisconsin

Mr. Fillin, substitute teacher in Woodside, CA

Brie Mercis, works at a cheese shop in Burlingame, CA

Cardinal Rapsong, Vatican spokesman against pop music

Drs. French & Fry, two dentists who share an office in Montgomery, AL

Dr. Chin, runs the Chin Ear, Nose & Throat Clinic in Malaysia

Mr. David Dollar, head of research, World Bank, NYC

PLACES

Pinch and **Tight,** neighboring towns in West Virginia

Pickles Gap, Arkansas

Oddville, Kentucky

Coolville, Ohio

Bowlegs, Oklahoma

Smartt, Tennessee

What Cheer, Iowa

Smut Eye, Alabama

Telephone, Texas

Bingo, Maine

BUSINESSES

Deadman Funeral Home, Manchester, TN

Gamble Insurance Agency, Central, SC

Crummy Plumbing Company, Ocean Shores, WA

STORES

A Pane in the Glass, Naples, FL

Wok-N-Roll, Chinese restaurant, Yarmouth Post, MA

The Hairtaker, Los Angeles

Great Buns, bakery, Las Vegas

Bye Bye Bifocals, optician, Dallas

Franks A Lot, restaurant, Kansas City, MO

MORE PEOPLE

Mary Rhoda Duck

Wavva White Flag

Janet Isadore Bell

Diana Brown Beard

Mary Hat Box

Eartha Quake

Dorothy May Grow

Alvin Will Pop

Very punny: Who won the 1995 Procrastinator of the Year award? Congressman Tom Delay.

LONELY PHONE BOOTH

*In the 1960s, some miners put a phone booth in the middle
of the Mojave Desert. Long after they left, the booth
remained... waiting for someone to call.*

HELLO? ANYBODY THERE?

Miles from the nearest town, the old phone booth stood at the junction of two dirt roads. Its windows were shot out; the overhead light was gone. Yet the phone lines on the endless rows of poles still popped and clicked in anticipation—just as they'd been doing for nearly 30 years. Finally, in 1997, it rang.

A guy named Deuce had read about the booth and called the number... and continued to call until a desert dweller named Lorene answered. Deuce wrote a story about his call to nowhere, posted it on his website... and the word spread through cyberspace. Someone else called. Then another person, and another—just to see if someone would answer. And quite often someone did. Only accessible by four wheel drive, the lonely phone booth soon became a destination. Travelers drove for hours just to answer the phone. One Texas man camped there for 32 days... and answered more than 500 calls.

REACH OUT AND TOUCH SOMEONE

Someone posted a call log in the booth to record where people were calling from: as close as Los Angeles and as far away as New Zealand and Kosovo. Why'd they call? Some liked the idea of two people who've never met—and probably never will—talking to each other. Just sending a call out into the Great Void and having someone answer was reward enough for most.

Unfortunately, in 2000 the National Park Service and Pacific Bell tore down the famous Mojave phone booth. Reason? It was getting too many calls. The traffic (20 to 30 visitors a day) was starting to have a negative impact on the fragile desert environment.

The old stop sign at the cattle grate still swings in the wind. And the phone lines still pop and click in anticipation. But all that's left of the loneliest phone on Earth is a ghost ring.

So if the urge strikes you to dial (760) 733-9969, be prepared to wait a very, very long time for someone to answer.

Polite tip from etiquette experts: If no one answers the phone after 6 rings, hang up.

THAT'S RICH!

Some interesting facts about gold and gemstones.

Where was the first U.S. Gold Rush? Not California—North Carolina, in 1803. (Started when a boy found a 17-pound nugget on his father's farm.) It supplied all the gold for the nation's mints until 1829.

It is estimated that only about 100,000 tons of gold have been mined during all of recorded history.

The word *garnet* comes from the Latin word for "pomegranate" (garnets were thought to resemble pomegranate seeds)

Legend says that one day Cupid cut Venus' fingernails while she was sleeping and left the clippings scattered on the ground. So that no part of Venus would ever disappear, the Fates turned them into stone. The stone: onyx, Greek for "fingernail."

The chemical formula for lapis lazuli: $(Na,Ca)8(Al,Si)12O24-(S,SO4)$. The chemical formula for diamond: C.

The name "turquoise" comes from the fact that it was first brought to Europe from the Mediterranean by Levantine traders, also known as...Turks.

The California Gold Rush yielded 125 million ounces of gold from 1850 to 1875—more than had been in the previous 350 years and worth more than $50 billion today.

From 330 B.C. to 1237 A.D., most of the world's emeralds came from "Cleopatra's Mine" in Egypt.

Organic gems:
- Amber (petrified tree sap, at least 30 million years old)
- Coral (exoskeletons of sea creatures—*coral polyps*—used as a gem since the Iron Age)
- Pearl (from oysters)
- Ivory (elephant tusks)
- Tagua nut (very hard, small blue-white nut of the tagua palm—a substitute for ivory)

Ancient Greeks named amber from the word "electron," because rubbing amber gives off static electricity.

Rarest gem: Painite, discovered in Burma. Fewer than 10 specimens exist in the world.

Gold is recycled. Result: jewelry purchased today may contain gold mined in prehistoric times.

OOPS!

Everybody enjoys reading about somebody else's blunders.
So go ahead and feel superior for a few minutes.

BUM WRAP

"Jean Baptiste de Chateaubrun (1685–1775) spent 40 years polishing and refining two plays, virtually his life's work, only to discover that his housekeeper had carelessly used the pages as wrapping paper, losing them forever."

—*The Best of the Worst*

MAJOR-LEAGUE DUST UP

"A deceased Seattle Mariners fan's last wishes went awry when the bag containing his cremated remains failed to open as a plane attempted to scatter them over Safeco Field, the Mariners' home stadium. Instead, the entire bag of ashes fell onto the closed roof of the stadium in one piece, bursting into a puff of gray smoke as it hit. A startled eyewitness called 911, and officials ordered the stadium to be evacuated.

"It took more than an hour for sheriff's deputies to trace the tail number of the plane and determine that the mysterious substance on the stadium roof was the ashes of a Mariners fan, not anthrax or some other kind of terrorist attack."

—*Seattle Times*

HARD OF EAR-ING

"A Russian criminal who tried to flee from Western Ukraine to Slovakia using another person's identity papers was unmasked when the fake ears he had used for a disguise fell off at passport control. They had been attached with cheap Russian medical glue."

—*The Fortean Times*

CALL HIM CHUCK

WATERTOWN, Conn., August 2002—"Mario Orsini, 73, faces assault charges for shooting and wounding his brother, Donato, 66, after mistaking him for a woodchuck, police said."

—*USA Today*

ALL WET

"A Philadelphia television weatherman whose dire predictions convinced countless viewers to take a snow day off work in March 2001, was inundated with hate mail and death threats after his 'Storm of the Decade' turned out to be a teapot-sized tempest. John Bolaris' heavily promoted forecasts, complete with graphics and theme music, did not envision the possibility that the storm would change course, which it did. An avalanche of angry e-mails and phone messages, which included such warnings as 'If I owned a gun, there would be one less person to worry about,' started almost immediately. Said Mr. Bolaris, 'I felt like leaving town.'"

—*The National Post*

GETTING SOME SHUT-EYE

"A Long Island woman accidentally squeezed a drop of glue in her daughter's eye, thinking she was holding a tube of prescription eye drops. Christine Giglio of Massapequa, New York, reached for the drops, a treatment for nine-year-old Nikki's pinkeye, but instead grabbed a tube of fingernail glue. When she realized what she had done, she called for emergency help. Giglio said she made the mistake because the two tubes looked very similar. Fortunately, the eye's protective mechanisms of blinking and tearing often prevents any lasting damage, said Dr. Richard Bagdonas, the attending emergency room surgeon. (Nikki made a full recovery.)"

—**Associated Press**

GOTTA KEEP 'EM SEPARATED

"Dean Sims, 26, was left unable to use the toilet after undergoing an operation at Woolwich Hospital to remove an abscess from his left buttock. The former factory worker returned home and was amazed to find that his buttocks had been taped together with surgical tape. Said Mr. Sims, 'How disgusting is that?' Sims phoned the hospital, only to be told he'd have to wait until the next day to have the bandage removed by a nurse. 'I've got to let them do it—I don't want it to get infected,' he added. 'Gangrene could set in.'

"His mum, Rita, said, 'He's in agony and getting cramps—he wants to go to the loo badly but can't.' A hospital spokesman said the bandaging was a mistake. Sims is demanding an apology."

—*News Shopper* (UK)

LET'S DO A STUDY!

If you're worried that the really important things in life aren't being researched by our scientists, keep worrying.

• Researchers at Georgetown University found that caterpillars can "shoot" their feces a distance of 40 times their body length.

• A 2002 study in Saudi Arabia concluded that women were responsible for 50% of the car accidents in the country. (Women aren't allowed to drive in Saudi Arabia.)

• In 2003 researchers at Plymouth University in England studied primate intelligence by giving macaque monkeys a computer. They reported that the monkeys attacked the machine, threw feces at it, and, contrary to their hopes, failed to produce a single word.

• Psychologists at the University of Texas conducted a study in 1996 to determine if calling children "boys" or "girls" is harmful.

• In 2001 scientists at Cambridge University studied kinetic energy, centrifugal force, and the coefficient of friction... to determine the least messy way to eat spaghetti.

• In 2002 food industry researchers reported that when children were told they couldn't have junk food, they wanted it even more. Industry spokespeople said that the study showed that children should decide for themselves how much junk food they should eat.

• Researchers at Northwestern University in Indiana used their federal grant money to study female sexuality...by paying female students to watch pornographic films ($75 per film).

• A 2001 study found that 60% of men in the Czech Republic do not buy their own underwear.

• According to a *British Medical Journal* report in 2003, Korean researchers have proven that karaoke is bad for your health.

• A 2002 study by the Department of Veterans Affairs Medical Center in Vermont found that studies are often misleading.

Q: What is the most nutritious "food" in the world? A: Blood.

COME HEAR BERTHA BELCH

What's the difference between good and evil? Maybe just a little grammar. The following are excerpts from real church bulletins.

"Ladies Bible Study will be held Thursday morning at 10:00. All are invited to lunch in the Fellowship after the B.S. is done."

"Evening Massage—6 p.m."

"The pastor would appreciate if the ladies of the congregation would lend him their electric girdles for pancake breakfast next Sunday."

"For those of you who have children and don't know it, we have a nursery downstairs."

"The pastor will preach his farewell message, after which the choir will sing 'Break Forth Into Joy.'"

"Barbara remains in the hospital and needs blood donors for more transfusions. She is also having trouble sleeping and requests tapes of Pastor Jack's sermons."

"Our youth basketball team is back in action Wednesday at 8 p.m. in the recreation hall. Come out and watch us kill Christ the King."

"Bertha Belch, a missionary from Africa, will be speaking tonight at Calvary Methodist. Come hear Bertha Belch all the way from Africa."

"The peacemaking meeting scheduled for today has been cancelled due to a conflict."

"The Lutheran Men's Group will meet at 6:00 p.m. Steak, mashed potatoes, green beans, bread, and dessert will be served for a nominal feel."

"Attend and you will hear an excellent speaker and heave a healthy lunch."

"The church will host an evening of fine dining, superb entertainment, and gracious hostility."

"This evening at 7 p.m. there will be a hymn sing in the park across from the church. Bring a blanket and come prepared to sin."

"Mrs. Johnson will be entering the hospital this week for testes."

Shortest verse in the Bible: John 11:35. ("Jesus wept.")

Q & A: ASK
THE EXPERTS

Everyone's got a question they'd like answered—basic stuff,
like "Why is the sky blue?" Here are a few questions,
with answers from the nation's top trivia experts.

CAN'T TOUCH THIS

Q: *Will you spread poison ivy if you touch the blisters?*

A: "You can't spread poison ivy (or poison oak) by touching, or even breaking, the blisters. The belief that poison ivy spreads through the bloodstream is equally false.

"So why do blisters often appear on different parts of the body days after the first signs? It probably wasn't just your skin that came in contact with the plant—it was also your clothing, shoes, gardening tools, etc. If it isn't washed off, the oil or resin from the plant can last almost indefinitely at full strength. If you were unaware you'd encountered poison ivy (it can take two to four days for the first red spots or blisters to show), the resin could have been spread to everything it touched." (From *Old Wives' Tales*, by Sue Castle)

NOW HEAR THIS

Q: *What makes our ears ring?*

A: "Sometimes, even in a quiet room, we hear noise that seems to come from inside our heads.

"Behind the eardrum is a bony chamber studded with three tiny, movable bones. These bones pick up vibrations from the eardrum. Deeper in the ear is a fluid-filled channel called the *cochlea*. Vibrations from the bones make waves in the fluid, where thousands of hair cells undulate in the sloshing fluid.

"These hair cells are crucial. Somehow, the ripples that pass through them trigger electrical impulses, which travel along the auditory nerve—the hearing nerve—to the brain. The brain translates the signals into sound.

"Hair cells can get hurt by loud noises, or by a knock on the head, impairing their ability to send electrical impulses through the hearing nerve. But some hair cells will be hurt in such a way that they

---

A group of frogs is called an *army*; a group of army officers is called a *mess*.

continuously send bursts of electricity to the hearing nerve. In effect, these hair cells are permanently turned on. When the brain receives their signals, it interprets them as sound and we hear a 'ringing,' even in a silent room." (From *How Come?*, by Kathy Wollard)

NUKE 'EM

Q: *Can the microwaves leak out of the box and cook the cook?*

A: "There is extremely little leakage from today's carefully designed ovens. Moreover, the instant the door is opened, the magnetron shuts off and the microwaves immediately disappear.

"What about the glass door? Microwaves can penetrate glass but not metal, so the glass door is covered with a perforated metal panel so you can see inside, but the microwaves can't get through because their wavelength ($4^{3}/_{4}$ inches) is simply too big to fit through the holes in the metal panel. There is no basis for the belief that it is hazardous to stand close to an operating microwave oven." (From *What Einstein Told His Cook*, by Robert L. Wolke)

POLLY WANT A FRIEND?

Q: *How do parrots talk?*

A: "Exactly why parrots can change their calls to make them sound like words is still not understood. Their ability to mimic may possibly be linked with the fact that they are highly social birds. A young parrot in captivity learns the sounds it hears around it and quickly realizes that repeating these sounds brings attention and companionship. This is perhaps a substitute for its normal social life.

"Although they are such good mimics in captivity, parrots do not imitate other sounds in the wild. There are, however, many other species that do: mynah birds and lyrebirds, for example, do mimic the sounds they hear in their everyday lives." (From *What Makes the World Go Round?*, edited by Jinny Johnson)

CAN YOU HEAR ME NOW?

Q: *Is there sound in space? If so, what's the speed of sound there?*

A: "No, there is no sound in space. That's because sound has to travel as a vibration in some material such as air or water or even stone. Since space is essentially empty, it cannot carry sound, at least not the sorts of sound that we are used to." (From *How Things Work*, by Louis A. Bloomfield)

How did the ancient Egyptians discover leavened bread? One theory...

CLASSIC PUBLICITY STUNTS

Advertising costs a lot of money. So why pay for it when you can get the press to spread the word for free? All it takes is a combination of imagination, determination, and no shame whatsoever. These guys were masters at it.

STUNTMAN: P. T. Barnum

STUNT: "That is not a real bearded lady," cried a paying customer at Barnum's Museum. "It's a bearded man wearing a dress!" The customer then had Barnum served with a subpoena and took him to court.

IT WORKED! The trial was a public spectacle as the bearded lady, her husband, and a doctor each testified as to her femininity. Meanwhile, thousands flocked to the museum to judge for themselves. After the trial it came out that Barnum had actually hired the man to sue him…solely to drum up business.

STUNTMAN: Press agent Marty Weiser

STUNT: In 1974 Weiser leased a drive-in theater in Los Angeles and invited the press to attend a movie premiere…for horses. Weiser featured a "horsepitality bar" full of "horse d'oeuvres" (popcorn buckets filled with oats). And true to his word, more than 250 horses and their riders paraded into the theater, "parked" in the stalls, and watched the movie.

IT WORKED! The odd story ran in every newspaper and newscast in town, which attracted huge crowds to the film Weiser was promoting, Mel Brooks's Western comedy spoof, *Blazing Saddles*.

STUNTMAN: Press agent Milton Crandall

STUNT: In 1923 Denver newspapers were tipped off that a whale had been sighted on top of Pikes Peak, a 14,000-foot-high mountain in Colorado. The reporters raced up to the site to see the whale. Sure enough, just beyond the peak, occasional sprays of water shot into the air, while hundreds of spectators gathered below, shouting, "Thar she blows!"

… By kneading dough with their feet—the yeast between their toes made it rise.

IT WORKED! The "whale" was actually Crandall hiding just behind the peak shooting sprays of seltzer in the air. And the shouting people were all paid to stand there in the cold for an hour. But it was worth it—for Crandall, anyway. He got just the publicity he was looking for to promote the 1922 movie, *Down to the Sea in Ships.*

STUNTMAN: A "researcher" calling himself Stuart Little

STUNT: In the 1940s, Mr. Little started a massive letter-writing campaign to the editors of newspapers across the nation. His beef: He refused to believe government statistics that claimed the average life span of a crow was only 12 years. Little was certain that crows lived longer than that. So in the letters he asked people from all over to send him authenticated reports of old crows. Little just wanted to set the record straight.

IT WORKED! Thousands responded. Soon *everyone* was talking about old crows. And the makers of Old Crow bourbon whiskey—and the press agent responsible for Stuart Little's letters—were smiling all the way to the bank.

STUNTMAN: Publicist Harry Reichenbach

STUNT: A group of teenage boys walked up to a store window in 1913 and saw a lithograph of a naked young woman standing in a lake. They ogled it for hours. Reichenbach complained to the head of the anti-vice society about the picture's effect on the young, demanding they come see the outrage. They did, and began a moral crusade against it.

IT WORKED! The picture was titled *September Morn.* The artist, Paul Chabas, had hired Reichenbach to drum up interest in it. Pretty soon the artist was unable to meet demand. The image showed up in magazines, on calendars, and on cigarette packs. Sailors had the woman tattooed on their forearms. The lithograph sold seven million copies, and the original painting is on display today in the Metropolitan Museum of Art in New York.

STUNTMAN: Publicist Jim Moran

STUNT: "Don't change horses in midstream," says the old adage. Moran set out to prove it wrong. Wearing an Uncle Sam top hat and tails, he was photographed in the middle of the Truckee

River, where he successfully leapt from a black horse to a white one. He'd had been hired by the Republican Party to inspire voters in the 1944 presidential campaign to change parties after three consecutive terms of Democrat Franklin D. Roosevelt.

IT WORKED! Actually, no, it didn't. FDR easily defeated Republican Thomas Dewey in the election.

STUNTMAN: Surrealist Salvador Dalí

STUNT: In 1939 Dalí was commissioned to create a window display for New York City's prestigious department store Bonwit Teller. The artist's design incorporated a female mannequin with a head of roses, ermine fingernails, a green feathered negligee, and a lobster telephone. A male mannequin wore a dinner jacket with 81 glasses of crème de menthe attached to it. Each glass was topped off with a dead fly and a straw. The only furniture in the window was a fur-lined claw-foot tub filled with water and floating narcissi (flowers).

IT WORKED! When the window was unveiled, the Bonwit Teller staff was outraged; they took it upon themselves to alter the scene without asking the artist. A furious Dalí stomped into the store, tipped the water out of the tub, and pushed it through the plate-glass window. After the police showed up and arrested him, the newspapers wrote about it and radio commentators talked about it. And Dalí's one-man show—which just happened to be opening that very evening—was packed.

STUNTMAN: Washington Irving

STUNT: In October 1809, a notice appeared in the New York *Evening Post*, describing "a small elderly gentleman dressed in an old black coat and cocked hat by the name of KNICKERBOCK-ER" who had gone missing. In November a notice from Knickerbocker's landlord stated that he had found a "very curious book" among the old gent's belongings and if the rent wasn't paid soon, he would sell it.

IT WORKED! Soon everyone in New York was talking about the missing author and his mysterious book. When Diedrich Knickerbocker's book, *A History of New York*, was published in December, everyone wanted to read it. Only later did they discover there was no Knickerbocker, lost or found. The real author of the book, the notices, and the publicity stunt…was Washington Irving.

Windmills originated in Iran.

LITTLE THINGS
MEAN A LOT

*"The devil's in the details," says an old proverb. It's true—
the littlest things can cause the biggest problems.*

A **PIECE OF TAPE**
In the early morning of June 17, 1972, an $80-a-week security guard named Frank Wills was patrolling the parking garage of an office complex in Washington, D.C., when he noticed that someone had used adhesive tape to prevent a stairwell door from latching. Wills removed the tape and continued on his rounds ...but when he returned to the same door at 2:00 a.m., he saw it had been taped *again*. So he called the police, who discovered a team of burglars planting bugs in an office leased by the Democratic National Committee. This "third-rate burglary"—and the coverup that followed—grew into the Watergate scandal that forced President Richard M. Nixon to resign from office in 1974.

A CONVERSION ERROR
On July 23, 1983 the pilots of Air Canada flight 143 was preparing to fly from Montreal to Edmonton, Canada. The device that calculates the amount of fuel needed wasn't working, so the pilots did the calculations by hand. Part of the process involved converting the volume of fuel to weight. They used the conversion factor of 1.77 pounds/liter...not realizing that on a Boeing 767, fuel is measured in *kilograms*, not pounds. (They should have used the conversion factor of .8 kilograms/liter.) Result: they didn't load enough fuel to get them to Edmonton. While the plane was cruising at 41,000 feet over Red Lake, Ontario, it suddenly ran out of fuel and both engines quit. The pilots had no choice but to *glide* the 767 to an emergency landing at a former airbase at Gimli, Manitoba, something that the pilots had never trained for and that was not covered in the 767's emergency manual, since no one ever thought that pilots would be dumb enough to let the plane run out of fuel in mid-air. No one was injured.

Geologically speaking, we live in the Cenozoic era, which began 65 million years ago.

YOU CALL THIS ART?

Ever been in an art gallery and seen something that made you wonder: "Is this really art?" So have we. Is it art just because someone puts it in a gallery? You decide.

THE ARTIST: Richard Lomas, a New Zealand painter
THE WORKS: *Bug Paintings*
THIS IS ART? In 1991 Lomas was distressed by a comment made by a fellow artist, that painting was dead. Lomas was traveling by van across North America at the time but still wanted to prove his friend wrong. So he strapped a still-wet canvas to the front of his van and drove and drove…and drove. When he finally stopped, the canvas had been reshaped by wind, sun, and a lot of splattered bugs. Inspired by his creation, he has since driven more than 8,000 miles making more "masterpieces." He's even strapped his canvases to the front of trains. "My paintings may contain dead matter," he says, "but they stimulate lively debate."

THE ARTIST: SAW Gallery in Ottawa, Canada
THE WORK: *Scatalogue: 30 Years of Crap in Contemporary Art*
THIS IS ART? The gallery's curator, Stefan St. Laurent, was lamenting that "people who live in this Western society can't really deal with their own excrement." So to help them, he commissioned works for an unusual exhibit. The pieces include a sculpture of former prime minister Brian Mulroney holding feces in his outstretched hand, a performance video featuring actors posing with toilets, and last (but not least), a genuine pair of soiled trousers. According to St. Laurent, the show tackled such issues as racism, homophobia, sexism, anti-Semitism, globalization, and consumerism. Visitors were also invited to check out the Scatalogue Boutique, where they could purchase cow-pie clocks.

THE ARTIST: Michael Landy, a London conceptual artist
THE WORK: *Break Down*
THIS IS ART? By age 37, Landy had become so fed up with materialism that he gathered every single thing he owned—7,006 items in all—and staged their destruction in a 14-day exhibit he

---

The Venus flytrap only grows wild in one place: a 100-mile stretch of Carolina swampland.

called an "examination of consumerism." As Landy supervised, 12 workers systematically destroyed everything from family heirlooms to dirty socks to his Saab 900. They smashed the big stuff with hammers and shredded the smaller stuff, reducing all of it to piles of pebble-sized trash, destined to end up in a landfill. More than 45,000 spectators witnessed the "art piece." His next work: Getting new credit cards, new keys, a new passport, a new birth certificate, new shoes, and a new suit. "I found it a bit soul-destroying," he said. "I really didn't want to buy anything."

THE ARTIST: Marilene Oliver, a London art student
THE WORK: *I Know You Inside Out*
THIS IS ART? In 1993 a convicted killer named Joseph Jernigan was put to death by lethal injection. After the execution, Jernigan's body was frozen, then sliced (crosswise) into 1,871 micro-thin cross-sections and photographed for medical students. The images were also posted on the Internet, which is where Marilene Oliver found them in 2001. She printed them out, cut them to shape, and stacked them to create a life-size figure of the murderer.

Still not satisfied, Oliver scanned her own skin on a flatbed scanner and created a touch screen display next to the Jernigan figure, kind of like Adam and Eve. This one she called *I Know Every Inch of Your Body*.

MORE "ART"
How to Make a Quick Buck: First, get a cup of coffee in a Styrofoam cup. Drink the coffee. Attach the coffee-stained cup to a piece of wood. Find a dead ladybug. Attach that to the same piece of wood. Call the piece *Untitled* and enter it into a New York City art auction. That's what modern artist Tom Friedman did in 1999. The winning bid: $29,900.

How to Get Rid of a Stack of Newspapers: At the same auction an unnamed artist entered a piece that consisted of a stack of newspapers. He called it *Stack of Newspapers*. Unfortunately for him, no bids were made on the "artwork."

And the idea wasn't even original—the previous year, artist Robert Gober had entered a tied stack of newspapers into a Sotheby's auction which he called, *Newspaper, 1992*. It sold for $19,000.

Bad sign: Mozambique has an AK-47 assault rifle on its flag.

THE TIME IT TAKES

It takes the average bathroom reader one minute and fifteen seconds to read the average page of a Bathroom Reader. *Here are some more examples of how long things take (or took).*

- **.05 second** for a human muscle to respond to stimulus

- **.06 second** for an automotive airbag to fully inflate

- **.2 second** for the Int'l Space Station to travel 1 mile

- **.46 second** for a 90-mph fastball to reach home plate

- **.6 second** for an adult to walk one step

- **1 second** for a hummingbird's wings to beat 70 times

- **1.25 seconds** for light to travel from the moon to Earth

- **3 seconds** for 475 lawsuits to be filed around the world

- **4 seconds** for 3,000,000 gallons of water to flow over Niagara Falls

- **10 seconds** for 50 people to be born

- **20 seconds** for a fast talker to say 100 words

- **58 seconds** for the elevator in Toronto's CN Tower to reach the top (1,815 feet)

- **1 minute** for a newborn baby's brain to grow 1.5 mg

- **45 minutes** to reach an actual person when calling the IRS during tax time

- **4 hours** for the *Titanic* to sink after it struck the iceberg

- **4 hrs, 30 min** to cook a 20-pound turkey at 325°F

- **92 hrs** to read both the Old and New Testaments aloud

- **96 hours** to completely recover from jet lag

- **6 days,** according to the Bible, to create the universe

- **7 days** for a newborn baby to wet or soil 80 diapers

- **19 days** until baby cardinals make their first flight

- **25 days** for Handel to compose "The Messiah"

- **29 days, 12 hrs, 44 mins, and 3 secs** from a new moon to a new moon

---

Dough doe? Animal Crackers come in 18 different "species."

- **30 days** for a human hair to grow half an inch

- **35 days** for a mouse to reach sexual maturity

- **38 days** for a slow boat to get to China (from New York)

- **12 weeks** for a U.S. Marine to go through boot camp

- **89 days, 1 hour,** for winter to come and go

- **91 days, 7 hrs, 26 mins, and 24 secs** for the Earth to fall into the Sun if it loses its orbit

- **258 days** for the gestation period of a yak

- **1 year** for Los Angeles to move two inches closer to San Francisco (due to the shifting of tectonic plates)

- **2 years** for cheddar cheese to reach its peak flavor

- **4 yrs, 8 mos** to receive your FBI file after making the appropriate request

- **6 years** in a snail's life span

- **25 years** equals the time the average American spends asleep in a lifetime

- **27 years** was the length of Nolan Ryan's pitching career

- **33 years** was the life expectancy of a Neanderthal man

- **69 years** for the Soviet Union to rise and fall

- **95 years** for Easter to recur on the same date

- **100 years** for tidal friction to slow Earth's rotation by 14 seconds

- **1,800 years** to complete the Great Wall of China

- **500,000 years** for plutonium-239 to become harmless

- **45.36 million years** to reach the nearest star, Proxima Centauri, in a car going 65 mph

- **1 billion years** for the sun to release as much energy as a supernova releases in 24 hours

*   *   *

POLITICAL DARWINISM

"In my lifetime, we've gone from Eisenhower to George W. Bush. We've gone from John F. Kennedy to Al Gore. If this is evolution, I believe that in 12 years, we'll be voting for plants."

—**Lewis Black**

How long American drivers wait at traffic lights in their lifetime: 14 days.

THE WILHELM SCREAM

Have you ever heard a sound effect in a film—a screeching eagle, a car crash, or a laughing crowd—that you swear you've heard before in other movies? You're probably right. Here's the story behind Hollywood's most famous "recycled" sound effect.

SOUNDS FAMILIAR

Like most American kids growing up in the 1950s, Ben Burtt went to the movies...*a lot.* Movie budgets were much smaller back then, and film studios reused whatever they could—props, sets, stock footage, sound effects, everything. If you watched and listened to the movies carefully, you might have noticed things you'd seen and heard in other movies.

Burtt noticed. He was good at picking out sounds—especially screams, and especially one scream in particular. "Every time someone died in a Warner Bros. movie, they'd scream this famous scream," he says.

By the 1970s, a grown-up Burtt was working in the movie business himself, as a sound designer—the guy who creates the sound effects. Years had passed, but he'd never forgotten that classic Warner Bros. scream. So when he got the chance, he decided to track down the original recording. It took a lot of digging, but he eventually found it on an old studio reel marked "Man Being Eaten by an Alligator." It turns out it had been recorded for the 1951 Warner Bros. western *Distant Drums* and used at least twice in that movie: once in a battle with some Indians, and then—of course—when a man is bitten and dragged underwater by an alligator.

A STAR IS BORN

No one could remember what actor had originally been hired to record the scream, so Burtt jokingly named it after a character in the 1953 movie, *Charge at Feather River.* The character, named Wilhelm, screams the scream after he is struck in the leg by an arrow. The "Wilhelm Scream" was used two more times in that film: once when a soldier is struck by a spear, and again when an Indian is stabbed and then rolls down a hill.

The Wilhelm Scream is now more than 50 years old, but if you heard it you'd probably recognize it, because Burtt, who's worked on almost every George Lucas film, uses it often—including in his Academy Award-winning sound design for *Star Wars*. "That scream gets in every picture I do, as a personal signature," he says.

So when you hear a Wilhelm Scream in a film, can you assume that Burtt did the sound effects? No—when other sound designers heard what he was doing, they started inserting the scream into their movies, too. Apparently, Burtt isn't the only person good at noticing reused sound effects, because movie buffs have caught on to what he is doing and discovered at least 66 films that use the Wilhelm Scream. A few examples:

AHHHHHHHHHEEEEEIIIIII!!!

Star Wars (1977) Just before Luke Skywalker and Princess Leia swing across the Death Star's chasm, a stormtrooper falls in.

The Empire Strikes Back (1980) 1) In the battle on the ice planet Hoth, a rebel soldier screams when his big satellite-dish laser gun is struck by laser fire and explodes. 2) As Han Solo is being frozen, Chewbacca knocks a stormtrooper off of the platform.

Return of the Jedi (1983) 1) In the desert scene, Luke slashes an enemy with his light saber. The victim screams as he falls into the Sarlac pit. 2) Later in the film, Han Solo knocks a man over a ledge. The man is Ben Burtt himself, making a cameo appearance—and that's him impersonating the Wilhelm Scream…with his own voice.

Batman Returns (1992) Batman punches a clown and knocks him out of the way. The clown screams.

Toy Story (1995) Buzz Lightyear screams when he gets knocked out of the bedroom window.

Titanic (1997) In the scene where the engine room is flooding, a crew member screams when he's hit with a jet of water.

Spaceballs (1987) Barf uses a section of tubes to reflect laser bolts back at three guards. The last one screams.

Lethal Weapon 4 (1998) A gunshot turns a terrorist's flame-thrower into a jet pack, and he flies into a gasoline truck.

Lord of the Rings: The Two Towers (2002) A soldier falls off the wall during the Battle of Helm's Deep…and lets out a Wilhelm.

NOT WHAT THEY SEEM TO BE

Things (and people) aren't always what they seem.
Here are some peeks behind the image.

JOHN JAMES AUDUBON

Image: Considered a pioneer of American wildlife conservation, this 19th-century naturalist spent days at a time searching for birds in the woods so he could paint them. The National Audubon Society was founded in 1905 in his honor.

Actually: Audubon found the birds, then shot them. In addition to painting, he was an avid hunter. According to David Wallechinsky in *Significa*, "He achieved unequaled realism by using freshly killed models held in lifelike poses by wires. Sometimes he shot dozens of birds just to complete a single picture."

WASHINGTON CROSSING THE DELAWARE

Image: One of the most famous paintings of American history depicts General George Washington—in a fierce battle against the redcoats—leading his men across the Delaware River on Christmas Eve 1776.

Actually: It was painted 75 years after the battle by a German artist named Leutze. He used American tourists as models and substituted the Rhine River for the Delaware. He got the style of boat wrong; the clothing was wrong; even the American flag was incorrect. Yet the drama of the daring offensive was vividly captured, making it one of our most recognized paintings.

WEBSTER'S DICTIONARY

Image: The oldest and most trusted dictionary in the United States, created in 1828 by Noah Webster.

Actually: "The truth is," says M. Hirsh Goldberg in *The Book of Lies*, "is that any dictionary maker can put *Webster's* in the name, because book titles can't be copyrighted." And a lot of shoddy publishers do just that. To know if your *Webster's* is authentic, make sure it's published by Merriam-Webster, Inc.

Widest waterfall in the world: Victoria Falls in Africa (almost a mile wide).

FLUBBED HEADLINES

These are 100% honest-to-goodness headlines.
Can you figure out what they're trying to say?

INFERTILITY UNLIKELY TO BE PASSED ON

CRITICS SAY SUNKEN SHIPS NOT SEAWORTHY

STUDY FINDS SEX, PREGNANCY LINK

AIR HEAD FIRED

Safety Experts Say School Bus Passengers Should Be Belted

SURVIVOR OF SIAMESE TWINS JOINS PARENTS

State Says Cost of Saving Money Too High

LUNG CANCER IN WOMEN MUSHROOMS

Man Steals Clock, Faces Time

Bank Drive-in Window Blocked by Board

ELIZABETH DOLE HAD NO CHOICE BUT TO RUN AS A WOMAN

DEER AND TURKEY HUNT FOR DISABLED PEOPLE

Axe For Media School's Head

Summer Schools Boost Scrores

Study Says Snoring Drivers Have More Accidents

WOMEN BOWLERS VOTE TO KEEP THEIR SKIRTS ON

Hillary Clinton on Welfare

IF STRIKE ISN'T SETTLED QUICKLY, IT MAY LAST A WHILE

ASTRONAUT TAKES BLAME FOR GAS IN SPACECRAFT

NEW STUDY OF OBESITY LOOKS FOR LARGER TEST GROUP

COLD WAVE LINKED TO TEMPERATURES

Pataki Proposes Allowing Pickups on State Parkways

Montezuma Mourns Banker Slain in Attack with Flowers

REAL ESTATE EXECUTIVE SOLD ON CITY MARKET

PECAN SCAB DISEASE CAUSING NUTS TO FALL OFF

Around 1 in 14,000 people is born with dwarfism.

UNCLE JOHN'S STALL OF FAME

*Uncle John is amazed—and pleased—by the creative way
people get involved with bathrooms, toilets, toilet paper,
etc. That's why he created the "Stall of Fame."*

Honoree: The Reverend Susan Brown, minister at the Church of Scotland's cathedral in Dornoch, Scotland
Notable Achievement: Giving the roll with a hole a holy role.

True Story: When she performs a marriage, Reverend Brown always gives the same wedding gift to the newlyweds: a twin-pack of toilet paper. Why toilet paper? And why a pack of *two* rolls, instead of one or three?

It's symbolic, Reverend Brown explains. "There are two rolls together, just like the couple. And the toilet paper is soft, gentle, long, and strong, which is what I hope their marriage will be." Reverend Brown married Madonna and director Guy Ritchie in December 2000; they got toilet paper, too.

Honoree: Dr. Tom Keating, also known as "Bathroom Man," a former teacher from Decatur, Georgia
Notable Achievement: Taking his daughter's restroom complaint and turning it into a personal crusade to clean up America's school bathrooms.

True Story: In the late 1980s, Dr. Keating's daughter, an eighth-grader, complained to him about the messy state of the bathrooms at her school. First he addressed the problem at her school...then he started checking the restroom conditions at other schools. It turned into an obsession, and soon Keating had founded a group called Project C.L.E.A.N.—Citizens, Learners, and Educators Against Neglect—which works with students, teachers, and administrators to improve the condition of their restrooms.

In a typical school visit, Keating tours the restrooms, notes all the problems—messiness, vandalism, missing toilet paper and other supplies—and works with school officials to come up with a strategy. Then, with the help of students, bathrooms are painted, lighting is improved, damage is repaired, and any fixtures prone to vandalism—such as soap and toilet paper dispensers—are replaced with vandal-resistant models.

"It all comes down to respect," Keating says. "Kids have to respect their school restrooms as if they were their own, and faculty, staff, and administration have to respect the students as young adults who can be trusted to take care of their basic, biological needs in an acceptable setting." And there's a bonus—Keating believes that cleaner bathrooms can lead to better grades. "Students will pay closer attention in class if they're not worried about 'holding it in' until school is over," he says.

Honoree: Monell Chemical Senses Center, a research facility in Philadelphia

Notable Achievement: Turning sour smells into sweet success

True Story: In November 2002, the U.S. National Research Council called for a massive increase in the amount of money the Pentagon spends on nonlethal weapons. So the army is now looking into malodorants, substances so stinky that the military can use them to disperse crowds, empty buildings, and keep enemies away from sensitive areas. And Monell is at the cutting edge of research. They cook up the stinkiest smells they can think of, then let volunteers of all nationalities and cultures sniff them to make sure they have worldwide dis-appeal. Monell's worst odors:

• "Who Me?" which smells like the odorant added to natural gas (if you've ever smelled a gas leak, that's the smell), combined with the smell of rotting mushrooms.

• "Bathroom Malodor," a nasty, poopy smell that's mixed with the smell of rotting rodents. The lab also sells this smell to makers of bathroom cleansers, who use it to test the effectiveness of new products.

• "Stench Soup," a combination of "Who Me?" and "Bathroom Malodor."

So which of these three smells is considered most offensive by the most people? "Bathroom Malodor," hands down—nothing else comes close. "We got cursed in a lot of different languages when we tested that," says researcher Pamela Dalton.

IT'S A WEIRD, WEIRD WORLD

Proof that truth really is stranger than fiction.

WHITE ON!

"A University of Northern Colorado intramural basketball team has been inundated with T-shirt requests since naming itself 'The Fightin' Whites.' The team, made up of Native Americans, Hispanics, and Anglos, chose the name because nearby Easton High refused to change *its* nickname from 'Reds' and drop its American Indian caricature logo. The team plans to donate profits from the shirts to an American Indian organization. The shirts show a 1950s-style caricature of a middle-aged white man with the phrase 'Every thang's gonna be all white!'"

—USA *Today*

OUT TO LUNCH

"At a hospital in Nashville, Tennessee, on election day, nurses went into the room of a 72-year-old woman to prepare her for open-heart surgery, only to find the woman wasn't there. Instead they found a note which read, 'Gone to vote, back in 30 minutes.' An election official later confirmed an elderly woman with IVs coming out of her arms had indeed come in to vote."

—Bloomington-Normal *Pantagraph*

FISHY BEHAVIOR

"A student at Carnegie Mellon University in Pittsburgh, Pa., has arranged an 'external study' in lieu of regular classes, consisting of his dressing as a lobster, building a shelter on campus from scrap lumber and living in it. Fine-arts major Bill Kofmehl III, also known as 'Lobster Boy,' moved into the shelter February 1, vowing not to speak to anyone for three months. He did, however, occasionally climb to the roof in his lobster costume and make noises through a cardboard tube and a bullhorn."

—Chicago *Sun-Times*

Hey, sweetie: Aspartame is 200 times sweeter than sugar; saccharin is 500 times sweeter.

HONEY, I'M HOME

"Trish and Vincent Caminiti of Bayport, NY, returned from a three-week vacation to find that 20,000 bees had established a hive in the walls of their home. According to neighbors, the swarm arrived in a dense, black, 10-foot-wide funnel cloud that buzzed so loud some thought it was an aircraft. The swarm then entered the home one at a time through a hole only a half-inch in diameter in the wall of the house."

—Strange Tails

DON'T BE CHICKEN

"The Associated Press reported that some Pittsburgh parents recently held chicken pox "parties" for their kids. The parties involve having one kid with a current outbreak of the disease mingle with other kids to infect them, too, so that they would acquire a lifetime immunity. These parents apparently want their kids to avoid standard immunizations because of the side effects."

—News of the Weird

TALIBAN(G)

"Hoping to defend his nation's honor, former Taliban foreign minister Wakil Ahmed Muttawakil challenged U.S. president George Bush and British prime minister Tony Blair to a duel, suggesting that they fight former Afghan leader Mullah Omar with Kalashnikov assault rifles. Needless to say, they didn't take him up on the offer."

—National Post

DUCK!

"Workers from White's Mobile Home Supply were hanging axles under a trailer when lightning struck nearby. They came out from under the home only to be greeted by a sight they'll never forget.

"'About 20 to 30 seconds after the lightning struck, stuff started falling from the sky,' owner Ron White said. 'At first they thought it was tennis shoes. Then they realized it was ducks.'

"The workers collected 20 mallards from the mobile home park. "'Lightning can hit ducks, but it is rare,' said Arkansas Game and Fish Commission biologist Mike Checkett. 'I think this is something they'll remember for the rest of their lives.'"

—SFGate

Water can flow through a plant at 4 mph.

ICKY LICKY STICKS

We were saving this page for our next Bathroom Reader
for Kids Only, *but then thought that everyone
should be warned. These are 100% real.*

SNOT SHOTS. Green bits of supersour, fruit-flavored bubble gum (also available: Blood Balls—gumballs filled with powdered candy that colors the mouth red).

CRAPPIN' CRITTERS. These are models of cows, sheep, and other animals, which emit chocolate-brown jelly beans.

TOXIC WASTE HAZARDOUSLY SOUR CANDY. Hard candies packaged in an industrial drum. After sucking through the supersour outer layer, you get a sweet center. But then—*yow!*—you get an even more painfully sour hidden center.

EVERY FLAVOR BEANS. Inspired by *Harry Potter*, these look like ordinary jelly beans...until you take a bite. Some of the 38 flavors—like banana, root beer, chocolate pudding, and buttered toast—are tasty. But there's also sardine, horseradish, grass, black pepper, dirt, vomit, and booger. *Warning:* The horseradish and coconut beans are both white.

ICKY LICKY STICKS. "Tasty sweet liquid candy packaged in grotesque human body parts! A wart-covered foot seeps cherry toe jam candy, a bloodshot eyeball oozes cherry eye mucous candy, and a runny, wart-covered nose leaks sour apple snot candy."

INSECTNSIDE. Made to look like fossilized amber—it's really a clear amber-colored toffee candy...with a *real* cricket sealed inside.

OH RATZ. It's a gummy rat, which you're supposed to dip into candy powder contained in a tiny plastic garbage can.

SOUR FLUSH. Candy powder in a plastic toilet bowl.

RAT PIZZA. A gummy pizza with a gummy rat on top. (They also make Worm Wiener, a gummy worm in a gummy hot dog bun.)

CHOCKA CA-CA. A piece of chocolate fudge that comes in a baby diaper. Packaged in a gift box—pink for girls, blue for boys.

The automobile was invented in 1886; the used car lot (17 cars) was invented in 1897.

THE IG NOBEL PRIZES

*Too dumb to win a Nobel Prize? Don't feel too bad—
there's still the Ig Nobel prizes. The science humor magazine
Annals of Improbable Research awards them at Harvard
University every year, to honor people whose achievements
in science, medicine, or technology "cannot or should
not be reproduced." Bonus: If you win, your prize
is handed to you by a genuine Nobel laureate!*

IG NOBEL PRIZE: Public Health (2001)

AWARD-WINNING TOPIC: "A Preliminary Survey of Rhinotillexomania in an Adolescent Sample," by Chittaranjan Andrade, et al. *Journal of Clinical Psychiatry,* June 2001.
Translation: "We studied nose-picking behavior in a sample of 200 adolescents from four urban schools."

FINDINGS:

• "Nose picking is common in adolescents.... Almost the entire sample admitted to nose picking, with a median frequency of four times per day."

• "Nearly 17% of subjects considered that they have a serious nose-picking problem."

• "Nose picking may merit closer nosologic scrutiny."

IG NOBEL PRIZE: Psychology (1995)

AWARD-WINNING TOPIC: "Pigeons' Discrimination of Paintings by Monet and Picasso," by Shigeru Watanabe, et al. *Journal of the Experimental Analysis of Behavior,* 1995.

FINDINGS:

• "Pigeons successfully learned to discriminate color slides of paintings by Monet and Picasso. Following this training, they discriminated novel paintings by Monet and Picasso that had never been presented during the discrimination training."

• The pigeons "showed generalization from Monet's to Cezanne's and Renoir's paintings [all Impressionist painters], or from Picasso's to Braque's and Matisse's paintings [Cubists and Fauvists]."

A poem written to celebrate a wedding is called an *epithalamium.*

- "Upside-down images of Monet's paintings disrupted the discrimination, whereas inverted images of Picasso's did not."

IG NOBEL PRIZE: Public Health (2000)

AWARD-WINNING TOPIC: "The Collapse of Toilets in Glasgow," by Jonathan Wyatt, et al. *The Scottish Medical Journal*, 1993.

FINDINGS:

- "Three cases are presented of porcelain toilets collapsing under body weight, producing wounds serious enough to require hospital treatment."
- "The excessive age of the toilets was a causative factor."
- "As many such toilets get older, episodes of collapse may become more common, resulting in further injuries."

IG NOBEL PRIZE: Psychology (2001)

AWARD-WINNING TOPIC: "An Ecological Study of Glee in Small Groups of Preschool Children," by Lawrence W. Sherman. *Child Development*, March 1975.

FINDINGS:

- "A phenomenon called group glee was studied in videotapes of 596 formal lessons in a preschool. This was characterized by joyful screaming, laughing, and intense physical acts which occurred in simultaneous bursts or which spread in a contagious fashion from one child to another."
- "While most events of glee did not disrupt the ongoing lesson, those which did tended to produce a protective reaction on the part of teachers [i.e., the teacher called the class back to order]."
- "Group glee tended to occur most often in large groups (seven to nine children) and in groups containing both sexes."

OTHER IG NOBEL LAUREATES

- **Physics (2002):** "Demonstration of the Exponential Decay Law Using Beer Froth," by Arnd Leike, *European Journal of Physics*, January 2002.
- **Mathematics (2002):** "Estimation of Total Surface Area in Indian Elephants," by K. P. Sreekumar, et al. *Veterinary Research Communications*, 1990.

The ears of an African elephant can weigh up to 110 pounds each.

FAMOUS LAST WORDS

If you had to choose your last words, what would they be?

"Hurrah, boys, we've got them! We'll finish them up and then go home to our station."
—**General George Custer**

"Let's go on to Chicago and win there."
—**Robert F. Kennedy**

"I wish to announce the first plank in my campaign for reelection…we're going to have the floors in this god-damned hospital smoothed out!"
—**Boston politician James Michael Curley**

"Moose…Indian."
—**Henry David Thoreau**

"Try to be forgotten. Go live in the country. Stay in mourning for two years, then remarry, but choose somebody decent."
—**Poet Alexander Pushkin**

"But the peasants…how do the peasants die?"
—**Russian author Leo Tolstoy**

"My work is done. Why wait?"
—**Kodak founder George Eastman,** *in a suicide note*

"My fun days are over."
—**James Dean**

"You can keep the things of bronze and stone and give me one man to remember me just once a year."
—**Journalist Damon Runyon**

"There ain't nobody gonna shoot me."
—**Lee Harvey Oswald,** *while being transferred to county jail*

"I am quite certain that the crimes of this guilty land will never be purged away but with blood. I had, as I now think, vainly flattered myself that without much bloodshed it might be done."
—**19th-century abolitionist John Brown**

"I still live."
—**Daniel Webster**

"Let's do it."
—**Gary Gilmore,** *executed by firing squad at Draper State Prison, Utah, 1977*

"Does nobody understand?"
—**Irish author James Joyce**

Every second, 100,000 chemical reactions occur in your brain.

THE HALIFAX EXPLOSION

*In late 1917, World War I was raging in Europe. Back in North America,
the port of Halifax, Nova Scotia, was the hub of Canada's war effort.
All the ships heading out to the Atlantic brought prosperity
to the small town...but they also brought disaster.*

U NLIKE TWO SHIPS PASSING IN THE NIGHT
In December 1917, the French cargo ship *Mont Blanc*
took on 5,000 tons of explosives in New York, including
more than 400,000 pounds of TNT. The 300-foot-long ship was
headed into Halifax Harbor to await a convoy of ships that would
accompany it to England. The *Mont Blanc's* captain, Aime Le
Medec, should have been flying a red flag to warn other ships of
the dangerous cargo, but he was afraid that enemy ships might see
the flag and start shooting.

At the same time, a 440-foot Norwegian ship, called the *Imo*—
much faster and larger than the *Mont Blanc*—was leaving Halifax
for New York. The *Imo's* captain, Haakon From, knew he was
behind schedule and ordered the ship full speed ahead.

Halifax Harbor has, roughly, an hourglass shape. The "waist" of
the hourglass is a slim channel of water called the Narrows. Halifax is on the southern side of this narrow channel; the town of
Darmouth sits on the north side. Two ships passing through the
Narrows must do so with caution—as the *Imo* and the *Mont Blanc*
were soon to learn.

COLLISION

On the cold, clear morning of December 6, shortly before nine,
the *Imo* and the *Mont Blanc* both entered the Narrows: the *Imo*
going east toward open sea (too fast, some said), the *Mont Blanc*
was going west to moor up. Harbor rules say that ships must pass
port to port—left side to left side—just like cars on the road. But
the *Imo* was veering too far north; it was headed directly toward
the *Mont Blanc* like a truck in the wrong lane. Captain Le Medec,
aboard the *Mont Blanc*, signaled the other ship, but, strangely,
Captain From didn't stop—he signaled that he was continuing farther north. After repeated and confused attempts to communicate
with horns and flags, Le Medec finally steered his ship south-

---

First-ever Christmas celebrated with electric tree lights: 1903.

ward... but Captain From did the same thing at the same time. Result: The smaller ship was broadsided. The collision sent the *Mont Blanc* straight toward the city of Halifax.

The impact started a fire on the deck of the *Mont Blanc*. Her crew, knowing the ship could blow up at any second, went straight to the lifeboats... without alerting the harbor patrol of the dangerous cargo. They rowed north toward Dartmouth, leaving the floating bomb heading straight for Halifax.

It was an astounding sight: a flaming ship drifting slowly toward shore. All morning activity stopped as people watched the spectacle—kids on their way to school, dockworkers on shore, shopkeepers, and homemakers who could see the harbor from their windows. The *Mont Blanc* drifted for about 20 minutes until it came to rest against Pier 6 in the Richmond district, the busy, industrial north end of Halifax. As firefighting crews rushed to put the fire out, the flames were getting closer and closer to the massive stores of TNT on the lower decks.

EXPLOSION

Then, shortly before 9:05 a.m., a blinding, white flash filled the harbor. The *Mont Blanc* exploded into bits and a giant mushroom cloud rose up over the town. More than 1,600 people were killed instantly. Thousands more were injured, many blinded from the glass and shrapnel that rained down on Halifax and Dartmouth. Schools, homes, factories, and churches were leveled by the ensuing shockwave. A 30-foot tidal wave swept away what was left of the waterfront, drowning many of the initial survivors and sinking dozens of ships in the harbor. Shattered pieces of the *Mont Blanc* were hurled as far as three miles away. A tugboat was thrown from the middle of the harbor onto the Dartmouth shore. The wave also rushed over the shores of Dartmouth and up Tufts Cove, where it completely washed away the settlement of an indigenous tribe called the Micmac.

The blast was so strong that windows were broken even in Charlottetown—120 miles away. It was the largest man-made explosion in human history, and its size and devastation wouldn't be eclipsed until the atomic bomb was dropped on Hiroshima in 1945.

More than 1,600 homes were gone; 12,000 more were damaged from the fires that spread through Halifax after the explosion. At least 6,000 people were left homeless at the onset of a powerful winter storm that would drop more than a foot of snow within the next 24 hours. Hundreds who had survived the blast, the tidal wave, and the ensuing fires would end up freezing to death.

RELIEF

Rescue efforts were slow at first. Power, water, gas, telephone, telegraph, and railroad lines were all obliterated. The dead and dying lined the streets, while thousands of others were buried under debris. And medical supplies were in pitifully short supply. But help was on the way. Money started pouring in from all over the world, from as far away as China and New Zealand. The Canadian government appropriated $18 million for relief efforts, and surrounding towns donated shelters, blankets, and other necessities. But much of the immediate help came from Massachusetts. A train full of supplies and medical personnel left for Halifax the day of the explosion. In all, Bostonians donated $750,000 through the Massachusetts-Halifax Relief Committee. (To this day, Halifax sends an annual Christmas tree to the city of Boston in gratitude.)

THE BLAME GAME

The survivors of the explosion were stunned. Something this horrible had to be somebody's fault. First, they blamed the Germans, because if Germany hadn't started the war, the disaster would not have happened. Every surviving German in town was rounded up and arrested, in spite of the fact that they had suffered the same as everyone else. But as rebuilding began and cooler heads prevailed, people realized that if anyone was to blame, it was the ships' captains.

Captain From and most of the crew of the *Imo* perished in the blast; Captain Le Medec of the *Mont Blanc* survived and was brought to trial. After months of inquiry and many civil suits, there was insufficient evidence to establish criminal negligence. Captain Le Medec's license was revoked, but in the end, no one was ever convicted.

On January 22, 1918, Canada appointed the Halifax Relief Commission to handle pensions, insurance claims, rehousing, and rebuilding, as well as the rehabilitation of survivors. The extent of the damage was so great that the Commission would remain open until 1976.

...man-made loss of life on North American soil... until 9/11/01.

COMIC RELIEF

*Our annual salute to those who stand up
so we may laugh while sitting down.*

"I met a beautiful girl at a barbeque, which was exciting. Blonde, I think—I don't know. Her hair was on fire. And all she talked about was herself. You know those kind of girls. It was just me, me, me. Help *me*. Put *me* out."
　　　—**Garry Shandling**

"You can say, 'Can I use your bathroom,' and nobody cares. But if you ask, 'Can I use the plop-plop machine,' it always breaks the conversation."
　　　—**Dave Attell**

"I can bend forks with my mind, but only the ones at Denny's. And you have to look away for a little while."
　　　—**Bobcat Goldthwaite**

"*Frisbeetarianism* is the belief that when you die, your soul goes up on the roof and gets stuck."
　　　—**George Carlin**

"Did you hear they finally made a device that makes cars run 95% quieter? It fits right over her mouth."
　　　—**Billy Crystal**

"My parents only had one argument in forty-five years. It lasted forty-three years."
　　　—**Cathy Ladman**

"First the doctor told me the good news: I was going to have a disease named after me."
　　　—**Steve Martin**

"I think I'm a pretty good judge of people, which is why I hate most of them."
　　　—**Roseanne**

"It's strange, isn't it. You stand in the middle of a library and go '*aaaaagghhhh*' and everyone just stares at you. But you do the same thing on an airplane, and everyone joins in."
　　　—**Tommy Cooper**

"I'm against picketing...but I don't know how to show it."
　　　—**Mitch Hedburg**

"A study in the *Washington Post* says that women have better verbal skills than men. I just want to say to the authors of that study: *Duh*."
　　　—**Conan O'Brien**

HOW PAPER
BECAME MONEY

*Today we take it for granted that a $20 bill is worth 20
dollars. But convincing people that paper can be just as
valuable as gold or silver took centuries and involved
many false starts. Take this one, for example.*

SPOILS OF WAR

In 1298 a Venetian traveler named Marco Polo signed on
as "gentleman commander" of a Venetian galley and led it
in battle against the fleet of its rival city, Genoa.

Lucky for us, Polo lost. After he was captured and thrown into
prison, he spent the next two years dictating a detailed account of
his 24 years of travel in India, Africa, and China (then part of the
Mongol empire ruled by Kublai Khan).

Until then, very little was known about that part of the world.
Few Europeans had been to the Far East, and even fewer had written about their experiences. Polo's memoirs changed everything.
The Travels of Marco Polo was widely read all over Europe and is
considered the most important account of the "outside" world
written during the Middle Ages.

HARD TO BELIEVE

But not everyone believed it. In its day, *The Travels of Marco Polo*
was also known as *Il Milióne,* or "The Million Lies," because so
many of the things that Polo described seemed preposterous to his
European readers. He told of a postal system that could transport a
letter 300 miles in a single day, fireproof cloth that could be
cleaned by throwing it into a fire (it was made from asbestos), and
baths that were heated by "stones that burn like logs" (coal).

But one of Polo's most preposterous-seeming claims: In Kublai
Khan's empire, people traded *paper* as if it were gold.

Here's how Polo described it:

In [the] city of Kanbalu, is the mint of the Grand Khan, who may
truly be said to possess the secret of the alchemists, as he has the
art of producing paper money.... When ready for use, he has it cut

into pieces of money of different sizes....The coinage of this paper money is authenticated with as much form and ceremony as if it were actually of pure gold or silver...and the act of counterfeiting it is punished as a capital offence.

This paper currency is circulated in every part of the Grand Khan's dominions; nor does any person, at the peril of his life, refuse to accept it in payment. All his subjects receive it without hesitation, because, wherever their business may call them, they can dispose of it again in the purchase of merchandise they have occasion for, such as pearls, jewels, gold, or silver. All his majesty's armies are paid with this currency, which is to them of the same value as if it were gold and silver.

Paper money? Europeans had never seen anything like it.

MADE IN CHINA

Kublai Khan's paper currency may have been news to Europeans, but for the Chinese it was just the latest attempt to establish paper as a legitimate form of money:

• Felted paper made from animal fibers was invented in China in about 177 B.C., and less than 40 years after that, the Chinese Emperor Wu-Ti (140–87 B.C.) began to issue the first notes made from paper. They were intended only as a temporary substitute for real money—precious metals and coins—when real money was in short supply. These first bills were more like cardboard than the foldable bills we use today.

• Another emperor, Hien Tsung, issued his own notes during a copper shortage in the early 800s. These, too, were intended only as temporary substitutes, but the idea caught on. More currency was issued in the year 910; after that, paper money came to be issued on a more regular basis.

• By 1020 so many paper notes were in circulation that China became the first country to experience "paper inflation." That's what happens when too much money is printed: it takes more currency to buy the same goods than it used to, so the purchasing power of each individual note goes down. If enough paper money is printed, the currency eventually becomes as worthless as... paper. To counteract the inflation, government officials began spraying the bills with perfume to make them more attractive. It didn't do any good—and neither did anything else they tried.

• When one issue of currency became worthless, government officials would replace it with a new issue of currency; but since they kept printing new bills, in time the new ones would become worthless too, and the cycle would repeat itself.

• By the time of the Mongol invasion in the early 13th century, China had already endured several rounds of paper inflation, but that didn't stop the Mongols from adopting the concept of paper money and spreading it across the entire Mongol empire.

• Kublai Khan issued his own series of paper notes in 1260. These were the ones that Marco Polo encountered when he visited China. By 1290, they were worthless, too.

THE END OF THE PAPER TRAIL

Although the Chinese used paper money over the next 150 years, by 1455 they were so disillusioned with it that it disappeared altogether and did not reappear in China for another 450 years.

"The Chinese people lost all faith in paper money and became more than ever convinced of the virtues of silver," historian Glyn Davies writes in A History of Money, "a conviction that lasted right up to the early part of the twentieth century."

Turn to Part II of "How Paper Became Money" on page 258.

Turn to Part II of "How Paper Became Money" on page 258.

*   *   *

WISDOM THEY DON'T TEACH IN SCHOOL
(but you can learn on the Internet)

• Scratch a dog and you'll find a permanent job.

• No one has more driving ambition than the boy who wants to buy a car.

• There are worse things than getting a call for a wrong number at 4 a.m. It could be a right number.

• Money may buy a dog; only kindness can make him wag his tail.

• The great thing about the future is that it always starts tomorrow.

• Seat belts are not as confining as wheelchairs.

• Learn from the mistakes of others. You won't live long enough to make them all yourself.

Albert Einstein was convinced his cat suffered from depression.

PHONE PHUNNIES

Riddle: What's the difference between a phone booth and a bathroom? (If you don't know, please don't use our phone booth.)

OVER THE HUMP

Next time you find yourself in rural India and need to phone home, don't bother looking for a phone booth; there are none—the cost of laying telephone cable in rural areas is prohibitive. Yet there are millions of potential customers, so enterprising telecommunications companies have to be creative. Enter Shyam Telelink. The solution: They own 200 mobile phones. Every day they send the phones out into the back country... mounted on camels. Customers say the service is very user-friendly. Cost: 2 cents a call.

DIAL-A-DOLPHIN

Stressed out and stuck in traffic with only your cell phone to keep you company? Call a dolphin. As you listen to their underwater clicks and whistles, your stress will disappear. At least that's what scientists at Ireland's Dolphin and Wildlife Foundation hope will happen once they've installed underwater microphones in the Shannon estuary, where dolphins reside year round. They're working with telecom giant Vodaphone to make it possible for cell phone users worldwide to "reach out and touch" the dolphins.

Some kinks still need to be worked out, though—dolphins use a wide frequency band to communicate... most of which is beyond the human range of hearing.

CALL ME STUPID

Michael LaRock, a thief who had been on the run for over a year, called the police in Ticonderoga, New York, to boast that he would never be caught. Apparently it didn't occur to him that the police might have caller I.D. The cops tracked the call to Auburn, Georgia, and quickly contacted the local police. While Officer Dan Charlton in New York was talking to LaRock on the phone, he heard the doorbell ring in the background. The next thing he heard was the Georgia police coming through the door to arrest the thief... right in his own home.

Most widely eaten fish in the world: herring.

SPACE, INC.

*To most people, the stars represent the infinite
cosmos. To some advertisers, they represent infinite
opportunity—or rather, product placement heaven.*

L OOK! UP IN THE SKY!
Companies have been trying to commercialize space since
the 1960s. But they took one giant step in 1993 when a
Georgia-based company called Space Marketing, Inc. floated the
idea of sending mile-long billboards into orbit. The Mylar billboards were designed to stay aloft for 30 days and project images
half the size of a full moon to potential customers down on Earth.
Fortunately, it never happened. Congress outlawed the billboards
later that year, as Massachusetts Congressman Edward Markey
raised the specter of every sunrise and sunset beaming down "the
logo of Coke or G.M. or the Marlboro man, turning our morning
and evening skies into the moral equivalent of the side of a bus."

While our skies seem safe from advertising for the moment, they
may not stay that way. Federal regulations prohibit federal employees—astronauts included—from endorsing products, but American
companies have found creative ways to finesse their own nation's
rules. And the cash-poor Russians have no such inhibitions. In
fact, they've thrown the doors wide open to advertisers in order to
help fund their space ventures. A brief chronology:

FISHER SPACE PEN (1968) Fisher was trying to build a better
ballpoint when it invented a cartridge that used pressurized nitro-
gen instead of gravity to feed ink to the pen point. Two years later,
NASA thought the pens would be perfect for taking notes in zero
gravity and sent some along on the Apollo 7 mission. The pens,
renamed AG-7 Space Pens, became standard equipment on both
American and Russian flights. Seizing a marketing opportunity, in
1998 Fisher peddled their pens during a live telecast from the
Russian space station Mir to home shopping network QVC.

THE COKE/PEPSI CHALLENGER (1985) Among the many
scientific experiments carried out on 1985's STS-51F *Challenger*
mission was one NASA called the Carbonated Beverage Dis-

Antarctica is the only continent that does not have land areas below sea level.

penser Evaluation (CBDE). In this carefully controlled trial, Coca-Cola and Pepsi each provided specially designed cans to deliver their beverages to thirsty astronauts. (The crew reported that without gravity or refrigeration, neither was very good.)

SLINKY SLINKS ONTO SPACE SHUTTLE (1985) Another experiment was conducted on the *Challenger* to show how a Slinky would behave in low-gravity conditions. Astronauts were filmed playing with the toys for an "educational" video.

GOT MILKSKI? (1997) Space vehicles carry milk in powdered form—they can't spare the energy for refrigeration. So what better way to show off the long shelf life of Israel's Tnuva Milk than to deliver it fresh to the space travelers' door? They spent $450,000 to fly their product to the Mir space station and film cosmonauts gulping it down, and then used the footage for a commercial on Israeli television.

PIE IN THE SKY (1999) Pizza Hut reportedly paid the Russians $1 million to paint a 30-foot version of its logo on the side of a Russian Proton rocket that was carrying a crew to the International Space Station (ISS). Then, piggybacking on a Russian cargo flight, Pizza Hut delivered a 15-inch salami and cheese pizza.

FRAMED! (2000) Radio Shack flew a "talking" picture frame to the ISS as a Father's Day gift for Commander Yuri Usachev. It held a picture of his 12-year-old daughter, Evgenia, and played this message: "Hey Dad, we are wishing you good fortune and success in your job and good relationships with the crew." A TV commercial featuring space-suited cosmonauts floating in through a hatch to deliver the gift to Usachev in a Radio Shack shopping bag debuted on American television on May 27, 2001.

BUILDING BLOCKS OF LIFE (2001) To promote their "Life on Mars" line, the LEGO company had a parcel containing 300 "miniature aliens" shuttled to the ISS and back again as part of a contest, in which the toys would be awarded as prizes. Cosmonauts were photographed playing with the toys before they were packed up for their return trip. According to Jay McGill, publisher of *Popular Mechanics* (which has also been marketed on the ISS), "Anything can be done for rubles."

DUMB CROOKS
OF THE OLD WEST

Here's proof that stupidity is timeless (and sometimes deadly).

THE DALTON BROTHERS

In the little town of Coffeyville, Kansas, in 1890, Bob, Emmett, and Gratton Dalton, along with two other men, formed a gang of outlaws. Inspired by the exploits of their cousins the Younger Brothers—who 15 years earlier had stolen nearly half a million dollars from trains and banks with the James Gang—the Daltons pulled a few small-time robberies. But they wanted a big payoff and the fame that goes with it—and that could only come from a bank heist. So they planned it all out... all wrong:

1. The Daltons aimed to rob two banks at once: two men would rob the First National Bank, while the other three hit Condon & Co. across the street. They thought they'd get double the loot, but they only doubled their chances of getting caught.

2. Instead of traveling to another town where no one knew them, they chose Coffeyville—where everyone knew them.

3. The street in front of the banks was being repaired the day of the heist. They could have postponed it, but went ahead anyway. Now they had to hitch their horses a block away, making a clean getaway that much more difficult.

4. *Smart:* They wore disguises. *Dumb:* The disguises were wispy stage mustaches and goatees. Locals saw right through them.

The bank robberies were a disaster. The townsfolk saw the Dalton boys coming and armed themselves. The Daltons did get $20,000 from First National, but came up empty at the other bank when a teller said she couldn't open the safe. When they emerged from the banks, an angry mob was waiting for them in the street. A hail of bullets followed, killing every member except Emmett Dalton, who spent the next 15 years in prison. He emerged from the penitentiary to discover that the Dalton Gang's story had indeed been immortalized, but not as legendary outlaws... only as hapless screwups.

Thomas Edison proposed to his second wife by Morse code.

LUCKY FINDS

Have you ever found something valuable? It's one of the best feelings in the world. Here's another installment of a regular Bathroom Reader *feature—a look at some folks who found really valuable stuff…and got to keep it.*

IT MAY BE UGLY, BUT IT'S MINE

The Find: Painting by Jackson Pollack

Where It Was Found: In a thrift shop

The Story: Retired truckdriver Teri Horton, 70, of Costa Mesa, California, bought an abstract painting for a friend at a local thrift shop. The price was $8, but Horton thought it was ugly and told the store owner, "I ain't paying eight dollars for this thing." She got it for $5. As it turned out, the painting wouldn't fit through her friend's front door, so Horton kept it. When another friend, an art professor, saw the painting, he told her it might actually be an original work by the 20th-century master Jackson Pollack. He was right: in July 2003, forensic specialists found one of Pollack's fingerprints on it—making it worth $20 million. "I still think it's ugly," Horton said, "but now I see dollar signs."

SHELL SHOCK

The Find: 40-carat emerald

Where It Was Found: In a conch shell

The Story: An elementary school teacher and part-time salvage diver was searching the wreck of a Spanish galleon that had sunk off the coast of Florida during a hurricane 380 years ago. Finding nothing of value, the diver collected a bucketful of seashells for his students instead. Later, as he was washing the shells, a 40-carat emerald estimated to be worth millions rolled out of a queen conch shell. According to Doug Pope, president of Amelia Research & Recovery, the man didn't even know what he'd found. "He thought it might be a piece of a Heineken bottle."

PRICEY WATERHOUSE

The Find: Victorian masterpiece painting

Where It Was Found: In an old farmhouse

Q: What animal has the longest tail in the world? A: The male giraffe—it can be up to 8 feet.

The Story: In 1973 a British couple bought a run-down farmhouse in Canada. They requested that an old painting in the house be included in the sale—because they thought it looked nice on the wall. Nineteen years later, they decided to have the painting appraised by Odon Wagner, an art dealer in Toronto. "Odon nearly fell off his chair," said a spokesman for Christie's auction house. It was *Gather Ye Rosebuds While Ye May*, a 1909 work by the Victorian master John William Waterhouse that had been missing for almost a century. "Nobody knew where it was," he said, "and we still don't know how it got to Canada." It was expected to sell for about $5 million. He said the couple was "very, very pleased."

YEAH! YEAH! YEAH!

The Find: More than 500 unknown photos of the Beatles

Where They Were Found: At a university in Scotland

The Story: Dundee University in Scotland was working to digitize its archives in 2002 when someone came across a cache of 130,000 photos by the late Hungarian photographer Michael Peto. Peto's son had given the collection to the university in 1971. Included were hundreds of black and whites of the Beatles from 1965, including candid shots of the band eating, drinking tea, and relaxing between takes on the set of the movie *Help!* Many of the images had never been seen by the public before. A spokesperson for Christie's auction house wouldn't put a dollar figure on the photos, but expected them to be worth a "significant" amount.

*　　*　　*

IT'S THE THOUGHT THAT COUNTS

Joe Purkey of Knoxville, Tennessee, lost his high school ring in 1964. Then he got a phone call about it...37 years later. It was Bob's Septic Service on the line. It seems that between when he bought the ring and when it was delivered, Purkey had lost 40 pounds. The ring was too loose and slipped off his finger...into the toilet *just as he was flushing it.* An employee of the septic service found it in their filtering system. She cleaned it off, researched the date and initials, and in November 2001 gave it back to its original owner. Purkey claimed to be grateful, but wasn't thrilled about wearing it again. "It was never really lost," he said, "I just didn't wanna go get it."

Worldwide, about 20% of all married couples are first cousins.

PRIMETIME PROVERBS

Reflections on life from some of today's most popular shows.

ON LAWYERS
Corporal Cortez: "They're not going to be glad to see us."
Harm: "I'm a lawyer, Corporal, no one's ever glad to see me."
—**J.A.G**

ON LISTENING
Kelly: "Dad, you haven't heard a single word I've said!"
Ozzy: "Can I explain something? You haven't been standing in front of 50 billion decibels for the past thirty years! Leave me a note!"
—**The Osbournes**

ON ENDANGERED SPECIES
Stan: "Dolphins are intelligent and friendly."
Cartman: "Intelligent and friendly on rye bread with some mayonnaise."
—**South park**

ON LOVE
"My love for you is like this scar: ugly, but permanent."
—**Grace, Will and Grace**

ON EATING
"Cheese: it's milk that you chew."
—**Chandler, Friends**

ON DEATH
Frasier: "There's nothing you can do when the cold hand of Death comes knocking on your door…"
(knock at door)
Frasier: "Would you get that?"
Niles: "I most certainly will not!"
—**Frasier**

ON HIGHER EDUCATION
"College is for ugly girls who can't get modeling contracts."
—**Kelso, That '70s Show**

ON ANIMALS
"If frogs could fly…well, we'd still be in this mess, but wouldn't it be neat?"
—**Drew, The Drew Carey Show**

ON HIGH SCHOOL
Andie: "You guys are a bunch of cynics, you know that? I mean, what kind of high school memories will you have if all you did in high school was bitch and moan about everything?"
Joey: "Bitching memories."
Dawson: "Moaning memories."
—**Dawson's Creek**

First coast-to-coast paved highway in U.S.: Lincoln Highway (N.Y–S.F.). It opened in 1913.

NAME THAT SLEUTH

*It took us a while, but using time-tested sleuthing
techniques, we finally solved... The Mystery
of the Fictional Detective Names.*

PERRY MASON (1933)
As a youngster, author Erle Stanley Gardner subscribed to a
boy's fiction magazine, *The Youth's Companion*, and learned a
lot about writing from the stories he read. *The Youth's Companion*
was published by... Perry Mason and Company.

SPENSER FOR HIRE (1973)
Robert B. Parker first introduced his streetwise, Chaucer-quoting,
beer-drinking, gourmet-cooking, Bostonian, ex-boxer private
investigator in *The Godwulf Manuscript*. Parker saw Spenser as a
tough guy but also as a knight in shining armor and named him
after the English poet (and Shakespeare contemporary) Edmund
Spenser.

MIKE HAMMER (1947)
Writer Mickey Spillane had been in and out of the comic book
business for years when he tried to sell a new detective strip to
some New York publishers in 1946. The character's name was
Mike Danger. When no one would buy, he decided to turn it into
a novel and changed the name to Mike Hammer, after one of his
favorite haunts, Hammer's Bar and Grill.

SHERLOCK HOLMES AND DR. JOHN WATSON (1887)
Dr. Watson is believed to have been inspired by author Arthur
Conan Doyle's friend Dr. James Watson. It's less clear how he
named the famous sleuth whom he originally named *Sherringford*
Holmes. Most experts say Doyle took "Holmes" from American
Supreme Court justice, physician and poet Oliver Wendell
Holmes, well-known for his probing intellect and attention to
detail. Sherringford was changed to Sherlock, Doyle enthusiasts
say, for a famous violinist of the time, Alfred Sherlock. Fittingly,
Doyle made his detective an amateur violinist.

Workplace Hazard: Beavers sometimes get crushed by the trees they gnaw down.

INSPECTOR MORSE (1975)

Morse's creator, Colin Dexter, was once a Morse Code operator in the English army—but that's not where he got the name for his character. Sir Jeremy Morse, the chairman of Lloyd's Bank, was a champion crossword-solver in England. Dexter, once a national crossword champion himself, named his melancholy inspector after Sir Jeremy.

HERCULE POIROT (1920)

Some say the meticulous Belgian detective was named after a vegetable—*poireau* means "leek" in French. But it's more likely that Poirot's creator, Agatha Christie, took the name from the stories of another female author of the time, Marie Belloc Lowndes. Her character: a French detective named Hercules Popeau.

TRAVIS MCGEE (1964)

John D. MacDonald began working on his Florida boat-bum character in 1962, calling him Dallas McGee. The next year, President John Kennedy was shot—in Dallas—and MacDonald changed the name to Travis.

KINSEY MILLHONE (1982)

Sue Grafton spent 15 years as a Hollywood scriptwriter before the birth of her first Kinsey Millhone novel, *A Is for Alibi*. Where'd she get the name? From the birth announcements page of her local newspaper.

JOHN SHAFT (1970)

Ernest Tidyman was trying to sell the idea of a bad-ass black detective to his publisher, but was stymied when the publisher asked the character's name—he didn't have one ready. Tidyman absent-mindedly looked out the window and saw a sign that said "Fire shaft." He looked back at the publisher and said, "Shaft. John Shaft."

*　　*　　*

"Ninety-eight percent of the adults in this country are decent, hard-working, honest citizens. It's the other 2% that get all the publicity. But then, we elected them."

—Lily Tomlin

Q: How many time zones are there in North America? A: 8.

CELEBRITY LAWSUITS

It seems that people will sue each other over practically anything. Here are a few real-life examples of unusual legal battles involving celebrities.

P **LAINTIFF:** President Theodore Roosevelt
DEFENDANT: Newspaper publisher George Newett
LAWSUIT: In 1912 Newett wrote an editorial in his Ishpeming, Michigan, paper, *The Iron Ore.* "Roosevelt lies, and curses in a most disgusting way," he wrote. "He gets drunk too, and that not infrequently, and all of his intimates know about it." Roosevelt happened to be campaigning for another presidential term at the time and jumped at the opportunity to be the center of a big news story. He sued Newett for libel, insisting that he hardly drank alcohol at all. Roosevelt arrived in the small town with a phalanx of security, some famous friends to act as character witnesses, and a horde of reporters and photographers. Huge crowds showed up for the trial. *The National Enquirer* even gave the start of arguments a banner headline: DRUNKEN ROOSEVELT TRIAL BEGINS! On the stand, Roosevelt mesmerized the judge, the jury, and the crowd with long stories about his many adventures around the world.

VERDICT: Newett must have realized he was outgunned. After five days, he gave up, reading a statement to the court admitting that he had wronged the former president. Roosevelt, having proved his point, asked the judge that he be awarded the lowest legal sum—6¢. The judge agreed. Asked by a reporter what he would do with his winnings, he replied, "That's about the price of a good paper." Cost of *The Iron Ore*: 3¢.

PLAINTIFF: Judy Z. Knight, aka JZ Knight
DEFENDANT: Julie Ravel
LAWSUIT: Knight claimed she could go into a trance and "channel" the spirit of a 35,000-year-old warrior from the lost continent of Atlantis named Ramtha. She charged fees of up to $1,500 per séance. By the 1980s she had attracted thousands of followers (including actresses Shirley MacLaine and Linda Evans), had pub-

lished books and videotapes, and had become very wealthy. When Ravel, also a clairvoyant, started channeling the same ancient Atlantian in 1992, Knight sued her in an Austrian courtroom. "I've had spiritual contact with Ramtha since 1978," Knight said. "I need him and he needs me."

"Ramtha feeds his thoughts and energies through me and me alone," Ravel replied. "I am his keeper."

VERDICT: Knight won. The judge ordered Ravel to stop using the Ramtha "brand" and to pay Knight $800 for interfering with her transmissions and for creating her subsequent period of "spiritual limbo."

PLAINTIFF: Shenandoah South Theater
DEFENDANT: Singer Wayne Newton
LAWSUIT: In 1994 Newton filed suit against the Branson, Missouri, theater for failing to pay him his full fee. Shenandoah owner Gary Snadon immediately filed a countersuit. Newton had appeared at the Shenandoah in 1993 and had been paid $5 million, Snadon said, while the theater had lost $500,000. Snadon's suit charged that Newton had ruined the theater's reputation. How? Because the singer told too many "fat" jokes and jokes about people from Pennsylvania.
VERDICT: Newton paid an undisclosed amount in a settlement before the trial ended. The Shenandoah South closed down later that year.

*　　*　　*

RANDOM FACTS TO BUG YOU

• The praying mantis is the only insect that can turn its head like a human.

• The word *bug* started out as the Anglo-Saxon word *bugge* or *bough*, meaning "a terror, a devil, or a ghost."

• The hairs on the butt of a cockroach are so sensitive that they can detect air currents made by the onrushing tongue of a toad.

• The praying mantis is the official state insect of Connecticut.

• Mating soapberry bugs remain locked in embrace for up to 11 days, which exceeds the life span of many other insects.

President Gerald R. Ford's birth name was Leslie Lynch King, Jr. (He was adopted.)

TODAY'S MENU

Funky foods from around the world.

CRACKLING ICE. Researchers from a Japanese steel company discovered that samples of Antarctic ice mixed in alcoholic drinks make distinctive, loud crackling sounds. When the ice is placed in alcohol, air bubbles trapped in the ice thousands of years ago are released with a loud popping sound. The stronger the alcohol, the louder the sound. Straight whiskey (80 proof) over the ice produces crackling sounds of around 70 decibels (equal to the noise of a loud radio) every second or so.

CRETE-DE-COQ. Cock's combs are often used by French and Italian chefs to garnish various poultry dishes. (The comb is the red, fleshy thing on top of a rooster's head.) According to experts, it's chewy but quite tasty.

CONCHA FINA. This shellfish looks like an oyster. But while oysters are often served raw (and dead), this Spanish delicacy is always served raw...and alive. Squeeze a little fresh lemon over the *concha fina.* When it starts fidgeting, pour it down your throat.

FRUIT BAT SOUP. A delicacy from Micronesia made with fruit bats (also called flying foxes). For the soup, the meat of the fruit bat is simmered in water, ginger, and onion and topped off with scallions, soy sauce, and coconut cream. When not in the soup, these furry bats are said to make affectionate pets.

CHIA PET SALAD. This dish features the edible sprouts of *Salvia columbariae*—related to the spice, sage. The "fur" that grows out of the ceramic cow, frog, hippo, puppy, or whatever is stripped from the pottery and tossed lightly with peppery nasturtiums and beanlike tulip flowers.

STUFFED ROAST CAMEL. It is served at traditional Bedouin wedding feasts in Middle Eastern and North African deserts. Ingredients include 1 medium-sized camel, 1 medium-sized North African goat, 1 spring lamb, 1 large chicken (some recipes substitute fish or monitor lizard), 1 boiled egg, 450 cloves of garlic, and

---

Holy cow! McDonald's uses 560 million pounds of beef each year.

1 large bunch of fresh coriander.

The chicken is stuffed with the boiled egg and coriander, then stuffed into the lamb, which is stuffed into the goat, which is stuffed into the camel. The camel is then spiked with garlic, brushed with butter, and roasted over an open fire. The finished dish is placed at the center of the table. Pieces of camel, goat, lamb, and chicken are pulled off and eaten with the hands. No utensils are required. Serves 100 to 150 guests.

SCHLAGSCHOCKEN. The recipe for this dessert from Zurich, Switzerland, calls for 12 pounds of cream, sugar, eggs, honey, and chocolate, all reduced down into a single four-inch square of Schlagschocken. *Warning:* The Swiss are used to this rich treat, but visitors have been known to pass out from eating a single serving.

CURRIED RAT. On your next trip to Vietnam, try this local delicacy. Severe flooding in 2000 nearly wiped out the rat population in rice fields along the Mekong River, but they're back on the menu thanks to their amazingly fast reproductive rate. Rat catchers make about $4 a day selling them to restaurants. Choice rat meat goes for $1.70 per kilo ($.77 per pound). Don't like curry? Try fried rat, rat on the grill, or rat sour soup.

IGUANA EGGS. A Central American favorite. Boil the eggs for 10 minutes, then sun-dry them. The result is a slightly rubbery egg with a cheeselike flavor. How do you get iguana eggs? Catch a pregnant female iguana, slit the abdomen open with a sharp knife, and gently remove the eggs. Then rub some ashes into the wound, sew it up with needle and thread, and let the iguana go. There's a good chance you'll see her again next year for another meal.

BIRD'S NEST SOUP. Have you seen this on a menu in some fancy Chinese restaurant? Forget it. *Real* bird's nest soup is made from bird spit—the gooey, stringy saliva that Chinese swiftlets use to attach their nests to the walls of caves. The hardened saliva is prized for its medicinal—and aphrodisiac—properties, which makes it very expensive. The license fee to harvest one cave: $100,000. The soup is a simple chicken broth, with one good dollop of bird spit in it.

FLYING FLOPS

Okay, so the last thing you want to read about is airplane trouble. But it's better to read about it in the bathroom than in an airplane. What? You took this book with you on a flight to Hawaii? Oh, well, our advice: skip this article for now and read it when you're back on solid porcelain.

CAPRONI CA-60 TRANSAEREO (1921)

If a plane with two wings is called a biplane, and a plane with three wings is called a triplane, what do you call a plane with nine wings? A *very* bad idea.

Count Gianni Caproni was an Italian nobleman who owned an airplane factory and built bombers for the Italian Air Force in 1914 and 1915. Yet for some reason, when he set out to build a seaplane that could fly from Italy all the way to New York, he ignored all of his practical experience. Instead of building a *plane* that could land on water, he took a *houseboat* and added wings—nine wings (three in the front, three in the middle and three in the back)—and eight engines (four on the front wings to pull the plane, and four on the back wings to push it).

On March 4, 1921, his test pilot fired up the engines, taxied across Lake Maggiore, and took off...sort of.

The craft got about 60 feet into the air, then suddenly nose-dived, broke into pieces, and slammed into the lake. The pilot survived, but Count Caproni's image did not. "His reputation for commercial aircraft thoroughly blackened," Bill Yenne writes in *The World's Worst Aircraft*, "Caproni skulked away into oblivion."

THE BREWSTER BUFFALO

In the 1930s, the U.S. Navy checked out prospective new fighter planes by putting them through a rigorous test flight. A test pilot would fly the prototype to its maximum altitude and then take it into a long, steep dive at full speed. If the pilot could pull out of the dive without ripping the plane's wings off, the Navy would consider buying it.

Reasonable or not, the test encouraged airplane manufacturers to build planes stronger than necessary, which made them heavy.

That, in turn, made them slow and difficult to maneuver—bad qualities for aircraft whose speed and agility could mean the difference between victory and defeat.

The worst example of this was the 2.5-ton Brewster Buffalo. It was so overbuilt in its structure that the manufacturer *under*built other parts of it—landing gear and machine guns, for example—just to save on weight.

England's Royal Air Force bought 150 Buffaloes, but then found them so worthless against the fast German fighters that it sent them to Britain's Far East colonies, to go up against Japanese fighters (considered "antiquated junk"). Big mistake—Japan's Mitsubishi Zeros proved to be faster, more maneuverable and better armed. They flew circles—literally—around the Buffaloes, whose four tiny machine guns were no match for the Zero's two larger machine guns and 20-millimeter cannons.

According to one expert, within a few months of the start of the war, "every Buffalo in the Far East had been lost, giving Brewster the distinction of having handed the Japanese complete air superiority over Southeast Asia on a silver platter."

Only a few American Buffaloes saw action and they didn't see it for long—13 of the 19 sent into combat during the Battle of Midway in June 1942 were shot out of the sky in less than half an hour. "It is my belief," wrote one Buffalo pilot who survived, "that any commander who orders pilots out for combat in a Brewster should consider the pilot as lost before leaving the ground."

CONVAIR XFY-1 POGO

One of the problems with flying an airplane, especially in a war, is that there isn't always a runway where you need one. The Convair Pogo, developed in the mid-1950s, was designed to be an airplane that didn't *need* a runway. It looked just like an ordinary plane, except that it was tilted up vertically on its tail like a rocket. It had an engine and propeller so powerful that it could take off straight up in the air and land the same way, just like a helicopter...or a pogo stick.

Taking off wasn't too difficult, but landing vertically was another story: the pilot had to literally set the plane back down on the ground while looking over his shoulder, which was almost impossible.

It was the same with a similar plane, the XFV-1, being developed at Lockheed. "We practiced landing looking over our shoulders," remembers Lockheed designer Kelly Johnson, "but we couldn't tell how fast we were coming down, or when we would hit. We wrote the Navy: 'We think it is inadvisable to *land* the airplane.' They came back with one paragraph that said, 'We agree.'"

CONVAIR XF2Y-1 SEA DART

The Sea Dart was built in the 1950s when it was easy to get money from the Pentagon and defense contractors were willing to try anything. So how about a supersonic jet fighter...on water skis?

Only five prototypes were ever made, only three were ever flown, and only two made it back safely. Vibration caused by the retractable skis made the Sea Dart unstable, but what really killed it was common sense. With the Pentagon's approval, Convair had pumped millions into the Sea Dart program without having any idea *why* such planes should be built in the first place. They never did come up with a reason, either.

"The program was terminated," Yenne writes, "without ever having demonstrated any operational rationale."

* * *

THOUGHTS FOR THE THRONE

If you could shrink the world down to 100 people—keeping the same ratios—there would be:

- 51 female, 49 male

- 57 Asians, 21 Europeans, 14 from the Americas, and 8 Africans

- 70 nonwhite, 30 white

- 70 non-Christian, 30 Christian

- 50% of the wealth in the hands of 6 people—all in the U.S.

- 80 living in substandard housing

- 70 who were illiterate

- 50 suffering from malnutrition

- 1 person near death, 1 near birth

- 1 with a college education

- Not one who owned a computer...or a *Bathroom Reader*

BOX OFFICE BLOOPERS

Some of our favorites from new and classic films.

Movie: *E.T. The Extra-Terrestrial* (1982)
Scene: When Elliott (Henry Thomas) first meets E.T. in his backyard, a crescent moon can be seen overhead.
Blooper: In the famous bike-flying scene, the silhouettes of Elliott and E.T. pass in front of a full moon, yet it's only three days later.

Movie: *Braveheart* (1995)
Scene: In the beginning of the film, young William Wallace (James Robinson) is throwing rocks with his left hand.
Blooper: In the next scene, a grown-up William Wallace (Mel Gibson) is throwing rocks with his right hand.

Movie: *Terminator 3: Rise of the Machines* (2003)
Scene: At the veterinary hospital, Kate (Claire Danes) is hiding only a few feet away from the T-X (Kristanna Loken).
Blooper: The T-X is *the* state-of-the-art Terminator, with heightened sensory awareness all around: sight, hearing, smell, even the ability to sense body heat. Yet somehow Kate—heavy breathing, sweating, and all—stays under the T-X's radar and escapes.

Movie: *Titanic* (1997)
Scene: The passengers are all boarding the lifeboats.
Blooper: One of them is wearing a digital watch.

Movie: *Maid in Manhattan* (2002)
Scene: Near the beginning of the movie, it's six days before Christmas. There's a fresh blanket of snow in the foreground.
Blooper: Someone forgot to tell the trees—in the next scene they all have green leaves.

Movie: *L.A. Confidential* (1997)
Scene: Toward the end of the movie, Lynn Bracken (Kim Basinger) is talking to Detective Exley (Guy Pearce).

Makes sense: *Frito* means "fried" in Spanish.

Blooper: An establishing shot shows them facing each other, but in each of their close-ups, the sun is behind their heads. Are there two suns in Los Angeles?

Movie: *Forrest Gump* (1994)
Scene: After Jenny (Robin Wright) dies, Forrest (Tom Hanks) is visiting her grave. He says, "You died on a Saturday."
Blooper: The gravestone reads March 12, 1982 (it's a Monday).

Movie: *Galaxy Quest* (1999)
Scene: When Commander Taggert (Tim Allen) and Lieutenant Madison (Sigourney Weaver) first encounter the "chompers," Madison exclaims, "Oh, screw that!"
Blooper: That's what we *hear*, but it doesn't take a professional lip reader to see that she actually says…a word other than "screw."

Movie: *The Rocky Horror Picture Show* (1975)
Scene: The audience is told that it is a "late November evening."
Blooper: In the very next scene, when Brad (Barry Bostwick) and Janet (Susan Sarandon) are in the car, Richard Nixon's resignation speech is playing on the radio. Nixon resigned in August.

Movie: *Pearl Harbor* (2001)
Scene: When Evelyn (Kate Beckinsale) first arrives at Pearl Harbor, she walks past a tall building.
Blooper: The building has a sign that says "Est. 1953"—12 years after the actual attack.

Movie: *When Harry Met Sally* (1989)
Scene: During a car ride when Harry (Billy Crystal) first gets to know Sally (Meg Ryan), Harry is spitting seeds out of an open window.
Blooper: An exterior shot shows that Harry's window is closed.

Movie: *There's Something About Mary* (1998)
Scene: Ted Stroehmann (Ben Stiller) gets "stuck" in his zipper.
Blooper: While trying to get free of the zipper, Ted somehow manages to alternate between wearing his tuxedo jacket and not wearing it, from close-ups to wide shots.

Good news: *Chrematophobia,* the fear of money, is curable. Send your dough to the BRI!

LAND OF THE GIANTS

Back in the early 1960s, little Uncle John saw a giant statue of Paul Bunyan at Freedomland USA, an amusement park outside New York City. Freedomland closed in 1964, but the Paul Bunyan statue is still around—standing behind a gas station in nearby Elmsford, New York. And it turns out there are a lot more Paul Bunyans around the country…if you know where to find them.

WHO'S THAT MAN?

If you've taken a lot of car trips you've seen them—18- to 25-foot figures of dark-haired, square-jawed men, dressed in a short-sleeved shirt and work pants. Their arms are extended at the elbow, with the right hand facing up and the left hand facing down, often holding something, like a muffler or a roll of carpet.

What you might not know is that there are more than 150 of these gigantic fiberglass figures dotting America's highways, advertising everything from tires to burger joints to amusement parks. Almost all of them were made by one man.

BIRTH OF THE BIG BOYS

It all started in 1962, when the Paul Bunyan Cafe on Route 66 in Flagstaff, Arizona, wanted a statue of their namesake to stand by the highway and attract hungry motorists. Prewitt Fiberglass in Venice, California, was happy to supply a figure of the giant lumberjack and created a molded Paul Bunyan character wearing a green cap, a dark beard, a red shirt, and jeans, and holding an axe.

That was it as far as Prewitt Fiberglass was concerned—one customer, one Paul Bunyan. But then owner Bob Prewitt decided to sell his business to a fiberglass boat builder named Steve Dashew. Dashew renamed the company International Fiberglass and, wanting to make a success of his new venture, started looking for business opportunities.

The leftover Paul Bunyan mold caught his eye. It was such an odd asset, he thought it might have value. Dashew began calling retail businesses around the country and asking them if they could use a giant advertising figure. A few said they could. When a story about one of Dashew's customers appeared in a retail trade magazine, stating that sales had doubled after the Paul Bunyan went up, business in the giant fiberglass figures began to boom.

PAUL BUNYAN'S FRIENDS

Dashew started to aggressively market the big statues across the country, and sold them by the score. At first they were all Paul Bunyans, but Dashew soon discovered he could modify the basic mold slightly to create other figures.

• He turned them into cowboys, Indians, and astronauts. All of the figures had the same arm configuration as the first Paul Bunyan, so they were almost always holding something, like a plate or some tires.

• International Fiberglass made other figures, too—such as giant chickens, dinosaurs, and tigers—selling each for $1,800 to $2,800.

• They made 300 "Big Friends" for Texaco, figures of smiling Texaco service attendants in green uniforms with green caps.

• They built Yogi Bear figures for Yogi Bear's Honey Fried Chicken restaurants in North and South Carolina.

• To advertise Uniroyal Tires, they made a series of hulking women who looked a lot like Jackie Kennedy, holding a tire in one of her upraised hands. These women were issued with a dress, which could be removed to reveal a bikini.

But the figures made from the original Paul Bunyan mold proved to be the most popular, not to mention the most cost-effective for Dashew, who used the same mold over and over again. By the mid-1960s, the figures had made their way into hundreds of towns across the United States and were great attention-getters for retail stores and restaurants of all kinds.

BYE-BYE, BUNYAN

But by the 1970s, the big figures that had seemed so impressive years earlier were getting dingy, weather-beaten, and silly looking to the next generation of consumers. As sales of the statues slowed, Dashew concentrated his energies on other business ventures. In 1976 he sold the business and the Paul Bunyan mold was destroyed.

Today, most of the fiberglass colossi are also gone, having been destroyed, removed, or beaten down by the elements. But they haven't all disappeared. In fact, almost every state in the Union has at least one. With businesses changing hands, the figures have been modified over the years:

• One Bunyan in Malibu, California, used to hold an immense hamburger. When a Mexican food joint bought out the burger place, he was given a sombrero and a serape, and his hamburger was replaced with a taco.

• A Bunyan at Lynch's Super Station in Havre de Grace, Maryland, was dressed in desert fatigues in 1991 to show support for the Gulf War.

• One former Uniroyal Gal stands in front of Martha's Cafe in Blackfoot, Idaho, holding a sandwich platter.

• Another Uniroyal Gal, in Rocky Mount, North Carolina, has been dressed in a pair of Daisy Duke shorts, given a beach ball to hold, fitted with a queen-size stainless-steel belly button ring, and placed in front of the Men's Night Out "private club."

BIG MEN IN THE MEDIA
If you can't get to see one of the giant statues in person, you can look for them in movies and on TV:

• A Paul Bunyan was featured in the 1969 movie *Easy Rider.*

• A modified Bunyan is pictured in the opening credits of the TV show *The Sopranos.* The figure, which holds a giant roll of carpet to advertise Wilson's Carpet in Jersey City, New Jersey, is now a stop on the New Jersey Sopranos bus tour.

• Bunyans have also made appearances in the TV show *The A-Team,* in the 2000 John Travolta flick *Battlefield Earth,* and in commercials for Saturn cars and Kleenex Tissues.

*   *   *

PATRIOTIC PAUL
In the small town of Cheshire, Connecticut, a Paul Bunyan statue ignited controversy because zoning laws declared him too tall for any purpose other than holding a flag. The statue now functions as a flagpole.

In Greek mythology, Nike is the goddess of victory.

A PASSING FANCY

Creativity—why should it be wasted on the living? Now,
thanks to some imaginative "grief counselors" (see
page 209), our dearly departed have quite a few
options as to where to spend eternity.

O UT OF THIS WORLD
The remains of more than 100 people have been shot
into space by Celestis of Houston, Texas. They pack a
small portion of cremated remains (or "cremains") into a lipstick-
sized aluminum container, load it into a NASA spacecraft, and
blast it into an Earth or moon orbit. Timothy Leary and *Star Trek*
creator Gene Roddenberry both chose this after-death option.
Cost: $995 to $12,500.

DIAMONDS ARE FOREVER

LifeGem of Chicago came up with a brilliant idea: They compress
portions of cremated remains into manufactured diamonds. It
sounds like a hoax but it's for real: after all, diamonds are carbon—
the same stuff humans are made of—and it's been possible to manufacture diamonds from carbon since the 1970s. So far they've
made the blue-tinted diamonds (which get their hue from the
boron present in human remains) for 50 clients, whose loved ones
usually have the diamonds set into jewelry. Cost: $4,000 and up.

PUSHING UP DAISIES

San Francisco's Creative Cremains mixes cremated ashes and
flower seeds into the paper they use to make their handmade
death-announcement cards. The cards are intended for grieving
friends or relatives, who can cut them into pieces and plant them
to create a flowering garden memorial. Cost: $300 and up.

SPEND ETERNITY WITH YOUR GOLF CLUB

A dizzying variety of companies will pack a portion of human
ashes into keepsake items, from fishing rods to pendants to musical instruments. The objects can also be engraved with details of
the deceased's life. Cost: $150 and up.

GOING OUT WITH A BANG

Celebrate Life of Lakeside, California, will pack the cremated remains of your loved one into fireworks and then explode them on a beach or off a boat at sunset. Fireworks shows can be coordinated to music ("When Irish Eyes Are Smiling," "Wind Beneath My Wings," etc.) and can even be rendered in red, white, and blue. Cost: $500 to $3,750.

GOOD G-REEF

Since late 1999, Georgia's Eternal Reefs Inc. has mixed the ashes of more than 200 ocean lovers with eco-friendly concrete to create artificial "reef balls." Once lowered into the ocean, the balls provide refuge for fish and other sea life. Eternal Reefs attempts to place the balls near areas of damaged coral to give plants a new home to cling to. Cost: $1,495 to $4,950.

DIG THIS!

The nutrients a decaying body gives off are typically wasted when enclosed in a traditional wood or metal coffin. The "green burial" movement encourages the deceased to go out in environmental style instead, buried in a biodegradable cardboard box or a simple shroud. This method is widely embraced in the United Kingdom, where some 150 burial grounds offer green burial. The United States has been slower to follow, but Memorial Ecosystems in South Carolina has buried 18 nonembalmed bodies in biodegradable caskets on its 33-acre site since 1998. Cost: $3,000 or less.

HANGING AROUND

Mississippi's Eternally Yours incorporates cremated remains into paintings, sprinkling a few tablespoons over original works of art that can be customized to match home decor or the deceased's interests. Cost: $350 to $950.

FREE AT LAST

Donated bodies, called "anatomical gifts" in the funeral biz, are used for research at medical schools across the country. Many medical facilities will pick up the "gift" at no charge to the deceased's estate. Once the research is complete, the body is cremated. Cost: Free.

DIE-HARD CHICKEN

Readers have been asking us to tell this story for years. It was so weird even we had a hard time swallowing it... but it's true.

OFF WITH HIS HEAD!
On September 10, 1945, Mike the rooster was making his usual rounds in the Olsen farmyard in Fruita, Colorado. He paused for a moment to join the other Wyandotte chickens as they hunted and pecked for grain outside the chicken coop. Mike didn't notice the dark shadow that fell across his path. It was Lloyd Olsen.

Clara Olsen had sent her husband out to the chicken coop on a mission: catch the rooster and prepare him for dinner. Lloyd Olsen grabbed Mike and put the rooster on the chopping block. Remembering that his mother-in-law (who was coming to dinner) loved chicken necks, Lloyd took special care to position the ax on Mike's neck so a generous portion of neck would remain. He gave that rooster one strong whack and cut off his head.

Mike the now-headless rooster ran around in circles, flapping his wings. At this point, most chickens would have dropped dead. Instead, Mike raced back to the coop, where he joined the rest of the chickens as they hunted and pecked for food.

Lloyd Olsen was flabbergasted. He kept expecting the rooster to keel over. It never happened. The next morning he checked again and found the feathered fellow—minus his head—asleep in the henhouse with the hens.

ONE FUNKY CHICKEN

Lloyd decided that if Mike was so determined to live, even without a head, he would figure out a way to give him food and water, so Lloyd used an eyedropper to drip food and water into Mike's gullet.

When Mike had managed to live an entire week, Lloyd and Clara took their headless wonder to scientists at the University of Utah to determine how it was possible for the bird to stay alive without a head. The scientists determined that the ax had missed the jugular vein, and a clot had kept Mike from bleeding to death. Although his head was gone, his brainstem and one ear were left on his body. Since a chicken's reflex actions are controlled by the brain stem, Mike's body was able to keep on ticking.

MIRACLE MIKE

Sensing that Mike had the possibility of becoming a real cash cow (or chicken), the Olsens hired a manager and took him on a national tour. Audiences in New York, Los Angeles, Atlantic City, and San Diego paid a quarter each to see "Miracle Mike." *Time* and *Life* magazines ran feature articles on the amazing fowl. Mike even made it into the *Guinness Book of World Records*. This "Wonder Chicken" was so valuable, he was insured for $10,000.

For 18 happy months Mike was a celebrity. Then one night in a motel in Arizona, Mike the headless chicken started choking on some food. Lloyd tried to save him, but he couldn't find the syringe he had often used to clear Mike's throat. Moments later Mike was dead—this time for real.

Those who knew Mike, which included many of the residents of Fruita, remembered him as a "robust chicken, and a fine specimen, except for not having a head." One recalled that Mike seemed "as happy as any other chicken."

GONE BUT NOT FORGOTTEN

Mike's been dead for almost 60 years, but his spirit lives on in Fruita. In 1999 the Chamber of Commerce was looking for something more interesting than "pioneers" as the theme for Colorado Heritage Week, when someone suggested Mike. Now, every third weekend in May, folks in this town of 6,500 gather to celebrate the remarkable rooster at the "Mike the Headless Chicken Festival."

The two-day-long celebration features the 5K Run Like a Chicken race, egg tosses, Pin the Head on the Chicken, a Cluck Off, Rubber Chicken Juggling, and the Chicken Dance. Chicken Bingo is played with chicken droppings on a grid and there is a Famous Fowl Pet Parade, for which owners dress their dogs, cats, and horses like chickens. Of course, great quantities of chicken— fried or barbecued—are enjoyed by all.

In 2000 Mike was memorialized in a statue made out of rakes, axes, and farm implements by artist Lyle Nichols, who said, "I made him proud-looking and cocky." And he gave the chamber a discount on the sculpture…because it didn't have a head.

If you have *alektorophobia,* you're chicken…of chickens.

NAME THAT COUNTRY

See if you can guess the name of the country before reading all the clues. (Answers on page 499.)

SAVED

1. It was originally inhabited by the Pipil tribe.
2. The Pipil are believed to be direct descendants of the Aztecs.
3. The Pipil were defeated by Spanish explorers looking for gold.
4. The Christian Spaniards named it in honor of Jesus.

Name the country

NOTHING TO IT

1. The local Nama people call it "an area where there is nothing."
2. The name describes the coastal desert area of the country.
3. It has been governed at different times by the British, the Germans, and the South Africans.
4. It gained independence in 1990 from South Africa.

Name the country

THE NAMELESS NAME

1. It got its European name long before Europeans knew it existed.
2. Early geographers insisted it must be there—if not, the Earth would "wobble."
3. The early name was Latin for "The Unknown Southern Land."
4. Captain James Cook "discovered" it in 1770.

Name the country

OVER THERE WHERE THE SUN COMES UP

1. Our word for this country originally comes from China.
2. It combines the words "sun" and "east," meaning "sunrise," or "sun's origin."
3. Portuguese traders learned the name from Malaysians in the 1500s.
4. Inhabitants of this country call it Nippon.

Name the country

It takes 16,550 kernels of durum wheat to make a pound of pasta.

GRECIAN FORMULA

1. Early inhabitants called themselves the Pritani.

2. The Greek sailor Pytheas named it after the inhabitants in 300 B.C.

3. When enemy tribes attacked in the 400s, many inhabitants fled this island, taking the name with them to the mainland.

4. To differentiate between the new "lesser" settlement on the mainland, the word "Greater" was added to the name of the island.

Name the island

ACUTE COUNTRY, BUT A BIT OBTUSE

1. This country, when grouped with two other countries, is known by another name.

2. When grouped with three other countries, it's known by yet another name.

3. The name comes from a Germanic tribe that invaded the country about 1,500 years ago.

4. It is believed that the tribe's name referred to their homeland in present-day Germany, which was shaped like a fishhook.

Name the country

WHY DON'T THEY SPEAK GERMAN?

1. This country was also named after an invading Germanic tribe.

2. The tribe's name came from a Latin word meaning "masculine."

3. Their allegiance with Rome, and use of its written Latin language, are two reasons why their language is so different from German.

4. They controlled so much of Europe at one point that the Arabic and Persian words for "European" are based on their name.

Name the country

OVERCOATIA

1. This country was named by the Portuguese in the 1470s.

2. The name comes from the Portuguese word for a traditional overcoat: *Gabao*.

3. The French gained control of this equatorial country in the late 1800s and helped to end its slave trade.

4. It's in western Africa.

Name the country

Myth conception: Rice thrown at weddings *won't* kill the birds that eat it.

MADE IN JAPAN: WEIRD GAME SHOWS

Reality shows like The Bachelor, Survivor *and* Fear Factor
*prove that people will do just about anything for money...and
they'll do it on national television. But even those shows
don't compare to crazy programs on Japanese television.*

Z **A GAMAN**
Object of the Game: University students compete in contests to see who can stand the most pain, eat the most unpleasant foods, and perform the most humiliating tasks.

Anything for Money: In one episode, "contestants were taken to an icy location, made to drink huge amounts of beer, and kept jogging up and down as their bladders swelled. The dubious winner was the drinker who lasted longest" without having to pee. (A restroom was provided.) In another segment, contestants rolled down a steep hill inside barrels; in another, they did headstands in the desert while officials with magnifying glasses focused sunlight on their nipples.

Update: *Za Gaman* was the inspiration for the British game show *Endurance U.K.*, in which eight players compete in humiliating and disgusting contests—bobbing for false teeth in buckets of pig eyeballs, eating quiches full of maggots—to win valuable prizes.

TAKESHI'S CASTLE

Object of the Game: This show was inspired by the obstacle courses in 1980s-era video games like Donkey Kong. One hundred players start each game—they're the "soldiers" of a character called "General Lee" and their goal is to storm Count Takeshi's castle, which is guarded by Takeshi and his henchmen. Wearing helmets and knee pads, the contestants scream out, "I'll do my best!" as they begin several rounds of physical challenges, with each successive round being harder than the one before it. Each round puts them closer to Takeshi's Castle.

In the first round, players might have to scale a wall or, with their hands tied behind their backs, bite a bun that is hanging on

---

British peerage, from lowest to highest rank: baron, viscount, earl, marquis, duke.

a string dangling over their heads. In the next round, they might play tag wearing giant blueberry suits or climb a steep hill while Takeshi's henchmen shoot water guns at the targets on their helmets. Then contestants might ride a giant rice bowl down a waterslide into a pond—if they fall out of the bowl, they're out.

Players who fail to complete a round lose the game. Prize for making it to the final round and storming the castle: 1 million yen—about $8,500.

Anything for Money: So how hard is it? The list of injuries suffered by contestants is long: broken arms, legs, fingers, toes, and jaws; concussions; bruises; and lacerations galore. Usually only 5 or 6 contestants out of the original 100 make it to the final round and attempt to storm Takeshi's Castle. And most of these attempts fail—the castle has been taken only a handful of times. Want to see the show for yourself? In mid-2003 it began airing on the Spike network under the name MXC—*Most Extreme Elimination Challenge*.

TV CHAMPION

Object of the Game: A different type of competition is aired each week—sushi rolling, cake baking, flower arranging, speed eating, trivia quizzes, etc. Some contests are screwier than others.

Anything for Money: In the "Lung Man Championship," contestants bowled by blowing a bowling ball into the pins; in the "Sweat King Championship," they collected their own sweat in a bottle.

FOOD BATTLE CLUB

Object of the Game: This show is like *TV Champion*, except that all of the contests are "gluttony" contests—players gorge themselves on food or beverages to see who can consume the most.

Anything for Money: "Contestants, mostly young men, double-fist platefuls of sushi, drain glasses of milk, and slurp up bowls of steaming ramen noodles. Some visibly hold back a vomit reflex as the cameras zoom in on the food and saliva dribbling down their chins."

Japan's craze for speed-eating shows took off in 1996, when a 144-pound speed-eating champ named Hirofumi Nakajima went to New York and won the Nathan's Famous Hot Dog eating contest by downing $24\frac{1}{4}$ hot dogs in 12 minutes, beating out 320-pound American Ed Krachie. Nakajima, who reportedly had never eaten a hot dog before, went on to win the contest three years in a row. Speed-eating contest shows like *The King of Gluttons* and *The National Big Eaters' Tournament* flooded Japanese airwaves after Nakajima's success, and they're still popular today.

MUSCLE RANKING

Object of the Game: This hour-long, primetime Saturday night show featured regular people "pitted against celebrities and athletes in offbeat tests of agility and strength." If you won a round you moved up in the "Muscle Ranking." Michael Jordan appeared on an episode in 1999.

Anything for Money: One week contestants might have to springboard over a 10-foot pyramid; on another, they'd have to hit baseballs through small holes in a wooden tic-tac-toe board. Then there was the time they flung themselves into Velcro-covered walls while wearing Velcro-covered suits.

Update: *Muscle Ranking* was pulled from the airwaves in May 2002 after two contestants suffered spinal injuries while taping the show—one was hurt when he fell into a moat while jumping on a giant styrofoam ball, the other while trying to stop a different giant ball from rolling down a slope. "The purpose of the show is to entertain, but if people are getting hurt in its making, the audience can't enjoy it," a spokesman told reporters.

*　　*　　*

CELEBRITY REVENGE

In 1938, legendary film producer David O. Selznick held auditions for a lead role in his upcoming film, *Gone With the Wind*. He wanted a redhead. A young starlet named Lucille Ball came in to audition, but it was raining outside and she was soaked. She was led to the producer's office and left alone to wait. Selznick walked in as she was trying to dry her hair. He had her quickly read the lines and dismissed her. She didn't get the part.

Revenge! Lucy never forgot. In 1957 Lucy and her husband, Desi Arnaz, by then two of the country's biggest stars, bought Selznick's old studio, renamed it Desilu, and set up their headquarters...in the office that Lucy remembered so well.

LOCAL HEROES

Here are the stories of ordinary people who were faced with
an extraordinary situation...and did something about it.

SPILT MILK

Local Hero: Steve Leech, a milkman in Cornwall, England

Heroic Deed: Putting out a dangerous fire

The Story: Leech was making his regular deliveries one morning when he noticed smoke pouring out of a gift shop along his route. He called 999 (the English equivalent of 911) but then decided not to wait for the fire fighters to arrive. "I saw the row of apartments up above the shop," he explains, "and I thought, bloody hell, I'd better do something!"

What did Leech do? He kicked open the door of the shop and started pouring milk on the fire. By the time the firefighters arrived 15 minutes later, the fire was under control—and Leech is credited with saving the row of eight shops, as well as the lives of the people living in the apartments above them. "It was hard work opening all those bottles, since they have tamper-proof lids," he says, "but it was even harder trying to explain to my boss where all the milk (320 pints) had gone."

Update: Leech needn't have worried about his boss—he not only kept his job, in January 2002 England's National Dairymen's Association named him the "Hero Milkman of the Millennium."

FIRST-RATE THIRD GRADER

Local Hero: Austin Rosedale, a third-grader at Sunny Hills Elementary School in Issaquah, Washington

Heroic Deed: Saving his teacher from choking

The Story: Austin was in the computer lab one day in November 2001 when his teacher, Mrs. Precht, started choking on a cough drop. She was just about to pass out when he sprang into action.

Luckily for Precht, Austin's parents had given him a Day Planner organizer that happened to have an instructional diagram of the Heimlich maneuver printed on the cover. Austin had read it so many times that helping Mrs. Precht was a snap. With two thrusts to her abdomen, he dislodged the cough drop. "I just visualized the pictures," he says, "and remembered what I'd read."

BLUE'S BROTHER

Local Hero: Art Aylesworth, a Montana insurance agent

Heroic Deed: Helping to save the mountain bluebird and the western bluebird from extinction

The Story: A longtime conservationist, Aylesworth had worked on a few wildlife habitat restoration projects. But in the mid-1970s he became alarmed when he learned that extensive logging in the state was pushing the bluebirds—which nest in the cavities of old trees—toward extinction. So he got some scrap lumber and built some nest boxes for the birds; then he founded an organization called the Mountain Bluebird Trails Group and recruited hundreds of volunteers to do the same thing.

The organization gave the boxes to anyone willing to put them up and keep an eye on them; it estimates that over the next 25 years, it gave away more than 35,000 boxes. Did it work? Yes— when Aylesworth started handing out the boxes in 1974, only a handful of the bluebirds were thought to still exist; by 1998 the count had grown to more than 17,000.

GUN CONTROL

Local Hero: Dale Rooks, a crossing guard at Suter Elementary School in Pensacola, Florida

Heroic Deed: Finding a unique way to get speeding motorists to slow down in front of the elementary school

The Story: For years Rooks had tried everything he could think of to get drivers to slow down in front of the school—including waving his hands and yelling—but nothing worked. Then inspiration struck him—he got an old hair dryer and covered it with gray duct tape so that it looked like a radar gun, and started pointing it at speeders. That did the trick. "People are slowing down, raising their hands at me apologetically," he says. "It's amazing how well it works."

Update: Inspired by his example, fifth-graders at the school set up a lemonade stand and raised $93 to buy Rooks a *real* radar gun. "I don't mean it to be funny," he says, "but it looks just like a hair dryer."

MONEY TALKS

A few priceless nuggets from our quote bank.

"Money's a horrid thing to follow, but a charming thing to meet."
—**Henry James**

"It's not money that brings happiness; it's lots of money."
—**Russian proverb**

"If you can actually count your money, then you are not really a rich man."
—**J. Paul Getty**

"Once in a while my wife complains about my jokes. I tell her to go cry in a big bag of money."
—**Ray Ramano**

"A feast is made for laughter, and wine maketh merry: but money answereth all things."
—**Bible**

"If there's no money in poetry, neither is there poetry in money."
—**Robert Graves**

"Who is rich? He that is content. Who is that? Nobody."
—**Ben Franklin**

"Money is a poor man's credit card."
—**Marshall McLuhan**

"Money is the worst currency that ever grew among mankind. It sacks cities, drives men from their homes, teaches and corrupts the worthiest minds to turn base deeds."
—**Sophocles**

"If you want to know what God thinks of money, just look at the people he gave it to."
—**Dorothy Parker**

"It isn't necessary to be rich and famous to be happy. It's only necessary to be rich."
—**Alan Alda**

"Make money your god and it will plague you like the devil."
—**Henry Fielding**

"Money speaks sense in a language all nations understand."
—**Aphra Behn**

"When it is a question of money, everyone is of the same religion."
—**Voltaire**

"A billion here, a billion there, pretty soon it adds up to real money."
—**Senator Everett Dirksen**

Winston Churchill called his wife "Kat." She called him "Pug."

SORRY ABOUT THAT

There are a few lessons we all learned when we were kids—be curteous to others, share your toys, and when you screw up, say you're sorry. Some people got it…and apparently some didn't.

HO! HO! HO!

Incident: In December 2002, Reverend Lee Rayfield of Maidenhead, England, had to send out letters of apology to his parishioners. Reverend Rayfield had held a special Christmas service just for children. A horrified shock went through the room when Rayfield delivered an unexpected message: Santa Claus, he told the kids, is *dead*. In order to deliver presents to all the children in the world, he explained, the reindeer would have to travel 3,000 times the speed of sound—which would make them all burn up in less than a second. The audience included "a lot of young children who still believe in Santa Claus," said one angry parent, "or did until last night."

Apology: "I guess I made a serious misjudgment," said Rayfield.

HOT WATER

Incident: After American-turned-Taliban John Walker Lindh was captured in Afganistan in November 2002, the press reported that he was from Marin County, California. That prompted former President Bush to describe Lindh as "some misguided Marin County hot-tubber." Jackie Kerwin, editor of the *Marin Independent Journal*, took exception to the insult and urged readers to write letters about it. And they did. Letters poured in, prompting newspapers, radio, and TV news programs to spread the story across the country.

Apology: "Dear Ms. Kerwin," Bush wrote to her, "Call off the dogs, please. I surrender. I will never use 'hot tub' and 'Marin County' in the same sentence again." He even made a personal phone call. "He gets on the phone and says 'Hot tubs for sale,'" Kerwin said, "and that pretty much set the tone for the rest of the conversation. But I think he was genuinely sorry."

HERE'S MUD (SLINGING) IN YOUR EYE

Incident: In the 2000 media guide for their men's basketball team, Ohio State University displayed photographs of some distinguished

---

Why do we all know Ann Turner Cook? Her face is on Gerber Baby Food jars.

alumni, including comedian Richard Lewis, who had graduated in 1969. But it turned out to be a dubious honor: the caption below his name said, "Actor, Writer, Comedian, Drunk." This was particularly insulting because Lewis is a recovering alcoholic. "I was really depressed that I would be so defamed," he said.

Apology: Red-faced officials apologized profusely…and then fired the editor, Gary Emig, who had put in "drunk" as a joke in an early draft, but forgot to take it out.

AN INFIELD HIT

Incident: Between innings at a June 2003 baseball game, the Milwaukee Brewers were staging one of their fans' favorite events: the Sausage Race. Dressed up as a bratwurst, a hot dog, an Italian sausage, and a Polish sausage, four Brewer employees raced around the infield. But as they passed the opposing team's dugout, Pittsburgh Pirate first baseman Randall Simon reached out and playfully whacked one of the runners with his bat. The employee fell to the ground, causing another runner to fall, too. The costumes were padded, so the victims received only minor knee scrapes, but Simon was taken from the park in handcuffs, charged with disorderly conduct, and fined $438.

Apology: An embarrassed Simon later called the injured sausages— Mandy Block and Veronica Piech—to personally apologize. Block, the Italian sausage that took the hit, accepted the apology and asked for an autographed bat from Simon—the one that he used to hit her. (She got it.)

I APOLOGIZE IN YOUR GENERAL DIRECTION

Incident: In an exhibit called "The Roman Experience," the Deva Museum in Chester, England, invited visitors to stroll through streets constructed to look as they did during Roman times. Hoping to provide an authentic experience, staff added an odor to the Roman latrines. They got one called "Flatulence" from Dale Air, a company that makes aromas for several museums. Unfortunately, it was too authentic: several schoolchildren immediately vomited.

Apology: Museum supervisor Christine Turner publicly apologized, saying, "It really was disgusting." But Dale Air director Frank Knight was somewhat less contrite. "We feel sorry for the kids," he said, "but it is nice to see that the smell is so realistic."

CRÈME *de la* CRUD

The best of the worst of the worst.

WORST MATADOR
"El Gallo" (Raphael Gomez Ortega), an early-20th-century bullfighter

El Gallo employed a technique called the *espantada* (sudden flight) that was unique in the history of professional bullfighting—when the bull entered the ring, he panicked, dropped his cape, and ran away. "All of us artists have bad days," he would explain. His fights were so hilarious that he was brought out of retirement seven times; in his last fight in October 1918, he claimed he spared the bull because "it winked at him." (The audience thought it was a big joke, but Ortega's relatives didn't—his brother was so ashamed during that last fight that he entered the ring and killed the bull himself...just to salvage the family's honor.)

WORST DRUG-SNIFFING DOG
"Falco," at the County Sheriff's Office, Knoxville, Tennessee

In August 2000 David and Pamela Stonebreaker were driving through Knoxville in their recreational vehicle when sheriff's deputies pulled them over for running a red light. The cops were suspicious and called for backup: a drug-sniffer named Falco. The dog sniffed outside the vehicle and signalled "positive," so deputies immediately searched the inside of the RV...and found more than a *quarter ton* of marijuana.

But in court, the Stonebreakers' attorney challenged the search—the dog couldn't be trusted. It turned out that between 1998 and 2000 Falco had signalled "positive" 225 times and the cops found drugs only 80 times. In other words, the dog was wrong nearly 70% of the time. Falco, the defense argued, was too incompetent to justify searching vehicles based on his "word" alone. The judge agreed and the Stonebreakers (their real name) went free.

LEAST-WATCHED TV SHOW IN HISTORY
"In 1978 an opinion poll showed that a French television program was watched by no viewers at all. The great day for French broad-

---

casting was August 14, when not one person saw the extensive interview with an Armenian woman on her 40th birthday. It ranged over the way she met her husband, her illnesses, and the joy of living....The program was broadcast in primetime."

—*The Incomplete Book of Failures,* by Stephen Pile

WORST JOCKEY

Beltran de Osorio y Diez de Rivera, "Iron" Duke of Albuquerque
The duke developed an obsession with winning England's Grand National Steeplechase horse race when he was only eight years old, after receiving a film of the race as a birthday present. "I said then that I would win that race one day," the amateur rider recounted years later.

• On his first attempt in 1952, he fell from his horse; he woke up later in the hospital with a cracked vertebra.

• He tried again in 1963; bookies placed odds of 66–1 against him finishing the race still on his horse. (The duke fell from the horse.)

• He raced again in 1965, and fell from his horse after it collapsed underneath him, breaking his leg.

• In 1974, having just had 16 screws removed from a leg he'd broken after falling from the horse in another race, he fell while training for the Grand National and broke his collarbone. He recovered in time to compete (in a plaster cast) and actually managed to finish the race while still on his horse—the only time he ever would. He placed eighth.

• In 1976 the duke fell again during a race—this time he was trampled by the other horses and suffered seven broken ribs, several broken vertebrae, a broken wrist, a broken thigh, and a severe concussion, which left him in a coma for two days.

• He eventually recovered, but when he announced at the age of 57 that he was going to try again, race organizers pulled his license "for his own safety."

The Iron Duke never did win the Grand National, as he promised himself he would, but he did break another record—he broke more bones trying to win it than any jockey before or since.

Desi Arnaz's mother was one of the heirs to the Bacardi Rum fortune.

FAMILIAR PHRASES

*Here's one of our regular features—the
origins of some common terms and phrases.*

THE BALL'S IN YOUR COURT

Meaning: It's your turn; it's up to you

Origin: "This term comes from tennis, where it signifies
that it is the opponent's turn to serve or play the ball. A British
equivalent is 'the ball's at your feet,' which comes from football
(soccer), and has been in use much longer. How much longer?
Lord Auckland used it figuratively in a letter written in about
1800: 'We have the ball at our feet.'" (From *Southpaws & Sunday
Punches*, by Christine Ammer)

TO BEAR DOWN

Meaning: To put pressure on someone or something

Origin: "For centuries sailors used the word *bear* in scores of
expressions to describe a ship's position in relation to the wind, the
land, or another ship. Most are still used by sailors today. *Bear up*,
for instance, means to head the ship into the wind. *Bear off* means
to head away from the wind, a phrase sailors came to use figuratively whenever they wanted anything thrust away from their person. *Bear down* in the original nautical sense meant to approach
from the weather, or windward, side. It later came to mean to
approach another ship rapidly, pressuring them to yield." (From
Scuttlebutt, by Teri Degler)

BY THE SKIN OF ONE'S TEETH

Meaning: By an extremely narrow margin; just barely

Origin: "A literal translation of a biblical phrase from Latin. The
biblical source is the passage where Job is complaining about how
illness has ravaged his body: 'My bone cleaveth to my skin and to
my flesh, and I am escaped with the skin of my teeth.' The point
is that Job is so sick that there's nothing left to his body. The passage is rendered differently in other translations; the Douay Bible,
for example—an English translation of the Vulgate (St. Jerome's
fourth-century translation)—gives: 'My bone hath cleaved to my

skin, and nothing but lips are left about my teeth.' The phrase first appeared in English in a mid-16th-century translation of the Bible. It did not become common until the 19th century." (From *Jesse's Word of the Day*, by Jesse Sheidlower)

TO EAT ONE OUT OF HOUSE AND HOME

Meaning: To eat large quantities of someone else's food

Origin: "Its first recorded use in English was by William Shakespeare, who used it in his play *Henry IV*, written in 1597–98. In Act II, Hostess Quickly of the Boar's Head Tavern is complaining about Sir John Falstaff, who has been lodging with her, eating huge quantities of food, and avoiding paying his bill: 'He hath eaten me out of house and home, he hath put all my substance into that fat belly of his…' The phrase *out of house and home* was in use as early as the 13th century, and during the 15th century people often said 'he hath eaten me out of house and harbor.' Shakespeare combined the two phrases." (From *Inventing English*, by Dale Corey)

NOT UP TO SNUFF

Meaning: Below standard

Origin: "Englishmen were so fond of finely powdered tobacco, or snuff, that its use was nearly universal throughout the kingdom. Connoisseurs would pride themselves on knowing their snuff. One derided as *not up to snuff* was considered an amateur at judging powdered tobacco. But soon the phrase expanded to any person or product considered to be less than discerning." (From *Everyday Phrases*, by Neil Ewart)

TO PAY THE PIPER

Meaning: To accept the consequences

Origin: "Street dancing was a common form of amusement during medieval times. Strolling musicians, including flute players, would play for a dance wherever they could gather a crowd.

"Frequently a dance was organized on the spur of the moment. Persons who heard the notes of a piper would drop their work and join in the fun. When they tired of the frolic, they would pass the hat for the musician. It became proverbial that a dancer had better have his fun while he could; sooner or later he would have to pay the piper." (From *I've Got Goose Pimples*, by Marvin Vanoni)

Scary thought: The great white shark is the only shark that can…

DUBIOUS ACHIEVERS

Here are some of the most bizarre world records we could find.
How bizarre? One of the record holders is a bacterium.

I 'M SENSING...SURGERY. Since 1979, Fulvia Celica Siguas Sandoval, a transsexual TV clairvoyant from Peru, has had plastic surgery 64 times. More than 25 of the operations have been to her face.

LIKE A ROCK. St. Simeon the Younger lived from 521 to 597 AD in Antioch, Syria. He spent his last 45 years sitting on top of a stone pillar.

CONAN THE BACTERIUM. *Deinococcus radiodurans* can withstand 10,000 times the radiation it would take to kill a human, earning it the title of "World's Toughest Bacterium." It was discovered living in swollen tins of irradiated meat in Oregon in the 1950s.

SOCK IT TO ME! Britain's Kirsten O'Brien managed to wear 41 socks at once...all on one foot. She performed the "feet" on the BBC's *Big Toe Radio Show* on May 20, 2003.

THE HOLE-IEST OF RECORDS. Having 600 body piercings is pretty impressive in itself, but in 2002, 28-year-old Kam Ma of Whitburn, England, got 600 piercings in 8 hours and 32 minutes.

CRIME AGAINST HUMANITY? On June 1, 2000, 566 accordian players gathered at the International Folklore Festival in the Netherlands. For 22 minutes they played folk songs in unison—becoming history's largest accordian ensemble ever (hopefully).

PANTS ON FIRE. John Graham (if that *is* his real name) holds the title "World's Biggest Liar." He earned it by telling the most tall tales at the Annual Lying Competition held in Cumbria, England. He's won the contest five times (or so he says).

POLITALKS

Politicians aren't getting much respect these days—but then, it sounds like they don't deserve much, either.

"That is true...but not absolutely true."
—**Montreal Mayor Jean Drapeau**

"My colleagues and I are upset by this blatant attempt to replace diversity with fairness."
—**N.J. assemblyman Joseph Doria**

"Solar energy is not something that is going to come in overnight."
—**Gerald Ford**

"Have we gone beyond the bounds of reasonable dishonesty?"
—**CIA memo**

"You can't just let nature run wild."
—**Gov. Wally Hickel (AK)**

"I intend to open this country up to democracy, and anyone who is against that, I will jail!"
—**President Joao Baptiste Figueiredo, Brazil**

"Things happen more frequently in the future than they do in the past."
—**Gov. Booth Gardner (WA)**

"Sometimes in order to make progress and move ahead, you have to stand up and do the wrong thing."
—**Rep. Gary Ackerman**

"If you let that sort of thing go on, your bread and butter will be cut right out from under your feet."
—**British foreign minister Ernest Bevin**

"If we don't succeed, we run the risk of failure."
—**Dan Quayle**

"We're going to move left and right at the same time."
—**Gov. Jerry Brown (CA)**

"Facts are stupid things."
—**Ronald Reagan**

"First they tax our beer, then they tax cigarettes. Now they are going to increase the tax on gasoline. All that's left are our women."
—**Sen. John East**

"Sixty years of progress, without change."
—**Saudi government's anniversary slogan**

"Gin" comes from the French *genièvre,* for "juniper." (Gin is made from juniper berries.)

HURRICANE HAZEL

Steve Pitt was born in Toronto on October 15, 1954, during the height of Hurricane Hazel. All his life, people have been telling him hurricane stories. Result: he's written a book (Rain Tonight), a documentary (Storm of the Century)...and this article.

BIRTH OF A KILLER
On October 5, 1954, meteorologists began tracking a massive tropical storm moving west toward the Caribbean island of Grenada. It was the eighth hurricane of the year, so they named it for the eighth letter in the alphabet: Hazel.

From the outset Hazel was a killer. On October 12, it swept over the island of Hispaniola (Haiti and the Dominican Republic), with devastating results. The storm surge washed away dozens of shoreline villages. Winds as high as 125 mph flattened inland towns. Torrential rains triggered mud slides that buried more than 250 people alive in the mountain town of Berley. At least 1,000 Haitians are estimated to have died within a few hours.

But the mountains of Hispaniola took their toll on Hazel as well. Hurricanes—essentially swirling masses of humid air—do not climb hills well; they lose energy with every foot. By the time Hazel was clear of Haiti, its wind speed had dropped to a mere 40 mph and meteorologists expected the storm to die before it touched land again. They were wrong. An unusually hot October sun helped recharge the storm, and by the time it passed over Bermuda, Hazel had become a Category 1 hurricane again. As it headed for North America, it grew to a Category 4.

HURRICANE ALLEY
Whenever hurricanes land on the eastern seaboard of the United States, they almost always follow the same route. Prevented from moving west by the Appalachian mountain range, they are pushed north by the rotation of the Earth. As a result, the low-lying coastal areas between South Carolina and New England have the rueful nickname "Hurricane Alley." So far that year, two hurricanes, Carol and Edna, had traveled exactly that route, and on the morning of October 15, Hazel followed in their wake. The eye of

---

Some Arctic and Antarctic fish have proteins in their blood that act as antifreeze.

the hurricane came ashore near the state line between North and South Carolina and the whole system immediately swung north toward Virginia.

Hazel caused a record 18-feet-high storm surge along the North Carolina coast, destroying hundreds of buildings and killing more than a dozen people. More records were set as winds gusted over 130 mph, damaging thousands of homes and knocking down whole forests. Crossing into Virginia, Hazel wrenched the battleship USS *Kentucky* from its moorings and ran it aground in the James River. Continuing north, the winds blasted through Washington, D.C., at 98 mph. Crossing into Pennsylvania, the storm killed 26 people across the state with flash floods and 94-mph winds. But as Hazel approached the Pennsylvania–New York line, its winds fell to less than 40 mph again and the rainfall tapered off dramatically. Hazel was now face-to-face with the Allegheny Mountains, one of the highest ridges in the Appalachian chain. As the hurricane began grinding itself against the 1,500-foot-tall barrier, meteorologists were once again confident that they had seen the last of Hazel.

IT AIN'T OVER 'TIL IT'S OVER

Then, like two obliging Boy Scouts pushing an overweight woman over a stone wall, two adjoining weather systems helped Hazel over the Alleghenies. A low-pressure system over central New York State pulled Hazel north and west, while a high-pressure system from the Midwest gave the storm a push from behind.

Twenty-one more people died from drowning, car accidents, and electrocution from downed power lines as Hazel moved across New York State. But the storm was definitely losing power every mile it moved north. As Hazel moved out over the Great Lakes, it was officially demoted from a "hurricane" to a "severe storm." Once more, meteorologists predicted the end of the storm. Once more they were wrong.

A few miles across the border in Toronto, Ontario, residents watched Hazel's approach with interest but not alarm. After all, Toronto was hundreds of miles from the ocean. Torontonians were used to massive snow storms in winter and blistering heat waves in summer…but hurricanes? The morning papers all predicted that Hazel would pass directly over the city. The official forecast said: "rain tonight."

Food for thought: Every year, about 8,000 people die from food poisoning in the U.S.

Throughout the day, rain fell fast and hard on Toronto. Some basements flooded and some roof shingles flew, but still no one paid much attention to the storm. When the rain stopped at around 10 p.m., most people thought Hazel was finished. Winds had knocked out telephone and power lines, so many people went to bed early. What they didn't know was that in less than eight hours, Hazel had deposited more than 300 million tons of water just north of the city. The rain landed on farm fields already saturated from a previous week of rain. Unable to be absorbed into the soil, the water began rolling south toward Toronto.

ROLLIN' ON THE RIVER

Toronto is a city built on river ravines. Just before midnight, people living in homes and trailers in those ravines heard a rumble. Looking out their windows, they were astonished to see normally placid streams and creeks suddenly burst over their banks and come rushing straight at their homes. Many people escaped their homes, but more than 80 people died as their homes, cars, and even a Sherman tank were swept down the rivers.

The next day the military was called out to search the valleys for survivors. There were few. What they found instead were bodies—some buried under four feet of silt and others caught in tree branches 20 feet off the ground. A few bodies, swept out into Lake Ontario, were recovered days later near Syracuse, New York.

Hazel continued moving north, eventually passing through the Arctic and finally petering out over Scandinavia.

SILVER LINING

There will never be another Hazel. Meteorologists officially retired the name out of respect for the families who suffered because of the storm.

The people of Toronto now know that hurricanes *can* attack their city. City planners use Hazel's high water lines as a benchmark for zoning. Land below the water line is zoned as parkland; no one is allowed to build homes or live there. So, from all the devastation Hazel caused, it brought at least one bit of good: Toronto now has one of the largest interconnected park and wildlife sanctuary systems in the world.

Kayaking is a required subject in Greenland's schools.

THE FABULOUS FLYING FLEA

If you designed and built your own airplane, would you name it after a small, bloodsucking insect? Believe it or not, one man did.

UPS AND DOWNS

One day during World War I, a young French soldier named Henri Mignet talked an airplane mechanic into letting him climb into the cockpit of an airplane and taxi down the runway.

Taxiing an airplane is simple enough, even for people (like Mignet) with no flying experience. But rather than stop at the end of the runway as he'd been told, Mignet gunned the engine and tried to fly the plane. He managed to get airborne but not for long: moments later both he and the plane were on their backs in a nearby cornfield.

JUST PLANE NUTS

Mignet was sent back to his unit and punished for wrecking the plane. Maybe he never lived down the humiliation, or maybe he bumped his head harder than people thought. Whatever the case, he spent the rest of his life trying to prove that the accepted scientific principles of aviation were a sham, and that people who built planes were liars and con men. He set out to prove that ordinary people could build airplanes themselves, without any help from the so-called experts.

In 1928 he wrote an article titled "Is Amateur Aviation Possible?" for a French aviation magazine. The timing couldn't have been better. Charles Lindbergh's famous flight from New York to Paris in May 1927 had generated huge worldwide interest in aviation, and Mignet's article told people exactly what they wanted to hear: that they could build their own airplane for next to nothing and learn to fly it themselves. "It is not necessary to have any technical knowledge to build an aeroplane," Mignet wrote. "If you can nail together a packing crate, you can construct an aeroplane."

The article generated so much attention that Mignet followed

In 1959 sci-fi author Arthur C. Clarke bet that man would land ...

up with a second article, including diagrams that people could use to build an airplane he called the HM 8.

Like the first seven planes he'd designed (and given his initials), number 8 could not actually fly. But Mignet's readers didn't know that—and he wouldn't admit it—and anyway he kept designing new planes, even after serious aviators banned him from local airfields.

By 1935 Mignet had progressed all the way to HM 14, which actually could fly a little. He named the aircraft *Pou du Ciel* (Sky Louse) and published his plans in a book called *Le Sport de l'Air*. The English edition was titled *The Flying Flea*. (Why name his creations after lice and fleas? Because, Mignet proudly explained, like his designs, these insects "made people scratch their heads.")

ON A WING AND A PRAYER

Built from wood scraps, held together by nails and glue, powered by an old motorcycle engine, and resembling "a coffin with an outboard motor in front," Mignet's Sky Louse lacked many features of conventional airplanes—ailerons, rudder pedals, engine cowls—that were necessary for safe flight but that he found offensive. "I cut them out!" he exclaimed. "No more sheet metal which flies off or rattles!" Mignet *did* like wings, so he gave his plane an extra set behind the cockpit.

People in Europe and the United States bought copies of Mignet's book by the thousands, and many of these enthusiasts built their own Sky Lice in their garages and barns. Thankfully, Mignet's designs were so awful (and his admirers so inept) that not many of these planes ever left the ground. Those few pilots unlucky enough to take to the air soon learned that Mignet's design had a fatal flaw—if they sent a Sky Louse into a steep enough dive, it either locked into the straight-down position or flipped upside down and locked into *that* position until the pilot ran out of gas or crashed.

Mounting casualties ended the Sky Louse craze by the late 1930s, but they didn't kill the movement entirely. In fact, Mignet's admirers are still at it: amateur aeronautic engineers in Europe, America, Australia, and New Zealand are still building—and flying—Flying Fleas today.

...on the moon by June 1969. He won. (Or did he? See page 278.)

THE WHO?

Ever wonder how bands get their names? So do we. After some digging around, we found the stories behind these famous names.

GENESIS. Named by producer Jonathan King, who signed the band in 1967. He chose the name because they were the first "serious" band he'd produced and he considered signing them to mark the official beginning of his production career.

HOLE. Named after a line in the Euripedes play *Medea*: "There's a hole burning deep inside me." Singer Courtney Love chose it because she says, "I knew it would confuse people."

THE BLACK CROWES. Originally a punk band called Mr. Crowe's Garden (after singer Chris Robinson's favorite kid's book). They later shortened the name and switched to southern rock.

AC/DC. Chosen because it fit the band's "high-voltage" sound.

CREAM. Eric Clapton, Jack Bruce, and Ginger Baker chose the name because they considered themselves the cream of the crop of British blues musicians.

THE CLASH. A political statement to demonstrate the band's antiestablishment attitude? No. According to bassist Paul Simonon: "I was looking through the *Evening Standard* with the idea of names on my mind, and noticed the word *clash* a few times. I thought The Clash would be good."

GUNS N' ROSES. The band chose Guns N' Roses by combining the names of two bands that members had previously played in: L.A. Guns and Hollywood Rose.

ELTON JOHN. Born Reginald Kenneth Dwight, he joined the backing band for blues singer Long John Baldry. Dwight later changed his name by combining the first names of John Baldry and saxophonist Elton Dean.

THE O'JAYS. Originally the Triumphs, they changed their name to the O'Jays in 1963 to honor Eddie O'Jay, a Cleveland disc jockey who was the group's mentor.

"I've got all the money I need... if I die by 4 o'clock this afternoon." —Henny Youngman

JANE'S ADDICTION. According to band legend, Jane was a hooker and heroin addict whom the band members met (and lived with) in Hollywood in the mid-1980s.

THEY MIGHT BE GIANTS. Named after an obscure 1971 B-movie starring George C. Scott and Joanne Woodward.

DAVID BOWIE. David Robert Jones changed his last name to Bowie to avoid being mistaken for Davy Jones of the Monkees. He chose Bowie after the hunting knife he'd seen in American films.

BAD COMPANY. Named after the 1972 Western starring Jeff Bridges.

THE POGUES. Began as Pogue Mahone, which is Gaelic for "kiss my arse."

ELVIS COSTELLO. Born Declan MacManus, he changed his name at the urging of manager Jake Riviera. According to Costello: "It was a marketing scheme. Jake said, 'We'll call you Elvis.' I thought he was completely out of his mind." Costello is a family name on his mother's side.

THE B52S. Not named after the Air Force jet. *B52* is a southern term for tall bouffant hairdos, which the women of the band wore early in the band's career.

THE POLICE. Named by drummer Stewart Copeland as an ironic reference to his father, Miles, who had served as chief of the CIA's Political Action Staff in the 1950s.

MÖTLEY CRÜE. Comes from Motley Croo, a band that guitarist Mick Mars worked for as a roadie in the early 1970s. According to bassist Nikki Sixx, they changed the spelling and added the umlauts because they "wanted to do something to be weird. It's German and strong, and that Nazi Germany mentality—'the future belongs to us'—intrigued me."

RADIOHEAD. Originally called On A Friday (because they could practice only on Fridays), EMI signed them in 1992. But EMI execs feared that On A Friday might be confusing to some. So the band quickly chose a new name. Their inspiration: an obscure Talking Heads song called "Radio Head."

THE LAST LAUGH: EPITAPHS

Some unusual epitaphs and tombstone rhymes from the United States and Europe, sent in by our crew of wandering BRI tombstone-ologists.

In Arizona:
Ezikel Height
Here lies young
Ezikel Height
Died from jumping
Jim Smith's claim;
Didn't happen at
  the mining site,
The claim he
  jumped, was Jim
  Smith's dame.

Anonymous
Here lies a wife
Of two husbands
  bereft
Robert on the right,
Richard on the left.

In Kansas:
Shoot 'em up Jake
Ran for Sheriff, 1872
Ran from Sheriff,
  1876.
Buried, 1876.

In England:
Will Smith
Here lies Will Smith
And, something
  rarish,
He was born, bred,
  and hanged,
All in the same
  parish.

In Mississippi:
Anonymous
Once I Wasn't.
Then I Was.
Now I ain't Again.

Jane Smith
Here lies Jane Smith,
  wife of Thomas
  Smith, Marble
  cutter.
Monuments of the
  same style, $350.

**H. J. Daniel's
Epitaph for His Wife**
To follow you I'm
  not content.
How do I know which
  way you went?

In Vermont:
John Barnes
Sacred to the memory
  of my husband
  John Barnes
Who died
  January 3, 1803.
His comely young
  widow,
Aged 23, has many
  qualifications
  of a good wife,
And yearns to be
  comforted.

In France:
Anonymous
I am anxiously
  expecting you —
  AD 1827
Here I am. —
  AD 1867

Wood
Here lies one Wood
Enclosed in Wood
One Wood within
  another.
One of these Woods,
Is very good
We cannot praise the
  other.

In England:
William Wiseman
Here lies the body
  of W. W.
He comes no more
To trouble you,
  trouble you
Where he's gone or
  how he fares,
Nobody knows &
  nobody cares.

*In Pawtucket, R.I.
(on a boulder):*
**William P. Rothwell,
M.D.**
This is on me.

Comic book quiz: Q. Who was Clark Kent's high school sweetheart? A. Lana Lang.

AT THE AUCTION

What do you think the very first G.I. Joe is worth? How about Orson Welles's Oscar for writing Citizen Kane? Elvis's tooth? (How much are the answers worth to you?)

AMERICA'S FIGHTING MAN

What would you pay for the very first action figure ever made? When G.I. Joe's creator, Don Levine, put it up for auction, he was certain it would fetch a lot—perhaps even break records.

The former Hasbro executive and Korean War veteran designed the toy in 1963 as a boy's answer to Mattel's Barbie Doll. And to make sure boys wouldn't be too embarrassed to play with a doll, Levine coined the term "action figure."

Forty years later, he decided to put his one-of-a-kind prototype, made of hand-painted ceramic plastic and wearing hand-sewn clothes and boots, up for sale at Heritage Comic's auction at the 2003 Comic-Con convention in San Diego. He expected to get about $600,000—which would have been more than any toy ever auctioned.

How much did he get? Nothing. The few bids the toy received didn't even meet the reserve price of $250,000. A disappointed Levine put it back in his display cabinet.

But wait! A month later, a comic book distributor named Stephen Geppi contacted Levine and offered him a whopping $200,000 for Joe #1. "I remember playing with G.I. Joe when I was a kid, and who'd have thought some 40 years later I would be buying the actual prototype," Geppi said. "What a coup."

AND THE LOSER IS...

In 1998 the American Film Institute rated *Citizen Kane* as the greatest American film ever made. Yet when the film was released in 1941, it won only one Academy Award—writer/director Orson Welles and co-writer Herman J. Mankiewicz received an Oscar for Best Original Screenplay.

Knowing that it would be highly prized in any Hollywood memorabilia collection, Welles's daughter Beatrice decided to put

---

Amharic, the language of Ethiopia, has an alphabet of 267 letters.

the *Kane* Oscar on Christie's auction block in June 2003. Ronald Colman's Best Actor Oscar for *A Double Life* netted a whopping $174,500 when Christie's sold it in 2002, and the auction house estimated that the *Kane* Oscar might bring as much as $400,000.

But everything came to a screeching halt when the Academy of Motion Picture Arts and Sciences stopped the auction, citing an obscure 1951 Academy bylaw. They claimed that Beatrice Welles had no right to sell the Oscar because the bylaw stipulates that if an Oscar winner (or the winner's heirs) ever offer the statuette for sale, it has to be offered to the Academy first...for $1.

The Plot Thickens

How was it possible that Ronald Colman's family could sell their Oscar but Orson Welles' daughter couldn't sell hers, even though both prizes were awarded before 1951?

When Orson Welles died in 1985, the *Kane* Oscar was not among his effects. Believing it lost, his daughter asked the Academy for a replacement. They gave her one but made her sign a waiver promising to return it if she ever decided she didn't want it.

Then in 1994, the original Oscar surfaced at Sotheby's. It turned out that Welles had given the Oscar to cinematographer Gary Graver as a gift during the shooting of his unfinished film, *The Other Side of the Wind*, in 1974. Twenty years later, Graver, who had not signed a waiver (neither had Ronald Colman), sold the Oscar for $50,000 to Bay Holdings, who then auctioned it at Sotheby's. When Beatrice Welles learned of the other statuette's existence, she sued Graver and Bay Holdings and won.

Graver was not pleased. "He gave it to me and told me to keep it," he said in a newspaper interview. "She never saw it before in her life. Orson had given it to me and she went to court and said, 'I want it.'"

But Beatrice Welles got a taste of her own medicine when the Academy forced her to withdraw the *Kane* Oscar from the auction block. She is now stuck with two Oscars, her father's original and the duplicate, together worth exactly...$2.

STAYIN' ALIVE

In 1977, 23-year-old John Travolta strutted into disco history in the film *Saturday Night Fever*. Besides being a blockbuster hit—the film

---

To ornithologists, the word *lore* refers to the space between a bird's eye and its bill.

made $145 million at the box office—it also enjoyed critical success. Gene Siskel, the Chicago film critic known for his "thumbs up" TV show with Roger Ebert, declared it his favorite film. In fact, he loved the film so much that when the famous white polyester suit Travolta wore came up for sale at a charity auction in the 1980s, he leapt at the chance to own it. His final bid of $2,000 beat out Jane Fonda. The suit was his.

Though some chuckled at Siskel's purchase, Siskel got the last laugh. In 1995 Christie's sold the suit at auction for $145,500—the highest amount ever paid for an article of clothing at that time. Ironically, the record was broken in 1997 by the $225,000 paid for Princess Di's blue velvet evening dress—the one she wore the night she danced with John Travolta at the White House.

*　　*　　*

OTHER CELEBRITY ITEMS UP FOR AUCTION

Elvis's tooth. In July 2003, Flo and Jesse Briggs, owners of a hair salon in Fort Lauderdale, Florida, put the King's tooth up for auction. The tooth purportedly once belonged to an old girlfriend, Linda Thompson (the Briggses got it from Startifacts, a company that sells celebrity memorabilia). Minimum bid for the tooth: $100,000. Number of legitimate bidders: 0. The tooth was pulled from auction.

JFK's boxer shorts. Former First Lady Jacqueline Kennedy's personal secretary and her personal attendant auctioned off 300 "intimate" items belonging the Kennedys, including a yellowed pair of President Kennedy's World War II Navy-issue cotton underwear. (No, not *that* kind of yellow.) They sold for $5,000. Also in the auction was a pair of JFK's pajama bottoms, which went for $2,000.

Carly Simon's secret. As part of a charity fundraiser, Simon offered to reveal who the song "You're So Vain" was written about. The catch: She agreed to tell only the highest bidder...and he's not allowed to tell anyone else. NBC exec Dick Ebersol paid $50,000 for the privilege (he also gets a live rendition of the song, a peanut butter-and-jelly sandwich, and a vodka on the rocks). Now he knows...and he's not telling.

WEDDING TRIVIA

From the Bathroom Reader *archives, here are a few tidbits about the best day in Mrs. Uncle John's life.*

Bridal shower. If a desperate bride's stingy father refused to give his daughter a dowry, friendly townspeople would "shower" her with gifts, allowing her to marry the man that she wanted.

Largest number of people married at the same time. In 1995, 35,000 couples exchanged vows in Olympic Stadium in Seoul, Korea. The Reverend Sun Myung Moon presided over the ceremony.

The thriller's gone. Actress Elizabeth Taylor has been married eight times (so far). Her most recent wedding took place in 1991 at the home of Michael Jackson. Jackson paid for it. Cost: $1.5 million.

Tying the knot. The phrase originated from the traditional girdle worn by Roman brides during the wedding ceremony. The girdle was tied together with hundreds of knots. (Untying the knots was the responsibility of her new husband.)

Longest engagement on record. 67 years, by a couple in Mexico City. (They were finally married in their 80s.)

White dress. In modern America, a white dress is commonly thought to be a symbol of purity, but originally it signified joy. In Japan, white is used for mourning, but Japanese brides can still wear it—to show they are "dead to their parents."

Milk bath. To purify themselves before their wedding, Moroccan brides bathe in milk.

July 29, 1981. The wedding of Prince Charles and Princess Diana was televised. Over 58 million Americans tuned in… even though it was on at 4 a.m.

Most decadent decorations? For the 1850 wedding of his daughter, Louisiana plantation owner Charles Durand bought a shipload of spiders from China and released them along the mile-long road to his mansion. Then he brought in sacks of silver and gold dust from California. Using bellows, his slaves blew the dust onto the webs the spiders had built, creating a sparkling canopy, under which 2,000 guests walked to reach the altar that he'd built in the front yard.

The E. Coli bacteria has the fewest chromosomes: 1 pair.

HOAXMEISTER

Think everything you read in the newspaper or see on the news has been checked for accuracy? Think again. Sometimes the media will repeat whatever they're told...and this guy set out to prove it.

MONKEY SEE, MONKEY SAY
Joey Skaggs's career as a hoax artist began in the mid-1960s when he first combined his art training with sociopolitical activism. He wanted to show that instead of being guardians of the truth, the media machine often runs stories without verifying the facts. And in proving his point, he perpetrated some pretty clever hoaxes.

HOAX #1: A Cathouse for Dogs
In 1976 Skaggs ran an ad in the *Village Voice* for a dog bordello. For $50 Skaggs promised satisfaction for any sexually deprived Fido. Then he hosted a special "night in the cathouse for dogs" just for the media. A beautiful woman and her Saluki, both clad in tight red sweaters and bows, paraded up and down in front of the panting "clientele" (male dogs belonging to Skaggs's friends). The ASPCA lodged a slew of protests and had Skaggs arrested (and indicted) for cruelty to animals. The event was even featured on an Emmy-nominated WABC News documentary. But the joke was on them—the "dog bordello" never existed.

HOAX #2: Save the Geoduck!
It's pronounced "gooey-duck" and it's a long-necked clam native to Puget Sound, Washington, with a digging muscle that bears a striking resemblance to the male reproductive organ of a horse. In 1987 Skaggs posed as a doctor (Dr. Long) and staged a protest rally in front of the Japan Society. Why? Because according to "Dr. Long," the geoduck was considered to be an aphrodisiac in Asia, and people were eating the mollusk into extinction. Although neither claim had the slightest basis in fact, Skaggs's "Clamscam" was good enough to sucker WNBC, UPI, the German news magazine *Der Spiegel*, and a number of Japanese papers into reporting the story as fact.

All toads are frogs, but not all frogs are toads.

HOAX #3: Miracle Roach Hormone Cure

Skaggs pretended to be an entomologist from Colombia named Dr. Josef Gregor in 1981. In an interview with WNBC-TV's *Live at Five,* "Dr. Gregor" claimed to have graduated from the University of Bogota, and said his "Miracle Roach Hormone Cure" cured the common cold, acne, and menstrual cramps. An amazed Skaggs remarked later, "Nobody ever checked my credentials." The interviewers didn't realize they were being had until Dr. Gregor played his theme song—*La Cucaracha.*

HOAX #4: Sergeant Bones and the Fat Squad

In 1986 Skaggs appeared on *Good Morning, America* as a former Marine Corps drill sergeant named Joe Bones, who was determined to stamp out obesity in the United States. Flanked by a squad of tough-looking commandos, Sergeant Bones announced that for "$300 a day plus expenses," his "Fat Squad" would infiltrate an overweight client's home and physically stop them from snacking. "You can hire us but you can't fire us," he deadpanned, staring into the camera. "Our commandos take no bribes." Reporters from the *Philadelphia Enquirer, Washington Post, Miami Herald,* and the *New York Daily News* all believed—and ran with—the story.

HOAX #5: Maqdananda, the Psychic Attorney

On April 1, 1994, Skaggs struck again with a 30-second TV spot in which he dressed like a swami. Seated on a pile of cushions, Maqdananda asked viewers, "Why deal with the legal system without knowing the outcome beforehand?" Along with normal third dimension legal issues—divorce, accidental injury, wills, trusts— Maqdananda claimed he could help renegotiate contracts made in past lives, sue for psychic surgery malpractice, and help rectify psychic injustices. "There is no statute of limitations in the psychic realm," he said. Viewers just had to call the number at the bottom of their screen: 1-808-UCA-DADA. In Hawaii, *CNN Headline News* ran the spot 40 times during the week. When people called the number (and dozens did), they were greeted by the swami's voice on an answering machine, saying, "I knew you'd call." Skaggs later revealed that the swami—and his political statement about the proliferation of New Age gurus and ambulance-chasing attorneys—was all a hoax.

FILTHY WATER PEOPLE

*Did you ever get a lousy nickname that stuck? You're
in good company. Many Native American tribes are
known today by unflattering names given to them
by their neighbors. Here are a few examples.*

CHEYENNE

Meaning: Red-Talkers

Origin: This Great Plains tribe called themselves the
Tsitsistas, which means the "Beautiful People." The neighboring
Dakota people may have agreed, but they couldn't understand
what the Tsitsistas were saying, because they spoke a different
language. They called the Tsitsistas the "Red-Talkers," meaning
"those who speak unintelligibly," or, in Dakota, the *Cheyenne*.

APACHE

Meaning: Enemy

Origin: Like many Native American tribes, this one, famous for
legendary chief Geronimo, called themselves "the People"—*Dine*
(di-nay) in their native language. But the neighboring tribe—victim of many of their war parties—the Zuni, called them "the
enemy," or *apachu*. Over time, that evolved into their permanent
name, the *Apache*.

ARAPAHO

Meaning: Tattooed People

Origin: These Plains Indians called themselves the *Inuna-ina*,
which translates to "the People." Their neighbors, the Crow, identified them by their distinctive body markings and called them
"Tattooed People," or, in their language, *Arapahos*.

HURON

Meaning: Boar's Head

Origin: This tribe lived in the area between Lakes Huron and
Ontario and called themselves the *Wyandot*, meaning "Those from
the Peninsula." But the French called them *Hures*, or "Boar's
Head," because the men in the tribe wore their hair in bristly

spikes that resembled boar's hair—and *Hures* eventually became *Huron.*

WINNEBAGO
Meaning: Filthy Water People
Origin: These Great Lakes Indians were named by the *Chippewa* people. Their own name was *Horogióthe*, or "Fish-Eaters." But the Chippewa called them the *Winnebago*—the "Filthy Water People," possibly because the Horogióthe painted themselves with clay when going to war, which made them appear to have bathed in muddy water.

MOHAWK
Meaning: Man-Eaters
Origin: This tribe from upper New York State and eastern Canada called themselves *Kaniengehagaóthe*, or "Flint People." That proved to be a very difficult word to pronounce for Europeans, who called them what their neighbors, the Narraganset, called them: *Mohawk*, or "Man-Eaters." Why? They engaged in ritualistic cannibalism.

GROS VENTRES
Meaning: Big Bellies
Origin: This tribe from what is now Montana and Saskatchewan called themselves the *Ahahninin*, or "White Clay People." When early French fur trappers and traders asked members of neighboring tribes about the name, they responded—in Native American sign language—by sweeping their hand out from their chest and downward, making what appeared to be a "belly" shape. What were they saying? Historians believe they were saying "Waterfall People," referring to the part of the Saskatchewan River where they lived. The French mistook the gesture and called them the name they are still called today, the *Gros Ventres*—"Big Bellies."

*   *   *

"Names are not always what they seem. The common Welsh name Bzjxxllwcp is pronounced Jackson."
                                                                —Mark Twain

---

The Gregorian calendar is accurate to within half a day per 1,000 years.

WHAT IS LOVE?

We have no idea. Here's what some other people think.

"Love is a fire. But whether it is going to warm your heart or burn down your house, you can never tell."
—**Joan Crawford**

"Love doesn't make the world go 'round. Love is what makes the ride worthwhile."
—**Franklin P. Jones**

"Love is the irresistible desire to be desired irresistibly."
—**Louis Ginsburg**

"Love is the great beautifier."
—**Louisa May Alcott**

"Love is the triumph of imagination over intelligence."
—**H. L. Mencken**

"All love is transference, nothing more than two normal neurotics mingling their infantile libidos with one another."
—**Sigmund Freud**

"Brief is life, but love is long."
—**Alfred, Lord Tennyson**

"Love is everything it's cracked up to be."
—**Erica Jong**

"Life is a flower of which love is the honey."
—**Victor Hugo**

"Love is an ideal thing, marriage a real thing; a confusion of the real with the ideal never goes unpunished."
—**Goethe**

"Love is only a dirty trick played on us to achieve the continuation of the species."
—**W. Somerset Maugham**

"Love is the reason you were born."
—**Dorothy Fields**

"The magic of first love is our ignorance that it can never end."
—**Benjamin Disraeli**

"True love is like ghosts, which everybody talks about and few have seen."
—**La Rochefoucauld**

"Love is life. All, everything that I understand, I understand only because I love."
—**Leo Tolstoy**

"Love stinks."
—**J. Geils Band**

Q: What has 18 legs and catches flies? A: A baseball team.

FOUNDING FATHERS

You already know the names. Here's who they belong to.

JOHANN ADAM BIRKENSTOCK

Background: Birkenstock was an 18th-century German shoemaker.

Famous Name: Birkenstock's family kept the shoemaking tradition going. In 1897 his grandson Konrad Birkenstock introduced a revolutionary concept in footware: the first shoe with a contoured insole that reflected the shape of the human foot. In 1965 Konrad's grandson Karl took the idea further and created the Birkenstock sandal. Introduced to the United States in 1966, it became the unofficial official footwear of the hippie generation.

ELMER (THE BULL)

Background: In the 1930s, Elsie the Cow was the logo for Borden dairy products. The company had a live cow named Elsie for personal appearances. There was so much demand for Elsie that Borden had to find another cow to make appearances, too. They found a bull instead, named him Elmer, and called him Elsie's "husband."

Famous Name: Borden's chemical division originally wanted to use Elsie as "spokescow" for their new white glue. But the dairy division didn't want Elsie to be associated with a nonfood product (especially one that *looked* like milk). So they decided to use Elsie's husband... and called it Elmer's Glue-All.

THOMAS JACOB HILFIGER

Background: Born in Elmira, New York, in 1951, Tommy knew what he wanted to do from an early age: design clothing.

Famous Name: While still in high school, he worked at a gas station, saved his money to buy used jeans, which he resold to other kids. He used the money he earned to open a chain of hip clothing stores called People's Place and got his start as a designer by telling the jeans-makers what styles would sell better. (He was right.) After working for other clothing companies for several years (Jordache fired him—they were wrong), he struck gold in 1985 with a line of urban-preppy clothing—Tommy Hilfiger.

P. T. Barnum staged the first international beauty contest.

RUDOLF DIESEL

Background: Born in Paris in 1858, Diesel studied mechanical engineering in college. He then dedicated his life to creating efficient heat engines, and in 1893 published his design for a new internal combustion engine.

Famous Name: At his wife's suggestion, Diesel named the engine after himself. But the moderate fame and fortune he received from his design were short-lived. Plagued by ill health and legal battles over his patents, he lost most of his money. While traveling on a ship to England in 1913, Diesel threw himself overboard.

MARGE SPENCER

Background: In 1947 a man named Max Adler decided to start a mail-order gift company. When designing his new catalog, he decided that Adler Gifts didn't sound quite right.

Famous Name: So he asked his secretary, Marge Spencer, if she wouldn't mind lending her name to the catalog. She agreed and Spencer Gifts was born.

ENZO FERRARI

Background: The man who created one of the world's most sought-after sports cars began his transportation career shoeing mules for the Italian army in World War I.

Famous Name: In the 1920s, Ferrari became one of Italy's most famous race car drivers and a designer for the Alfa Romeo racing team. In 1929 he started his own racing team, building sports cars only to help finance the team. When he died in 1988, Ferrari had sold fewer than 50,000 cars.

TADAO KASHIO

Background: In 1946 Tadao founded Kashio Seisakusho, a company that specialized in manufacturing aircraft parts.

Famous Name: His younger brother Toshio suggested they work on developing a calculator instead. So the Kashio brothers—there were four of them—used technology from telephone relay switching equipment to create an all-electric "gearless" calculator. (Up until that time, calculators used electricity to drive internal gears.) It took a decade of tinkering, but they introduced the Model 14-A calculator in 1957 and changed their name to...Casio Computer.

That stings! Human DNA and jellyfish DNA are 90% identical.

THE MAD BOMBER, PT. I

*From our Dustbin of History files, the story of a city,
a criminal psychiatrist, and a psycho with a grudge.*

SPECIAL DELIVERY

On November 16, 1940, an unexploded bomb was found on a window ledge of the Consolidated Edison Building in Manhattan. It was wrapped in a very neatly hand-written note that read,

CON EDISON CROOKS—THIS IS FOR YOU.

The police were baffled: surely whoever delivered the bomb would know that the note would be destroyed if the bomb detonated. Was the bomb not meant to go off? Was the person stupid…or was he just sending a message?

No discernable fingerprints were found on the device and a brief search of company records brought no leads, so the police treated the case as an isolated incident by a crackpot, possibly someone who had a grievance with "Con Ed"—the huge company that provided New York City with all of its gas and electric power.

WAKE-UP CALL

Nearly a year later, another unexploded bomb was found lying in the street a few blocks from the Con Ed building, this one with an alarm clock fusing mechanism that had not been wound. Again the police had no leads and again they filed the case away—there were larger problems at hand: the war in Europe was escalating and U.S. involvement seemed imminent. Sure enough, three months later, the Japanese attacked Pearl Harbor, triggering America's entry into World War II.

Shortly thereafter a strange, neatly written letter arrived at police headquarters in Manhattan:

I WILL MAKE NO MORE BOMB UNITS FOR THE DURATION OF THE WAR—MY PATRIOTIC FEELINGS HAVE MADE ME DECIDE THIS—I WILL BRING THE CON EDISON TO JUSTICE—THEY WILL PAY FOR THEIR DASTARDLY DEEDS…F. P.

True to his (or her) words, no more bombs showed up during the war, or for five years after that. But in that time at least 16 threat

---

Huh? Number of U.S. marine wildlife sanctuaries where fishing is illegal: zero.

letters, all from "F. P.", were delivered to Con Ed, as well as to movie theaters, the police, and even private individuals. Still, there were no bombs...until March 29, 1950.

CITY UNDER SIEGE

That day, a third unexploded bomb much more advanced than the previous two was found on the lower level of Grand Central Station. "F. P." seemed to be sending the message that he (or she) had been honing his (or her) bomb-building skills over the last decade. Still, so far none of them had exploded. And police wondered: were these all just empty threats? That question was answered a month later when a bomb tore apart a phone booth at the New York Public Library. Over the next two years, four more bombs exploded around New York City. And try as they might to downplay the threat, the police couldn't keep the press from running with the story. "The Mad Bomber" started to dominate headlines.

More bombs were found, and more angry letters—some neatly written, others created from block letters clipped from magazines—promised to continue the terror until Con Edison was "BROUGHT TO JUSTICE."

Heading up the case was Police Inspector Howard E. Finney. He and his detectives had used every conventional police method they knew of, but the Mad Bomber was too smart for them. In December 1956, after a powerful explosion injured six people in Brooklyn's Paramount Theater, Inspector Finney decided to do something unconventional.

PSYCH-OUT

Finney called in Dr. James A. Brussel, a brilliant psychiatrist who had worked with the military and the FBI. Brussel had an uncanny understanding of the criminal mind, and like everyone else in New York, this eloquent, pipe-smoking psychiatrist was curious about what made the Mad Bomber tick. But because none of the letters had been released to the press, Brussel knew very little about the case. That all changed when police handed him the evidence they had gathered since 1941.

The pressure was on: citizens were growing more panicked with each new bomb, and more impatient with the cops' inability to catch the Mad Bomber. After poring through letters, phone call

transcripts and police reports, and studying the unexploded
bombs, Dr. Brussel presented this profile to Inspector Finney:

> It's a man. Paranoiac. He's middle-aged, forty to fifty years old, intro-
> vert. Well proportioned in build. He's single. A loner, perhaps living
> with an older female relative. He is very neat, tidy, and clean-
> shaven. Good education, but of foreign extraction. Skilled mechan-
> ic, neat with tools. Not interested in women. He's a Slav. Religious.
> Might flare up violently at work when criticized. Possible motive:
> discharge or reprimand. Feels superior to his critics. Resentment
> keeps growing. His letters are posted from Westchester, and he
> wouldn't be stupid enough to post them from where he lives. He
> probably mails the letter between his home and New York City. One
> of the biggest concentration of Poles is in Bridgeport, Connecticut,
> and to get from there to New York you have to pass through
> Westchester. He has had a bad disease—possibly heart trouble.

GOING PUBLIC

Finney was impressed…but skeptical. His team had drawn some of
the same conclusions, but even so, there had to be thousands of
middle-aged men who fit that profile. What good would it do?

"I think you ought to publicize the description I've given you,"
suggested Dr. Brussel. "Publicize the whole Bomber investigation,
in fact. Spread it in the newspapers, on radio and television."
Finney disagreed. It was standard procedure to keep details of
investigations away from the press. But Brussel maintained that if
they handled the case correctly, the Mad Bomber would do most
of the work for them. He said that, unconsciously, "he wants to be
found out." Finney finally agreed. And as he left the office, Brussel
added one more thing: "When you catch him, he'll be wearing a
double-breasted suit, and it will be buttoned."

So the papers published the profile and the chase went into
high gear. As Finney predicted, "a million crackpots" came out of
the woodwork, all claiming to be the Mad Bomber, but none of
them had the Mad Bomber's skill or his distinctively neat handwrit-
ing. A slew of legitimate leads came from concerned citizens about
their odd neighbors, yet nothing solid surfaced. Still, Brussel was
confident that the real Bomber's arrogance would be his undoing.

*Did Brussel's strategy work? Turn to
Part II on page 320 to find out.*

Neanderthals are believed to have buried their dead.

UNCLE JOHN'S SECOND FAVORITE ROLL

A friend of Uncle John's recently called to report that her son had just made a backpack...completely out of duct tape. That started us wondering about other ways people use duct tape. Here's a small fraction of what we found.

DUCK TAPE

Originally called "duck" tape (because it was made from a kind of cotton canvas known as "duck"...and it was waterproof), this household staple was developed for the military to keep moisture out of ammunition cases. Don't have any leaky ammo cases? You can use it for a Band-Aid or to repair a tent, even as a fly strip. Russian cosmonauts used it to help keep the aging Mir Space Station lashed together. And now it even comes in a rainbow of designer colors, including camouflage.

Here are some other creative uses people have found for the tape:

• Researchers say it's good for removing warts. Duct tape irritates the wart, which causes the immune system to kick in and attack the virus that created it. Recommended course of treatment: Tape the wart for six days, then rip off the tape, soak the area in water, and file the wart with a pumice stone or emery board. Reapply duct tape and keep it on for another six days. Repeat the cycle for two months or until the wart goes away.

• The Tesoro Iron Dog is a 2,000-mile snowmobile race in Alaska. With temperatures hovering around -20°F, racers apply duct tape to their exposed skin to protect it from frostbite.

• When one of his cows suffered a deep cut that caused "some of its insides to fall out," a farmer in Maine used duct tape to close the wound. He found that medical tape couldn't hold the gash together under all the conditions a cow faced on the farm—but duct tape did. Another farmer stuffed the innards back into an injured hen and taped her up with duct tape. When the duct tape finally fell off (months later), the hen was as good as new.

The U.S. national flowers are the goldenrod and the columbine.

• When calves are born in severely cold weather, their ears sometimes freeze. Instead of using fleece-lined earmuffs, which the cows scratch off, a Canadian rancher duct tapes the calves' ears to their heads. The ears stay warm and the cows can't get the tape off.

• During the 2002 Winter Olympics at Salt Lake City, snowboarder Chris Klug broke a boot buckle just before his final race. After having survived a liver transplant only 19 months earlier, Klug wasn't about to let a broken buckle stop him. With less than two minutes to spare, he grabbed a roll of duct tape, jury-rigged a quick repair, and went on to win a bronze medal in the giant slalom event.

• On the NASCAR pro circuit, a special grade of duct tape is used for split-second auto body repairs. In fact, some cars are literally covered in it, which is why this grade is known as the "200-mph tape." (Another grade of duct tape, known as "nuclear tape," is used to repair nuclear reactors.)

• Starlets, beauty queens, and fashion models have long used duct tape to enhance cleavage in low-cut gowns. First they apply surgical tape across their breasts to protect them, then duct tape, which is strong and flexible enough to lift, shape, and hold everything in place. The technique was once demonstrated on *Oprah*.

SPACE CASES

• When *Apollo 17* astronauts Harrison Schmitt and Eugene Cernan drove their lunar vehicle across the moon, the fine grit kicked up by the vehicle's wheels wreaked havoc on their equipment. They fixed the problem by building extended fenders out of spare maps, clamps, and duct tape. (Or did they? See page 278.)

• After a month of living on the International Space Station without a kitchen table, astronaut Bill Shepherd and cosmonauts Sergei Krikalev and Yuri Gidzenko began piecing together scraps of aluminum. Once they got a frame together, they covered the top with duct tape. The table became the social center of the space station—the best place to eat, work, or just hang out.

*   *   *

"Duct tape is like the Force: It has a dark side and a light side—and it holds the universe together."

—Pop philosopher Carl Zwanzig

Catnip can affect lions and cougars as well as house cats.

UNCLE JOHN'S PAGE OF LISTS

Some random facts from our files.

5 Roman Delicacies, circa 200 A.D.
1. Parrot tongue
2. Ostrich brain
3. Thrush tongue
4. Peacock comb
5. Nightingale tongue

8 Things Rupert Murdoch Owns
1. *The N.Y. Post*
2. *The Times* (London)
3. *The Australian* (Sydney)
4. *TV Guide*
5. Twentieth-Century Fox
6. Madison Square Garden
7. Fox News Channel
8. L.A. Dodgers

4 Jell-O Flavor Flops
1. Cola
2. Coffee
3. Apple
4. Celery

5 Greatest American Generals (Gallup Poll, 2000)
1. George Patton
2. Dwight Eisenhower
3. Douglas MacArthur
4. Colin Powell
5. George Washington

5 States with the Most Nuclear Waste Sites
1. Illinois—10
2. California—9
3. New York—9
4. Michigan—6
5. Pennsylvania—6

4 Most Expensive Ad Spots on a Race Car
1. Hood
2. Lower rear quarter panel
3. Behind rear window
4. Behind driver's window

10 Animals That Have Been in Space
1. Dog
2. Chimp
3. Bullfrog 4. Cat
5. Tortoise
6. Bee 7. Cricket
8. Spider 9. Fish
10. Worm

4 Most Copied Hollywood Noses (Beverly Hills plastic surgeons)
1. Heather Locklear
2. Nicole Kidman
3. Marisa Tomei
4. Catherine Zeta-Jones

7 Actors in *The Magnificent Seven*
1. Robert Vaughn
2. Steve McQueen
3. Brad Dexter
4. James Coburn
5. Horst Bucholz
6. Yul Brynner
7. Charles Bronson

A variety of mimosa is called the "sensitive plant" because it wilts when touched.

RETURN OF THE SEQUEL

Hollywood can't seem to leave well enough alone—not when it looks like there's money to be made. Here's a look at some of the worst movie sequels ever made.

HOME ALONE 3 (1997)

Background: The first *Home Alone* (1990) earned more than $280 million at the box office, turning child actor Macaulay Culkin into a household name and the biggest child star since Shirley Temple.

The Plot Thickens: Macaulay appeared in *Home Alone 2* (1992), but by the time *Home Alone 3* went into production, he was too old—17—and too expensive for the part. So the filmmakers cut their losses and started over with an entirely new family and an entirely new son: Alex, played by newcomer Alex D. Linz. Plot: He's home with the chicken pox when international thieves break into the house to retrieve a missile-system computer chip that has found its way into one of his toys.

The Critics Speak: "Better to stay home alone." (Steve Persall, *St. Petersburg Times*)

THE NEXT KARATE KID (1994)

Background: The original *Karate Kid*, starring Ralph Macchio as teenager Daniel LaRusso, was the sleeper hit of the summer of 1984. It made more than $90 million at the box office; two years later *Karate Kid II* pulled in more than $115 million. Why not try for more?

The Plot Thickens: By the time *Karate Kid III* hit screens in 1989, the kids in the audience had moved on but Macchio, 27, had not. He looked ridiculous trying to pass himself off as 17, so for sequel #3 the filmmakers dumped him and brought in a girl—Mr. Miyagi befriends Julie, a "churlish orphan" played by newcomer Hilary Swank. That Swank eventually became a star was no thanks to this dud: It died at the box office and took the entire franchise down with it.

The Critics Speak: "The sound of one mouth yawning." (Mike Clark, *USA Today*)

Saturn's not alone: Jupiter, Neptune, and Uranus also have rings.

BOOK OF SHADOWS: BLAIR WITCH 2 (2000)

Background: *The Blair Witch Project* (1999) cost $35,000 to make and went on to earn more than *$250 million* worldwide, making it not only the most successful independent film ever made, but also the most profitable motion picture in Hollywood history. Newcomers Daniel Myrick and Eduardo Sanchez, who directed the first film, made the covers of *Time* and *Newsweek* and were hailed as the brightest young talents in Hollywood.

The Plot Thickens: Then Artisan Entertainment (the major studio that bought *The Blair Witch Project* after it premiered at the Sundance Film Festival) decided to rush out a sequel. Myrick and Sanchez were starting work on a comedy called *Heart of Love,* but rather than wait for them to finish, Artisan hired a documentary filmmaker named Joe Berlinger to direct the sequel instead.

Big mistake—*Book of Shadows,* the story of five fans of the original documentary who return to the same patch of woods to see if the Blair Witch legend is true, is probably the most hated of the most anticipated sequels ever made. Myrick and Sanchez had very little to do with it, but their careers stalled anyway; as of the summer of 2003, they hadn't gotten *Heart of Love* off the ground and hadn't made any other films.

The Critics Speak: "The characters are boring, the violence generic, the suspense nonexistent." (Jack Matthews, *NY Daily News*)

PSYCHO (1998)

Background: In its day Alfred Hitchcock's *Psycho* (1960) was disparaged by critics as a "sensationalist slasher movie." But in the years since, the film has grown in stature and today is considered to be the second most influential film in the history of American cinema after Orson Welles's *Citizen Kane.*

The Plot Thickens: In 1998 Gus Van Sant, director of *Good Will Hunting* and *My Own Private Idaho,* decided to make a frame-by-frame, line-by-line remake of the original *Psycho,* filmed in color instead of black and white, and set in the 1990s. Why copy a classic? Universal figured that even if the idea was dumb, at least it would have built-in box-office appeal and get lots of free publicity, which would translate into ticket sales.

For his part, Van Sant figured that if pop singers can make cover versions of classic songs, why shouldn't filmmakers cover classic movies? He called the remake "experimental art."

Van Sant made his dumb idea even dumber by failing to stick to it—not satisfied with merely replicating Hitchcock's masterpiece, he hyped up the sex and inserted one particularly lurid scene that provides a sexual dimension to Norman Bates's weird obsessions. That's what the scene was *supposed* to do, anyway—all it really did was make Van Sant look sadly misguided.

The Critics Speak: "Van Sant called his film 'a forgery. Like we're making a copy of the *Mona Lisa* or the statue of *David*.' Which, of course, raises the question: Who wants to see a forgery when you can see the real deal?" (Renee Graham, *The Boston Globe*)

JAWS: THE REVENGE (JAWS 4)

Background: According to Hollywood legend, when Steven Spielberg was asked to direct the movie adaptation of Peter Benchley's bestselling novel *Jaws*, he agreed on one condition: that the shark not be seen for the first hour of the film. True or not, the shark movie without too much shark became Spielberg's first big hit and one of the most successful thrillers ever made, precisely because the limited shark sightings kept audiences in suspense.

The Plot Thickens: In its time *Jaws* (1975) was the highest-grossing movie ever made, so it's understandable that Universal execs wanted more. But did they really understand what made the first film work so well? Apparently not, because each succeeding sequel had more and more shark, less and less suspense—and dwindling ticket sales. It probably didn't help that the scripts, acting, directors, and special effects also got progressively worse. Even with the addition of Michael Caine as a love interest for Chief Brody's widow (Roy Scheider bailed out after *Jaws 2*), *Jaws: The Revenge* was such a box-office failure that Universal didn't bother with #5.

The Critics Speak: "*Jaws: The Revenge* is not simply a bad movie, but also a stupid and incompetent one. . . . The screenplay is simply a series of meaningless episodes of human behavior, punctuated by shark attacks." (Roger Ebert, *Chicago Sun-Times*)

The Last Laugh: "I have never seen *Jaws: The Revenge*, but by all accounts it is terrible. However, I have seen the house that it built, and it is terrific." (Actor Michael Caine, referring to his mansion in Oxfordshire, England)

LET'S PLAY TOILET GOLF

It may be heresy for us to say, but sometimes you just don't want to read in the bathroom. For those rare moments, here are a few products that will help make your next pit stop as fun as a trip to a theme park.

N OW *THAT'S A BATHTUB*
In 2003 the Jacuzzi company introduced "La Scala," a bathtub spa with a built-in, 43-inch flat-screen TV, a CD player, a DVD player, and a floating remote control. Price: $29,000 (installation is extra).

But what about the rest of us, who don't have $29,000 to spend on a tub? Shouldn't we be able to have fun in the bathroom, too? Never fear—the BRI is here! We've been looking around for things that anyone can use to turn their bathroom into an entertainment center. Here's what we found:

ROLL MODEL
Product: Don't P Me Off Roll Playing Puzzle
Description: Have you ever solved one of those puzzles where you have to separate a couple of twisted pieces of metal that seem impossibly locked together? This is that kind of puzzle—only with a sadistic twist. The cylindrical wooden box completely encases a roll of toilet paper, so your houseguests can't get at it...unless they solve the puzzle. How hard is it? The manufacturer's advice: "We suggest that you have an extra roll on hand."

STREAM OF CONSCIOUSNESS
Product: Peeball
Description: You need a urinal to play, so unless your bathroom is well equipped, your Peeball career will be limited to away games. Peeball is a little smaller than a Ping-Pong ball and is made of bicarbonate of soda, similar to the stuff that Alka-Seltzer is made of.
How to Play: Toss the ball into the urinal, aim, and fire! The player who dissolves their Peeball in the shortest amount of time is the winner.

A shrimp's heart is in its head.

Background: Peeball was developed by England's Prostate Cancer Charity. Because "difficulty peeing and weak flow" are typical symptoms of prostate cancer, Peeball educates players about the disease and encourages anyone who has the symptoms to get a checkup. "The message is that if men can't dissolve the Peeball in a certain period of time, they might need to see a doctor," says spokesperson Gina Growden.

LOO-TERATURE

Product: Toilet Paper Literature

Description: Klo-Verlag, a German publishing company, takes novels, detective stories, fairy tales, poetry, and other written works and publishes them on rolls of toilet paper. The company prefers shorter pieces that can be printed several times on the same roll, so that when one "end user" finishes off part of the roll, the next person in the bathroom will still find the remaining material interesting to read. "We want our books to be used," company head Georges Hemmerstoffer explains. "That's our philosophy."

TEE PEE

Product: Toilet Golf

Description: The game consists of a green bathroom rug shaped like a putting green, a miniature putter, and two golf balls. The rug wraps around the base of a toilet, so you can practice your putt while on the pot. (Also available: Toilet Bowling and Toilet Fishing.)

SOUND SYSTEMS

• **Talking Toilet Paper.** A digital voice recorder is built into the spool of this toilet paper holder. Record any message you want—then, every time someone touches the toilet paper, they'll get a surprise. Manufacturer's suggested messages: "This is a bathroom, not a library" or "Whoa! Somebody light a match!"

• **Fart Clock.** Every hour on the hour the Fart Clock lets out one of 12 different fart sounds. Includes a light sensor to turn it off when the room darkens.

• **Fart Phone.** It farts instead of rings. This phone will provide a mystery every time someone calls—is that the phone, or did somebody step on a duck?

There are 4.5 million wild turkeys in the U.S. (Not including the ones in liquor stores.)

LE HOT DOG?

*The French are sensitive about their language—it was once
the international language of kings and diplomats. English
has taken over, and, to the chagrin of the French, many
English words are now finding their way into the
lexicon. But the French are fighting back.*

VIVE LA FRANCE!
When The French Academy (L'Académie Française) was
founded in 1635 by Cardinal Richelieu, its mission was
high-minded—to keep the French tongue pure and uncorrupted.
Richelieu charged the Academy with compiling a definitive dictionary of the French language. Instead, however, the members
became obsessed with rooting out vulgar (which means English)
influences on their mother tongue. And they were—and are—
very serious about it.

In 1757 an academic named Forgeret de Monbron wrote a
scathing attack on the influx of English words into the French
language. And even more recently, in 1964, René Etiemble, a professor at the Sorbonne, declared, "To violate the French language
is a crime. During the war persons were shot for treason. These
traitors should now be punished for degrading the French language."

In 1992 the French parliament passed a law actually making it
illegal to use non-French words in contracts, billboards, advertising, and instructions for appliances. The following are some English words in common use in France that have been banned by the
Academy: *le baby-sitter, le boss, le bulldozer, bye-bye, le cash flow, le
cocktail, le cowboy, le drive-in, le fast-food, le hamburger, le holdup,
le hotdog, le jogging, le jukebox, le flashback, le marketing, le parking,
le remake, le rip-off, le rock, le shopping, le showbiz, le software, le
soda, le sponsor, le stress, le supermarket, le weekend, le zoom.*

L'EMAIL, NON!

The rise of the Internet has spurred an even greater invasion of
English words into common French usage. But the Academy has
begun to strike back. Nobody in Paris checks their "e-mail"—that
word is no longer used. Instead, the Academy wants people to

Face facts: *Cosmetics* means "skilled in decorating" in Greek.

check their *courriel*, an abbreviation of the French term *courrier electronique* ("electronic mail"). They can say good-bye to "chat rooms," too, unless they log into a *causette*. Here are some other tech terms that have been banned, with their approved French equivalents: computer—*un ordinateur*; software—*le logiciel*; start-up—*une jeune pousse*; cookie—*un témoin de connexion*.

COLONIAL OVERKILL

While the French are railing against English-language encroach-ment, the government of Quebec is actually doing something about it. Technically, Canada is a bilingual country—English and French are to be treated equally. But in Quebec, French takes precedence. The province even has its own French-language office whose mission is the "francization" of Quebec. Officers travel the province making sure that shop signs are not only in both French and English but that the letters of the French words are twice the size of the English ones. Violators are hauled into court and fined. For example:

• Bill McCleary ran a gas station in Shawville, Quebec. In 1998 he was informed by mail that he was in violation of provincial law because the French words on his "Full Service" sign weren't larger than the English. But the letter he received was in French only. He demanded to be notified in a language he could understand. Bad move. He was fined $690. When the bailiff showed up to collect the fine, McCleary refused to pay. Very bad move. The officer seized his pickup truck, SkiDoo, snowblower, two ATVs, lawn tractor, house trailer, and McCleary's 1986 Mustang.

• In 1997 shopkeepers in Montreal's Chinatown were told to make the French letters twice as large as the Chinese letters on their signs. The storekeepers responded that they would enlarge the French if the rest of the province put Chinese characters on *their* signs. The language office was not amused.

• A popular coffee shop chain called The Second Cup had three of its locations *fire-bombed* by a terrorist group called the French Self-Defense Brigade. The coffee chain's offense? The registered trademark on their signs hadn't been translated into French.

Meanwhile, Back in France: More than 360 years later, L'A-cadémie Française has yet to finish their French dictionary.

Cotton candy in France is called *barbe à papa* ("Papa's beard").

THE PARANOID'S FIELD GUIDE TO SECRET SOCIETIES

Secret societies actually do exist. In fact, there are dozens of them, from the Freemasons to the Ku Klux Klan. But are they really responsible for the world's ills, as some people believe? Probably not, but on the other hand, you never know...

THE ILLUMINATI

Who They Are: This group was founded in 1776 by Adam Weishaupt, a Jesuit priest, in Bavaria. His mission: to advance the 18th-century ideals of revolution, social reform, and rational thought (the name means "the Enlightened Ones" in Latin). Weishaupt and his cronies were fiercely opposed by the monarchs of Europe and by the Catholic Church, which is why they had to meet and communicate in secret. German author Johann Goethe was a member. In the United States, both Benjamin Franklin and Thomas Jefferson were accused of being members and denied it, but both wrote favorably about Weishaupt and his efforts.

What They're Blamed For: This group has been associated with more conspiracy theories than any other. Considered the silent evil behind such paranoid bugaboos as One World Government and the New World Order, the Illuminati have been blamed for starting the French and Russian revolutions, as well as both world wars, and almost every global conflict in between. They are said to use bribery, blackmail, and murder to infiltrate every level of power in society—business, banking, and government—to achieve their ultimate goal: world domination.

BILDERBERG GROUP

Who They Are: Founded in 1952 by Prince Bernhard of the Netherlands, the Bilderberg Group (named after the hotel in Oosterbeck, Holland, where the first meeting was held) was founded to promote cooperation and understanding between

Western Europe and North America. To that end, leaders from both regions are invited to meet every year for off-the-record discussions on current issues. The list of attendees has included presidents (every one from Eisenhower to Clinton), British prime ministers (Lord Home, Lord Callaghan, Sir Edward Heath, Margaret Thatcher), captains of industry like Fiat's Giovanni Agnelli, and financiers like David Rockefeller. Invitees are members of the power elite in their countries, mostly rich and male. Meetings are closed. No resolutions are passed, no votes are taken, and no public statements are ever made.

What They're Blamed For: The fact that so many of the world's most powerful players refuse to disclose anything about the group's meetings strikes many outsiders as downright subversive. What are they doing? The group has been accused of hand picking Western leaders to be their puppets, pointing to circumstantial evidence like the fact that Bill Clinton was invited to attend a meeting before he became president, as was Britain's Tony Blair before he became prime minister. Conspiracy buffs have even accused the Bilderbergers of masterminding the global AIDS epidemic as a way of controlling world population to the benefit of the European/American elite.

TRILATERAL COMMISSION

Who They Are: Founded in 1973 by David Rockefeller and former National Security Council chief Zbigniew Brzezinski, this organization is composed of 350 prominent private citizens (none currently hold government positions) from Europe, North America, and Japan (the tri-lateral global power triangle). Like the Bilderberg Group, their stated goal is to discuss global issues and to promote understanding and cooperation. Unlike other groups, this one is more visible: it publishes reports, and members are identified. It's also more diverse, with women and ethnic groups represented. However, membership is by invitation only, usually on the recommendation of serving members, making it one of the most exclusive private clubs in the world. There are no representatives from developing nations.

What They're Blamed For: Many conspiracy theorists view the Trilateral Commission as the "sunny" face of the evil machinations of international bankers and business moguls who are working to make the world their own little oyster, with one financial system, one defense system, one government, and one religion—which they will control. Again, all members are major players in business and government. Americans of note include Bill Clinton, Jimmy Carter, Henry Kissinger, and George Bush (the elder), former Federal Reserve Chairman Paul Volcker, former Speaker of the House Tom Foley, and former U.S. Trade Representative Carla Hills, to name a few. Since there is considerable crossover between the Trilateral Commission and the Bilderberg Group, the commission is thought by some to be under the control of the Illuminati. That it is completely private, with no direct role in government (read "no accountability"), only adds fuel to the fires of suspicious minds.

SKULL & BONES SOCIETY

Who They Are: This society was founded at Yale University in 1833. Only 15 senior-year students are admitted annually; they meet twice a week in a grim, windowless building called the Tombs. Unlike most campus fraternities, Skull & Bones appears to focus on positioning its members for success after college. But no one knows for sure, because members are sworn to total secrecy for life. The names of past and current members include many of America's power elite: both George Bushes, William Howard Taft, as well as the descendants of such famous American families as the Pillsburys, Weyerhausers, Rockefellers, Vanderbilts, and Whitneys.

What They're Blamed For: What's wrong with a little good ol' boy networking? Nothing, perhaps, but Skull & Bones members have also been accused of practicing satanic rites within the walls of the Tombs. Initiation reportedly requires pledges to lie down in coffins, confess sordid details of their sex lives, and endure painful torture so that he may "die to the world, to be born again into the Order." Like the Illuminati, the Order (as it's called by its members) supposedly works to create a world controlled and ruled by the elite—members of Skull & Bones.

BOHEMIAN GROVE

Who They Are: Founded in 1872 by five San Francisco *Examiner* newsmen as a social boozing club, the Bohemian Grove has been called "one of the world's most prestigious summer camps" by *Newsweek*. Prospective members may wait up to 15 years to get in and then have to pony up a $2,500 membership fee. The Grove

---

Buculets are those little bumpers on the underside of your toilet seat.

itself is a 2,700-acre retreat set deep in a California redwood forest. Members' privacy is zealously guarded: no strangers are allowed near the site, and reporters are expressly forbidden entry. The Bohemian Grove motto is from Shakespeare: "Weaving spiders come not here," a reminder that all deal making is to be left at the gates. The members relax and entertain each other by putting on plays, lecturing on subjects of the day, and wining and dining lavishly.

So why does anyone care about the Bohemian Grove? Well, the membership is a virtual Who's Who of the most powerful people (mostly Republican) in American government and business. Members past and present include Dick Cheney, Donald Rumsfeld, Karl Rove, George W. Bush, Richard Nixon, Gerald Ford, Henry Kissinger, Caspar Weinberger, Stephen Bechtel, Joseph Coors, Alexander Haig, Ronald Reagan, and hundreds more. Critics claim there is no way men like these (no women are allowed) can hang out together and *not* make back-room deals.

What They're Blamed For: Conspiracy theorist claim that the Manhattan Project was set up at the Grove and that the decision to make Eisenhower the Republican presidential candidate for 1952 was hammered out between drinks on the lawn.

Darker charges have been made against the Grove as well. Members are purported to practice some odd rituals, such as wearing red hoods and marching in procession like ancient druids, chanting hymns to the Great Owl. Members say it's all in good fun, but outsiders wonder at the cultlike overtones. Outrageous rumors were rampant in the 1980s: sacrificial murders, drunken revels, even pedophilia, sodomy, kidnapping, and rape. Of course, none of this has ever been proven, but as limousines and private jets swoop into this secret enclave in the woods, the "big boys" continue to party and the rest of the world remains in the dark about just exactly what goes on.

*　　　*　　　*

THE SECRET RECIPE FOR ~~COCA~~ COLA

The Bathroom Readers Institute is pleased to reveal the closely-guarded secret recipe of ~~Coca~~ Cola. Here it is: 3 ½ ~~~~ of ~~~~, 2 ~~~~ of ~~~~, 14 ~~~~, 13 ⅓ ~~~~ of ~~~~ ~~~~, and a dash of salt. (Now you know—don't tell anyone.)

THE RHINOCEROS PARTY

Who says politics has to be stodgy and humorless? Not Canada.

BACKGROUND
In the early 1960s, Quebec was wracked by violent protests against the federal government and the Anglo-Saxon establishment that dominated the province. In the midst of this turmoil, Dr. Jacques Ferron, a physician and writer, launched a new political party—a satirical alternative "to serve as a peaceful outlet for disgruntled Quebecois." And he chose the rhinoceros as the party's symbol. Why a rhino? Ferron said it epitomized the professional politician—"a slow-witted animal that can move fast as hell when in danger."

It existed for only 30 years, but the Rhinoceros Party "put the 'mock' back in 'demockracy.'" And for a fringe group, it attracted a surprising number of votes. Here are some of their more creative campaign promises:

• They vowed to sell Canada's Senate at an antiques auction in California.

• They promised to plant coffee, chocolate, and oranges in southern Ontario, so Canada could become a banana republic.

• In the 1980 election, the Rhinos promised to break all their promises and introduce an era of "indecision and incompetence."

• Fielding candidates with names like "Richard the Troll" and "Albert the Cad," the Rhinos ran on a platform of "sex, drugs, and rock 'n' roll" for the masses.

• Other parties talked about a guaranteed annual income; the Rhinos vowed to introduce a "Guaranteed Annual Orgasm" and to sell seats in Canada's Senate for $15 each.

• In 1988 they made national headlines by running a candidate named John Turner against the incumbent opposition leader... John Turner. Turner was not amused (everyone else was).

• They promised to repeal the law of gravity, provide free trips to bordellos, and nationalize all pay toilets.

• When the Canadian government was trying to decide where to

Q: Why aren't there any zebras in Prague? A: Czechs and stripes don't mix.

locate its embassy in Israel, the Rhinoceros Party proposed to locate it in a Winnebago, which could travel continuously between Jerusalem and Tel Aviv.

MORE PROMISES AND PROPOSALS

• As an energy-saving measure, they proposed larger wheels for the backs of all cars, so they would always be going downhill.

• They proposed legislating a lower boiling point of water (another energy-saving measure).

• They also proposed moving half the Rockies one meter to the west, as a make-work project.

• They promised to make bubble gum the currency of Canada and to provide tax credits for enthusiastic sleepers.

• They promised to spend $50 million on reform schools for politicians.

• They pledged that "None of our candidates will be running on steroids."

• Another promise: to have the Rocky Mountains bulldozed so that Alberta could get a few extra minutes of daylight.

• They promised to turn the parliamentary restaurant into a national franchise operation.

• One Rhino candidate proposed "to create a cartel of the world's snow-producing countries, call it Snow-pec, and export snow to cool down the Middle East conflict."

• They promised to bring back "the good old English system of driving on the left-hand side of the road, but in the first year only, buses and trucks will drive on the right-hand side."

END OF AN ERA

When the government passed a law in 1993 requiring a $50,000 deposit from every party in a national election—essentially killing off the Rhinoceros Party—the Rhinos asked Canadians to write their own names on the ballot and vote for themselves.

"We cannot fool all of the people some of the time or even some of the people all of the time," said Charlie McKenzie, the party's general secretary, "but if we can fool a majority of the people at election time, that's all the time we need."

The only American praised by Hitler in *Mein Kampf*? Henry Ford.

HOUSEHOLD ORIGINS

Some things are so commonplace that it's difficult to imagine life without them. Here's where these everyday items came from.

P LASTIC WRAP
Invented by accident in 1933, when Ralph Wiley, a researcher at Dow Chemical, was washing his lab equipment at the end of the day and found that a thin plastic film coating the inside of one vial wasn't coming off. The stuff was polyvinylidene chloride, and after further experimentation, Wiley found that the stuff was clingy, resisted chemicals, and was impervious to air and water. It was so tough, in fact, that he wanted to call it "eonite," after an imaginary indestructible substance in the *Little Orphan Annie* comic strip. Dow decided to call it Saran Wrap instead.

WATER BEDS

Believe it or not, people have been sleeping on water-filled bags for more than 3,500 years. The Persians were apparently the first—they sewed goatskins together, filled them with water, and left them in the sun to get warm. The direct ancestor of the modern water bed was invented in 1853 by Dr. William Hooper of Portsmouth, England, who saw the beds as a medical device that could be used to treat bedridden patients suffering from bedsores, as well as burn victims, and arthritis and rheumatism sufferers. His water bed wasn't much more than a rubber hot water bottle big enough to sleep on. It wasn't until 1967 that San Francisco design student Charles Hall made an improved model out of vinyl and added an electric heater to keep the bed warm all the time.

ELECTRIC PLUGS AND SOCKETS

Electricity was first introduced into homes in the 1880s, but every lamp or appliance had to be "hard-wired" into the wall by an electrician. That lasted until 1904, when a Connecticut inventor named Harvey Hubbell was in a penny arcade and noticed a janitor struggling to disconnect the wires of a boxing game so that he could clean behind it. Hubbell knew there had to be a better—not to mention a safer—way to detach and reattach wires to walls.

Looney law: In Brooklyn, it's illegal to let a dog sleep in your bathtub.

After experimenting with metal and wood (which served as an insulator before plastic came into use), he came up with a two-pronged plug-and-socket system that isn't all that different from the one used today. In fact, since then there have only been two major updates to his design, both safety features: 1) many plugs and sockets have a third prong that serves as a ground, and 2) one prong is wider than the other so that the plug can only be plugged into the socket one way—keeping "neutral" on the correct side.

BINOCULARS

In 1608 a Dutch maker of eyeglasses named Hans Lippershey noticed that when he held up two lenses and looked through both of them at a church steeple, the steeple looked bigger—it was magnified. So he made a tube, fitted a lens at each end, and tried to obtain a patent for this telescope, which he called a "looker." The patent application was rejected by Dutch authorities because other people had noticed the same thing before he did and made their own telescopes. (To this day it is not certain who invented the very first telescope.) In addition to rejecting Lippershey's patent, Dutch authorities complained that squinting through one eyepiece gave them eyestrain, and they asked him to join two telescopes together so that using it wouldn't give them such a headache. He took their suggestion, and the first binoculars were invented.

STAPLERS

The hardest part about inventing the stapler wasn't the device itself, it was getting all those little staples to stick together. The precursors of modern staplers were invented in the 19th century and were used by printers to bind pages of books and magazines together. These machines used rolls of wire instead of staples, which the machine cut and bent into shape as it was binding the pages together. The first machines to use pre-bent, U-shaped pieces of wire came in the 1860s, but they held only one staple at a time and had to be reloaded by hand before each use. The first stapler to hold more than one staple was invented in 1894, but it used staples set onto a wooden core that came loose easily and jammed the stapler. In 1923 Thomas Briggs, founder of the Boston Wire Stitcher Company (later shortened to Bostitch), figured out a way to glue the staples together into a long strip that could be loaded into a stapler. Bostitch still makes staplers today.

Half the world's population lives in temperate zones, which make up 7% of Earth's land area.

DIAMOND GEMS

Why does Uncle John love baseball? It's loaded with facts, stories, odd characters, obscure histories, and weird statistics...just like a Bathroom Reader. Even if you're not a fan, you might like these gems.

ONE IN A MILLION

Ever heard of Bob Watson? He has the distinction of scoring major-league baseball's one millionth run. It happened on May 4, 1975, while he was playing for the Houston Astros. His prize: one million Tootsie Rolls.

THE FIRST...AND HOPEFULLY LAST

The only major leaguer ever to be killed playing baseball was the Cleveland Indians' shortstop Ray Chapman. On August 16, 1920, before players wore batting helmets, Chapman was beaned in the head by a pitch from Yankee's hurler Carl Mays. He fell, slowly stood up, walked around in a daze, then collapsed again. Chapman was pronounced dead at 4:40 a.m. the next morning. Mays, who had always had a surly reputation, lamented about it after his playing days. "I won over 200 big-league games, but no one remembers that. When they think of me, I'm the guy who killed Chapman."

INFLATION

After fan Sal Durante caught Roger Maris's historic 61st home run in 1961, he tried to return the ball to the quiet Yankee, but Maris told the truck driver to keep the ball and sell it if he wanted to. Durante sold it for $5,000. Maris' record stood for 37 years until Mark McGwire broke it in 1998, hitting 70 home runs. The 70th was caught by 26-year-old Phil Ozersky, who sold the ball for $3 million.

THE OTHER ROBINSON

Jackie Robinson, as most people know, broke major-league baseball's color barrier in 1947. But few people outside baseball have heard of Frank Robinson (they're not related). In his Hall of Fame career, Frank Robinson won the Most Valuable Player award (in both the American and the National League), was a Triple Crown winner (led the league in homers, RBIs, and batting average), and won the All-Star Game and World Series MVP awards. But he wasn't done yet: In 1974 he became the first African American to manage a big league ball club, and in 1989 became the first African American to be named Manager of the Year.

HUMBLE BEGINNINGS
Superstar slugger Sammy Sosa was once a shoeshine boy. At only eight years old, he gave the money he earned to his widowed mother so she could buy food for the family.

BY THE NUMBERS
The Baltimore Orioles' Cal Ripken Jr. played in a record 2,632 consecutive major-league games from 1982 to 1998. During Ripken's streak:

• 3,695 major leaguers went on the disabled list.

• 522 shortstops started for the other 27 teams.

• 33 second basemen played second base next to Ripken at shortstop (including his younger brother Billy Ripken).

Ripken also holds the record for the most consecutive innings played, with 8,243. He didn't miss a single inning from June 5, 1982, to September 14, 1987. His potential wasn't recognized early on, though—47 players were selected ahead of Ripken in the June 1978 draft.

A LEAGUE OF HER OWN
On July 31, 1935, the Cincinnati Reds oversold tickets for their night game. To avoid a potential riot, they allowed the extra fans—8,000 in all—to stand along the foul lines. It was so packed that the players had to muscle their way through the crowd to get to the field. When Reds batter Babe Herman was trying to make his way to the plate in the bottom of the eighth, a nightclub singer named Kitty Burke grabbed the bat from the surprised player and told her friends, "Hang on to him, boys, I'm going to take his turn at bat." Sure enough, she went to the plate against Cardinal Paul "Daffy" Dean. The bewildered pitcher shrugged and lobbed a ball to the blonde bombshell. Burke swung ferociously but only hit a slow roller toward first base. Dean scooped up the ball and tagged her out (to a round of boos from the crowd). Although the at-bat didn't officially count, it was—and still is—the only time a woman has hit in a major-league game.

STRANGE LAWSUITS

These days, it seems that people will sue each other over practically anything. Here are some real-life examples of unusual legal battles.

THE PLAINTIFF: Tom Morgan, a Portland, Oregon, grocery cashier

THE DEFENDANT: Randy Maresh, a cashier at the same store

THE LAWSUIT: Apparently Morgan believed that Maresh lived to torment him. He sued Maresh for $100,000, claiming that his co-worker "willfully and maliciously inflicted severe mental stress and humiliation by continually, intentionally, and repeatedly passing gas directed at the plaintiff." Maresh's lawyer didn't sit quietly—he argued that farting is a form of free speech and protected by the First Amendment.

THE VERDICT: Case dismissed. The judge called the defendant's behavior "juvenile and boorish" but conceded that there was no law against farting.

THE PLAINTIFF: John Cage Trust

THE DEFENDANT: Mike Batt, a British composer

THE LAWSUIT: In 1952 composer John Cage wrote a piece he called "4'33"." It was four minutes and 33 seconds of silence. In 2002 Batt included a track called "A One Minute Silence" on an album by his rock band The Planets, crediting it to "Batt/Cage." That's when Cage's estate came in—they accused Batt of copyright infringement.

Batt's response: "Has the world gone mad? I'm prepared to do time rather than pay out." Besides, he said, his piece was much better than Cage's because "I have been able to say in one minute what Cage could only say in four minutes and 33 seconds."

THE VERDICT: The suit ended with a six-figure out-of-court settlement. "We feel that honour has been settled," said Nicholas Riddle, Cage's publisher, "because the concept of a silent piece is a very valuable artistic concept."

THE PLAINTIFF: James Crangle

THE DEFENDANT: District of Columbia, a.k.a., "Police State Leviathan"

THE LAWSUIT: On December 22, 1989, Crangle found himself accidentally driving the wrong way down a one-way street in Washington, D.C. When the District police tried to pull him over, Crangle attempted to elude them…and ended up crashing into a utility pole. Still unwilling to give up, he climbed on top of a mailbox, claiming sanctuary. After his arrest, he filed suit against the cops, saying that local police had no authority to arrest him since he was on "federal property"—the mailbox.

THE VERDICT: The suit was dismissed.

THE PLAINTIFF: Kimberly M. Cloutier

THE DEFENDANT: Costco Wholesale Corp.

THE LAWSUIT: In 2001 Costco fired Cloutier for wearing an eyebrow ring—a violation of their dress code, which bars facial jewelry. All she had to do was remove the ring while she was at work, but she refused. Why? She considers wearing the ring an essential part of her religion, the "Church of Body Modification." Costco managers were unwilling to accommodate the church's view that piercings "are essential to our spiritual salvation," so Cloutier filed a religious discrimination charge under the 1964 Civil Rights Act and sued Costco for $2 million.

THE VERDICT: Despite voicing "grave doubts" about the viability of the case, a judge threw out an early challenge by Costco to the lawsuit. The case is still pending.

THE PLAINTIFF: Coca-Cola Co.

THE DEFENDANT: Frederick Coke-Is-It of Brattleboro, Vt.

THE LAWSUIT: Born Frederick Koch, he pronounced his name "kotch," but got fed up with people pronouncing it "Coke." Out of frustration he had his name legally changed to Frederick "Coke-Is-It." When the Coca-Cola Company heard about Mr. Coke-Is-It, they sued him on the grounds that he changed his name specifically to "infringe on their rights."

THE VERDICT: They settled out of court…and amazingly, Koch, er, Coke-Is-It, is *still* it—he won the right to keep his new name.

The first Rolls-Royce sold for $600 in 1906. Today they sell for more than $200,000.

THINGS YOU DIDN'T KNOW ABOUT WWII

From our Forgotten History files, here are three little-known anecdotes about the world's worst armed conflict.

JAPAN'S SECRET WEAPON: BALLOONS

On May 5, 1945, a group of picnickers in Oregon fell victim to one of the oddest weapons used in World War II. The party found a 32-foot balloon in the woods. When they tried to move it, it exploded, killing six of them—the only fatalities of World War II to occur on American soil.

In 1944, feeling intense pressure from American air raids, Japan came up with a seemingly brilliant way of striking back. Their planes couldn't fly all the way to the States, so they started sending balloons made of rubberized silk, each carrying an explosive device. The balloons were supposed to ride high-altitude winds across the Pacific and come down to wreak havoc in the American heartland.

The U.S. Air Force estimates that Japan launched 9,000 balloon bombs between November 1944 and April 1945. About 1,000 of those actually made it to the United States, but they inflicted only minor damage. Designed to be a weapon of mass terror, Japan's balloon bomb campaign was a total…uh…bomb.

But it could have been much worse: Japan conducted extensive biological warfare research during the war. Had the Japanese added "germ bombs" to their balloons, casualties might have been immense. It's likely that they balked at such a step for fear the United States would retaliate with their own germ weapons.

THE BROWN SCARE

Back in the 1930s, left-wing Communists were called "Reds," while right-wing Nazis were called "Browns" (the color of the uniforms worn by the "SA," the street thugs who helped Hitler rise to power).

During the Great Depression, "Browns" began to gain strength in America. One of the largest pro-Nazi organizations was the German-American *Bund*. Supposedly representing the interests of German immigrants, the Bund actually espoused a racist, anti-Jewish party line. By 1938 Bund membership stood at roughly 6,500

---

with thousands of additional sympathizers—enough to pack Madison Square Garden for a rally in February 1939.

As Europe edged closer to war, U.S. citizens became increasingly alarmed by the influence of extremist groups. President Roosevelt blasted homegrown Fascists as traitors, a theme picked up by the popular media. Congress held hearings on right-wing extremists; the FBI monitored the activities of domestic Nazis.

When the U. S. entered the war in 1941, the Justice Department finally had a reason to take action. They indicted dozens of far-right leaders on sedition charges. Meanwhile, the Bund fell apart after its leader, Fritz Kuhn, was hustled off to jail for forgery. And that pretty much shattered the power of the "Browns."

In years to come, the press, public, and politicians would shift their focus and begin to attack left-wing groups in the much better-known "Red Scare" of the 1950s.

FIGHTING IN GREENLAND

The Nazi invasion of Denmark in 1940 put the Arctic island of Greenland in an awkward situation. As a Danish colony, technically they should have surrendered to Germany following the German occupation of Denmark. But that might have allowed the Nazis to set up bases along the island's expansive coastline and relay information to their submarines. Eske Brun, the chief administrative officer of Greenland, would not allow it.

Brun decided to fight. He put together an army to resist any Nazi attacks. (The "army" consisted of a grand total of nine men, traversing the snow-covered coastline on dog sledges.) Dubbed "the Sledge Patrol," the Greenland army radioed weather data to the Allies and kept an eye out for Nazi invaders. And they soon arrived. In 1943 a small German naval detachment was sent to establish a weather base and battle the mighty Greenland army.

The invading Nazis and the Sledge Patrol spent more time fighting snowstorms than fighting each other. But in the end, the Greenland army was triumphant and the Germans were prevented from establishing a permanent weather base.

The Sledge Patrol still exists—they consist of one small squad under the command of the Danish Navy, performing surveillance duties along Greenland's coast. And yes, they still use dog sleds to get around.

Europe is the only continent without a desert.

I ♥ THE '80s!

Yo, Rambo, remember the Gimme Decade? The Teflon President, and "Who Shot JR?" Relax, it's like, totally awesome! (Part 2 on page 391.)

1980
- Ronald Reagan elected 40th U.S. president (defeats Jimmy Carter)
- John Lennon assassinated
- Mount St. Helens erupts
- #1 movie: *The Empire Strikes Back*
- U.S. hockey team wins Olympic Gold over Soviet Union
- Country Grammy: Willie Nelson's "On The Road Again"
- 1% of American homes have a PC

1981
- President Reagan and Pope John Paul II shot; both recover
- Prince Charles weds Lady Diana
- Sandra Day O'Connor becomes first woman appointed to Supreme Court
- 52 U.S. hostages released from Iran
- AIDS identified for the first time
- MTV debuts

- Best Picture Oscar: *Chariots of Fire*

1982
- Falklands War begins and ends
- First issue of *USA Today* hits stands
- Graceland opens to the public (adults: $6.50; kids: $4.50)
- First permanent artificial heart transplant performed on Barney Clark
- *Time* magazine man of the year: Pac-Man
- *Late Night with David Letterman* debuts on NBC
- #1 movie: *E.T.: The Extra-Terrestrial*

1983
- U.S. invades Grenada
- President Reagan first proposes SDI (Star Wars) program
- Vanessa Williams becomes first black Miss America
- America's first poet laureate: Robert Penn Warren

- Truck bomb in Lebanon kills 241 U.S. soldiers
- Michael Jackson's *Thriller* becomes bestselling album of all time
- M*A*S*H ends after 251 episodes
- *Terms of Endearment* wins 5 Oscars

1984
- First photos of missing children on milk cartons
- Bishop Desmond Tutu awarded the Nobel Peace Prize
- Indian Prime Minister Indira Gandhi assassinated
- Soviet Union boycotts summer Olympics in L.A.
- Dan Marino (Miami Dolphins) throws single-season record 48 TD passes
- #1 movie: *Ghostbusters*
- #1 single: Prince's "When Doves Cry"
- *Newsweek* magazine dubs 1984 the "Year of the Yuppie"

Q: On what sitcom did Nancy Reagan appear to tell kids to "Just Say No?" A: *Diff'rent Strokes.*

DUMB CROOKS

Here's proof that crime doesn't pay.

REVOLVING DUMMIES

"In August 1975 three men were on their way in to rob the Royal Bank of Scotland at Rothesay, when they got stuck in the revolving doors. They had to be helped free by the staff and, after thanking everyone, sheepishly left the building.

"A few minutes later they returned and announced their intention of robbing the bank, but none of the bank employees believed them. When they demanded £5,000, the head cashier laughed at them, convinced that it was a practical joke.

"Disheartened, the gang leader reduced his demand first to £500, then to £50 and ultimately to 50 pence. By this stage the cashier could barely control her laughter.

"Then one of the men jumped over the counter and fell awkwardly on the floor, clutching at his ankle. The other two attempted a getaway, but got trapped in the revolving doors for a second time, desperately pushing the wrong way."

—*The Incomplete Book of Failures*

SMILE

"A Mexico City mugger known to police as 'Teeth' stopped a news photographer at gunpoint, demanding everything the photographer was carrying, including his camera. But first, Teeth wanted his picture taken. The lensman clicked away...and then ran. The next day his newspaper, *Reforma*, ran the 'mug shot' on page one."

—*Christian Science Monitor*

PHOTO FINISH

"Sheriff's detectives arrested 28-year-old Einetta Denise Brown of Tampa, Florida, on identity theft charges. They said Brown, who is unemployed, has made her living since 1996 off credit card scams worth tens of thousands of dollars, leaving behind scores of angry victims.

"Detective Skip Pask said he first learned of Brown in 1998, but he was unable to catch up with her until December 2000, when

---

Q: What is a *bilateral perorbital hematoma*? A: A black eye.

she foolishly used a stolen credit card to pay for Christmas portraits of herself and her two young daughters.

"'She had been doing it for so long, she got comfortable,' Pask said. 'And careless.'"

—*St. Petersburg Times*

"I AM A CROOK"

"William Nixon did not know he had carried out a robbery—he was drunk at the time. Then he saw himself on a security video tape on television. Nixon, 36, immediately surrendered himself to police and admitted robbing the Carrickfergus, Northern Ireland, filling station several weeks earlier. He pled guilty to the robbery of about £250 ($400) from two women assistants, using an imitation firearm. Nixon had already spent the full amount from his welfare check on drink and could be seen staggering during the robbery. The proceeds of the robbery also went to alcohol.

"After the hold-up, he left the shop with a cigarette in his hand saying: 'All the best,' to the women, and sauntered off down the road."

—*Belfast News Letter*

TRY ACTING SMART

"Actor Brad Renfro (*The Client* and *Sleepers*) and a pal were charged with grand theft after trying to take a $175,000 yacht on a joy ride. Catching them might have been harder if they hadn't forgotten to untie the boat, causing it to smash back into the dock."

—*Stuff* magazine

BOOK HIM

"Gregory Roberts, 43, of Las Cruces, New Mexico, was arrested at the public library shortly after 2 a.m. Tuesday, for breaking and entering. Officers found his shoeprints on broken glass where he allegedly entered by kicking in a windowpane.

"Once inside the library, Roberts got himself trapped between the outer and inner doors of the foyer. He couldn't get back in, and he couldn't get back out. What could he do? He called police from a pay phone in the foyer. They got him out, but now Roberts is trapped behind another door: a jail door."

—*Albuquerque Journal*

A flea can jump 30,000 times in a row without taking a break.

FAMOUS CLOSE CALLS

*Too many world leaders—Gandhi, JFK, and Anwar Sadat to name
a few—have lost their lives to assassins. But the death toll would
be even higher if fate hadn't thwarted a few assassination
plots. Here are some intriguing examples.*

GENERAL ULYSSES S. GRANT (1822–1885)
THE ATTEMPT: On April 14, 1865, Abraham Lincoln
invited General Grant and his wife, Julia, to accompany
him and Mrs. Lincoln to Ford's Theatre. The Grants declined.
That night, of course, Lincoln was assassinated. "Had his assassination plot gone according to plan," Carl Sifakis writes in *The
Encyclopedia of Assassinations*, John Wilkes Booth "would have
killed not only the president, but a future president as well, General Ulysses S. Grant."

WHAT HAPPENED: Why didn't the Grants go? Because Julia
Grant *detested* Mary Lincoln. A few weeks earlier while touring
Grant's headquarters together, Mary snubbed Julia so many times in
front of so many important people that she refused to spend another night in her company. Grant, biographer William S. McFeely
writes, "was left to make to the president the most classic—and
limp—of excuses: He couldn't go because of the children."

PRESIDENT CHARLES DE GAULLE (1890–1970)
THE ATTEMPT(S): De Gaulle, president of France from 1959
to 1969, may have set a record as the modern world leader with
the most attempts on his life—31. Some examples:

• **September 1961.** Assassins planted plastic explosives and napalm
at the side of a road and set the bomb to go off when de Gaulle's car
approached. But they detonated it too soon. De Gaulle's driver sped
the undamaged car straight through the flames to safety.

• **August 1962.** A team of assassins, using submachine guns and
hand grenades, planned to attack de Gaulle's motorcade. But the
lookout failed to spot the cars until they were already speeding by.
The killers only managed to shoot out a window and a tire on de
Gaulle's car, and de Gaulle escaped unharmed…except for a cut
on his finger that he got brushing broken glass off his clothes.

In 1910 about 32 million Americans lived on farms. Today, less than 5 million do.

• **July 1966.** The last attempt made on de Gaulle's life and perhaps his luckiest break. Would-be assassins packed more than a ton of dynamite into a car and parked it on the road to Orly Airport. They made plans to set it off as de Gaulle was driven to the airport for a flight to the USSR.

WHAT HAPPENED: At the appointed time, de Gaulle's car drove past the car bomb…and nothing happened. Why not? The night before the attack was to take place, the "assassins" decided to commit a robbery to raise the money they would need to make their getaway. But they got caught—and were sitting in jail, unable to trigger the bomb.

KING HASSAN II (1929–1999)

THE ATTEMPT: On August 16, 1972, King Hassan of Morocco was flying home from France aboard his private Boeing 727. As the plane approached the airport in the capital city of Rabat, it was attacked by four jet fighters of the Royal Moroccan Air Force.

WHAT HAPPENED: In the middle of the attack, someone claiming to be a mechanic on the royal plane radioed to the attackers, "Stop firing! The tyrant is dead!" The fighters backed off, and the royal 727 was allowed to land.

The "mechanic" turned out to be the king himself. Unharmed, he exited the plane and then participated in the scheduled welcoming ceremonies as if nothing had happened. When the plotters realized they'd been fooled, eight more fighter planes attacked the ceremonies with machine gun fire, killing 8 people and wounding more than 40…but missing the king (he hid under some trees). Later that day still more fighters attacked a guest house next to the royal palace, where it was thought the king was hiding. Hassan survived all three attempts, executed the general behind the plot, and remained on the throne until July 1999, when he died from a heart attack at age 70.

CZAR ALEXANDER II (1818–1881)

THE ATTEMPT: In 1879 a violent anarchist group called Will of the People tried to bomb the czar's train outside Moscow.

WHAT HAPPENED: It was common for the czar's entourage to consist of two trains—one in front to test the rails and a second in back to carry the czar. So when the first train rolled by, the attackers let it go and blew up the second train...only to learn later that Alexander had been riding on the *first* train. The second one was a decoy.

AFTERMATH: In 1881 Will of the People made another attempt, as Alexander was returning by carriage to the Winter Palace. They tunneled under a road along the czar's intended route and packed the space with explosives. But they were thwarted at the last minute when the czar's guards changed the route.

This time, however, there were backup bombers, and as the czar passed by, one of them tossed a bomb at the imperial carriage, blowing it apart and killing two of the czar's guards. Alexander somehow escaped unscathed and might well have survived the entire attack had he not lingered at the scene to tend to the wounded. But moments later a second bomb killed him.

So in murdering Alexander II, did the anarchists get the revolution they were hoping for? No—the czar, a reformer by czarist standards, was succeeded by his son Alexander III, considered one of the most repressive czars of the 19th century.

PRIME MINISTER MARGARET THATCHER (1925–   )

THE ATTEMPT: Four weeks before a scheduled meeting of Thatcher's Conservative Party in the seaside town of Brighton, an Irish Republican Army bomber named Patrick Magee checked into the Grand Hotel, where Thatcher and numerous other high government officials would be staying. He then rented a room five stories above Thatcher's and planted 30 pounds of explosives.

WHAT HAPPENED: The bomb was programmed to explode at 3:00 a.m. on the last night of the conference. It was assumed that Thatcher would be in bed. She might have been, too, had her speechwriters done a better job preparing the speech she was to deliver the next day. But at 3:00 a.m. she was still working on it. Just moments after she left of her room, the powerful bomb ripped through the hotel, destroying much of the building...including part of Thatcher's suite. By then, however, she was in another part of the hotel, unharmed.

Five people, including a member of Parliament, were killed in the blast and 30 more were injured. Authorities speculated that the death toll would have been much higher had so many officials not been downstairs in the hotel bar.

WEIRD CANADA

Canada: land of beautiful mountains, clear lakes, bustling cities...and some really weird news reports. Here are some of the oddest entries from the BRI news file.

WHO WOULD HAVE SUSPECTED?

In April 2001, police in Vancouver, British Columbia, ended a three-year crime spree when they arrested 64-year-old Eugene Mah and his 32-year-old son, Avery. The Mahs had been stealing assorted lawn and garden items from homes in their neighborhood, including garbage cans, lawn decorations, recycling boxes, and realty signs. Why did they steal them? Nobody knows. Eugene Mah is a real estate tycoon worth a reported $13 million. One local psychiatrist said the thefts may be due to an obsessive-compulsive hoarding disorder. They reportedly stole a neighbor's doormat...and each of the 14 other doormats the neighbor bought as replacements.

BEAVER FEVER!

In June 2003, two disc jockeys in Toronto caused a SARS panic—in the Dominican Republic. Z103.5 Morning Show hosts Scott Fox and Dave Blezard thought it would be funny to call the resort where their co-worker, Melanie Martin, was vacationing. They told the desk clerk that Martin had smuggled a "rare Canadian beaver" into their country. But the desk clerk, who didn't speak much English, thought he'd heard the word "fever." With SARS (Severe Acute Respiratory Syndrome) being big news at the time and Toronto being one of the cities where the disease had spread, the clerk panicked—and locked the woman in her room. The entire hotel wasn't quarantined, according to the station's news manager, but staff were at the point of contacting medical authorities when the disc jockeys finally convinced them that it was all a misunderstanding. Martin was released from her room that afternoon.

COMING IN FOR A LANDING

Lucette St. Louis, a 66-year-old woman from Corbeil, Ontario, was rounding up three runaway pigs owned by her son, Marc, when she became the victim of a bizarre accident. One of the 180-pound pigs had wandered into the road and a passing car hit it. The impact sent the pig airborne, landing on top of Mrs. St. Louis and breaking her leg in two places. "Well, at least," she said, "I can tell my grandchildren that pigs really do fly."

DEATH MERCHANT

Roman Panchyshyn, a 47-year-old Winnipeg retailer, upset some of his fellow residents when he started selling $65 sweatshirts that read "Winnipeg, Murder Capital of Canada—Escape The Fear" in his store. The shirts showed the city skyline dripping in blood. "We spend hundreds of thousands of dollars yearly to promote Winnipeg to the world," complained City Councillor Harry Lazarenko, "and I don't want this to give us a black eye." So he contacted the premier to see if Panchyshyn could be stopped. He couldn't—the shirts are accurate. Winnipeg has the highest murder rate in Canada. Said the unapologetic Panchyshyn, "The truth hurts."

WEIRD CANADIAN RECORDS

• On August 30, 1995, Sean Shannon of Canada recited Hamlet's "To be or not to be" soliloquy in 23.8 seconds—an average of 655 words a minute.

• On August 17, 1991, 512 dancers of the Royal Scottish Dance Society (Toronto branch) set the record for the largest genuine Scottish country dance (a reel).

• In 1988 Palm Dairies of Edmonton created the world's largest ice cream sundae—24,900 kg. (54,895 lbs.).

• In 1993 the Kitchener-Waterloo Hospital Auxiliary filled a bowl with 2,390 kg (5,269 lbs.) of strawberries.

• Four hundred mothers in Vancouver broke the record for mass breast feeding in 2002.

• In Feb. 2000, 1,588 couples at the Sarnia Sports Centre broke the record for most kissing in one place at one time.

• Dave Pearson holds the record for clearing all 15 balls from a standard pool table in 26.5 seconds at Pepper's Bar in Windsor, Ontario, in 1997.

• In 1998 1,000 University of Guelph students formed the longest human conveyor belt, laying down in a row and rolling a surfboard over their bodies. In 1999 they set the record for simultaneous soap-bubble blowing.

A regulation tennis ball must weigh between 2 and 2$\frac{1}{16}$ ounces.

FILE UNDER "UNDERWEAR"

*Here at the BRI, we believe it's important to keep up with
world events... especially when they involve underpants.*

GERMANY

• BERLIN—In July 2003, a group of naked men riding in a van on the autobahn caused a traffic accident. One of the men tossed his underpants out of the window of the van, striking the driver of a Volkswagen Passat in the face. The underpants blocked the Passat driver's view, causing him to slam into the truck in front of him. There were no injuries. At last report, "police were hunting the owner of the underpants for leaving the scene of an accident."

• MUNICH—In June 1999, a policeman was severely disciplined for stripping off his clothes at work and exercising in his underwear late in the day when he thought he was alone in the station. Wrong—a female officer saw him and reported him for sexual harassment. "I had no idea anybody else was still in the office," the man explained, telling the court that he stripped out of his clothes because he sweats a lot. The court docked his pay 12.5% for the next *five years*. Total amount of the fine: about $53,000.

MALAYSIA

KUALA LUMPUR—Malaysian police arrested Doomsday cult leader Petrus Ratu Doren, self-described "holiest of them all," after he predicted that the end of the world would come in October 1995 and that his followers could protect themselves by wearing their underpants on their heads. In custody, Doren admitted that he made the whole thing up "because he wanted fame and power."

Police rounded up more than 200 of Doren's followers, who fled into the jungle with their weapons (and their underpants) to await the end of the world. "We want to get to the root of the matter about this guy who has used the name of God in vain," police told reporters. "Especially that bit on underwear."

THAILAND

BANGKOK—In January 2003, fifty-eight college students were arrested at Bangkok's Ramkhamhaeng University for hiding pagers in their underpants and using them to cheat on a final exam. The pagers were set to vibrate the correct answers on the multiple choice test: one buzz if the first choice was correct, two buzzes if the second choice was correct, etc. Four teachers were also arrested and charged with helping the students cheat. Illegal use of a pager is a serious crime in Thailand; if convicted, each of the conspirators faces two years in prison and a $2,300 fine.

CHINA

HONG KONG—In December 2002, a 45-year-old man was fined the equivalent of $128 for making hundreds of crank calls to the local fire station over a period of more than five years. According to court records, each time a firefighter answered the phone, the man—whose name was not released—asked him "if he'd put on his underpants."

ENGLAND

LONDON—Police searching the apartment of an underwear thief in September 1998 discovered a cache of more than 10,000 stolen bras, underpants, and leotards piled four feet high in the man's tiny one-room flat. Police arrested the man as he was stealing even more underwear from a clothesline. According to news reports, at the time of his arrest the 37-year-old suspect was wearing "a stolen swimsuit and someone else's pants."

MEXICO

MEXICO CITY—In June 2003, dozens of farmers from the province of Veracruz staged a protest by stripping down to their underpants in front of a national monument on one of Mexico City's busiest streets. The farmers were protesting the policies of former Veracruz governor Patricio Chirinos, whom they accused of unjust land seizures. Why protest in underpants? "Stripping is the only way to get attention," farmer Agustín Morales explained. "We don't have money to buy an ad in the newspapers."

Sing along: There are 158 verses in the Greek national anthem.

RISE OF THE MACHINES

We're not saying they're about to take over, but robots are becoming more integral to our world all the time. Here are some innovative ways they are being used today.

Name: ROBOP

Profile: Garry O'Hagan, manager of the Easter Roads Stadium in Scotland, was fed up with invading flocks of pigeons. They fouled the seats, annoyed the fans, and sometimes even disrupted play on the field. He wanted to find a humane way to get rid of the unwanted birds, so O'Hagan hired a pest-control expert who spent nine months developing Robop, an electronic robot peregrine falcon. But pigeons aren't easily fooled by most fake falcons, so this one was designed to flap its wings, move its head, and utter a realistic screech. It works. Robop now stands guard over the stadium and scares the pigeons away.

Name: ROBONAUT

Profile: Still in the design stages at NASA, this humanoid figure looks like something out of *Star Wars*. Slated to take on the most dangerous extravehicular jobs on the International Space Station, Robonaut will be run by "telepresence," a virtual-reality system controlled by astronauts in the station. How will they do it? They'll don a special suit to maneuver the robots: every movement the astronaut makes, Robonaut will make, too.

Name: ROBORAT

Profile: Engineers have been trying to build small robots that can navigate through rubble to find disaster victims, without much success. Meanwhile, rats have shown that they have the brains and agility to perform search missions—but only in a laboratory setting. Let them outside the lab, and the rats do pretty much whatever they want.

So physiologists at the University of New York have combined the best of both worlds to create RoboRat, a cyborg (part animal, part machine) rodent that will go anywhere it's told. A tiny backpack carries a miniature video camera; tiny electrodes go into its brain. A human controller can guide RoboRat with a laptop com-

---

What is *ichthyosis*? A disease that gives human skin the appearance of fish scales.

puter, sending signals directly to the pleasure center of the rat's brain. The scientists are surprised how easily this is done—they've even been able to get them to climb trees, something most rats don't do.

Name: THE MILKER
Profile: Taking the farmer out of farming, all that this fully automatic machine requires is a cow. Once a cow gets to the milking station, she "spends a few minutes munching grain while the robot's quietly moving parts prod at the animal's udders." First, a laser finds the cow's teats, then a roller disinfects them. After that comes the "milking claw"—an apparatus with long, white suction cups. The robot is self-cleaning and will even call itself in for repairs.

Name: MONROE
Profile: It's easy for humans, but tough for robots. What is it? Walking. It's taken 30 years of experimentation—with a lot of trips and falls along the way—but the persistence has paid off: biped walking robots are here. One such leggy bot named Monroe (after Marilyn Monroe) has been developed by the Mechatronics Design Laboratory in Japan. Each of Monroe's legs has a hip joint, a knee joint, an ankle joint, and a toe joint. A complex system of sensors and gyros helps it maintain balance. The lab is also working on robots that can run and jump. Their ultimate goal: an android—an autonomous robot that can walk, talk, see, and manipulate objects with its hands.

Name: CYBERFLORA
Profile: "So many robots are seen only as mechanical drones that do physical labor," says Cynthia Breazeal, a professor of arts and sciences at the MIT Media Lab. "I wanted to communicate a more humane vision of technology." So she created cyberflora. Her futuristic garden consists of "flowers" that are actually metal skeletons fitted with silicon and electronic sensors capable of reacting to light and body heat. To walk among them is a completely unique experience. These robotic blossoms change colors, sway in the wind, and open their buds to capture light. And in addition to producing sweet odors, some also emit soft, ambient music for those patient enough to stop and…listen to the flowers.

URBAN LEGENDS

Hey—did you hear about the guy who invented a car that can run for months on a single tank of gas? We've looked into some urban legends to see if there's any truth to them.

LEGEND: If you eat a lot of cup-of-soups, you *must* remove the noodles from the Styrofoam cup and put them in a bowl before you add boiling water. Why? There's a layer of wax lining the cup that will liquefy when you pour in hot water. The wax can accumulate in your system, causing a deadly "waxy buildup."

HOW IT SPREAD: Via word of mouth, for more than 20 years. The latest version is an e-mail that describes how a college student lived on the stuff for months to save money, only to die when so much wax built up in his stomach that surgeons were unable to remove it.

THE TRUTH: Cup-A-Noodle cups and those of similar soups don't have a wax lining—they're just ordinary Styrofoam cups. And even if the cups *did* contain wax, wax is so easy to digest that it's a fairly common ingredient in candy and other foods.

LEGEND: On the day he retires, a longtime General Motors employee is invited down to the factory lot to pick out any car he wants as a retirement gift. He picks a Chevy Caprice. But after weeks of long drives in the country he finds he still hasn't used up the first tank of gas. When he calls GM to praise the car's performance, they react suspiciously...and the very next morning he looks out into his driveway and sees two mysterious men in white lab coats working under the hood of his car. The retiree chases the men away, but from then on his car gets only normal gas mileage.

It turns out that the car he picked was actually a 200+ mpg prototype that GM is hiding from consumers, so that they have to buy more gas than is really necessary. When GM realized the Caprice had gotten out of the factory, they dispatched two company engineers to "fix" it.

HOW IT SPREAD: The story has been floating around since the 1920s, spreading first by word of mouth, then by photocopies

---

Exhibitionists: Houseflies prefer to breed in the middle of a room.

posted on bulletin boards and lately by e-mail. The tale resurfaces every few years with fresh new details—new auto companies and updated makes of car—that keep it believable.

THE TRUTH: This story fails the common sense test: why would any auto company suppress technology that would give it such a huge advantage over its competitors? If GM could make a 200+ mpg car using patented technology that its competitors didn't have, it would dominate the industry.

This legend has been kept alive by generations of con artists who claim to have invented 200+ mpg carburetors or magic pills that can turn tap water into auto fuel. When frustrated investors demand to see proof that the "inventions" really do work, the con artists frequently claim that the invention has been stolen by mysterious men in black suits or that it's been suppressed by the auto industry. Rather than admit they've been conned, gullible investors sometimes pass these claims along as true.

(Similar urban legends haunt the tire industry, which is supposedly suppressing tires that will last for a million miles, and the drug industry, which is accused of buying up the patents to electric headache cures so that the public has to keep buying aspirin.)

LEGEND: The screams of a UCLA coed being sexually assaulted are ignored because the assault takes place during a midnight "scream session," when students scream out their dorm windows to relieve the stress of final exams. The attack forced a change in university policy: "To this day, anyone screaming unnecessarily during finals week at UCLA is subject to expulsion."

HOW IT SPREAD: Originally by word of mouth, then by e-mail, from one college student to another.

THE TRUTH: No such attack ever happened—and UCLA doesn't expel students for screaming during finals. This legend, which has been attributed to many different universities around the country, is kept alive by the insecurities of incoming freshmen, nervous about living away from home for the first time.

LEGEND: On October 2, 1994, Lauren Archer let her three-year-old son Kevin play in the "ball pit" of a McDonald's play area. Afterward Kevin started whimpering, telling his mommy, "It hurts." That night when Archer bathed her son, she noticed an odd welt on his butt. It looked like he had a large splinter. She immediately made an appointment with the doctor to have it removed the next day, but when Kevin became violently ill later that evening—she rushed him to the emergency room.

Too late. Kevin died from what an autopsy revealed to be a heroin overdose...and the "splinter" in his rear end turned out to be the broken-off needle of a drug-filled syringe. How did it get there? Police investigators emptied out the McDonald's ball pit and found, according to one version of the story, "Rotten food, several hypodermic needles, knives, half-eaten candy, diapers, feces, and the stench of urine."

HOW IT SPREAD: First by e-mail beginning in the mid-1990s, then by word of mouth from one frightened parent to another. The story's credibility is supported by the fact that the original e-mail gives specific names and dates, and even cites a newspaper article that supposedly appeared in the October 10, 1994 issue of the *Houston Chronicle*.

THE TRUTH: It's a hoax. No such incident ever happened and no such article ever appeared in the *Houston Chronicle*. Don't take our word for it—after years of denying the rumors, the *Chronicle* finally printed an official denial in February 2000. A similar story about rattlesnakes in a ball pit—at Burger King—is also false.

*   *   *

CELEBRITY EXCUSES

"Crack is cheap. I make too much money to use crack."
> —**Whitney Houston,** *on why crack wasn't on the long list of drugs she admitted to having used*

"I was told that I should shoplift. My director said I should try it out."
> —**Wynona Ryder,** *to the security guard who busted her at Saks Fifth Avenue*

"I've killed enough of the world's trees."
> —**Stephen King,** *on why he's quitting writing*

The Tin Woodsman's real name in the Oz books was Nick Chopper.

BUDDHA'S WISDOM

Siddhartha Gautama, known as the Buddha, or "Enlightened One," died in 480 B.C., but his wisdom lives on.

"Do not dwell in the past, do not dream of the future, concentrate the mind on the present moment."

"Nothing ever exists entirely alone; everything is in relation to everything else."

"Believe nothing, no matter where you read it, or who said it, unless it agrees with your own reason and your own common sense."

"Holding on to anger is like grasping a hot coal with the intent of throwing it at someone else; you are the one who gets burned."

"Better than a thousand hollow words, is one word that brings peace."

"Every human being is the author of his own disease."

"In the sky, there is no distinction of east and west; people create distinctions out of their own minds and then believe them to be true."

"It is a man's own mind, not his enemy or foe, that lures him to evil ways."

"We are what we think."

"Let us be thankful, for if we didn't learn a lot today, at least we learned a little, and if we didn't learn a little, at least we didn't get sick, and if we got sick, at least we didn't die. So, let us all be thankful."

"There are only two mistakes one can make along the road to truth; not going all the way, and not starting."

"Work out your own salvation. Do not depend on others."

"Thousands of candles can be lighted from a single candle, and the life of the candle will not be shortened. Happiness never decreases by being shared."

"Your work is to discover your world and then with all your heart give yourself to it."

THE BIRTH OF THE DEMOCRATIC PARTY

Major political parties aren't born overnight. They usually begin when a group of dissenters gets so fed up with the party they belong to that they break away to form a new one.

ONE-PARTY SYSTEM

The two-party political system was a basic element in the founding of the United States, right? Wrong. As we told you in *Uncle John's Supremely Satisfying Bathroom Reader*, America's Founding Fathers were vehemently opposed to the idea of political parties. Why? England's political parties seemed to spend their time battling one another instead of working together to advance the national interest, and the Founding Fathers hoped to avoid that.

But they couldn't—by 1787, as the Constitutional Convention was being held in Philadelphia to draw up the country's new constitution, political factions were already beginning to emerge. There were "Federalists," who wanted to create a strong federal government by giving it powers that had previously belonged to the state governments. And there were "Anti-Federalists," who opposed the new constitution, which in its final form promised to do just that.

The Federalists won that debate, and the new constitution went into effect on March 4, 1789. In 1796 they succeeded in electing Vice President John Adams president after George Washington, who was non-partisan, declined to run for a third term.

THE JEFFERSONIAN REPUBLICANS

And who did Adams beat? The leader of the Anti-Federalists: Thomas Jefferson (he lost by only three electoral votes). As the Federalists won one debate after another, Jefferson's supporters decided to make a clean break and resurfaced as the "Democratic-Republican" Party, also known as the "Republicans" or the "Jeffersonian Republicans." Ironically, these Republicans are considered the direct antecedents of the modern *Democratic* Party, not the Republican Party.

The Jeffersonian Republicans opposed the Alien and Sedition

Wonder Woman's bullet-proof bracelets were made of a metal called *feminum*.

Acts, new laws that outlawed associations whose purpose was "to oppose any measure of the government of the United States." The Acts also imposed stiff punishments for writing, printing, or saying anything against the U.S. government. The Republicans saw these acts as targeted at them and also as a grave threat to democracy. Jefferson put his hat in the ring for the 1800 presidential election, and after the Republicans mounted a fierce campaign, he won.

SWAN SONG

The Federalists went on to lose again in 1804, then again in 1808, and again in 1812. That year they made the mistake of publicly opposing the War of 1812, and even secretly discussed seceding from the Union because of it. When this came to light in 1814, they were finished as a political force. They lost the presidency again in 1816, and by 1820 they were so far gone that they didn't even field a candidate for president. That year, President James Monroe ran for reelection unopposed.

For the moment, it seemed that American democracy might be returning to a one-party system. What prevented that from happening? The fact that four men—Secretary of War John C. Calhoun, Secretary of the Treasury William Crawford, Secretary of State John Quincy Adams, and Speaker of the House Henry Clay all wanted to succeed Monroe as president.

Calhoun and Crawford were not above using the patronage and other perks of their offices to gain an advantage in the race. And both of them leaked details of the other's doings to news reporters. In the process, the entire Monroe administration became tainted with a reputation for corruption.

ACTION JACKSON

Many Americans were outraged by Calhoun's and Crawford's scheming. One such man was General Andrew Jackson, hero of the Battle of New Orleans in 1815 and a man so tough his soldiers called him Old Hickory after "the hardest wood in creation." As the first war hero since George Washington, Jackson was the most popular living American, and for years his admirers had urged him to run for president. For years he had turned them down.

But the corruption of the Monroe administration changed his mind. It convinced Jackson that it was "his public duty to campaign for the presidency and engage in what he called 'a general cleansing' of the federal capital," historian Paul Johnson writes in *A History of the American People*. "Jackson became the first presidential candidate to grasp with both hands what was to become the most popular campaigning theme in American history—'Turn the rascals out.'"

Jackson became the fifth candidate to enter the race for president in 1824. Although he was the least politically experienced of the candidates, he was the most popular man in the country. Result: on election day, Jackson won more votes and carried more states than any other candidate.

But amazingly, it wasn't enough.

POLITICAL SCRAMBLING

Because the electoral college vote was split among four candidates, none of them, not even Jackson, won an absolute majority of electoral votes. According to the Twelfth Amendment to the Constitution, that meant that the House of Representatives would have to choose between the top three finishers: Jackson, Adams, and Crawford. Each state's delegation would get one vote.

Because he came in fourth, Henry Clay was excluded from consideration for the presidency. But as Speaker of the House, he was well positioned to steer it to the candidate of his choice, and his choice was John Quincy Adams. Crawford had suffered a stroke during the campaign and was in no condition to assume presidential duties, and Clay saw Jackson as "a mere military chieftain" with a bad temper and not nearly enough political experience to be president. By comparison, Adams was the Harvard-educated son of a former president, and had served stints as secretary of state and U.S. ambassador to Russia.

Clay worked hard to deliver the presidency to Adams, but when the time came to vote in the House of Representatives, he was still one vote short—he needed New York. But the New York delegation was evenly split, which, according to the rules, meant that its vote wouldn't even be counted unless someone in the delegation changed their vote.

THAT'S THE TICKET

Henry Clay put enormous pressure on an elderly New York congressman named Stephen Van Rensselaer to change his vote in favor of Adams...but Van Rensselaer couldn't make up his mind. So when the vote was called, he lowered his head, closed his eyes, and whispered a short prayer, asking for divine guidance.

When Van Rensselaer opened his eyes, the first thing he saw was a ticket for John Quincy Adams on the floor beneath his desk. That was all he needed—Van Rensselaer picked up the ticket, carried it over to the ballot box, and put Adams in the White House.

Jackson, who'd won more votes and carried more states than anyone else, was convinced that he'd just been cheated out of the presidency. The Adams presidency, he charged, was the result of a "corrupt bargain": essentially Henry Clay had delivered the presidency to Adams and Adams appointed Clay Secretary of State, which in those days was considered heir apparent to the presidency. Jackson and his supporters vowed to get revenge.

The Jeffersonian Republican Party was so deeply divided over the election of 1824 that it split in two. Jackson's supporters now began to refer to themselves as the "*Democratic*-Republican" Party—Democrats for short. Adams's supporters called themselves the "*National* Republicans."

The two-party system was back, this time to stay.

MUD FIGHT

What followed was one of the nastiest political battles in the history of the United States. Adams, his reputation tarnished by the charges of corruption, was determined to muddy Jackson's reputation as well. Adams's supporters attacked Jackson's military career, accusing him of misconduct during the War of 1812. They also dug up an old charge (possibly true) that he'd married his wife Rachel before her divorce from her first husband was final. That made her a bigamist, which was not only illegal but scandalous.

Nothing was sacred. Adams's people even attacked Jackson's deceased mother. The pro-Adams *National Journal* called her "a *Common Prostitute,* brought to this country by British soldiers! She afterwards married a *Mulatto Man,* by whom she had several children of which number *General Jackson is one!*"

Jackson's forces fought back, attacking President Adams as an out-of-touch, elitist aristocrat, as well as an alcoholic and a "Sabbath-breaker" who, when he did go to church, went barefoot.

LIFE OF THE PARTY

But what really made the election of 1828 remarkable was that it was the first truly *national* presidential campaign. Traditionally, the slow pace of communication across the U.S. necessitated that political campaigns be run at the state and local level, with no national strategy or tactics. That began to change in 1826, when Senator Martin Van Buren, the political boss of New York known as "the Little Magician," joined forces with the Jackson camp.

Van Buren launched a centrally controlled communications strategy. The campaign formed its own newspaper, called the *United States Telegraph*, and hired a staff of writers to write pro-Jackson articles that were then published in the *Telegraph* and 50 other pro-Jackson papers around the country.

At the same time, local and state committees organized pro-Jackson dinners, barbecues, parades, and other events where local politicos would deliver stump speeches written by the national campaign. Campaign workers sang campaign songs—another innovation for 1828—planted hickory trees in town squares and along major roads, and distributed hickory brooms, hickory canes, and even hickory leaves that people could wear to show their support for Old Hickory. Then, on election day, local Jackson organizations marched their voters to the polls under banners reading "Jackson and Reform."

DEMOCRATS IN POWER

The old-fashioned Adams campaign could not match the strategy or intensity of the Jackson campaign. Old Hickory won 56% of the popular vote and 178 out of 261 electoral votes, including every state west of New Jersey and south of the Potomac River. "Organization is the secret of victory," one pro-Adams newspaper observed, and "by want of it, we have been overthrown."

"Jackson's victory brought a full-blown party system into existence," Arthur Schlesinger writes in *Of the People*. "Martin Van Buren...was the champion of the organized party with party machinery, national conventions and national committees, all held together by party discipline and the cult of party loyalty."

The Democrats were the first to benefit from Van Buren's system, but other parties would soon follow. Read about the birth of the Whig party on page 452.

FIRST EDITIONS

As you might imagine, Uncle John is a book hound. He loves "first editions." So you can imagine how flushed he got when he found a list of some real first editions.

• **World's First Dictionary:** *Explaining Words, Analyzing Characters* (100 A.D.), by Xu Shen. Chinese words and definitions.

• **World's First Fantasy Story:** *The Castaway*, published in Egypt circa 1950 B.C. The story of a man who is shipwrecked on an island ruled by a giant bearded serpent with a deep voice and an ability to predict the future.

• **World's First Sci-Fi Story:** *True History*, by Lucian of Samosata, published in the second century A.D. Adventures in outer space, in unknown seas, and on the moon. Everyone in space speaks Greek.

• **World's First Book of Firsts:** *Origins of Ages* (100 B.C.), author unknown. Lists the founders of the ruling families of China.

• **World's First Novel:** *Cyropaedia* (360 B.C.), by the Greek author Xenophon. An account of the life of Cyrus, founder of the Persian empire. The book offers "an idealized account of Persian society, contrasting with the unsympathetic views of most Greeks."

• **World's First Autobiography:** *Memoirs of Aratus of Sicyon*, published after his death by poisoning in 213 B.C. Critics commend Aratus for admitting his own weaknesses in the book, but fault him for being "insultingly critical of people he disliked."

• **World's First Book of Ghost Stories:** *Tales of Marvels* (early third century), by Chinese author Tsao Pi. Stories include a haunted house and a man who convinces a ghost that he's a ghost, too.

• **World's First Joke Book:** *Forest of Jokes*, by Harn Darn Jun, a Chinese author, around 200 A.D. Here's one of the jokes:

> In Lu, a man with a long pole tried to go in through a city gate. But whether he held the pole upright or side on, he couldn't get through. He was at his wit's end. Then an old man came up and gave him advice which he acted on: "I may not be a sage, but I have had plenty of experience. Why don't you saw the pole in half and carry it through that way?"

Humorist Will Rogers once served as honorary mayor of Beverly Hills.

THE SOPRANOS QUIZ

The Sopranos, a TV drama about mobsters, is one of the hottest shows ever created by HBO. You may be a fan, but how much do you really *know about the show?*

1. From the start the show's creator, David Chase, wanted to call the show *The Sopranos*, but HBO said no. Why?

♦ **a)** HBO executives thought the word *Soprano* sounded Greek, not Italian. Who would watch a show about Greek mobsters?

b) Not "authentic enough." HBO insisted on *The Fratiannos*, but they backed off when deceased mobster Jimmy "the Weasel" Fratianno's relatives threatened to sue.

c) They were afraid viewers would think the show was about opera singers. They were going to call the series *Family Man*, but backed off when Fox introduced the animated series *Family Guy*.

2. Which of the following other titles were also considered for the show before HBO backed down and let Chase call it *The Sopranos*?
a) *Red Sauce*
b) *Made in New Jersey*
c) *The Tony Files*
d) All of the above

3. How did James Gandolfini (Tony Soprano) take up acting?
a) "I was shy in high school. I thought acting would be a good way to meet girls. It was."
b) "I didn't want a job where I'd work in an office all day."
c) "I got tired of working for the phone company. It was either acting or singing, so I flipped a coin. It came up heads—acting."
d) "A friend took me to his acting class, and I was scared to death. That really made me mad, so I stayed. I don't know why."

4. Who said, "Hit them over the head with a baseball bat, and they come around" and "I'm gonna come back here and carve my initials in your forehead. You better show me the respect I deserve."
a) Jamie-Lynn Sigler (Meadow Soprano) said it to David Chase.

More steel is used in the U.S. to make bottle caps than to make cars.

According to Chase, she said it when he refused to give her a raise.

b) Tony Sirico, the actor who plays Paulie Walnuts. In the early 1970s, he really was a Mob thug. He made the threats during a confrontation with the owner of a New York discotheque.

c) Dominic Chianese, who plays Uncle Junior, had an uncle who believed that the best way to get good service in a restaurant was by threatening the waiters. He told the story to Chase, who put some of the uncle's lines in episode 10 of the first season, when Junior threatens an attendant at Livia Soprano's nursing home.

d) Chase heard Nancy Marchand (Livia Soprano) say it to her husband on the phone, so he used it in episode 6, when Tony Soprano threatens Anthony Jr.'s football coach.

5. What is a *goomah?*
a) The same as a *borgata*—a crime family.
b) The same as a *jamook*—an idiot or a loser.
c) The same as a *comare*—a mobster's mistress.
d) The same as a *mannagge*—a war with another clan or family.

6. What was one of the challenges actor Michael Imperioli had to master to play Tony Soprano's nephew, Christopher Moltisanti?
a) Learning how to drive.
b) Learning how to act. He'd played small parts in movies (he was Spider in *Goodfellas*), but he'd never really studied the craft.
c) Overcoming his stutter.
d) The New Jersey accent. He was raised in North Dakota.

7. What is an "executive game"?
a) A financial scam that cheats wealthy investors by selling them stock in fake companies.
b) An exclusive, high-stakes poker game for celebrities and rich people.
c) A code name for a sporting event that has been fixed in advance by paying key players to lose.
d) The title of episode 12, where Tony wants to join a private country club but can't because golf is an "executive game" and he's "the wrong kind of executive."

Answers on page 498.

Cleopatra was married to Ptolemy XIII and Ptolemy XIV—both her brothers.

WEIRD-MART

*You've probably come up with a business idea you
thought was terrific, only to be told it would never
work. Well, that didn't stop these folks.*

AS NOT SEEN ON TV

Toy stores in the United States and Great Britain started selling a new action figure in 2001: Invisible Jim. Like other action figures, Invisible Jim is packaged in a box of clear plastic and colorful cardboard. The only difference is that there's nothing inside the box. The makers of the "toy" say it's good for kid's imaginations and perfect for "anyone with a sense of humor."

"We get the odd phone call from someone who says, 'We got an Invisible Jim but he must have fallen out. Could you send me another doll?'" said distributor Chris Marler, adding, "When we got the first shipment, we weren't sure it had actually arrived."

IT'S A MALL WORLD AFTER ALL

Fearing they might be losing business from women whose husbands hated to shop, the Braehead Shopping Centre in Glasgow, Scotland, came up with an unusual idea in 2002: "The Shopping Boyfriend," a real-life person who acts as a temporary boyfriend or husband to be dragged along from store to store. "The Shopping Boyfriend is the ultimate retail therapist," said a mall spokesperson. They are "enthusiastic, attentive, admiring, and complimentary," and, if necessary, they'll even say "her bum looks small."

GHOST WRITER

Do you live in a haunted house? Ultraviolet, a company in England, offers "Spooksafe" insurance policies that will pay up to $100,000 for "death, injury or damage to personal effects caused by a ghost or poltergeist." (Or aliens.) And if you can prove medically that you've been transformed into a vampire or werewolf, the policy pays $1 million. According to Simon Burgess, chief underwriter, the company has already paid out on one ghost-related murder. "We had a firm of investigators look into it," he said, "and they were convinced that a ghost was responsible."

More children are accidentally poisoned by toxic houseplants than by household chemicals.

THEY JUST CALLED TO SAY I'M SORRY

It's difficult for some people to say "I'm sorry" (see pages 83 and 325). So for the equivalent of $2.50, the Apology and Gift Center in Tianjin, China, will send someone to apologize for you. The company claims to be thriving; in Chinese culture many people fear that making an apology will make them "lose face." And for anyone who can't afford $2.50, there's another alternative: saying "I'm sorry" live on the popular Beijing People's Radio show *Apologize in Public Tonight.*

URINE THE MONEY

Kenneth Curtis, a pipefitter in Marietta, South Carolina, got fed up with having to submit to regular urinalysis drug tests at his worksites. He didn't use drugs and saw the tests an invasion of his privacy. So in 1996 he decided to get even with the testers—he started an online company, Privacy Protection Services, to sell his "clean" urine. For $69, Curtis offers 5.5 ounces of drug-free urine, a tube, and a small heated pouch to strap to your leg. "Use our kit in a natural urinating position," ads boast. "You cannot be detected even if directly observed." Curtis claims to have sold more than 100,000 kits.

Update: When South Carolina made selling urine illegal in 1999, Curtis appealed it all the way to the U.S. Supreme Court...but finally lost in 2001. Undaunted, Curtis found a way around the law—he moved to North Carolina, where he continued to sell drug-free pee. "If you can't sell urine, what can you sell?" he asks.

HE CHARGES AN ARM AND A LEG

The *South China Morning Post* reported in 2003 that a 19-year-old security guard from Changsha, Hunan province, was selling himself—one piece at a time. The young man put posters up advertising his body parts for sale to the highest bidder: $18,000 for a kidney, the same amount for one testicle, and $9,000 for an eye. He said he hadn't had any offers yet, but did have some inquiries. Why was he doing it? According to the news reports, he wanted to "get rich."

*   *   *

"A business that makes nothing but money is a poor business."

—**Henry Ford**

BEFORE THEY
WERE INFAMOUS

*Great leaders make choices early in life that pave the way
for their illustrious careers. But what about the world's
worst tyrants? Here's a look at the early lives of
some rotten apples in the history barrel.*

JOSEPH STALIN (1879–1953)

Place in History: Soviet ruler from 1924 to 1953. Fueled by a mad paranoia, Stalin is responsible for the murder and mass starvation of millions of Soviet citizens. His forced collectivization of Soviet agriculture starved as many as 5 million people from 1932 to 1933; the political purges that followed from 1936 to 1938 may have killed as many as 7 million more. His diplomatic and military blunders leading up to World War II contributed mightily to the 20 million Soviet military and civilian casualties during the war.

Before He Was Infamous: Born Iosif Vissarionovich Dzhugashvili, young Joseph entered a Russian Orthodox seminary in 1894, but he was kicked out at the age of 20. He went underground, became a Bolshevik revolutionary, and later adopted the pseudonym Stalin, which means "Man of Steel." Between 1902 and 1913, the man of steel was arrested and jailed seven times, and sent to Siberia twice. In 1917, he became the editor of *Pravda*, the Communist Party newspaper. Stalin did not play a prominent role in the communist revolution of November 1917, but in 1922 he was elected general secretary of Communist Party, a post that became his power base. Vladimir Lenin died in 1924, but it wasn't until after six years of maneuvering against opponents that Stalin emerged as Lenin's unrivaled successor in 1930.

MAO TSE-TUNG (1893–1976)

Place in History: Leader of the Chinese Communist Party (1935) and founder of the People's Republic of China, which he ruled from 1949 until his death in 1976. Under such disastrous programs as The Great Leap Forward (1958-60) and The Cultural Revolution (1966-76), more than 30 million people starved to death or were murdered outright by Mao's government and its policies.

Snot funny: The Japanese have been blowing their noses on tissue paper for over 300 years.

Before He Was Infamous: At 13, this child of peasant farmers left home to get an education. He tried police school, soap-making school, law school, and economics before settling on becoming a teacher. He attended the University of Beijing, where he became a Marxist and in 1921, at the age of 27, a founding member of the Chinese Communist Party. In 1927 he alienated orthodox Marxists by arguing that peasants, not workers, would be the main force in the communist revolution. It wasn't until 1935, following the 6,000 mile "Long March" to escape the Chinese government's brutal campaign against the communists, that he emerged as the party's leader.

ADOLF HITLER (1889–1945)

Place in History: Elected German Chancellor in 1933 and ruled Nazi Germany from 1933 until his death in 1945. The Nazis murdered an estimated 6 million Jews and other people it considered inferior, including Gypsies, Jehovah's Witnesses, communists and homosexuals. Hitler also started World War II, which killed as many as 55 million people.

Before He Was Infamous: As a small boy, Hitler dreamed of becoming a priest, but by age 14 he'd lost his interest in religion. As a young man he enjoyed architecture and art and dreamed of becoming a great artist, but when he applied for admission to the Academy of Fine Arts in Vienna, he was turned down—twice—for lack of talent. He bummed around Vienna until 1913, living off an orphan's pension and what little money he made from odd jobs like beating carpets, and from selling paintings and drawings of Viennese landmarks. When World War I broke out in 1914 he was living in Munich, where he volunteered for the Bavarian Army and was later awarded the Iron Cross.

Germany lost the war in 1918; the following year Hitler joined the German Workers Party at a time when it had only about 25 members. He soon became its leader, and in 1920 the party changed its name to the National Socialist German Workers' Party—better known as the Nazis.

POL POT (1925–1998)

Place in History: Leader of the Cambodian *Khmer Rouge* guerrilla movement, which seized control of the Cambodian government in

1975 and ruled the country until January 1979. On Pol Pot's orders the cities were emptied and the urban population forced out into the countryside to work on collective farms that became known as "killing fields." Nearly 1.7 million Cambodians—20% of the entire population—were starved, worked to death or murdered by the Khmer Rouge.

Before He Was Infamous: Born Saloth Sar, Pol Pot lived in a Buddhist monastery for six years, and was a practicing monk. He worked briefly as a carpenter before moving to Paris at the age of 24 to study radio electronics on a full scholarship. While there he joined the French Communist Party. He later lost his scholarship and returned home in 1953, the same year that Cambodia won independence from France. Over the next decade Sar rose through the ranks of the Cambodian Communist Party (the Khmer Rouge), and in 1963 he became its head. In the mid 1970s he adopted the pseudonym, Pol Pot.

IDI AMIN DADA (ca. 1924–2003)

Place in History: Ugandan dictator from 1971 to 1979. In those years he expelled the entire Asian population of Uganda (more than 70,000 people) and is believed to have murdered as many as 400,000 people during his eight-year reign of terror. In 1979 he invaded the neighboring country of Tanzania; when the invasion failed and the Tanzanians counterattacked he fled into exile, eventually settling in Saudi Arabia. He died there in August 2003.

Before He Was Infamous: Amin, a member of the small Kakwa tribe of northwestern Uganda, was born in 1925 and raised by his mother, a self-proclaimed sorceress. As a child he sold doughnuts (*mandazi*) in the streets. In 1943 he joined the King's African Rifles of the British colonial army and went on to serve in the Allied Forces' Burma campaign during World War II. After the war he became a boxer and was the heavyweight champion of Uganda for nine years (1951–1960).

Amin continued his rise through the ranks of the military, and by the time Uganda became independent from England in 1962 he was one of only two African officers in the entire Ugandan armed forces. President Milton Obote appointed him head of the army and navy in 1966; five years later Amin seized power in a coup and declared himself president for life.

The phrase "the sky's the limit" comes from Cervantes' *Don Quixote*.

MANEKI NEKO

There are countless superstitions involving cats, most of them focused on the bad luck that they supposedly bring. In Japan and other Asian countries, however, the cat is a symbol of good fortune.

THE BECKONING CAT

If you've ever walked into a Chinese or Japanese business and noticed a figure of a cat with an upraised paw, you've met Maneki Neko (pronounced MAH-ne-key NAY-ko). "The Beckoning Cat" is displayed to invite good fortune, a tradition that began with a legendary Japanese cat many centuries ago.

According to legend, that cat, called Tama, lived in a poverty-stricken temple in 17th-century Tokyo. The temple priest often scolded Tama for contributing nothing to the upkeep of the temple. Then one day, a powerful feudal lord named Naotaka Ii was caught in a rainstorm near the temple while returning home from a hunting trip. As the lord took refuge under a big tree, he noticed Tama with her paw raised, beckoning to him, inviting him to enter the temple's front gate. Intrigued, the lord decided to get a closer look at this remarkable cat. Suddenly, the tree was struck by lightning and fell on the exact spot where Naotaka had just been standing. Tama had saved his life! In gratitude, Naotaka made the little temple his family temple and became its benefactor. Tama and the priest never went hungry again. After a long life, Tama was buried with great respect at the renamed Goutokuji temple. Goutokuji still exists, housing dozens of statues of the Beckoning Cat.

LUCKY CHARMS

Figures of Maneki Neko became popular in Japan under shogun rule in the 19th century. At that time, most "houses of amusement" (brothels) and many private homes had a good-luck shelf filled with lucky charms, many in the shape of male sexual organs. When Japan began to associate with Western countries in the 1860s, the charms began to be seen as vulgar. In an effort to modernize Japan and improve its image, Emperor Meiji outlawed the production, sale, and display of phallic talismans in 1872. People still wanted lucky objects, however, so the less controversial Maneki Neko figures became popular.

Eventually the image of the lucky cat spread to China and then to Southeast Asia. How popular did the Beckoning Cat become? In Thailand, the ancient goddess of prosperity, Nang Kwak, was traditionally shown kneeling with a money bag on her lap. Now she's usually shown making the cat's raised-hand gesture and occasionally sporting a cat's tail.

In Europe and North America, images of Maneki Neko can be found in Asian-owned businesses, such as Chinese restaurants. And back in Japan, a new cat icon adorns clothing, toys, and various objects: Hello Kitty—a literal translation of Maneki Neko, or "Beckoning Cat."

MANEKI NEKO FACTS

• Sometimes Maneki Neko has his left paw up, sometimes the right. The left paw signifies that the business owner is inviting in customers. The right invites in money or good fortune.

• Most Maneki Nekos are calico cats; the male calico is so rare it's considered lucky in Japan. But Maneki Neko may be white, black, red, gold, or pink to ward off illness, bad luck, or evil spirits and bring financial success, good luck, health, and love.

• Maneki Nekos made in Japan show the palm of the paw, imitating the manner in which Japanese people beckon. American Maneki Nekos show the back of the paw, reflecting the way we gesture "come here."

• The higher Maneki Neko holds his paw, the more good fortune is being invited.

*　　　*　　　*

"I don't need a reading lamp in my living room. I don't have a toilet in there."

—**Norm Macdonald**

No laughing matter: Hyenas are more closely related to cats than dogs.

AMAZING ANAGRAMS

Bathroom readers seem to love anagrams…words or phrases whose letters can be rearranged to form new words or phrases. Bonus: The new phrase has a meaning that relates to the old one.

NEGATION *becomes…*
GET A "NO" IN

ENDEARMENTS *becomes…*
TENDER NAMES

HARVESTING SEASON *becomes…* **SAVE THE GRAIN, SONS**

BURY THE HATCHET *becomes…* **BUTCHER THY HATE**

SUPREME COURT *becomes…*
CORRUPT? SUE ME

THE ASSASSINATION OF PRESIDENT ABRAHAM LINCOLN *becomes…*
A PISTOL IN AN ACTOR'S REBEL HANDS; A FINE MAN IS SHOT

PUBLIC RELATIONS *becomes…* **CRAP, BUILT ON LIES**

SOUTHERN CALIFORNIA *becomes…* **HOT SUN, OR LIFE IN A CAR**

MARRIAGE *becomes…*
A GRIM ERA

INFORMATION SUPERHIGHWAY *becomes…* **NEW UTOPIA? HORRIFYING SHAM**

North America *becomes…*
MACHO TERRAIN

SENATOR *becomes…*
TREASON

GARBAGE MAN *becomes…*
BAG MANAGER

A SURGICAL OPERATION *becomes…* **PAIN OR GORE. ALAS, I CUT.**

A PSYCHIATRIST *becomes…*
SIT, CHAT, PAY, SIR.

MERRIAM WEBSTER DICTIONARY *becomes…* **MAY CITE BRAINIER WORD TERMS**

TELEVISION *becomes…*
TV IS ONE LIE

First movie star to appear on a postage stamp: Gene Kelly.

THE DUSTBIN OF HISTORY

*Leon Livingston had many titles—A-No.1, the
Rambler, Emperor of the North—but none fit
him better than "King of the Hoboes."*

Forgotten Figure: Leon Ray Livingston
Claim to Fame: Being King of the Hoboes
Background: Leon began his hobo lifestyle when he ran
away from home in San Francisco in 1883. Only 11 years old, the
boy was too young to find work, so he took up with a hobo named
Frenchy, an ex-convict and experienced wanderer who taught little Leon the ways of the open road:

• How to survive on handouts from local charities.

• Where to sleep—parks, freight cars, or the "hobo jungles" outside railroad yards.

• How to make "mulligan stew," a traditional hobo meal consisting of a stolen chicken and whatever few vegetables they could
gather, all cooked in a large tin can on a campfire.

• How to move about the country for free: generally in empty
freight cars.

• Ways to avoid the railroad police, known as "bulls," who
patrolled the train yards looking for freeloaders. Being caught usually meant getting a beating with the bulls' nightsticks. Worse,
sometimes it meant being tossed off a moving train.

FAME (BUT NO FORTUNE)

Leon, who became known as A-No.1, got to be adept at hopping a
train after it had left the station (other "brethren of the road" who
weren't as skilled often lost their lives, falling under the wheels of
the train). He loved the hobo life and kept a scrapbook of the travels that took him from the Klondike to the Amazon. And everywhere he went, he wrote his name, "A-No.1," on fences, on barns,
on storefronts, and in train yards. Every bare wall he encountered
bore witness to the fact that A-No.1 had been there.

Scientists say: The easiest sound for the human ear to hear is "ah."

Word of mouth turned him into America's most famous tramp. And because he neither drank nor smoked, because he valued honesty and cleanliness, the other hoboes looked up to A-No.1, and gave him another nickname, "King of the Hoboes."

ROAD SCHOLAR

As he got older, A-No.1 rambled from coast to coast with the famous writer Jack London, whose hobo moniker was "Sailor Jack." London inspired A-No.1 to become a writer himself. His first published book was *The Life and Adventures of A-No.1*, followed closely by *Hobo Camp Fire Tales*. He wrote 12 books in all.

A-No.1 claimed that his only real goal in life was to keep American boys and girls from running away from home and living the sort of life he led. He gave lectures on the evils of the vagabond life and used the money he made from his books to send runaway kids back home.

"When I started out, the wanderlust was upon me and I enjoyed the zest of adventure," A-No.1 said. "Later I traveled because it became a habit, and now, although I hate the life, I travel because I cannot stop."

A-No.1 died in 1944 and was buried in the place he had come to love most—a small town in Pennsylvania called Cambridge Springs. On his tombstone is written, A-No.1 AT REST AT LAST.

*   *   *

FAMOUS LAST WORDS

"I have just had to tell your mother that I shall be dead in a quarter of an hour. Hitler is charging me with high treason. In view of my services in Africa I am to have the chance of dying by poison. The two generals have brought it with them. It is fatal in three seconds. If I accept, none of the usual steps will be taken against my family. I'm to be given a state funeral. It's all been prepared to the last detail. In a quarter of an hour you will receive a call from the hospital in Ulm to say that I've had a brain seizure on the way to a conference."

—Suicide note of "Desert Fox"
Erwin Rommel after participating
in a plot to assassinate Hitler

In Arabic countries, *Sesame Street* is known as *Iftah Ya Simsim*.

MYTH-CONCEPTIONS

"Common knowledge" is frequently wrong. Here are
some examples of things that many people believe—
but that according to our sources, just aren't true.

Myth: If you touch a baby bird, its mother will abandon it.
Fact: Whether or not a mother can detect the scent of a human depends on the animal's sense of smell. Birds have a poor sense of smell and would never know from it whether a human had touched their nest.

Myth: Julius Caesar was a Roman emperor.
Fact: In Caesar's time, Rome was a republic and had no emperor. The Roman Empire didn't exist until 17 years after Caesar's death.

Myth: You should drink at least eight 8-ounce glasses of water a day.
Fact: The bottled-water industry loves this myth, but according to kidney specialist Dr. Heinz Valtin, there is no scientific evidence to support the claim.

Myth: Diamonds are the most valuable gem.
Fact: Carat for carat, rubies are far more valuable than diamonds.

Myth: Ticks are insects.
Fact: Insects have six legs and three body parts. Ticks, on the other hand, have eight legs and two body parts, which classifies them as arachnids, not insects.

Myth: The chameleon changes color to match its background.
Fact: Chameleons really *can* change color instantaneously, but it's a reaction to fear or to extreme temperature and light changes—it has nothing to do with matching the colors of its background.

Myth: Arabic numerals come from Arabia.
Fact: The numbering system we use today actually originated in India. It was later brought to Arab lands, where westerners first encountered them and labeled the numbers "Arabic."

Impotence is grounds for divorce in 24 U.S. states.

THE MAN FROM C.R.A.P.

An acronym is a word made up of the initial letters of other words—and some of them end up being pretty funny. And if you don't like them, don't blame us—see someone at C.R.A.P. (the Committee to Resist Acronym Proliferation).

EGADS
Stands For: Electronic Ground Automatic Destruct System (*military command given to destroy a missile already in flight*)

BOGSATT
Stands For: Bunch Of Guys Sitting Around The Table (*Pentagonese for where the important decisions are made*)

CHAOTIC
Stands For: Computer-Human-Assisted Organization of a Technical Information Center

LIE
Stands For: Limited Information Estimation (*it's true*)

MANIAC
Stands For: Mathematical Analyzer, Numerical Integrator, And Computer

OOPS
Stands For: Occasionless Ordered Preemptive Strike (*World War III begun by accident*)

SIMPLE
Stands For: Simulation of Industrial Management Problems with Lots of Equations

NO FUN
Stands For: NO First Use of Nuclear Weapons

BUFF
Stands For: Big Ugly Fat Fellow (*Air Force slang for a B-52 bomber*)

WOMBAT
Stands For: Waste Of Money, Brains, And Time (*A computer programmer "wrestles with a wombat" when the solution proves more complex than the problem*)

OOH, OOH
Stands For: On the One Hand, On the Other Hand

WOE
Stands For: Withdrawal Of Enthusiasm (*The bored tone of an airline pilot's "Welcome aboard" on the third or fourth straight flight*)

Do you get ingrown toenails? It's hereditary—odds are someone else in your family does, too.

I GOT IT BACK!

Have you ever lost something special? Well, don't give up hope—you may find it again. These folks did.

ON GUARD

Lost Item: A wallet

The Story: In November 2002, a Swedish man named Holger Granlund got a call from the army saying that they had found his wallet...the one he'd lost 56 years earlier. It was found in the hayloft of a stable where Granlund had been on guard duty in 1946. Amazingly, almost everything was still in it—his driver's license, a food ration card, and photos of young women he'd known. The only item missing: a 20-kroner bill (worth about $2).

RING ME LATER

Lost Item: A University of Notre Dame class ring

The Story: When Robert Lensing graduated from Indiana's Notre Dame University in 1959, he received the traditional sapphire class ring...which mysteriously disappeared from a jacket pocket. (He suspected his mother's cleaning lady.) A few years later, a landscaper named Frank Foster bought a used camper from a family in Petersburg, Indiana. Foster and his wife found the ring under some seat cushions, put it in a jewelry box, and forgot about it—for almost four decades. Not long after Foster's wife died in 2000, he remarried. His new wife found the ring and insisted they return it to the owner. They contacted Notre Dame, who used the ring's inscription to find Lensing, and in February 2002, 42 years after it was lost, he got his ring back. "This just shows that there's a lot of good in people," said Lensing.

A NOT-SO-BRIEF CASE

Lost Item: A briefcase

The Story: In September 1989, Frank Keating got on a United Airlines flight from Washington, D.C., to Tulsa, Oklahoma. But, when he got off, he inadvertently left his briefcase on the plane. The airline sent it to him...in November 2002. "I had forgotten all about it," said Keating, who had become governor of Okla-

---

Most common physical complaint in the U.S.: lower back pain.

homa in the meantime. The case had been sitting on a shelf in a security closet in San Francisco. United spokesman Jeff Green said, "We're glad we got it back to him. Sorry it took 13 years." Contents of the case: some papers, wrapped birthday presents for his mother-in-law, and a calculator (the batteries were dead).

PYRAMID SCHEME

Lost Item: A cat

The Story: Cathryn Chartez really likes her cat. So much so that she took it with her on vacation to Egypt in October 2002. But the cat escaped in the Cairo airport as she was headed home to the United States. The Egyptian tourist police tried to help her find it, to no avail. Chartez went home catless. Two months later, she went back to Egypt to look for her cat again, putting up posters, taking out advertisements, and offering a $110 reward. It worked. A week later an electrical worker found the kitty hiding from the rain in a nearby terminal and notified the police…and the worker refused to accept any reward money.

THANKS!

Lost Item: A gold ring

The Story: In 1945 the mayor of Jersey City, New Jersey, gave the sheriff a gift: a gold ring, inscribed "From Mayor Frank Hague to Sheriff Teddy Fleming 1945." Years later Fleming passed the ring on to his son, the historian Thomas Fleming. In 1968 Fleming was visiting the famous French battlefield, the Argonne, on the 50th anniversary of his father's service there during World War I. While climbing a steep hill, he slipped and fell—and lost the ring.

In 1985 Frenchman Gil Malmasson was metal-detecting in the Argonne and found it. He immediately contacted the American embassy, but couldn't track down the Flemings. Thirteen more years passed. Then in 1998 Malmasson was surfing the Internet and found the website for Jersey City…and the name "Mayor Frank Hague." He got in touch with the current mayor, Bret Schundler, who made some phone calls and located Fleming within hours. Fleming flew to Paris and met Malmasson—who happily put the ring back on his finger.

Not as fragile as you thought: Egg shells are proportionately as strong as bone.

JUST PLANE WEIRD

Close calls, close encounters, and other strange events in the sky.

GOT JUICE?

During the landing phase of Aeroflot Flight #2315 on May 9, 1994, over Arkhangelsk, Russia, loss of hydraulic fluid caused the landing gear system to fail; the right leg of the plane would not come down. In desperation, the crew poured every beverage they could find into the hydraulic system—soda, water, wine, milk, juice, and liquor. That made it possible for the crew to lower the gear, but only partway. When the plane landed, it veered to the right and went off the side of the runway, but a serious crash had been avoided. (According to experts, in an emergency any fluid will help—even urine.)

YOU SNOOZE, YOU LOSE (ALTITUDE)

On February 17, 1994, the pilot of a private Piper PA-34 fell asleep at the controls as he was flying from Springfield, Kentucky, to Crossville, Tennessee. This was normally a short flight, but five hours later he woke up over the Gulf of Mexico, with only 20 minutes of fuel remaining. Lucky break: He was able to reach the Coast Guard by radio just as he ran out of fuel. A helicopter pulled him out of the water 70 miles west of St. Petersburg, Florida.

BLINDED BY THE LIGHT

On October 30, 1995, a Southwest Airlines flight was climbing after takeoff from McCarran International Airport in Las Vegas when a blinding beam of light swept into the cockpit. The first officer, who was piloting the aircraft, was completely blinded for 30 seconds. For another two minutes he suffered flash blindness in the right eye and after-image effects in his left eye. He was unable to focus or interpret any of the instrument readings and was "completely disoriented."

The source of the beam: an outdoor laser light show at one of the Vegas hotels. But because so many hotels entertain guests with nightly light shows, it was impossible to determine which one was responsible. The captain (who was not affected) took over the controls until the first officer recovered.

Looney law: In Oklahoma, you can be fined for making funny faces at dogs.

BETTER LATE THAN STUPID

America West Flight #6361 had been in the air less than two minutes one day in 2003, when the pilot received a call from the tower: there was a bomb onboard. The pilot immediately returned to the Medford, Oregon, airport where the passengers and crew were evacuated. A bomb squad searched the plane and luggage, but found nothing.

A little while later, when a man arrived at the check-in counter and insisted that he be allowed to board the delayed flight, America West clerks became suspicious. It turned out that the man had been on his way to the airport when he realized he was going to miss the flight. Brilliant solution: He called in the bomb threat on his cell phone, hoping to delay the plane a few minutes. The police were notified, the call was traced, and the man was promptly arrested. (The plane took off without him...again.)

WHERE THERE'S SMOKE...

While taxiing for takeoff in Detroit, Michigan, on April 17, 1986, a TWA passenger saw some mist coming out of the plane's air vents. It was nothing abnormal, just condensation from an overheated air conditioner pack. But the passenger, believing that the plane was on fire, panicked and shouted, "Open the door!" The lead flight attendant responded to the emergency orders (which she thought came from the cockpit) and opened an exit door. Passengers sitting near exit doors also prepared for evacuation by opening *their* doors. Fortunately, the plane was still on the ground—21 passengers jumped off before the captain could intervene.

*   *   *

"IT WAS MY CADDY...REALLY"

"At the 1959 Memphis Invitational Open, pro golfer Tommy Bolt was assessed one of the strangest fines in PGA tour history. Just when his playing partner was about to putt, Bolt loudly passed gas. Officials were not amused and fined him $250 for unsportsmanlike behavior."

—*Dubious Achievements in Golf's History*

MANAGEMENT EXPECTS...

*JoAnn Padgett of the Bathroom Readers' Hysterical Society
sent us this page from an old almanac with a note: "And
you guys think you've got it bad." (No, we don't.)*

**In 1870, after the government passed new, "liberal" labor laws,
one business released the following manifesto to its employees.**

NOTICE

1. Staff members must be present between the hours of 7:00 a.m.
and 6:00 p.m. on weekdays and only until noon on Saturday.

2. Daily prayers will be held each morning in the main office
with the clerical staff in attendance.

3. The staff will not disport themselves in raiment of bright colors, nor will they wear hose "unless in good repair."

4. A stove is provided for the clerical staff. Coal and wood must
be kept in the locker. Each member of the staff should bring four
pounds of coal each day during cold weather.

5. No member of the staff may leave the room without permission. Calls of nature are permitted and the staff may use the garden below the second gate. This area must be kept in good order.

6. Now that business hours have been reduced drastically, the
partaking of food is allowed between 11:30 and noon, but work
will not, on any account, cease.

7. A new pencil sharpener is available on application to Mr.
Rogers.

8. Trainees will report 40 minutes before prayer and will report
to Mr. Rogers after closing hours to clean private offices with
brushes, brooms, and scrubbers provided by the management.

9. Management recognizes the generosity of the new labor laws,
but will expect a much greater work output to compensate for
these near utopian conditions.

Bozo the Clown wore size 83AAA shoes.

UNSCRIPTED

When actors have to come up with their own lines...

"I have no experience, but I guess they're different from dogs and horses."
　—**Bo Derek, on children**

"If I'm androgynous, I'd say I lean toward macho-androgynous."
　—**John Travolta**

"I loved making the movie *Rising Sun*. I got into the psychology of why she liked to get tied up in plastic bags. It has to do with low self-esteem."
　—**Tatjana Patitz**

"The only happy artist is a dead artist, because only then you can't change. After I die, I'll probably come back as a paintbrush."
　—**Sylvester Stallone**

"Good looking people turn me off. Myself included."
　—**Patrick Swayze**

"There is no capital of Uruguay, you dummy—it's a country."
　—**Lorenzo Lamas, to Jon Stewart on *The Daily Show***

"I feel my best when I'm happy."
　—**Winona Ryder**

"Sure the body count in this movie (*Die Harder*) bothers me, but it's what everybody likes. At least it's not an awful body count—it's a fun body count."
　—**Bonnie Bedelia**

"In an action film you act in the action, in a drama film you act in the drama."
　—**Jean-Claude Van Damme**

"You can hardly tell where the computer models finish and the real dinosaurs begin."
　—**Laura Dern, on *Jurassic Park***

"I think that the film *Clueless* was very deep. I think it was deep in the way that it was very light. I think lightness has to come from a very deep place if it's true lightness."
　—**Alicia Silverstone**

"He's the chief, right? What else is there to say? It's not bad sleeping with Einstein."
　—**Lara Flynn Boyle on then-boyfriend Jack Nicholson**

"My main hope for myself is to be where I am."
　—**Woody Harrelson**

Scientists say: Gesturing with your hands while speaking improves your memory.

THE FEDERAL WITNESS PROTECTION PROGRAM

If you've ever wondered what being in the federal government's witness protection program is like, check out the book WITSEC: Inside the Federal Witness Protection Program, *by Pete Earley and Gerald Shur. It will tell you everything you ever wanted to know...and more.*

DOUBLE CROSS

In 1967 a Mafia hitman named Joe "The Animal" Barboza was arrested on minor charges and thrown in jail. His boss, Massachusetts mobster Raymond Patriarca, was supposed to bail him out, but Patriarca turned on Barboza instead, having three of Barboza's friends assassinated.

Barboza figured he was next and decided he wasn't going to just sit around and wait for someone to kill him. He immediately contacted the FBI and offered to testify against Patriarca...on one condition: the government had to protect Barboza, his wife, and their daughter against retaliation from the Mafia. For the rest of their lives. Breaking the Mafia's code of silence was an automatic death sentence, not just for Barboza but for his family as well. The FBI agreed and handed the job over to the U.S. Marshals Service, the federal agency charged with overseeing the security of the federal courts.

ON THE MOVE

Once the deal was made, deputies transferred Barboza to a new jail and registered him under a false name, so that nobody would know who he was. Another team of deputies set up a 24-hour guard at his house, an arrangement that lasted until Patriarca took out a $300,000 "contract" on Barboza. Fearing for the family's safety, the marshals moved the Barbozas to an abandoned lightkeeper's house on a small island off the coast of Massachusetts and stationed 16 armed guards there to protect them 24 hours a day. They stayed on the island until a Boston newspaper found out and revealed where they were hiding. Then they moved again.

Ernest Hemingway rewrote the final page of *A Farewell To Arms* 39 times.

YOUR TAX DOLLARS AT WORK

Barboza and his family remained in hiding and under round-the-clock protection for more than a year before Barboza testified against Patriarca in court. In the months that followed, he testified against more than a dozen other mobsters as well. By the time all the trials were over, Patriarca was behind bars and his criminal organization had been crippled.

It was an impressive victory for the Justice Department, but protecting Barboza had cost a fortune—more than 300 deputies had rotated in and out of two-week shifts guarding the family, and now that the trials were over, a way had to be found to protect the Barbozas for the rest of their lives.

But how? For now the Barbozas were hiding out in military housing at Fort Knox, Kentucky, but they couldn't stay there forever. A lifetime of 24-hour guards was out of the question: It cost too much money, consumed too much manpower, and put too many lives at risk. There had to be a better way.

HIDING IN PLAIN SIGHT

Gerald Shur, an attorney with the Justice Department's organized crime division, had been thinking about the problem for several years and came up with an answer: Why not just give the witnesses new identities and move them to a new part of the country?

In those days, mobsters were pretty territorial—they rarely left the cities where they lived. A witness from the New York City mob was a dead man if he stayed in New York, but if he moved to Portland, Oregon, he'd probably be safe—nobody there would know who he was. And if he changed his name and avoided contact with friends and relatives back home, nobody would be able to track him down. Round-the-clock armed guards would be unnecessary.

Shur was convinced that this was the best way to protect government witnesses like Barboza. He knew it could work because some deputies in the Marshals Service were already beginning to move mobsters around the country on their own initiative. But Shur wanted to put an official program in place. He figured that if potential witnesses knew that such a program existed, they were more likely to cooperate with prosecutors.

Not many people agreed with Shur. But when President Lyndon Johnson's political opponents accused Johnson of being soft on crime, a presidential commission on law enforcement started looking for new ways to nab criminals. In 1967 Shur pitched his witness protection idea to the commission. They recommended it to President Johnson, but it didn't become law until President Nixon signed the Witness Security Program (WITSEC) as part of the Organized Crime Control Act of 1970.

WITSEC BY THE NUMBERS

Initially Shur figured that no more than a few dozen new witnesses would enter the program each year. His guess was way off. For one thing, government prosecutors were eager to use witness testimony to win convictions. But just as importantly, every time a mob witness was able to break *omertà*—the Mafia's code of silence—and survive, it became more likely that other disgruntled or imprisoned mobsters would agree to rat out their crime bosses. By 1972 witnesses were entering the program at a rate of 200 a year; two years later the number had doubled.

To date, WITSEC has relocated more than 7,000 government witnesses and 9,000 of their family members. The Marshals Service estimates that more than 10,000 convictions have been obtained with the help of WITSEC witnesses. So far none of the witnesses in the program have been murdered in retaliation for their testimony, although 30 witnesses who left the program have been murdered... including the mobster who helped to start it all: In February 1976, Joe "The Animal" Barboza left the program and returned to a life of drug dealing, extortion, and murder. He was gunned down in San Francisco, California, in a drive-by shooting that police believe was a mob hit.

Though WITSEC was originally set up to battle the Mafia, today more than half of the people who enter the program are witnesses in drug trials; fewer than one in six are connected to the Mafia.

STARTING OVER

• *Any* relatives or loved ones of a witness are eligible to enter the program if they are potential targets. This includes grandparents, in-laws, girlfriends, boyfriends, even mistresses.

• When a witness enters WITSEC, they get a new name, assistance moving to a new city, and help with rent and other expenses until they find a job. They also get a new birth certificate, social

---

Have you heard? According to experts, a dog can't hear the lowest key on a piano.

security card, and driver's license, but that's about it. The Marshals Service doesn't create elaborate fake pasts or phony job histories, and it doesn't provide fake credit histories, either.

GETTING A JOB

• It's not easy finding a job without a résumé or job history. "You go to get a job, you got no references and they're not going to lie for you," says former mobster Joseph "Joe Dogs" Iannuzzi. "They don't help you get references for an apartment. You have to go and muscle it for yourself."

• But the Marshals Service does what it can to help. It has compiled a list of companies whose CEOs have agreed to provide jobs to government witnesses.

• When a witness is placed with a company only the CEO or some other high corporate official knows that the employee is a government witness, and even they are not told the person's true identity. They are, however, given details of the employee's criminal history. "You go to the head of the corporation," says retired deputy marshal Donald McPherson, "and you tell him the crimes. You have that obligation. You're not going to help a bank robber get a job as a bank teller."

STAYING IN TOUCH

• Witnesses are strictly forbidden from revealing their new identities, addresses, or even the region of the country they live in to friends and loved ones back home. If family members don't know the names and whereabouts of their relatives in the program, the mob is less likely to come after them and try to get the information.

• It's a myth that when witnesses enter the program they are forbidden from ever contacting loved ones outside the program again. They're only forbidden from making *direct* contact—letters and phone calls can be forwarded through the Marshals Service. In-person meetings can be arranged at safe, neutral sites, such as federal buildings or safehouses.

• Does the program work? It's estimated that as many as one in five return to a life of crime after entering the witness protection program. That's about half the recidivism rate of convicts released from prison.

FABULOUS FLOPS

Some folks have an eye for business, and
some businesses have an "i" for idiot.

YOU SAY TO-MA-TO, I SAY TO-BLAH-TO

In 1994 a small biotech company called Calgene got FDA approval for the first genetically engineered whole food to hit the stores in the United States—the *Flavr Savr* tomato. It was genetically altered to delay ripening, which allowed growers to keep the plant on the vine longer, shippers to keep it in the trucks longer, and grocers to keep it on shelves longer. It sounds good, but the tomatoes had problems: they didn't taste very good; crop yields were below expectations; and the machines used for packing them, built for still-green and firm tomatoes, mashed the Flavr Savrs to mush. After two years on the market, the original "Frankenfood" was pulled from stores. Calgene's loss: an estimated $150 million.

PUT A SOCK IN IT

Remember the Pets.com sock puppet? He appeared in 2000 in TV commercials for the online pet store and was wildly popular. He showed up on *Good Morning America* and floated in the Macy's Thanksgiving Day parade as a 36-foot balloon. Unfortunately, Pet.com's concept—selling pet supplies over the Internet—wasn't as popular as the puppet. After little more than a year, Pets.com was gone...and so was $100 million in start-up funds.

Flop-Flip: And the sock puppet? He reappeared in 2002 in ads for 1-800-BarNone, a company that offered loans to people with bad credit, and has written an autobiography, *Me By Me.*

BEERZ IN THE HOOD

In June of 1991, G. Heileman Brewing Company, makers of Colt 45, came out with a new beverage: PowerMaster, a malt liquor with a 5.8% alcohol content (the average American beer has 3.5%; most malt liquors have 4.5%.) Black community leaders immediately protested, charging that the product was aimed specifically and irresponsibly at urban African Americans. For proof, they pointed to the billboard ads for the beverage that were

---

Original name for the Bank of America: the Bank of Italy.

popping up in black neighborhoods. The protests quickly spread around the country, and by July the Bureau of Alcohol, Tobacco and Firearms ruled that the "Power" in PowerMaster had to go. A beer's name, they said, cannot reflect the strength of its alcohol content (even though they had approved the name just a month earlier). Heileman was forced to pull PowerMaster, at a marketing loss of more than $2 million.

Flop-flip: A year later, the brewer quietly introduced Colt 45 Premium, a malt liquor with a 5.9% alcohol content. The can was black with a red horse on it—the same design as PowerMaster.

HOPE SPRINGS ETERNAL

Pharmaceutical giant Pfizer Inc. spent 10 years and tons of money developing a "fountain of youth" drug designed to slow the aging process and keep people feeling young and vital well into old age. Initial research showed promise, prompting the company to pour even more money into the project. The reasoning was obvious: if it worked, the drug could make them millions, or even billions of dollars. In 2001 an independent testing lab performed a study that Pfizer executives expected would vault the drug toward FDA approval…but it didn't work out that way. The study actually concluded that people who took the "fountain of youth" drug had about the same results as those who'd taken sugar pills. By June 2002, the project had been canned. Cost of the decade of work: $71 million.

FELT TIP FOLLIES

In late 2001, Sony Music came out with a "copy-proof" CD. It was a much-heralded step toward preventing the piracy of their artists' music, which they claimed hurt sales. Sony spent millions developing the technology and in the first few months of 2002 shipped more than 11 million of the discs. But by May the innovation proved to be a total flop. Word had spread like wildfire on the Internet that the high-tech copy-proofing could be thwarted…by scribbling around the rim of the CDs with an 89¢ felt-tip marker.

*   *   *

"Wise men learn by other men's mistakes, fools by their own."

—**Anonymous**

Buenos Aires has more psychoanalysts per capita than any other city in the world.

KIBBLE ME THIS

What would Porter the Wonder Dog have eaten 200 years ago, before there was Alpo or Dog Chow? Here's the history of the multi-billion-dollar dog food industry.

CHOW DOWN

- More than 2,000 years ago, Roman poet and philosopher Marcus Terentius Varro wrote the first farming manual. In it he advised giving farm dogs barley bread soaked in milk, and bones from dead sheep.

- During the Middle Ages, it was common for European royalty to have kennels for their hounds. Kennel cooks would make huge stews, mostly grains and vegetables with some meat or meat by-products—the hearts, livers, and lungs of various livestock.

- Dogs in common households had meager diets. They were fed only what their owners could spare. A normal domesticated dog's diet consisted of crusts of bread, bare bones, potatoes, cabbage, or whatever they could scrounge on their own.

- In the 18th century, farm dogs, which had to be fairly healthy to do their jobs, were regularly fed mixes of grains and lard. In cities, you could make a living by searching the streets for dead horses, cutting them up, and selling the meat to wealthy dog owners.

- There were exceptions: The very wealthy, throughout history, have fed their pet dogs fare that was much better than what most humans ate. In the 1800s Empress Tzu Hsi of China was known to feed her Pekingese shark fins, quail breasts, and antelope milk. European nobility fed their dogs roast duck, cakes, candies, and even liquor.

LUXURY FOOD

Then in the mid-1800s, as the Industrial Revolution created a growing middle class with more money and more leisure time, pets began to be regarded as "luxury items" by everyday folk. Result: pet food became more closely scrutinized.

More pets and more money meant a new profession: veterinary medicine. It was officially founded in the United States in 1895, but many self-styled experts were already giving advice on dog diets. Many said that dogs needed to be "civilized," and since wild dogs ate raw meat, domesticated dogs shouldn't. (That advice influenced the pet food industry for decades after.)

In the late 1850s, a young electrician from Cincinnati named James Spratt went to London to sell lightning rods. When his ship arrived, crew members threw the leftover "ship's biscuits" onto the dock, where they were devoured by hordes of waiting dogs. That gave Spratt an idea. "Ship's biscuits," or hard tack, were the standard fare for sailors for centuries. Flour, water, and salt were mixed into a stiff dough, baked, and left to harden and dry. The biscuits were easily stored and had an extremely long shelf life, which was important in the days before refrigeration. And they looked a lot like today's dog biscuits.

Spratt had the idea that he could make cheap, easy-to-serve biscuits and sell them to the growing number of urban dog owners. His recipe: a baked mixture of wheat, beet root, and vegetables bound together with beef blood. When Spratt's Patent Meal Fibrine Dog Cakes came on the market in 1860, the pet-food industry was born. Spratt's Dog Cakes were a hit in England, so in 1870 he took the business to New York...and began the American pet food industry.

A GROWING TREND

Others followed in Spratt's footsteps:

• In the 1880s, a Boston veterinarian introduced A.C. Daniels' Medicated Dog Bread.

• The F. H. Bennett Biscuit company opened in 1908, making biscuits shaped like bones. Bennett also made the first puppy food, and was the first to package different-sized kibble for different breeds.

• In 1931 the National Biscuit Company (Nabisco) bought Bennett's company and renamed the biscuits Milkbones. Then they hired 3,000 salesmen with the specific goal of getting Milkbones into food stores—and the national consciousness. For the first time, dog biscuits were part of regular grocery shopping.

• In 1922 Chappel Brothers of Rockford, Illinois, introduced Ken-L Ration, the first canned dog food in the United States. It was horse meat. In 1930 they started sponsoring a popular radio show, *The Adventures of Rin Tin Tin*. Ken-L Ration became such a success that by the mid-1930s they were breeding horses just for dog food and slaughtering 50,000 of them a year.

Many restaurants in France allow dogs and even offer special menus for them.

AW, DRY UP

By 1941 canned dog food had a 90% share of the market...until the United States entered World War II and the government started rationing tin and meat. Then dry dog food became popular again.

In 1950 the Ralston Purina Company started using a cooking extruder to make their Chex cereal. Here's how it worked: ingredients were pushed through a tube, cooked under high pressure, and puffed up with air. This allowed Chex to stay crisp when milk was added.

At about the same time, manufacturers were getting complaints about the appearance, texture, and digestibility of dry dog food. Purina's pet food division borrowed an extruder from the cereal division and experimented with it in secret for three years. The result: Purina Dog Chow. Dogs loved it, it digested well, and it quickly became the number one dog food in the nation—and still is today.

NO PEOPLE FOOD FOR YOU

In the early 1950s, Ken-L Ration made the jump from radio to TV advertising, running commercials on wholesome shows like *The Adventures of the Ozzie and Harriet.* ("This dog food uses only USDA, government-inspected horse meat!")

In 1964 the Pet Food Institute, a lobbying group for the now-gigantic pet food industry, began a campaign to get people to stop feeding their dogs anything *but* packaged dog food. They funded "reports" that appeared in magazines, detailing the benefits of processed dog food, and even produced a radio spot about "the dangers of table scraps."

The dog food industry was spending an incredible $50 million a year on advertising. Commercials centered around the "beef wars," with competing companies all claiming to have the most pure beef. (*Bonanza* star Lorne Greene did a TV commercial for Alpo...holding a sirloin steak.)

In the 1960s and 1970s, factors such as increased numbers of breeds and rising crime rates made dog ownership skyrocket. By 1975 there were more than 1,500 dog foods on the market.

Today, more than 1,600 square miles of soybeans, 2,100 square miles of corn, and 1.7 million tons of meat and poultry products are made into pet food every year. There are more than 65 million dogs in the U.S., and pet food is an $11 billion industry...and growing.

COOL BILLIONS

There are 1,000,000,000 reasons to read this page.

• If you had $1 billion and spent $1,000 a day, it would take 2,740 years to spend it.

• One billion people would fill roughly 305 Chicagos.

• It took from the beginning of time until 1800 for the world's population to reach one billion, but only 130 years more for it to reach two billion—in 1930.

• One billion people lined up side by side would stretch for 568,200 miles.

• First magazine in history to sell a billion copies: *TV Guide*, in 1974.

• More than one billion people on Earth are between the ages of 15 and 24.

• One Styrofoam cup contains one billion molecules of CFCs (chlorofluorocarbons)—harmful to the Earth's ozone layer.

• Nearly one billion Barbie dolls (including friends and family) have been sold since 1959. Placed head to toe, the dolls would circle the Earth more than three times.

• To cook one billion pounds of pasta, you'd need two billion gallons of water—enough to fill nearly 75,000 Olympic-size swimming pools.

• The first billion-dollar corporation in the U.S. emerged in 1901—United States Steel.

• The ratio of billionaires to the rest of the U.S. population is 1 to 4.5 million.

• A single ragweed plant can release a billion grains of pollen.

• One teaspoon of yogurt contains more than one billion live and active bacteria.

• The first year in which the U.S. national debt exceeded $1 billion was 1863.

• There are about one billion red blood cells in two to three drops of blood.

• It's estimated that by 2005 there will be more than one billion cell phone users.

• Earth's oceans will completely disappear in about one billion years due to rising temperatures from a maturing sun.

Soak up this fact: Sponges form an amazing 99% of all marine species.

DUMB JOCKS?

Sports stars say the darnedest things. Are they trying to be funny...or just not all there? You be the judge.

"My wife doesn't care what I do when I'm away as long as I don't have a good time."
—**Lee Trevino**

"Be sure to put some of them neutrons on it."
—**Mike Smith, baseball player,** *instructing a waitress on how to prepare his salad*

"This taught me a lesson, but I'm not sure what it is."
—**John McEnroe**

"I want all the kids to do what I do, to look up to me. I want all the kids to copulate me."
—**Andre Dawson, Chicago Cubs outfielder**

"They shouldn't throw at me. I'm the father of five or six kids."
—**Tito Fuentes, baseball player,** *after getting hit by a pitch*

"That's so when I forget how to spell my name, I can still find my clothes."
—**Stu Grimson, hockey player,** *on why he has a photo of himself above his locker*

"I've won on every level, except college and pro."
—**Shaquille O'Neal**

"I could have been a Rhodes Scholar, except for my grades."
—**Duffy Daugherty, Michigan State football coach**

"People think we make $3 million and $4 million a year. They don't realize that most of us only make $500,000."
—**Pete Incaviglia, baseball player**

"If history repeats itself, I think we can expect the same thing again."
—**Terry Venables, professional skier**

"After a day like this, I've got the three Cs: I'm comfortable, I'm confident, and I'm seeing the ball well."
—**Jay Buhner, outfielder,** *after a perfect 5-for-5 day*

"Just remember the words of Patrick Henry—'Kill me or let me live.'"
—**coach Bill Peterson,** *giving a halftime pep talk*

Huh? The following statement is true. The previous statement was false.

CELEBRITY RUMORS

*Oh, those poor celebrities. Just because they're out in the public
eye, people want to make up weird stories about them. At the
BRI we hear rumors about celebrities all the time, and we
decided to look into some to see if they were true.*

RUMOR: Movie critic Gene Siskel, half of TV's Siskel and
Ebert, was buried with his thumb pointing upward ("Two
Thumbs Up" was the Siskel and Ebert trademark), as he'd
requested in his will.

HOW IT SPREAD: From a UPI news story that began circulat-
ing over the Internet shortly after Siskel's death in February 1999.
"Gene wanted to be remembered as a Thumbs-Up kind of guy,"
Siskel's attorney was quoted as telling the wire service.

THE TRUTH: The "news" article is fake. It was probably
intended as a joke, but at some point people started passing it
around as if it were true. Just to be safe, though, reporters at *Time
Out New York* obtained a copy of Siskel's will from the Chicago
court where it was filed. Their finding: "There are no digit-place-
ment requests in the critic's last wishes."

RUMOR: Vanna White of *Wheel of Fortune* fame starred in a
stage version of *The Diary of Anne Frank*. Her performance was so
bad that when the Nazis came in the house, people in the audience stood up and shouted, "She's in the attic!"

HOW IT SPREAD: By word of mouth and on the Internet.

THE TRUTH: Another example of a story that started out as a
joke but came to be passed along as true. White has never played
Anne Frank on stage, on TV, in the movies, or anyplace else.
Over the years, the "She's in the attic!" story has been attributed
to numerous actresses of questionable talent, including Pia Zadora.

RUMOR: Cher had her lowest pair of ribs surgically removed to
make her waist look slimmer.

HOW IT SPREAD: In 1988 *Paris Match* magazine published a
story claiming that she'd had the procedure done. From there the
story was published in newspapers and magazines all over the

world. (Jane Fonda, Tori Spelling, Janet Jackson, and even Marilyn Manson are rumored to have had the same procedure.)

THE TRUTH: Neither Cher nor anyone else could have the procedure done even if they wanted to, because no such procedure exists. Cher got so fed up with the rumor that she sued *Paris Match* (they retracted the story). She even hired a physician to examine her for evidence of the "procedure" (there was none) and release his findings to the public. It didn't do any good—the rumor persists to this day.

RUMOR: *Playboy* magazine founder Hugh Hefner used to place a number of small stars on the cover of his magazine to indicate how many times he'd slept with that month's cover girl. If he found her satisfactory, he placed them *inside* the "P" of the magazine's masthead. If he was disappointed, he placed them *next* to the "P."

HOW IT SPREAD: By word of mouth from one fantasizing *Playboy* reader to another. The story was helped along by the fact that from 1955 until 1979, there really *were* a series of small stars on the cover, sometimes inside the "P"... and sometimes alongside it.

THE TRUTH: The stars were marketing codes—*Playboy* was published in several different regional editions, and the company used different numbers of stars to identify the different editions. The stars were always printed in a dark color. If the cover was a dark color, the masthead was white and the stars went inside the "P." But on a light-colored cover, the stars went alongside it.

RUMOR: Iron Eyes Cody, the famous "crying Indian" of the Keep America Beautiful anti-littering ad campaign of the 1970s... was actually Italian.

HOW IT SPREAD: By word of mouth. Cody, who died at the age of 94 in 1999, went to his grave insisting his father was a member of the Cherokee tribe and his mother was full-blooded Cree.

THE TRUTH: When reporters from the *New Orleans Times-Picayune* went to Cody's hometown of Kaplan, Louisiana, in 1996 to check birth records, they found that he'd actually been born Espero DeCorti, to Italian immigrant parents. DeCorti assumed Indian identities in the 1920s to get jobs in Hollywood westerns. Once "Iron Eyes" became a Native American, he never stopped pretending. As DeCorti's half-sister May Abshire remembered of their childhood, "He always said he wanted to be an Indian."

HOW'D YOU METER?

A few strange—yet 100% real—measuring devices

LICK-O-METER

Remember the commercial that asked, "How many licks does it take to get to the Tootsie Roll center of a Tootsie Pop?" This device from WonderfullyWacky.com answers the all-important question. Insert a lollipop into the counter and start licking—an LCD readout tells you how many licks you've licked. Bonus: It's also a key chain.

BOA CONSTRICT-O-METER

As a gimmick for an upcoming TV special, producers asked scientists at Carnegie Mellon University for a way to measure a snake's squeezing power. Connected to a laptop computer, the quarter-sized device was put between a Burmese python and its prey—a frozen 10-pound rabbit. The results: About 12 pounds per square inch.

STING-O-METER

The USDA patented this inexpensive device for beekeepers so they can tell whether they're dealing with gentle European honeybees or the dangerous "Africanized" kind (they look virtually the same). This simple black plastic container is swung in front of the hive. An electronic sensor inside counts how many "hits" are made by attacking bees over 10 seconds. Too many hits? Run.

SPAWN-O-METER

Dr. Phil Lobel of the Woods Hole Oceanographic Institution in Massachusetts designed this underwater microphone to listen in on sounds made by fish. What's he listening for? According to Lobel, some species produce a shrill shuddering whistle when they mate.

GRUNT-O-METER

The British newspaper *The Sun* claimed to have set up this device to measure the loudness of the grunts made by tennis star Monica Seles during play at Wimbledon. The paper reported that the star had a grunt volume of 82 decibels, somewhere "between a pneumatic drill and a diesel train."

In the 1860s, Thomas Edison developed a device to electrocute cockroaches.

REAL TOYS OF THE CIA

Uncle John loves those clever spy gadgets in the James Bond movies devised by Q. It turns out that some of them are real. Here are a few actual spy tools.

IT LOOKS LIKE: A cigarette
BUT IT'S REALLY: A .22-caliber gun
DESCRIPTION: This brand of cigarette packs a powerful puff. Intended as an escape tool, the weapon only carries a single round, but with good aim it can inflict a lethal wound from close range. To fire the cigarette, the operator must twist the filtered end counterclockwise, then squeeze the same end between the thumb and forefinger. Warning: Don't shoot the weapon in front of your face or body—it has a nasty recoil.

IT LOOKS LIKE: A pencil
BUT IT'S REALLY: A .22-caliber pistol
DESCRIPTION: Like the cigarette gun, this camouflaged .22 comes preloaded with a single shot. The weapon is fired in the same manner as the cigarette: simply turn the pencil's eraser counterclockwise and squeeze. The only difference between the weapons is that the pencil has a greater firing distance—up to 30 feet.

IT LOOKS LIKE: A belt buckle
BUT IT'S REALLY: A hacksaw
DESCRIPTION: Fitted inside a hollow belt buckle is a miniature hacksaw. When the buckle is opened, a small amount of pressure is released from the saw's frame, exerting tension on the blade. This makes the saw a more efficient cutting machine, keeping the blade taut when sawing through, for example, handcuffs. The belt buckle saw will cut through anything from steel to concrete in about 15 minutes and will tear through rope and nylon. Don't wear belts? Buckles can be put on coats and luggage, too.

IT LOOKS LIKE: Eyeglasses
BUT IT'S REALLY: A dagger
DESCRIPTION: Concealed in the temple arms of these CIA

"Q" stands for *quartermaster*, a military name for the officer in charge of supplies.

glasses are two sharp blades. Disguised as the reinforcing wire found in most eyeglass frames, the daggers are designed to be used once and broken off at the hilt, inside the victim. The lenses are cutting tools, too. The lower edges are ground to razor sharpness and can be removed by heating or breaking the frames.

IT LOOKS LIKE: A felt-tip marker
BUT IT'S REALLY: A blister-causing weapon
DESCRIPTION: Don't mistake this pen for your Sharpie, and be careful: you wouldn't want it leaking in your pocket. A little over three inches long, the marker distributes an ointment that creates blisters on the skin. In order to activate the applicator, press the tip down on a surface for one minute—then simply apply a thin coating of the colorless oil over any area, such as a keyboard or door handle. The ointment will penetrate clothing and even shoes, and will cause temporary blindness if it comes in contact with the eyes. Blisters will cover the skin wherever contact is made within 24 hours and will last for about a week.

IT LOOKS LIKE: Dentures
BUT IT'S REALLY: A concealment device (and much more)
DESCRIPTION: What could possibly fit inside a dental plate? A lot more than you'd think. Items such as a cutting wire or a compass can be placed in a small concealment tube and hidden under a false tooth. A rubber-coated poison pill can be carried in the same manner. The poison can either be ingested to avoid capture or poured into an enemy's food and utilized as a weapon. Radio transceivers can be placed in dental plates, with audio being transmitted through bone conduction. The CIA has even created a dental plate that alters the sound of one's voice. If all of these gadgets prove ineffective, then the dental plate itself can be removed and its sharp scalloped edge used for digging, cutting, or engaging in hand-to-hand combat.

*   *   *

James Bond: "They always said, 'The pen is mightier than the sword.'"
Q: "Thanks to me, they were right."

—*Goldeneye*

A one-day weather forecast requires about 10 billion mathematical calculations.

LIFE IMITATES ART

Everyone loves the movies. They're entertaining—usually a good escape from reality. No one expects the story to come true...but sometimes it does. Here are a few examples.

THE BIRTH OF A NATION (1915)

THE MOVIE: *The Birth of a Nation* is considered one of the greatest American movies ever made—and one of the most racist. Director D. W. Griffith's classic tells the triumphs and travails of a white southern family before and after the Civil War. The film also uses cinematic techniques that were revolutionary for the time, such as tracking shots, extreme close-ups, fade-outs, extensive cross-cutting, and panoramic long shots.

Yet unfortunately, *The Birth of a Nation* offers an incredibly demeaning portrayal of African Americans. It depicts black northern soldiers (actually white actors in blackface) as sex-crazed rapists and glorifies the Ku Klux Klan for keeping former slaves "in their place" (i.e., away from the ballot box).

REAL LIFE: The original Klan was a secret society founded after the Civil War to enforce white supremacy in the South. And it only lasted a few short years before dying out in the 1870s.

But in the fall of 1915, following the release of *The Birth of a Nation*, a Methodist preacher named William Simmons decided to revive the Ku Klux Klan in Georgia. By the mid-1920s, the revitalized Klan boasted of three million members across the United States, thanks in large part to the popularity of the groundbreaking silent film.

THE MANCHURIAN CANDIDATE (1962)

THE MOVIE: This Cold War classic features Laurence Harvey as a brainwashed U.S. soldier who finds himself at the center of an elaborate conspiracy involving Communists and conservatives. The goal of this conspiracy: to kill the president of the United States. To achieve this end, Harvey smuggles a rifle with a telescopic sight into a political rally where the president will be speaking.

REAL LIFE: A year after the film was released, President John F. Kennedy was assassinated in Dallas, allegedly by former Marine

---

Antarctica is the only continent without reptiles.

Lee Harvey Oswald using a rifle with a telescopic scope. And in the decades that followed, speculation abounded that more than one person was involved in the shooting, that Oswald was a mere dupe, and that just like the movie, the president's murder was actually engineered by a shadowy cabal of extremists. To make things even weirder, *The Manchurian Candidate* co-starred Kennedy's buddy, Frank Sinatra, as a fellow soldier who unravels the assassination conspiracy.

Following the film's release, a contractual dispute between Sinatra and the filmmakers forced *The Manchurian Candidate* to be withdrawn from theaters and not shown to the public for decades. The suppression of the film only enhanced its reputation as an eerily prophetic political thriller.

DEATH WISH (1974)

THE MOVIE: This film stars Charles Bronson as a mild-mannered guy who turns into a pistol-wielding vigilante after his family is brutally assaulted by thugs. In one pivotal scene, Bronson is sitting by himself on a New York City subway car and is accosted by a mugger. Instead of handing over his cash, Bronson shoots the mugger and then casually walks out of the car.

REAL LIFE: On December 22, 1984, Bernhard Goetz, a meek, self-employed electrical engineer, smuggled a five-shot .38-caliber revolver onto the New York subway. Goetz took a seat near a group of four young men. When one of the youths approached him and demanded money, Goetz stood up, drew his gun, and shot all four of them. Goetz then pocketed his gun and walked off the subway. He later surrendered to police.

While Goetz appears to have been motivated by fear (he had been mugged previously), his actions eerily paralleled those of Bronson's character. Like Bronson in *Death Wish*, Goetz was seen by many as a hero, an "ordinary Joe" who lashed out in justifiable rage against deserving creeps.

The outcome of the two men's actions, however, couldn't have been more different: at the end of *Death Wish*, Bronson is free and eager to impose lethal justice on a fresh batch of miscreants. Goetz stood trial for his crimes and although acquitted of attempted murder, he served eight months in jail for illegal gun possession.

"LET US BEGIN ANEW"

A Bathroom Reader is mostly light reading, but every once in a while
we like to throw in a few serious things. Here's a piece of history for you:
It was January 20, 1961. The United States was about to enter one of
the most exciting and tumultuous eras in its history. When newly elected
President John F. Kennedy made this now-famous inaugural speech, he
had no idea what was in store for the nation. But he conveyed
the hope for the future that many Americans felt.

WE OBSERVE TODAY not a victory of party but a celebration of freedom—symbolizing an end as well as a
beginning, signifying renewal as well as change. For I
have sworn before you and Almighty God the same solemn oath
our forebears prescribed nearly a century and three-quarters ago.

The world is very different now. For man holds in his mortal
hands the power to abolish all forms of human poverty and all
forms of human life. And yet the same revolutionary beliefs for
which our forebears fought are still at issue around the globe: the
belief that the rights of man come not from the generosity of the
state but from the hand of God.

We dare not forget today that we are the heirs of that first revolution. Let the word go forth from this time and place, to friend
and foe alike, that the torch has been passed to a new generation
of Americans—born in this century, tempered by war, disciplined
by a hard and bitter peace, proud of our ancient heritage—and
unwilling to witness or permit the slow undoing of those human
rights to which this nation has always been committed, and to
which we are committed today at home and around the world.

LET EVERY NATION KNOW, whether it wishes us well or ill,
that we shall pay any price, bear any burden, meet any hardship,
support any friend, oppose any foe to assure the survival and the
success of liberty.

This much we pledge—and more.

To those old allies whose cultural and spiritual origins we share,
we pledge the loyalty of faithful friends. United, there is little we
cannot do in a host of cooperative ventures. Divided, there is lit-

tle we can do—for we dare not meet a powerful challenge at odds and split asunder.

To those new states whom we welcome to the ranks of the free, we pledge our word that one form of colonial control shall not have passed away merely to be replaced by a far more iron tyranny. We shall not always expect to find them supporting our view. But we shall always hope to find them strongly supporting their own freedom—and to remember that, in the past, those who foolishly sought power by riding the back of the tiger ended up inside.

TO THOSE PEOPLE in the huts and villages of half the globe struggling to break the bonds of mass misery, we pledge our best efforts to help them help themselves, for whatever period is required—not because the Communists may be doing it, not because we seek their votes, but because it is right. If a free society cannot help the many who are poor, it cannot save the few who are rich.

To our sister republics south of the border, we offer a special pledge: to convert our good words into good deeds—in a new alliance for progress—to assist free men and free governments in casting off the chains of poverty. But this peaceful revolution of hope cannot become the prey of hostile powers.

Let all our neighbors know that we shall join with them to oppose aggression or subversion anywhere in the Americas. And let every other power know that this hemisphere intends to remain the master of its own house.

To that world assembly of sovereign states, the United Nations, our last best hope in an age where the instruments of war have far outpaced the instruments of peace, we renew our pledge of support—to prevent it from becoming merely a forum for invective, to strengthen its shield of the new and the weak, and to enlarge the area in which its writ may run.

FINALLY, TO THOSE NATIONS who would make themselves our adversary, we offer not a pledge but a request: that both sides begin anew the quest for peace, before the dark powers of destruction unleashed by science engulf all humanity in planned or accidental self-destruction.

We dare not tempt them with weakness. For only when our arms are sufficient beyond doubt can we be certain beyond doubt

---

Q: What is it called when your eyes go different directions? A: *Strabismus.*

that they will never be employed.

But neither can two great and powerful groups of nations take comfort from our present course—both sides overburdened by the cost of modern weapons, both rightly alarmed by the steady spread of the deadly atom, yet both racing to alter that uncertain balance of terror that stays the hand of mankind's final war.

SO LET US BEGIN ANEW, remembering on both sides that civility is not a sign of weakness, and sincerity is always subject to proof. Let us never negotiate out of fear. But let us never fear to negotiate.

Let both sides explore what problems unite us instead of belaboring those problems which divide us.

Let both sides, for the first time, formulate serious and precise proposals for the inspection and control of arms—and bring the absolute power to destroy other nations under the absolute control of all nations.

Let both sides seek to invoke the wonders of science instead of its terrors. Together let us explore the stars, conquer the deserts, eradicate disease, tap the ocean depths, and encourage the arts and commerce.

Let both sides unite to heed in all corners of the earth the command of Isaiah—to "undo the heavy burdens... [and] let the oppressed go free."

And if a beachhead of cooperation may push back the jungle of suspicion, let both sides join in creating a new endeavor, not a new balance of power, but a new world of law, where the strong are just and the weak secure and the peace preserved.

All this will not be finished in the first one hundred days. Nor will it be finished in the first one thousand days, nor in the life of this administration, nor even perhaps in our lifetime on this planet. But let us begin.

IN YOUR HANDS, my fellow citizens, more than mine, will rest the final success or failure of our course. Since this country was founded, each generation of Americans has been summoned to give testimony to its national loyalty. The graves of young Americans who answered the call to service surround the globe.

Now the trumpet summons us again—not as a call to bear arms,

$$111,111,111 \times 111,111,111 = 12,345,678,987,654,321$$

though arms we need; not as a call to battle, though embattled we are—but a call to bear the burden of a long twilight struggle, year in and year out, "rejoicing in hope, patient in tribulation," a struggle against the common enemies of man: tyranny, poverty, disease, and war itself.

Can we forge against these enemies a grand and global alliance, north and south, east and west, that can assure a more fruitful life for all mankind? Will you join in that historic effort?

In the long history of the world, only a few generations have been granted the role of defending freedom in its hour of maximum danger. I do not shrink from this responsibility—I welcome it. I do not believe that any of us would exchange places with any other people or any other generation. The energy, the faith, the devotion which we bring to this endeavor will light our country and all who serve it—and the glow from that fire can truly light the world.

AND SO, MY FELLOW AMERICANS: Ask not what your country can do for you—ask what you can do for your country.

My fellow citizens of the world: Ask not what America will do for you, but what together we can do for the freedom of man.

Finally, whether you are citizens of America or citizens of the world, ask of us here the same high standards of strength and sacrifice which we ask of you. With a good conscience our only sure reward, with history the final judge of our deeds, let us go forth to lead the land we love, asking His blessing and His help, but knowing that here on earth God's work must truly be our own.

*   *   *

MORE CHURCH BULLETIN BLOOPERS

- "Eight new choir robes are currently needed, due to the addition of several new members and to the deterioration of some older ones."

- "Our next song is: 'Angels We Have Heard Get High.'"

- "The cost for attending the Fasting & Prayer Conference includes meals."

Hummingbirds can fly upside down.

STAR TREK WISDOM

Is there intelligent life in TV's outer space? You decide.

"Is there anyone on this ship who, even remotely, looks like Satan?"

—**Kirk**

Tuvok: "The phaser beam would ricochet along an unpredictable path, possibly impacting our ship in the process."
Janeway: "All right, we won't try that."

"Mr. Spock, the women on your planet are logical. That's the only planet in the galaxy that can make that claim."

—**Kirk**

"I'm a doctor, not an escalator."

—**McCoy**

"I must say, there's nothing like the vacuum of space for preserving a handsome corpse."

—**Doctor**

"I'm attempting to construct a mnemonic memory circuit, using stone knives and bearskins."

—**Spock**

"The best diplomat I know is a fully-loaded phaser bank."

—**Scotty**

"Mr. Neelix, do you think you could possibly behave a little less like yourself?"

—**Tuvok**

"What am I, a doctor or a moon shuttle conductor?"

—**McCoy**

"Time travel, from my first day on the job I promised myself I'd never let myself get caught up in one of these God-forsaken paradoxes. The future is the past; the past is the future. It all gives me a headache."

—**Janeway**

"It's difficult to work in a group when you're omnipotent."

—**Q**

Data: "Tell me, are you using a polymer-based neuro-relay to transmit organic nerve impulses to the central processor of my positronic net?"
Borg Queen: "Do you always talk this much?"

"The weak innocents...they always seem to be located on the natural invasion routes."

—**Kirk**

"I'm a doctor, not a bricklayer."

—**McCoy**

Survival of the fittest? Charles Darwin and Albert Einstein married their first cousins.

WHERE THERE'S A WILL...THERE'S GRACE

Here's the story of a network sitcom that used laughter to overcome a social taboo.

COMING OUT

Primetime TV's first homosexual character was Jodie Dallas, played by Billy Crystal on ABC's *Soap* in 1977. Over the next two decades, a few shows with supporting gay characters came and went, but it wasn't until 1998 that homosexuality on network TV made headlines.

That April, actress and comedian Ellen DeGeneres, star of the highly rated show, *Ellen*, revealed a very intimate detail of her private life—she announced publicly that she's gay. And *Ellen*, which had been a popular TV comedy since 1994, suddenly turned into a political forum for gay issues. Result: The ratings plummeted. Major advertisers pulled their support; outraged viewers began boycotting Disney, ABC's parent company; and religious groups prepared for a full-scale, nationwide protest. But was it the politics that hurt the new *Ellen*? Critics said it was the lack of comedy that came *with* the politics. "We know you're a lesbian," British rocker Elton John said. "Now, shut up and be funny!" But *Ellen* wasn't, so ABC pulled the plug.

A NEW APPROACH

Around the same time, David Kohan and Max Mutchnick, creators of the critically acclaimed shows *Boston Common* and *Dream On*, approached NBC with an idea for a new sitcom that would feature homosexuality. The show would be about three couples, two straight and one gay. One of the gay men (Will) was best friends with one of the straight women (Grace).

In a surprising move, NBC brass suggested that Kohan and Mutchnick "get rid of the heterosexual couples and develop the show for Will and Grace." But with the *Ellen* backlash still in the news, they had to be careful...or the new show might die a quick death. From the beginning, they knew two things would make the show successful: don't make it just about homosexuality, and more importantly, make it funny.

Goldilocks was originally named Silver Hair.

SKIPPING TO THE GOOD PART

Here's the premise they came up with: boy meets girl, boy asks girl to marry him, boy realizes he's gay, they overcome a tough breakup and eventually become best friends.

Kohan, who's straight, and Mutchnick, who's gay, opted to fast-forward through the romance and "coming out." The pilot episode, which aired in September 1998, began with Will Truman (played by Eric McCormack), a lawyer who's comfortable with his homosexuality, offering his support and the spare room of his Manhattan apartment to Grace Adler (Debra Messing), a self-employed interior designer, who has recently left her fiancé at the altar.

Grace accepts the offer, but not without attitude from Will's flamboyant, man-chasing best friend, Jack McFarland (Sean Hayes), who was promised first dibs on the room. The fourth character in the ensemble was Karen Walker (Megan Mullally), Grace's spoiled, smart-mouthed, pill-popping assistant.

REELING IN THE CAST

• Eric McCormack, best known for his role in the syndicated series *Lonesome Dove: The Outlaw Years*, worried about being type-cast as gay (he's straight). But when he actually read for the part, he realized how perfect he was for the role. "Will was me in every way except sexuality," said McCormack.

• Debra Messing had two successive flops under her belt—Fox's *Ned & Stacey* and ABC's *Prey*—and was fearful of adding a third, so she rejected the offer to star. It took a house call from Mutchnick and Kohan (and a bottle of vodka) to get her onboard.

• Sean Hayes was originally asked to read for the Will role but was out of town during the auditions. So he ended up reading for the role of Jack, which required a more in-your-face style which comes natural to Hayes. "As I was walking out of the audition," said Hayes, "I turned around and said, 'Hey, Max, don't be checking out my ass.' And they said, 'Okay, *that's* Jack McFarland.'" (In real life, Hayes keeps his sexuality a secret. "I like the mystery. When you see me play Jack, I want you to believe that that's a gay character...when I play a straight character, I want you to believe that, too.")

• Megan Mullally, who had recurring roles on *Seinfeld, Frasier, Just*

In the 13th century, suits of armor weighed as much as 90 pounds.

Shoot Me, and several other hit TV shows, was so underwhelmed by the role of Karen that she intentionally missed her audition. The producers called her at home and coaxed her into the studio. "At the last minute," said Mullally, "something told me to go for it." Good thing she did. Karen has developed a cult following that rivals *Seinfeld's* Cosmo Kramer.

AGAINST THE ODDS

Although NBC gave the show the green light, they decided not to promote it heavily and they put it in one of the toughest time slots: pitted against Fox's *Ally McBeal*, a favorite among female viewers, and ABC's *Monday Night Football*, the seasonal reason-to-live for many male viewers. But *Will & Grace* did have one very good thing going for it: longtime comedy director James Burrows. Highly regarded for his award-winning work on *Cheers, Frasier, Friends, Third Rock from the Sun, Taxi,* and *The Mary Tyler Moore Show*, Burrows equals laughs in the world of network sitcoms.

Will & Grace became the highest rated new sitcom of the 1998 fall season, averaging 10.9 million viewers per episode. NBC quickly moved it to the coveted Thursday night at 9:00 p.m., "Must-See TV" time slot, where it has remained for six consecutive seasons.

And all this without causing a smidgen of controversy.

Advertisers didn't flee; religious activist groups left it alone; no boycotts were threatened. *Will & Grace* had become a true crossover hit, gaining a loyal following of gay and straight viewers alike.

PAVING THE WAY

In the wake of *Will & Grace's* success, other popular network shows such as *Dawson's Creek* and *Party of Five* added gay characters and integrated gay topics into their story lines—all without incident. *Queer Eye for the Straight Guy*, a show where five gay men give fashion advice to straight men, debuted in 2003 as the highest-rated show in Bravo cable network history.

In its fifth season, *Will & Grace* was primetime's #3 show among adults 18 to 49 and the #2 comedy. In 2003 the show received 12 Emmy nominations, including one for outstanding casting for a comedy series, proof that a little humor really can go a long way. "The only thing we're trying to force down people's throats," says Kohan, "is comedy."

The IRS estimates that $20–$40 billion are lost to tax fraud every year.

CURTAINS!

When you go to the theater, you expect to see a well-rehearsed play, but that's not always what you get. Sometimes actors forget lines or the scenery falls and the cast has to find a way to keep the show going...sometimes with hilarious results.

A KNOCKOUT PERFORMANCE

During a performance of *Rumplestiltskin* at The Afternoon Players of Salt Lake City, the actor playing Rumplestiltskin made an unscripted leaping exit—and knocked himself out on a door frame. The actress playing the Princess had no idea that he'd been hurt. According to the plot, the Princess has to guess Rumplestiltskin's name by midnight or he'll take away her baby. The actress sat onstage and waited for the Rumplestiltskin character to reappear. When he didn't, she began to improvise.

"I wonder where that funny little man is?" she asked, loudly. "That funny little man was supposed to come back here and I was supposed to guess his name." Still no Rumplestiltskin. While she improvised, the actors backstage were frantically trying to think of what to do. Finally two of them put on silly hats and ran onstage. "You know that funny little man?" one of them said, in a very meaningful way. "Well, he's *never* coming back."

The Princess's eyes widened in horror. "You mean, he's *never* coming back?"

"No. He's *never* coming back." The three stood there in dead silence. Finally the other actor spoke. "But he told us to tell you that he knew you had guessed his name. It's Rumplestiltskin. And now you can keep your baby! Hooray!" Curtain down. End of play.

"IT'S A MIRACLE!"

The Miracle Worker tells the story of Helen Keller, who was deaf, dumb, and blind. In one production in the Midwest, the actor playing the Doctor was discovered to have a drinking problem. But as his character was only in the first scene, the director took pity on him and cast him anyway.

At the start of the play, the Doctor is supposed to inform the Keller family that a fever has left their infant without the use of her eyes, ears, or vocal chords. Unfortunately, on opening night, the actor drunkenly blurted, "Mr. and Mrs. Keller, I've got bad news. Your daughter is…dead."

The other actors were stunned. If Helen was dead, the play couldn't go on. Thinking quickly, the actress playing Mrs. Keller ad-libbed, "I think we need a second opinion."

The curtain came down, and the drunken actor was yanked off the stage. The stage manager put on the Doctor's white coat and took his place on stage. When the curtain went up again, the new Doctor declared, "Your baby is alive, but she'll be deaf, dumb, and blind for the rest of her life."

The actor playing Mr. Keller was so relieved to hear the correct lines that he clasped his hands together and cried, "Thank God!"

A CROSS TO BEAR

Every summer, Passion plays are performed throughout the South. These spectacles tell the story of Jesus using huge casts, massive sets, and lots of special effects. In one production in Texas, an actor playing a Roman guard was supposed to stab the actor playing Jesus with a spear that had a special retractable blade. Oops—the guard grabbed the wrong prop backstage and poked a *real* spear into Jesus' ribcage. Jesus cried out in agony, "Jesus Christ! I've been stabbed!"

The stage manager quickly brought down the curtain and called an ambulance. As sirens wailed in the distance, the curtain rose to reveal a new Jesus—a 260-pound stagehand in a loincloth.

When the time came for him to be lifted to heaven on special ropes, the new actor said, "And now I shall ascend!" The ropes were attached to a special counterweight system—that had been rigged for a man who weighed 100 pounds less. The stagehand pulling the rope couldn't lift him. He added more weights to the system as the actor repeated, "And now I shall ascend." This time Jesus was lifted a few feet above the cross, but quickly dropped back down again. The desperate stagehand quickly put all the weights he could find onto the system and pulled the rope as the actor playing Jesus said, "And now I shall…AAAAIIIIEEEEE!"

Jesus' scream could be heard across town as he was catapulted straight up into the metal grid at the top of the theater and knocked senseless.

Another ambulance was called, and the show was canceled.

WHOOSH! Olympic downhill skiers reach 80 mph.

POP CULTURE QUIZ

So you're an avid bathroom reader and you think you know a thing or two. Well, see if you can match wits with Uncle John—he knew almost all of these.

1. What beer did E.T. the Extra-Terrestrial drink in the 1982 film?

a) Budweiser **b)** Miller Genuine Draft
c) Coors Light **d)** Milwaukee's Best

2. What country's flag consists of one solid color?

a) Zimbabwe **b)** Costa Rica **c)** Greece **d)** Libya

3. Who's autobiography is entitled *Wheel of Fortune*?

a) Pat Sajak **b)** Vanna White **c)** Edith Piaf **d)** B. F. Goodrich

4. What's an *ananym*?

a) A name someone uses to remain anonymous
b) A name spelled backward
c) A word that means the opposite of another word
d) A quotation that precedes a book, chapter, or article

5. How long did the 1991 Persian Gulf War last?

a) 32 days—January 16 to February 17
b) 39 days—January 16 to February 24
c) 43 days—January 16 to February 28
d) 54 days—January 16 to March 11

6. Who was the first ghost to visit Scrooge in Charles Dickens's *A Christmas Carol*?

a) Bob Cratchit **b)** Jacob Marley
c) The Ghost of Christmas Past **d)** Tiny Tim

7. The first African American to win a Nobel prize for peace:

a) Martin Luther King Jr. **b)** Jesse Jackson
c) Frederick Douglass **d)** Louis Armstrong

Big Bird's address: 123 1/2 Sesame Street (Zip Code unknown).

8. In Denmark, the "Peanuts" comic strip is known as:

a) "Karl Brun und Venindes" b) "Horned Toads"
c) "Gud Gryf" d) "Radishes"

9. Who once boxed under the name "Packy East?"

a) Frank Sinatra b) Bob Hope
c) Mickey Rourke d) Ronald Reagan

10. What is the name of the dog on the box of Cracker Jacks?

a) Crackers b) Bozo c) Bingo d) Porter

11. When M&Ms introduced their blue candies in 1995, what color did they discontinue?

a) tan b) orange c) purple d) white

12. Who was the shortest Beatle?

a) John b) Paul c) George d) Ringo

13. The only member of the *Lord of the Rings* movie cast to have actually met the author of the books, J. R. R. Tolkien, was:

a) Ian Holm (Bilbo Baggins) b) Ian McKellan (Gandalf)
c) Christopher Lee (Saruman) d) John Rhys-Davies (Gimli)

14. What does the "L" stand for in Samuel L. Jackson's name?

a) Lawrence b) Leroy c) Luscious
d) Nothing—he has no middle name, but
added an initial for "mystique."

Answers

1. c; 2. d; 3. c (Piaf was a French singer, known as "The Little Sparrow."); 4. b (Ananyms are often used as pseudonyms, as in Oprah Winfrey's production company: Harpo); 5. c; 6. b; 7. a; 8. d; 9. b; 10. c; 11. a; 12. d (He's 5'8"; He's also the oldest, born on July 7, 1940.); 13. c (Lee also knew the books better than anyone else on the set, and was a creative consultant to director Peter Jackson.); 14. b.

The Cartheginians fought off Roman ships in 300 B.C. by catapulting live snakes at them.

"PAGING MR. POST"

The funeral business (known as "the dismal trade" in the 18th century) necessarily deals with concepts that many people find distasteful. That led to the evolution of a unique set of euphemisms in the death biz.

Passed into the arms of God. Dead. Other euphemisms: *passed away, gone to meet his/her Maker, expired, deceased.*

Temporary preservation. Embalming—the common treatment of dead bodies in which bodily fluids are replaced with preservative fluid. Other euphemisms: *sanitary treatment, hygienic treatment.*

Grief therapy. The "therapeutic" effect of having an expensive funeral "viewing."

Burn and scatter. Slang for services that scatter cremated remains at sea. Also known as *bake and shake.*

Casket coach. Hearse.

Consigned to earth. Buried.

Pre-need sales. Funeral services sold to someone who hasn't died yet.

Corpse cooler. A specialized coffin with a window, once used to preserve the body for viewing. An ice compartment kept the corpse cool.

Interment space. A grave. Used in phrases such as *opening the interment space* (digging the grave) and *closing the interment space* (filling the grave).

Cremains. Cremated remains; ashes.

Babyland. The part of a cemetery reserved for small children and infants.

Slumber room. The room in which the loved one's body is displayed.

Memorial park. Cemetery.

Lawn-type cemetery. A cemetery that bans headstones in favor of ground markers, allowing caretakers to simply mow the lawn rather than trim each grave by hand.

Funeral director. Undertaker.

O-sign. A dead body sometimes displays what hospital workers call the "O-sign," meaning the mouth is hanging open, forming an "O." The "Q-sign" is the same— but with the tongue hanging out.

Gotta hand it to her: Queen Elizabeth I owned 2,000 pairs of gloves.

Protective caskets. Coffin sealed with rubber gaskets to keep out bugs and other invaders. Unfortunately, methane gas has been known to build up inside such caskets, causing them to explode and spew out their contents. This prompted the introduction of *burping caskets* that allow gas to escape.

Grief counselor. Mortuary salesperson.

Mr. Post. Morgue attendant. Used by many hospitals to page the morgue when a body has to be removed from a room.

Nose squeezer. Flat-topped coffin.

Beautiful memory picture. An embalmed body displayed in an expensive casket.

Body. This term for a dead person is generally discouraged, along with *corpse*. Preferred: the dead person's name, or *remains*.

Plantings. Graves.

Selection room. Room in which buyers look at displayed caskets. This term replaces *back room, showroom, casket room.*

Companion space. An over/under grave set for husband-and-wife couples; one body is placed deep in the ground and the second buried above it.

* * *

LET'S DO ANOTHER STUDY

• Colorado State University scientists concluded that Western Civilization causes acne.

• A 2003 study carried out by scientists at Edinburgh University found that fish feel pain.

• In 1994 the Japanese meteorological agency concluded a seven-year study into whether or not earthquakes are caused by catfish wiggling their tails. (They're not.)

• Physicists at the University of Nijmegen in the Netherlands released a report in 2000 on their study of diamagnetics, during which they claimed to have "levitated" a frog, a grasshopper, a pizza…and a sumo wrestler.

"His mother should have thrown him away and kept the stork." —Mae West

THE SANTA CHRONICLES

You probably don't give Santa a second look when you
see him in a department store or on a street corner
every December...but maybe you should.

SANTA COPS

By December 2001, Mafia fugitive Francesco Farina had been on the run from Sicilian police for more than five years. Holed up in what he thought was a great hideout—a flat in downtown Catania—Farina was able to look out his window and see whether the cops were closing in on him. But all he saw were the regular assortment of Christmas shoppers, schoolchildren, and a Santa Claus ho-ho-hoing on the street corner. A few days before Christmas, thinking the coast was clear, Farina decided to go out on the town. Bad idea: the guy in the red suit wasn't Santa after all. A succession of surveillance cops dressed as Santa had kept their eyes on Farina, who ended up spending Christmas in jail.

SANTA'S FISTS OF FURY

An unidentified Santa was cruising down a LeHigh Acres, Florida, street in his convertible when he was approached by 20-year-old Jonathan Danzey, who asked Santa for a present. Informed that there was nothing for him in Santa's sack, Danzey got angry. Words were exchanged, Santa got out of the car, and Danzey tried to punch him. According to Katherine Phillips, who witnessed the altercation, "Santa Claus whipped his butt." He ripped Danzey's shirt, knocked him to the ground, and then drove away. The cops soon arrived and arrested Danzey on drunk and disorderly charges. "He won," Danzey conceded, "but he was stronger and more soberer."

SANTAS ON THE RUN

One of the oddest sights in the history of sports took place in Newtown, Wales, in December 2002. More than 1,000 runners—both male and female—participated in a four-mile race for charity...all dressed in full Santa Claus garb: black boots, red pants, red coat, and a big white beard. Said one of the runners: "It's a lot easier to run in a Santa suit than to try to hold a normal conversation in one."

Two states, Oregon and Michigan, provide the majority of the nation's Christmas trees.

SANTA PROTESTORS

What if Santa were banned from Christmas? That's what they tried to do in the small town of Kensington, Maryland, in 2001. Some of the townspeople complained that it made them feel uncomfortable having a "religious figure" participate in the annual tree-lighting ceremony, so the town fathers decided to ask Santa to stay home. Unfortunately, not everyone in town agreed with the decision. Result: 50 Santas showed up and marched on City Hall. Pro- and anti-Santa factions clashed; one Santa was arrested.

SANTA MELTDOWN

Shortly before Christmas in 1999, Kelley Fornatoro placed her 19-month-old son next to Santa for a holiday portrait in a Woodland Hills, California, shopping mall. The baby immediately started crying. So Fornatoro suggested that Santa put his arm around the boy to calm him down. That's when Santa had a fit of his own. "I will not imprison your child!" he yelled at her. "Was it worth it for you to torture your child for a picture? You must be an evil person." As Fornatoro retrieved her baby, she said she'd be filing a formal complaint. "You can complain about me if you want, but I am Santa Claus. I am the best person in the world!" Then he got *really* mad. While parents rushed to cover their shocked children's eyes, Santa began undressing. He took off his hat, beard, wig, coat, and belt, and was down to his red, baggy pants and a tank top when security guards escorted him out of the building.

THE SANTA

In a quest to find Great Britain's ultimate Santa, organizers at Guinness World Records sponsored the first-ever "Santathon" in December 2001. The event included a field of eight top contenders donned in full beards, red suits, and black boots. Competitive events included sack hauling, pie eating, chimney climbing, stocking filling, and ho-ho-hoing. First prize was awarded to David Broughton-Davis, 43, from Croydon, a professional department store Santa. "I'm not very proud to admit that my best event was eating three large mince pies," Broughton-Davis lamented after being awarded the Golden Boots trophy. "I just wish that event hadn't taken place before the chimney climb. It was hard on the stomach."

The S.S. in a ship's name stands for "steamship."

ANIMAL NAME ORIGINS

When we came up with the idea for this page we figured that after 15 Bathroom Readers, we must have done it before. We were wrong.

GORILLA

"First used in a Greek translation of 5th century BC Carthaginian explorer Hanno's account of a voyage to West Africa. He reported encountering a tribe of wild hairy people, whose females were, according to a local interpreter, called gorillas. In 1847 the American missionary and scientist Thomas Savage adopted the word as the species name of the great ape and by the 1850s it had passed into general use." (From *Dictionary of Word Origins*, by John Ayto)

FERRET

"*Ferret* comes from Latin *furritus*, for 'little thief,' which probably alludes to the fact that ferrets, which are related to pole cats, like to steal hens' eggs. Its name also developed into a verb, *to ferret out*, meaning 'to dig out or bring something to light.'" (From *Cool Cats, Top Dogs, and Other Beastly Expressions*, by Christine Ammer)

SKUNK

"Because the little striped mammal could squirt his foul yellow spray up to 12 feet, American Indians called him *segankw*, or *segonku*, the Algonquin dialect word meaning simply 'he who squirts.' Early pioneers corrupted the hard-to-pronounce Algonquin word to *skunk*, and that way it has remained ever since." (From *Animal Crackers*, by Robert Hendrickson)

HOUND

"Before the Norman conquest of England, French hunters bred a keen-nosed dog that they called the St. Hubert. One of their rulers, William, took a pack to England and hunted deer—following the dogs on foot. Saxons had never before seen a dog fierce enough to seize its prey, so they named William's animals *hunts*, meaning 'seizure.' Altered over time to *hound*, it was long applied to all hunting dogs. Then the meaning narrowed to stand for breeds that follow their quarry by scent." (From *Why You Say It*, by Webb Garrison)

Literally translated, *hors d'oeuvre* means "outside of work."

LEOPARD

"It was once wrongly believed that the leopard was a cross between a 'leo' (a lion) and a 'pard' (a white panther)—hence the name 'leopard.'" (From *Why Do We Say It?*, by Nigel Rees)

PYTHON

"According to Greek legend, the god Apollo's earliest adventure was the single-handed slaying of Python, a flame-breathing dragon who blocked his way to Pytho (now Delphi), the site he had chosen for an oracle. From the name of this monster derives the name of the large snake of Asia, Africa, and Australia, the python." (From *Thou Improper, Thou Uncommon Noun*, by Willard R. Espy)

CARDINAL

"One would think that such an attractive creature would have given its name to many things, but in fact it is the other way around. The bird's name comes from the red-robed official of the Roman Catholic Church, who in turn was named for being so important—that is, from the adjective *cardinal*, from the Latin cardo, meaning 'hinge' or 'pivot.' Anything cardinal was so important that events depended (hinged or pivoted) on it." (From *It's Raining Cats and Dogs*, by Christine Ammer)

MOOSE

"Captain John Smith, one of the original leaders at Jamestown, wrote accounts of the colony and life in Virginia, in which he defined the creature as *Moos, a beast bigger than a stagge*. *Moos* was from Natick (Indian) dialect and probably derived from *moosu*, 'he trims, he shaves,' a reference to the way the animal rips the bark and lower branches from trees while feeding." (From *The Chronology of Words and Phrases*, by Linda and Roger Flavell)

FLAMINGO

"This long-legged pink wading bird is named for the people of Flanders, the *Flemings*, as they were called. Flemings were widely known for their lively personalities, their flushed complexions, and their love of bright clothing. Spaniard explorers in the New World thought it was a great joke naming the bird *flamingo*, which means 'a Fleming' in Spanish." (From *Facts On File Encyclopedia of Word and Phrase Origins*, by Robert Hendrickson)

Florence, Italy, was the first city to have all of its streets paved...in 1339 B.C.

BIRTH OF THE BAGEL

Uncle John was in his office munching on a bagel (toasted, with cream cheese) when he realized that the last time he wrote about that fabulous food was all the way back in the very first Bathroom Reader! And that wasn't the (w)hole story!

WHAT EXACTLY IS A BAGEL?

There are lots of different kinds of bagels made today, but to the purist, real bagels contain only flour, water, yeast, malt, and salt. No sugar, no eggs, no raisins, no onions, no sesame seeds, no cinnamon, no garlic, no jalapeño peppers, no cheddar cheese, and no sun-dried tomatoes.

The dough is rolled into a cylinder and then twisted into a ring with a hole in the middle. The rings are allowed to rise, and then (the key to making real bagels) they're cooked quickly in boiling water before they're baked. The boiling process gelatinizes the gluten in the dough, giving the bagel its unique hard and shiny surface and thus sealing the inside to preserve its density and chewiness.

WHERE DID BAGELS COME FROM?

Bagels are believed to have been invented in the 17th century, but there is some debate about their exact origin. They might be Polish—text from Kraków, Poland, written in 1610 refers to *beygls* being good gifts for new mothers—possibly because they make good teething rings, which many people still use them for today.

Another theory says that an Austrian baker wanted to make a gift for King John III Sobieski of Poland after he saved the city of Vienna from Turkish invaders in 1683. King John was famous for his horsemanship, so the baker made a roll in the shape of a stirrup. (Bagels used to be much thinner, with bigger holes.) The Austrian-German word for stirrup: *beugel,* or *bügel.*

However they began, bagels were a hit. They spread all through Eastern Europe over the next two centuries—even into Russia, where they were called *bubliki.* Many different peoples baked bagels in the old days, but over time, Jewish bakers became bagel specialists.

French flies: *Entomagraphy* is the practice of eating insects.

BAGELS IN THE NEW WORLD

In the 1880s, thousands of eastern European Jews emigrated to North America, bringing the bagel with them. The chewy bread soon became a staple in stores and street markets on New York's Lower East Side, as well as in Montreal and Toronto. (Each of these cities claims to have the best bagels today.)

In 1907 the International Bakers Union was founded in New York City. By 1915 bagels had become so popular that bagel-makers formed their own union: Bagel Bakers Local #338. It was a very exclusive group (the only way to get in was to be the son of one of the 300 members). Their recipes were closely guarded secrets, and bagel-baking techniques—hand rolling and twisting—remained unchanged for decades.

THE THOMPSON MACHINE

It wasn't until the early 1960s that this process changed. Dan Thompson—whose father started baking bagels in Los Angeles in the 1920s—started tinkering with a bagel-making contraption after watching his dad try in vain to invent one. In 1963 he succeeded. The Thompson Bagel Making Machine was the first commercially-practical bagel-making device. Using nonunion, unskilled workers, Thompson's machine could make over 1,000 bagels an hour.

Who leased the first one? Lender's Bagels, a small shop that had been in operation in New Haven, Connecticut, since 1927. In 1963 they were going into the frozen bagel business, and Dan Thompson's invention came along at just the right time. Lender's Bagels became a familiar item in supermarkets across the country, and Lender's became the biggest bagel maker in the world.

MODERN-DAY BAGELS

Today there are bagel shops all over the country and bagels come in all different flavors, shapes, and sizes: there are chocolate-chip bagels, spinach bagels, pumpkin bagels, miniature bagels, pizza bagels, and even square bagels. Bagel-making machines can now turn out more than 50,000 bagels an hour.

But nostalgia is affecting business today too, so many shops have gone back to the old style, making all their bagels by hand or with simple machines, boiling them in a bagel kettle, and using the simple authentic recipe. If you ever get to Englewood, New Jersey, stop by Englewood Hot Bagels. That's where Uncle John got his bagels as a boy, and he hasn't found a better one since. Enjoy.

BAGEL BITS

• Classic combo: Cream cheese was invented in 1872; Philadelphia Cream Cheese hit the market in 1880. But it wasn't until Joseph and Isaac Breakstone began selling their Breakstone Cream Cheese brand in 1920 that New York bagel eaters discovered it—and cream cheese became *the* bagel spread.

• In 2000 several rioters at a Fourth of July celebration in Morristown, New Jersey, were arrested for throwing "dangerous" projectiles into the crowd and at police. The projectiles: "batteries, golf balls, and stale bagels."

• According to the *Guinness Book of World Records*, the world's largest bagel was made by Larry Wilkerson and Jeff Maninfior in 1998, at the Lender's Bagel Bakery in Mattoon, Illinois. Weight: 714 pounds. Diameter: 6 feet. Flavor: blueberry.

• During the 2002 American League Championship Series between the New York Yankees and Anaheim Angels, Anaheim mayor Tom Daly bet New York mayor Michael Bloomberg a crate of oranges and chilies that the Angels would win. Bloomberg's bet: a crate of Nathan's hot dogs and 48 H&H bagels. (Daly won.)

• In 2002 John and Cecelia O'Hare sued a McDonald's restaurant in Panama City Beach, Florida, claiming that an improperly cooked bagel damaged Mr. O'Hare's teeth...and somehow ruined their marriage as well. They sued for $15,000 in damages. (Case pending.)

*　　*　　*

BIRTH OF A STRANGE LAW

To attract patrons to his circus, P. T. Barnum would often hitch a plow to an elephant and have it work fields next to the big top. One farmer got so angry about his field being torn up that he pushed a bill through the state legislature. To this day it's illegal to plow a field with an elephant in North Carolina.

ON TOUR WITH ELVIS

Next time you're traveling, here are some Elvis-related sites to see.

MISSISSIPPI-ALABAMA FAIRGROUND
Address: West Main and Mulberry Alley, Tupelo, Mississippi

Claim to Fame: Site of the King's very first public performance on October 3, 1945, when he was only 10 years old. His teacher entered him in a talent contest—he sang a song titled "Old Shep" and won $5.

OVERTON SHELL
Address: 1928 Popular Ave., Memphis, Tennessee

Claim to Fame: The first place Elvis "the Pelvis" swiveled his hips—on July 30, 1954. Also, his first paid performance, which explains why he swiveled—he was scared. "He said he thought he was gonna faint out there on stage," recalled singer Webb Pierce. "So he started flapping his legs, just to keep from passing out. Then he noticed the crowd reacting to it, so he just kept doing it."

SUN STUDIO
Address: 706 Union Ave., Memphis, Tennessee

Claim to Fame: The place where Elvis recorded his very first single, "That's All Right," on July 5, 1954.

LAS VEGAS HILTON
Address: 3000 S. Paradise Rd. (Elvis usually stayed in the Presidential Suite on the 30th floor.)

Claim to Fame: Elvis was notorious for shooting appliances, TVs (especially if Robert Goulet was on), and just about anything else. In 1974 he squeezed off a round at a light switch in the Presidential Suite and nearly hit his girlfriend, Linda Thompson. After that Elvis changed the rules. "We're in the penthouse," he reminded his entourage, "nobody's gonna get hit as long as you shoot straight up."

MARKET SQUARE ARENA
Address: 300 East Market St., Indianapolis, Indiana

What do Rush Limbaugh and Howard Stern have in common? Both were born on January 12.

Claim to Fame: Site of Elvis's last concert, on June 26, 1977. He died less than two months later, on August 16. The arena has since been torn down and replaced by a parking lot.

OFFICE OF DR. GEORGE NICHOPOULOS
Address: 6027 Walnut Grove Rd., Memphis, Tennessee
Claim to Fame: "Dr. Nick" prescribed the King more than 5,300 pills in the last seven months of his life. In 1980 Nichopoulos went on trial for overprescribing drugs to himself, Elvis, Jerry Lee Lewis, and eight other people. He was acquitted.

BAPTIST MEMORIAL HOSPITAL
Address: 899 Madison Ave., Memphis, Tennessee
Claim to Fame: The place where Elvis went in 1973, 1975, and 1977 to wean himself from the pills that were prescribed by Dr. Nick.

HARDING'S GROCERY
Address: 120 West Prairie, Vicksburg, Michigan (now Felpausch's)
Claim to Fame: The place where housewife Louise Welling, 51, claims she saw Elvis—*alive!*—in September 1988, 11 years after his death. "He was dressed in a white jumpsuit," she says. "He'd lost weight, and he didn't have sideburns. He bought a fuse."

J.C. PENNEY
Address: Crossroads Mall in Kalamazoo, Michigan
Claim to Fame: Where Welling says she saw Elvis a second time, in November 1988. She doesn't know what he was buying at Penney's, or even if he shopped there. He may have just been passing through on his way to another store in the mall.

COLUMBIA PLAZA HOTEL
Address: 305 East Michigan Ave., Kalamazoo, Michigan
Claim to Fame: Elvis's Kalamazoo hideway, according to Mrs. Welling. After so many sightings in one town, she figured he must be living there, so she traced him to the hotel. He was registered under one of his favorite pseudonyms: John Burrows.

World's largest harbor: Rotterdam Harbor in the Netherlands.

CAT TALES

*Legends of cats with mysterious powers have been
told for thousands of years. Nearly every culture
has at least one. Here is some feline folklore
that's been passed down over the centuries.*

GRIMALKIN. Its name comes from its color, *gray*, plus
malkin, an archaic word for cat. Scottish legend tells of
this wraith, a human by day, a fierce wild panther roaming the Highlands by night. The huge gray cat has magical powers:
it can also appear in the form of a hare and can disappear at will.
During the Middle Ages, the name grimalkin—and cats in general—became associated with the devil and witchcraft. Women tried
as witches during the 16th, 17th, and 18th centuries were often
accused of having a "familiar," a devilish companion animal.
What kind of animal? Usually a grimalkin.

JAGUAR SUN. The Mayans of Central America worshiped
the Jaguar Sun that rose each day in the east and journeyed west.
After the sun set, the cat god would have to fight lords of the
underworld all night. But he would win the battle and rise again
in the morning. Warriors wore jaguar skins to help them in battle;
shamans were said to be able to shape-shift into the big cats.

MATAGOT. According to European folklore, matagots are magical cats. The French say that a matagot can be lured home with a
plump chicken. Once in the house, treat it well and it will bring
good luck. For example, give it the first bite of every meal, and it
will reward you with a gold coin each morning. In England, people
whispered that Dick Whittington, a humble boy who grew up to
become mayor of London in the 15th century, owed his good luck
to his matagot.

EL BROOSHA. The ancient myths of the Sephardic Jews
(ancient Hebrews who left Israel and went to what is now Spain
and Portugal) tell of Lilith, Adam's first wife, created before Eve.
According to the legend, when Lilith refused to submit to Adam,
she was banished from paradise. Lilith still haunts Earth as a

demon in the shape of a huge black vampire-cat named El Broosha (or sometimes El Brooja—*bruja* means "witch" in Spanish), who sucks the blood of newborn babies.

BAST. The ancient Egyptians began worshiping this cat-headed goddess more than 5,000 years ago. Her name means "devouring lady" and she was worshiped in temples throughout Egypt—especially on October 31, Bast's Feast Day. Bast was said to be the daughter of the sun god Ra, and was associated with the moon, music, dancing, motherhood—and violent vengeance. In the Egyptian Book of the Dead she was said to have destroyed the bodies of the deceased with her "royal flame" if they failed entry tests for the underworld. Out of respect for Bast, it became an honor to stage expensive funerals for cats, during which gold and gem-studded cat figurines were buried along with the mummified body of the deceased kitty.

LI SHOU. Li Shou was a cat goddess worshiped by the ancient Chinese, who believed that at one time cats had the ability to speak, but gave the gift to humans so that they could lay around all day. Li Shou was a fertility goddess who brought rain and protected crops. At harvest time, peasants would hold an orgiastic festival in her honor, offering sacrifices to the cats that had protected the grain from rats and mice.

CAT FACTS

• Some famous Italian paintings of the Last Supper show a cat at the feet of Judas. The fickle cat symbolizes Judas' role as traitor.

• Charles I ruled England from 1625 to 1649. According to legend, he had a lucky black cat. As civil war ripped the country, Charles became so convinced that his cat kept him safe, he assigned guards to watch it. Strangely enough, only one day after the black cat died, Charles was arrested and eventually sentenced to death by beheading.

• In 1760 a "racy" book called *The Life and Adventures of a Cat* was published in England. The main character was a *ram* cat (as males were known back then), named Tom the Cat. The book was so popular that ever since then, males have been known as *tomcats*.

Zip code 12345 is assigned to General Electric in Schenectady, New York.

EYE OF THE HURRICANE

Hurricanes are the largest, most powerful, most unpredictable, and deadliest phenomena on Earth. (Kind of like Uncle John about an hour after dinner on "bean night"—but that's another story.)

WHAT'S IN A NAME?

Hurricanes, typhoons, and cyclones are the same thing—it just depends on what part of the world you're from. The word *hurricane* comes from "Hurikan," the Mayan name for the god of evil. The Mayans believed the Hurikan was a huge winged serpent whose breath could flatten trees and dry up oceans. In the Northwest Pacific, meteorologists use the Chinese word *typhoon* (from *taaifung*, which means "big wind") for the same kind of weather system. Meteorologists also use the term *cyclone* (from the Greek word for "coil"), especially for smaller hurricanes and typhoons. Cyclone describes the way a hurricane's wind coils around a low pressure system. (See page 341 to find out how hurricanes are named.)

HOW THEY'RE BORN

The mother of all hurricanes is the sun. Hurricanes are born when a unique set of circumstances come together in exactly the right order. For a hurricane to form, several conditions must be met:

• First the sun must heat up a large area of tropical ocean where the water temperature is a minimum of 80°F (the 80-degree layer has to be 150 feet deep or the storm will die). Billions of tons of water start to evaporate and rise into the atmosphere.

• The winds coming from different directions have to converge on the rising air, forcing it further upwards.

• As the warm air rises, it meets cooler air above. The moisture in the air mass condenses and turns into heavy rain. The heat energy created during condensation is pumped back into the air mass, making it rise even faster.

• The next step, according to Jack Williams in *The USA Today Weather Book*, is a violent mid-air collision.

> The air in such high pressure areas is flowing outward. That helps disperse the air that's rising in the storm, which creates a

semi-vacuum and encourages even more air to rise from the ground. A hurricane's winds are formed by air near the ocean rushing inward to replace air that's rising in the storm.

• Result: a huge doughnut-shaped weather system that continues to grow as long as the sun and ocean feed in energy and moisture.

• Finally, the rotation of the earth causes this enormous cloud to spin from a force known as the Coriolis Effect.

Weather in Motion

The Coriolis Effect is named after Gustave Gaspard Coriolis, a 19th-century French scientist who is credited with explaining why Napoleon's cannon balls always deflected slightly to the right of the targets at which they were fired. The reason, Coriolis determined, is that the rotation of the earth affects objects in motion. The Coriolis Effect gives northbound air masses a counterclockwise spin—and southbound air masses a clockwise spin.

HOW HURRICANES KILL

Over the past 30 years the damage and loss of life from hurricanes has diminished as meteorologists have become better at tracking storms. The hurricane death toll has also decreased, but there are still hundreds of victims every year, sometimes even thousands. Here are the three major ways people die during hurricanes:

Storm surge. As a hurricane approaches land, the storm's rushing winds push a wall of water ahead of it like a tank moving forward through a muddy ditch. Some hurricanes are capable of producing a storm surge 15 feet high. This can be extremely hazardous because some of the most densely-populated—and hurricane-prone—parts of the Atlantic and Gulf coastlines are less than 10 feet above sea level.

Coupled with normal tides, a hurricane can create a "storm surge" super-tide which can rise as high as a three-story building. Shoreline communities can be engulfed in a matter of minutes while huge wind-driven waves pound buildings to kindling, and boats, houses, and people are dragged miles out to sea as the surge retreats. In 1900 more than 6,000 people died in Galveston, Texas, when a 15-foot storm surge overwhelmed the entire city. In 1995 a 24-foot storm surge caused $3 billion worth of damage to beachfront property near Pensacola, Florida, although thanks to early warning from meteorologists, no lives were lost.

Moving Air. Hurricane winds can reach sustained speeds in excess of 150 mph for hours at a time. That's enough to level most buildings, overturn a bus, and turn virtually any seemingly harmless object into a deadly projectile. But if that isn't bad enough, tornadoes will often form on the fringes of hurricanes, raising hurricane-related wind speeds to more than 300 mph.

Floods. As hurricanes come ashore, they almost always encounter cold weather systems on higher ground. Warm humid air colliding with huge masses of cold air causes torrential rainfall. In a matter of hours, millions of tons of water can be deposited over an inland community creating flash floods in places where residents never expect high water. To make matters worse, people often underestimate the power of moving water. They are tempted to wade through a knee deep stream or drive over a flooded bridge, unaware that 18 inches of water moving at 20 mph can sweep away an 18-wheeler. Over the past 30 years, nearly 60% of all hurricane fatalities were caused by inland flooding.

THE NUMBERS

• In an average year, hurricanes cause nearly five billion dollars of damage to the United States.

• The highest storm surge ever recorded was a 42-foot surge in Bathurst Bay, Australia, in 1899.

• The largest amount of rain in less than 12 hours was 45 inches dumped on La Reunion Island by tropical Cyclone Denise in 1966. La Reunion Island is a good place to live if you like rain—it holds five world records for cyclone-induced rain including 97.1 inches over a 48-hour period (unnamed cyclone, 1958) and 223.5 inches over a 10-day period (Cyclone Hyacinthe, 1980).

• What's the most destructive hurricane of all time? In 1992 Hurricane Andrew damaged or destroyed nearly 100,000 homes and caused $26 billion worth of property damage. But that's not the record—in 1926 an unnamed hurricane rampaged through Florida and Alabama. If that storm's damage were measured in today's dollars, it's estimated that it would have cost more than $84 billion.

WHAT'S A JEROBOAM?

You know those huge, phony-looking wine bottles in restaurant windows and liquor stores? We did a little research and found out that they're not phony—they're really filled with wine.

TAKING THE FIFTH

One of the most recognizable shapes in the world is the glass wine bottle, which came into common use 300 years ago. Back then the bottle (called a *fifth*) was considered the ideal size because it held what was thought to be a reasonable amount for the average man to consume with dinner—a fifth of a gallon.

But the fifth wasn't the only size. Many vintners, particularly in the Champagne region of France, have always made larger bottles for special occasions. The first step up, the *magnum*, was a logical extension of the standard bottle—it held double the amount of wine. For reasons lost to history, as larger and larger sizes appeared, vintners began giving the new wine behemoths biblical names.

Originally the bottle sizes were measured in ounces, but in the 1970s, the wine industry adopted the metric system and everything changed. A fifth, for example, was rounded off to 750 milliliters, the size you'll find on most dining tables around the world today. Here's a handy reference chart for the budding oenophile who doesn't want to confuse a *jeroboam* with a *nebuchadnezzar*.

Name	Quantity
Magnum	1.5 liters (2 bottles)
Jeroboam	3 liters (4 bottles)
Rehoboam	4.5 liters (6 bottles)
Methuselah	6 liters (8 bottles)
Salmanazar	9 liters (12 bottles)
Balthazar	12 liters (16 bottles)
Nebuchadnezzar	15 liters (20 bottles)
Melchior	18 liters (24 bottles)

PUT A CORK IN IT

To muddy the waters thoroughly, here are some exceptions:

Steepest snowboard descent: 72° by Tom Burt on Donner Pass in California.

- A methuselah is called an imperial in Bordeaux, France.
- Bordeaux vintners also call a jeroboam a *double magnum*.
- The melchior is sometimes called a *solomon*.
- The *fillette* is a half bottle (375 milliliters) used in the Loire Valley.

SO WHO WERE THESE GUYS?

- **Jeroboam:** The first king of Israel, 976 to 945 B.C.
- **Rehoboam:** The son of Solomon, and king of Judah from 975 to 958 B.C.
- **Methuselah:** A Hebrew patriarch, said to have lived to be 969 years old.
- **Salmanazar:** Five kings of Assyria shared this name. The most important was Salmanazar III, who ruled from 859 to 824 B.C.
- **Balthazar:** Two choices—one was the regent of Babylon, killed by Cyrus around 539 B.C. The other was one of the three wise men who followed the star to Bethlehem, for Jesus' birth.
- **Nebuchadnezzar:** The most powerful of the Babylonian kings, ruler from 605 to 562 B.C. He razed the temple in Jerusalem and carried the Jewish people off into captivity.
- **Melchior:** Another one of the three wise men in the Bible.

ODD LOTS

- The *Marie-jeanne* is a 3-bottle-size used occasionally by Bordeaux vintners.
- The largest bottle in common use is the *primat*, a 27-liter (36-bottle) monster that weighs 143 pounds (65 kg) when full.
- The largest bottle ever blown came from Staffordshire, England, in 1958. It held 26 gallons of sherry (about 6-1/2 nebuchadnezzars) and when filled weighed 220 pounds. It was called an *adelaide*.
- Champagne maker Pol Roger produced an imperial pint bottle (600 milliliters) just for Winston Churchill, which he drank every day at exactly 11 a.m.

*   *   *

"God made only water, but man made wine."

—Victor Hugo

Wine is mentioned in every book of the Bible, except Jonah.

I'VE BEEN CORNOBBLED!

You won't find these archaic words in most dictionaries, but take our word for it—they're real. And just for fun, try to use them in a sentence. (We did—check out page 457.)

Hobberdehoy, A youth entering manhood

Faffle, To stutter or mumble

Dasypygal, Having hairy buttocks

Cornobbled, Hit with a fish

Collieshangie, A noisy or confused fight

Wem, A stain, flaw, or scar

Calcographer, One who draws with chalk

Bodewash, Cow dung

Twiddlepoop, An effeminate-looking man

Liripoop, A silly creature

Leptorrhinian, Having a long narrow nose

Bridelope, When the new bride is "both symbolically and physically swept off on horseback" to the husband's home

Mundungus, Garbage; stinky tobacco

Chirogymnast, A finger-exercise machine for pianists

Toxophily, love of archery

Pismire, An ant

Valgus, Bowlegged or knock-kneed

Xystus, An indoor porch for exercising in winter

Jumentous, Having a strong animal smell

Saprostomous, Having bad breath

Balbriggan, A fine cotton used mainly for underwear

Atmatertera, A great-grandfather's grandmother's sister

Anisognathous, Having the upper and lower teeth unlike

Whipjack, A beggar pretending to have been shipwrecked

Spodogenous, Pertaining to or due to the presence of waste matter

Crapandina, A mineral such as toadstone or bufonite said to have healing properties

Galligaskin, Baggy trousers

What's for dinner, honey? A hive of honeybees eats up to 30 pounds of honey over the winter.

BATHROOM NEWS

*Here are a few fascinating bits of bathroom trivia
that we've flushed out from around the world.*

OPEN AND SHUT CASE

In March 1997, a Russian Antonov-24 charter plane broke apart in midair and crashed just 30 minutes after takeoff. Investigators looking into the crash concluded that moisture leaking from a toilet had damaged the structural integrity of the plane. Then, apparently somebody on the fatal flight slammed the restroom door a little too hard, "causing a chain reaction of disintegration in the structure beneath the toilet, which was rotten due to the prolonged water leakage."

KEEP IT CLEAN

In July 2003, Vietnam's Ministry of Culture and Information banned the broadcast of commercials for toilet paper between the hours of 6:00 p.m. and 8:00 p.m. Reason: Viewers complained that seeing T.P. commercials at dinnertime caused them to lose their appetite. Airing such ads at the dinner hour "is not suitable to the national psychology, manners, and customs" of Vietnam, the country's state-controlled *Tien Phong* newspaper reported. The ban also applies to commercials for condoms, sanitary napkins, and skin disease medications.

SHELTER FROM THE STORM

The town of Van Wert, Ohio, was struck by not one but *four* tornadoes on November 11, 2002. One of the tornadoes bore down on the town movie theater just as a matinee crowd of about 50 people were getting ready to watch *The Santa Clause 2*. The twister ripped the roof off the theater and tossed two automobiles into the seats, where patrons had been sitting just moments before. Amazingly, no one was injured because the management had evacuated everyone into the only part of the building strong enough to withstand the tornado—the restrooms. "Could have been a real tragedy," said Jack Snyder, spokesman for the Van Wert County Emergency Management Agency. "We consider ourselves very lucky."

THE NIGHT SHIFT

In June 2003, Danish researchers released a scientific study on a medical condition known as *nocturia*—having to get up several times a night to pee. Their findings:

• Sleep deprivation caused by nocturia can result in "daytime sleepiness, depression...poor memory, and difficulties managing work."

• The average worker with nocturia suffers a 10% drop in productivity. Estimated cost to the European economy: nearly $16 million per year.

MORE THAN HE CAN BEAR

Ed Yurkovich made a trip to the bathroom at his home in Willard, Wisconsin, in June 2003. His pit stop would have been unremarkable except for two things: 1) he left the bathroom window ajar, and 2) there are bears in Willard, Wisconsin.

Yurkovich left the house, and while he was gone a 300-pound bear pried the bathroom window completely open and climbed into the house. Once inside, the bear couldn't figure out how to get back out, so it roamed from room to room, pooping on the floor and scratching at other windows, trying to get out. When Yurkovich returned home, the bear was lying on the living room floor. As soon as he opened the front door the bear ambled out and disappeared into the trees. Estimated damage: $1,000.

*　　*　　*

GOING OUT WITH A BANG

What happens when a congressman running for reelection accidentally discharges a gun at a neighborhood reception? He loses. In 2002, Republican Congressman Bob Barr attended a rally hosted by Bruce Widener, a local lobbyist and gun collector. As Widener handed Barr an antique .38-caliber pistol from his collection, it suddenly went off, shattering a glass door. Barr, a board member of the National Rifle Association, was in a tight primary battle against another congressman, John Linder, and the incident helped Linder paint Barr as an extremist. "We were handling it safely," Widener explained. "Except that it was loaded."

Q: What is an *undecennial*? A: An 11th anniversary.

MADE A FORTUNE...

Uncle John grew up near an old, crumbling outhouse way out in the woods...but now he has a lavish two-holer right in his backyard. Here are some other people who have come from humble beginnings to achieve great wealth.

JIM CARREY

From Rags... He had to drop out of high school and take a job as a janitor in a factory. In fact, his entire family worked in that factory, living in a small cottage on the grounds. At his lowest low, Carrey wrote a $10 million check to himself...to be redeemed when he made the big time.

...to Riches: After working the comedy circuit for years, Carrey landed a role on *In Living Color*, which led to a movie deal. In 1996 he became the highest paid actor ever when he received $20 million to star in *Cable Guy*. When his father died, Carrey placed the check he had written to himself in his dad's burial suit.

J. K. ROWLING

From Rags... As a single mother living on public assistance, Rowling started writing *Harry Potter and the Philosopher's Stone* in a café while her baby daughter napped. Why the café? Because it was warmer than the tiny flat she lived in. When Bloomsbury Books bought her manuscript in 1996, she was thrilled. The £1,500 (about $2,400) she was advanced was more money than she'd ever received at one time in her life.

...to Riches: Four years and three more books later, Rowling was worth more than $400 million...and she's not done yet.

OPRAH WINFREY

From Rags... Born in Mississippi to unwed teenage parents, Winfrey grew up in poverty. While living in Milwaukee, she was molested by relatives. Not knowing what else to do, her mother sent her to live in a detention home.

To Riches: Fortunately, the detention home was full and Winfrey went to live with her father. He nurtured her abilities and helped her get to college. Now, as the queen of the talk show, Winfrey is worth an estimated $1 billion.

Baby seals are called *weaners*.

...LOST A FORTUNE

Like the celebrities on the opposite page, these people came from humble beginnings. But we think what happened to them after they made their fortunes is much more interesting.

WILLIE NELSON

From Riches... By 1988 Willie Nelson had been a country music star for nearly 20 years and had two multiplatinum albums under his belt.

...to Rags: Due to years of "creative" accounting, in 1990 Nelson owed the IRS $16.7 million. To pay it, he had to auction off just about everything he owned.

M. C. HAMMER

From Riches... "U Can't Touch This," released in 1990, became a pop phenomenon, making Hammer an overnight superstar. A world tour and endorsement deals with Pepsi and KFC followed.

...to Rags: Hammer went on a $30 million spending spree that included mansions and a $500,000-a-month payroll. After two mediocre follow-up albums and some poor investments, Hammer declared bankruptcy in 1996, more than $13 million in debt.

NIKOLA TESLA

From Riches... In his heyday in the 1890s, Tesla was a rich and famous inventor and held more than 700 patents. He is best-known for developing alternating current (AC) electricity.

...to Rags: He was also naive. Thomas Edison, who saw Tesla as competition, did all he could to undermine Tesla's work. It worked. A series of patent lawsuits left Tesla with no money or credit, despite his many inventions. He died broke in 1943.

MIKE TYSON

From Riches... The youngest heavyweight champion in boxing history had earned $300 million.

...to Rags: By 2003 it was all gone. Tyson blames his former promoter, Don King, for mismanaging his earnings. King claims that Tyson blew the money himself. The two will duke it out in court.

Willie Nelson's first gig: playing guitar in a polka band.

GROANERS

A good pun is its own reword.

Dijon vu—the same mustard as before.

Marathon runners with bad footwear suffer the agony of defeat.

A lot of money is tainted. It taint yours and it taint mine.

When two egoists meet, it's an I for an I.

Every calendar's days are numbered.

The reading of a will is a dead giveaway.

It was an emotional wedding. Even the cake was in tiers.

When chemists die, we barium.

Why couldn't the bicycle stand on its own? Because it was two-tired.

She had a boyfriend with a wooden leg…until she broke it off.

A chicken crossing the road is poultry in motion.

Those who jump off a Paris bridge are in Seine.

Energizer Bunny arrested— charged with battery.

When a clock gets hungry, it goes back four seconds.

When the actress saw her first strands of gray hair, she thought she'd dye.

Reading while sunbathing makes you well-red.

Without geometry, life is pointless.

A man's home is his castle, in a manor of speaking.

A pessimist's blood type: always B-negative.

Show me a piano falling down a mine shaft, and I'll show you A flat minor.

Once you've seen one shopping center, you've seen a mall.

What you seize is what you get.

* * *

A man walks into a bar with a salamander in his hand. The bartender asks the man what he calls it. "Tiny" replies the man. "Why's that?" asks the barkeep. "Because he's my newt!"

LACROSSE

What's the national sport of Canada? Bet you said "hockey."
(Uncle John himself said it in the Ahh-Inspiring Bathroom
Reader.) But you're both wrong. Here's the story
of the oldest known sport in North America.

BAGGATTAWAY

In 1636 French Jesuit missionary Jean de Brebeuf watched Huron Indians of southeastern Canada play an unusual game called *baggattaway*, meaning "they bump hips." He wrote in his journal that the players used curved sticks with net pouches on the end to hurl a small ball. The stick reminded him of the cross carried by French bishops, called the crosier, or *la crosse*. That's the first documented mention—and the origin of the modern name— of one of the fastest-growing sports in the world today, lacrosse. Its roots go back at least to the 1400s and possibly much earlier. Today, organized lacrosse is played in more than 20 countries on five continents, with teams in such diverse places as Japan, Germany, Argentina, South Korea, and the Czech Republic.

And, it's still an important game to Native Canadians.

THE BIG LEAGUES

At the time Europeans discovered it, baggattaway was already a very popular sport in North America. Different versions with different names were being played by tribes throughout southeastern Canada, around the Great Lakes, and all the way into the southeastern United States. The rules and equipment varied from region to region, but in general the game was as follows:

Players used a wooden stick about three to four feet long with a big curve on one end, kind of like a shepherd's staff. A mesh pouch made of strips of boiled bark was attached to the curve and tied back down the handle of the stick. The stick could be used to pick up, carry, bat, throw, or catch a small ball, which was made of wood, baked clay, or deerskin stuffed with hair. (They could also use the stick to whack their opponents.)

Players would move down the field, then organize strategies, sometimes using all-out attacks, trying to put the ball through a

---

First sport on film: boxing (Thomas Edison filmed it in 1894).

goal. Goal markers could be a pole or two poles, or rocks or trees at either end of the playing field. As for the playing field: there were no sidelines, and the goals could be hundreds of yards—or several miles—apart. The games could last as long as three days, and, in probably the most stunning aspect of the early game, the teams could number from 5 to 1,000 players on each side.

SPORTS MEDICINE

Baggattaway wasn't just a game to native North Americans, it was an important part of spiritual life as well. Tribal mythology says that the sport was a gift given to them by the Creator. Its purpose was healing, and it was (and still is) known as a "medicine game," because it promoted good health, mental toughness, and community teamwork. It was traditionally played by men, but entire villages would take part in the contests, which were often prepared for with elaborate rituals led by spiritual leaders.

Often it was a war ritual, and the games were prepared for by chanting, dreaming, and dancing—the same way a tribe prepared for battle. The Cherokee in the southeast even named the game accordingly: "Little Brother of War." Its grueling nature and violent style of play—which often resulted in serious injuries—was seen as perfect training for warriors. French fur trader Nicholas Peffot wrote in the late 1600s, "legs and arms are sometimes broken, and it has happened that a player has been killed."

Sometimes it even substituted for battle, with tribes settling disputes with a game—although that strategy didn't always work. One account says that a game was played in 1790 between the Choctaws and the Creeks to settle a territorial dispute. When the Creeks were declared the winners, the unhappy Choctaw players attacked them, and they ended up in a full-scale war.

ALL LACROSSE THE WORLD

But it wasn't until 200 years after Father de Brebeuf first noted the game that Europeans became active players. In 1834 the Canadian Caughnawaga tribe played a demonstration game for European settlers in Montreal, and lacrosse started its worldwide spread. After it was reported in the newspapers, interest grew among non-natives, and leagues started to form. Then it got its biggest boost: in 1856 Dr. George Beers, a dentist from Montreal, founded the Montreal

Lacrosse Club. He wrote down the rules, setting field size, team size, etc., campaigned tirelessly, and set lacrosse on the path to becoming the highly organized and successful sport it is today. Beers is still called the "Father of Lacrosse." It became so popular that by 1859, an act of Canadian Parliament named lacrosse Canada's national sport.

In 1867 white Canadian and native teams did an exhibition tour throughout Great Britain. People loved it, and leagues started to spring up around the British Isles. The Caughnawaga even played for a special audience: Queen Victoria. She gave the game her blessing, and by the end of the century it had spread to Australia, New Zealand, and South Africa. It had also spread to the United States, becoming part of high school and university programs in the Northeast, with the first intercollegiate tournament held at the Westchester Polo Grounds in New York in 1881. In 1904 and 1908, lacrosse was played in the Olympic Games in St. Louis and London.

LACROSSE FACTS

• The official name for the lacrosse stick: the crosse. In men's lacrosse, it's still legal to whack your opponent with it.

• In the 1960s, Czech Boy Scout groups saw pictures of Native Americans playing lacrosse in *National Geographic* magazine. They made their own sticks, wrote their own rules, and began playing "Czech-lacrosse." It was actually closer to baggattaway than today's official lacrosse game.

• NFL Hall of Fame running back (and movie star) Jim Brown is considered by many the best football player to ever play the game. Many say the same thing about his lacrosse play: he was an All-American at Syracuse University in the 1950s and is a member of the Lacrosse Hall of Fame.

• In 1763 the Chippewa and Sauk tribes played a game outside Fort Michilimackinac, a British stronghold in Michigan. When the ball was "accidentally" kicked over the fort walls, the players all rushed after it and, as planned, attacked the soldiers inside. When it was over, 20 British soldiers had been killed, 15 taken prisoner, and the fort belonged to the Indians.

• The Iroquois Nationals, a multi-tribe team from the New York–Ontario area, is the only team from an indigenous nation participating in international sports competition.

Say it three times fast: *Geschwindigkeitsbegrenzung* is German for "speed limit."

CONSPIRACY THEORY

Conspiracy Theory is one of Uncle John's favorite movies. Why? Because the main character, Jerry (Mel Gibson), weaves some theories that are even loonier than what Uncle John comes up with. Here are some samples from the film.

NOBEL PRIZE CONSPIRACY: "All the fathers of Nobel prize winners were rounded up by United National Military and actually forced at gunpoint to give semen samples in little plastic jars which are now stored below Rockefeller Center underneath the ice skating rink. You don't want to be there for the thaw."

$100 BILL CONSPIRACY: "Hey, is that one of those new hundreds? Get rid of it as soon as you can, lady. Hold it up to the light—see the metal strip in it? That's a tracking device."

MIDDLE NAME CONSPIRACY: "Serial killers only have two names. Ever notice that? But lone assassins always have three. John Wilkes Booth, Lee Harvey Oswald, Mark David Chapman..."
Alice: "John Hinckley. He shot Reagan. He only has two names."
Jerry: "Yeah, but Reagan didn't die. If Reagan had died, I'm pretty sure we would know what Hinckley's middle name was."

VIETNAM CONSPIRACY: "The whole Vietnam war was fought on a bet between Howard Hughes and Aristotle Onassis."

GRATEFUL DEAD CONSPIRACY: "You know why the Grateful Dead are always on tour? They're all British intelligence agents. They're all spies. Jerry Garcia himself has a double-O rating, just like James Bond."
Alice: "Jerry Garcia is dead."
Jerry: "That's what they want you to think."

CONSPIRACY CONSPIRACY:
Alice: "Can you prove any of this?"
Jerry: "No, absolutely not. A good conspiracy is an unprovable one."

Technically speaking, the liver is a gland, not an organ.

THE ADVENTURES OF EGGPLANT

*On page 329 we told you about the first reality TV show.
On page 77 we told you about Japanese game shows. Mix
them together with the plot of the movie* The Truman
Show, *and you've got this unbelievable true story.*

MADE IN JAPAN
In January 1998, a struggling 23-year-old standup comedian known only by his stage name Nasubi (Eggplant) heard about an audition for a mysterious "show business–related job" and decided to try out for it.

The audition was the strangest one he'd ever been to. The producers of a popular Japanese TV show called *Susunu! Denpa Sho-Nen (Don't Go for It, Electric Boy!)* were looking for someone who was willing to be locked away in a one-bedroom apartment for however long it took to win one million yen (then the equivalent of about $10,000) worth of prizes in magazine contests.

Cameras would be set up in the apartment, and if the contestant was able to win the prizes, the footage would be edited into a segment called "Sweepstakes Boy." The contestant would be invited on the show to tell his story and, with any luck, the national TV exposure would give a boost to his career. That was it—that was the reward (along with the magazine prizes).

SUCH A DEAL
As if that wasn't a weak enough offer, there was a catch—the contestant would have to live off the prizes he won. The apartment would be completely empty, and the contestant wouldn't be allowed to bring anything with him—no clothes, no food, nothing. If he wanted to eat, he had to win food. If he wanted to wear clothes, he had to win those, too. Nasubi passed the audition and agreed to take the job.

On day one of the contest, the producers blindfolded him and took him to a tiny one-bedroom apartment in an undisclosed location somewhere in Tokyo. The apartment was furnished with a magazine rack and thousands of neatly stacked postcards (for entering the contests), as well as a table, a cushion to sit on, a telephone, notepads, and some pens. Other than that, it was completely empty.

Nasubi stripped naked and handed his clothes and other personal effects to the producers. He stepped into the apartment, the door was locked behind him, and his strange adventure began.

HOME ALONE

Nasubi spent his days entering magazine sweepstakes, filling out between 3,000 and 8,000 postcards a month. It took him two weeks to win his first prize—a jar of jelly. Two weeks later, he won a five-pound bag of rice.

But how could he cook it? He hadn't won any cooking utensils. He tried eating the rice raw, and when that failed he put some in a tin can, added some water, and put it next to a burner on the stove. Using this method, he cooked about half a cup of rice each day, and ate it using two of his pens for chopsticks. (The producers are believed to have given Nasubi some sort of food assistance, otherwise he would not have eaten anything for the first two weeks of the show. To this day it is unclear exactly how much assistance he received, but judging from the amount of weight he lost during the show, it wasn't much.)

SECRET ADMIRERS

Nasubi didn't know it at the time, but he was being watched. Sure, he knew about the cameras in the apartment, but the producers had told him that the footage would be used on *Susunu! Denpa Sho-Nen* after (and if) he completed his mission. And he had believed them.

But the producers had lied—he'd been on TV from the very beginning. Each Sunday night, edited highlights of the week's activities were broadcast in a one-hour show on NTV, one of Japan's national networks. The show was a big hit, and in the process Nasubi became a national celebrity, one of the hottest new stars in Japan. A naked star at that, albeit one whose private parts were kept continuously concealed by a cartoon eggplant that the producers superimposed on the screen.

NASUBI'S BOOTY

Viewers were there when Nasubi won each of his two vacuum cleaners, and they were there when he won each of his four bags of rice, his watermelon, his automobile tires, his belt, and his ladies underwear (the only articles of clothing he won during months in captivity), his four tickets to a Spice Girls movie (which he could not leave the apartment to see), his bike (which he could not ride outside), and countless other items, including chocolates, stuffed animals, headphones, videos, golf balls, a tent, a case of potato chips, a barbecue, and a shipment of duck meat.

Nasubi also won a TV, but the joy of winning it was shattered when he discovered that his apartment had neither antenna nor cable hookup. (The producers feared that if he watched TV, he'd find out he was *on* TV.)

And he won a few rolls of toilet paper—10 *months* after his ordeal began.

Nasubi sang a song and danced a victory dance every time a new prize came in the mail; when he did, many viewers at home sang and danced with him. When his food ran out, they gagged and sobbed with him as he ate from the bag of dog food he won; when he prayed for a new bag of rice, viewers prayed, too.

ROUND-THE-CLOCK EXPOSURE

Nasubi was such a media sensation that reporters tried to find out where he was living. It took six months, but someone finally located his apartment building in June 1998. Before they could make contact with him, however, the producers whisked Nasubi off to a new apartment in the dead of night, telling him the move was intended "to change his luck."

In July the producers set up a live website with a video feed and a staff of more than 50 people (many of whom were there just to make sure the moving digital dot stayed over Nasubi's private parts at all times). Now people could watch Nasubi 24 hours a day.

Finally, in December 1998, one year after he was first locked into the apartment, Nasubi won the prize—a bag of rice—that pushed his total winnings over a million yen. So was he free? Not exactly: The show's producers gave him his clothes, fed him a bowl of ramen noodles, and then whisked him off to Korea, where he couldn't speak the language and no one would recognize him.

Was it a mis-de-mooo-ner? In 1740 a French judge found a cow guilty of sorcery.

Then he was placed in *another* empty apartment, where he had to win prizes to pay for his airfare back home.

When Nasubi finally accomplished *that*, he was flown back to Tokyo, taken to a building, and led into another empty room (it was really just a box, but he didn't know it).

INSTANT CELEBRITY

Out of habit, he stripped naked and waited for something to happen. Suddenly the roof lifted, the walls fell away, and Nasubi found himself, still naked, his hair uncut and his face unshaved for more than 15 months (he never did win clippers or a shaver), standing in an NTV broadcast studio in front of a live audience. Seventeen million more people were watching at home.

More than 15 months had passed since Nasubi had been locked into his apartment, and it was only now, as he held a cushion over his privates, that he learned he'd been on TV since day one. His weekly show had made him Japan's hottest new star, the producers explained to him. The diary he'd kept? It had already been published and was a bestselling book, one that had earned him millions of yen (tens of thousands of dollars) in royalties. That bowl of ramen soup the producers fed him the day he came out of isolation? The footage had been turned into a popular soup commercial. They told him about the website—it made money, too. All of this resulted in a lot of money for Nasubi.

It took quite a while for all of this information to sink in. "I'm so shocked," Nasubi finally said. "I can't express what I feel."

ONE OF A KIND

Today Nasubi is a happy, successful celebrity. Nevertheless, as crazy as Japanese game shows can be, it's unlikely that any other person will experience what he went through. Even if someone were crazy enough to agree to be locked in an apartment for such a long time, they would know from the beginning what was up.

But there's another reason: that much isolation just isn't healthy. Sure, he looked relatively happy on the show, and he certainly had moments of joy. But the footage had been edited to make Nasubi's experience seem better than it really was. In press interviews, he admitted there were times when he thought he was going to go nuts. "I thought of escaping several times," he told reporters later. "I was on edge, especially toward the end."

An American living in Japan in 1869 invented the rickshaw to transport his invalid wife.

ONE-OF-A-KIND HOTELS

*You could reserve a suite at the Ritz, but for the night's sleep
you'll never forget, try one of these one-of-a-kind hotels.*

JULE'S UNDERSEA LODGE

There's only one way to check into this pleasure palace—by
scuba diving to it. Set at a depth of five fathoms (30 feet)
below the clear waters off Key Largo, Florida, this two-bedroom
facility is the only underwater hotel in the world. As you flipper
down from the surface, you will pass through schools of fish on
your way to the barnacle-encrusted building, a former scientific
habitat. You'll pop up into the lobby through a small pool (compressed air pumped into the lodge keeps the sea water out).
Moments later a "mer-porter" delivers your luggage in watertight
containers. There's a lounge with a comfy couch and a TV/VCR,
but most guests prefer to watch sharks through the 42-inch picture
windows in each bedroom. A "mer-chef" will dive down to cook
and serve your lobster dinner. You can take an evening stroll along
the bottom of the coral lagoon, your way lit up by millions of phos-
phorescent plankton. A notary public will even dive down to
marry you, should you so desire, but your witnesses had better be
certified divers.

OUT 'N' ABOUT TREE RESORT

This is one place where you can literally go out on a limb for your
vacation. Set in the deeply wooded Illinois Valley of Oregon, this
"treesort" has 14 different treehouses, some as high as 36 feet up.
Since many are connected by swinging bridges and rope ladders,
once you're aloft, you never have to put your foot on the ground
until you check out.

At one time local authorities closed the treehouses to the general public because they didn't conform to county codes. However,
the owner's friends were welcome to stay there. Michael Garnier
called his friends "Treemusketeers." Soon Treemusketeers from all
over the world were buying T-shirts with specific dates on them.
When they arrived to pick up their T-shirts, Garnier would invite

his new "friends" to spend the night in one of his treehouses. (The county finally gave up in the face of this scheme and issued a permit.)

DREAM CAVE HOTEL, CAPPADOCIA

If you've ever wanted to live like a Hobbit, this is the place for you! The Cappadocia region of Turkey is home to some of the most amazing dwellings in the world. Over thousands of years, the ancient volcanic landscape has been carved by the wind and rain, dotting the area with curious tall cinder cones known locally as "fairy chimneys." Native people have been carving houses and churches out of these cone-shaped rocks for centuries—at first for protection from marauding armies, and later out of tradition. There are two entire cities carved underground that once sheltered as many as 20,000 people. The Dream Cave is one of dozens of modest B&Bs in the town of Goreme that can put you up right in the cool heart of one of these ancient rock homes.

LIBRARY HOTEL, NEW YORK CITY

Now you can combine the thrill of staying in a hotel with the excitement of going to the library. Based on the Dewey Decimal System, the Library Hotel gives each floor a topic and each room a sub-topic. "For example," says hotel patron Mike Warren, "I am on the 12th Floor (Religion), staying in Room 3 (The Occult), so they have about 30 books in my room on the occult, plus weird pictures on the wall."

OTHER GREAT STAYS

• **The Ice Hotel**, Jukkasjarvi, Lapland, Sweden
Rooms for 100 people, a chapel, a cinema, the world-famous Absolut Ice Bar—it's all here, and it's all made entirely of ice.

• **Walrus Islands State Game Sanctuary**, Round Island, Alaska
For $50 you can spend the night surrounded by 15,000 snorting male walruses having what must be the bachelor party of all time.

*   *   *

There's plenty of room at the **Hotel California**. Any time of year (any time of year), you can find it here (you can find it here).

FUNNY BUSINESS

Big corporations play by an interesting set of rules: their own.

THE ANTI-ANTISMOKING CAMPAIGN

In the early 1980s, Merrell Dow, a subsidiary of Dow Chemical, released Nicorette, a cigarette-substitute chewing gum. To promote it they published *The Smoking Cessation Newsletter*, which they sent to doctors' offices, did studies on the dangers of cigarettes, and even encouraged their own employees to quit smoking. Meanwhile, tobacco giant Philip Morris was spending millions annually on chemicals for the manufacture of their tobacco products, which they purchased from... Dow Chemical. Using their economic muscle to squash Nicorette, in 1984 Philip Morris ceased all purchasing from Dow. It worked. An internal memo later revealed that Merrell Dow president David Sharrock personally assured Philip Morris executives that he would screen all advertising and eliminate any anti-tobacco statements. Result: The newsletter was reduced to a one-sentence blurb: "If you want to quit smoking for good, see your doctor."

THE CHICKEN SAYS "MOO"

Given up eating red meat? Next time you're in England you may want to think twice before you order chicken. Recent tests by the British *Food Standards Agency* on imported chicken show they're not exactly what you'd expect. Poultry companies in Holland and Belgium have been pumping water into their birds to inflate their weight and then advertising it as "more meat." But how do you artificially inflate chickens? Inject the birds with extra protein, which allows the meat to retain more water. Chicken protein? No—the tests revealed that pork and beef protein had been put into the chickens.

SMOKE AND MIRRORS

Remember the huge tobacco lawsuits of the late 1990s? Threatened with having to foot the bill for *all* smoking-related illnesses, the nation's largest tobacco companies agreed to pay 46 states an unbelievable $206 billion. The idea was that the states would use the money 1) to pay for smoking prevention programs, and 2) to defray the costs of health care for smokers who got ill. So far, however, less than 5% of the $33 billion paid out has gone to prevent smoking. And it gets worse: several states have earmarked their share of the money to help…the tobacco industry. In North Carolina, for example, $43 million of the $59 million they've received has gone to marketing and producing tobacco, the state's biggest crop. They bought equipment for farmers, built a new tobacco auction hall, and put $400,000 toward a new tobacco processing plant. Other states have used the money won from tobacco companies to buy stock—in tobacco companies.

THE HOMELAND LAWSUIT SECURITY AGENCY

In November 2002, just before President Bush signed the Homeland Security Bill into law, an interesting one-page "rider" was found buried in the bill: a provision that would protect companies that manufactured vaccine *ingredients* from being sued (vaccine makers were already protected). What does that have to do with homeland security? Nothing. Who would benefit from the provision? Pharmaceutical giant Eli Lilly. A vaccine ingredient they manufactured was suspected of causing autism in thousands of children, and Lilly was facing hundreds of lawsuits that could potentially cost them millions—maybe billions—of dollars. It was as if the law were tailor-made for Eli Lilly. Parents of autistic children, medical experts, and many lawmakers were outraged.

And nobody would admit to adding the rider to the bill.

Finally, weeks later, House Majority Leader Dick Armey (R-Texas) admitted he had done it, explaining, "It's a matter of national security. We need vaccines if the country is attacked with germ weapons." Adding to the intrigue, he said he had put the rider in at the request of the White House. What connection did the White House have to Eli Lilly? In the 1970s, former President George H. W. Bush sat on the board of Eli Lilly; White House budget director Mitch Daniels was a former Eli Lilly exec; and current Eli Lilly CEO Sidney Taurel served on the president's Homeland Security Advisory Council.

UPDATE: In January 2003, amid complaints from parents of autistic children and growing media speculation about corporate influence on lawmaking, Republicans announced that the rider would be repealed.

HAPPY TOILETS

*While some governments fret over trivial matters
such as national security and unemployment, other
governments focus on what's truly important.*

KEEP IT CLEAN

In the past, Singapore's government has launched campaigns against gum-chewers. Now they're going to flush out dirty toilets. Why? Environmental minister Lim Swee Say and the government-sponsored Restroom Association of Singapore believe it's important to maintain the country's reputation as a "magnet for human talent and a top location for investment. A country with dirty toilets has no future." To ensure Singapore's future, they have launched the "Happy Toilet" campaign—a plan to rate every one of the 70,000 public restrooms located in this tiny Asian country's shopping malls, food courts, and public buildings.

"Today when you go to a public toilet you do not know what to expect inside," says Jack Sim, president of the Restroom Association. "Sometimes you are very happy but sometimes you are very shocked—disgusted. When toilets are clean, people are happy."

THE STAR SYSTEM

The association has established a five-star rating system, with the inspectors judging toilets for cleanliness, layout, and ergonomics. Just the basics gets a restroom three stars: clean and stocked with toilet paper, soap, and paper towels. For the highest rating? The restroom "has to have a good ambiance," says Mr. Sim. "Probably with plants and pictures."

One 5-star restroom features a poster of a woman dressed like a giant cockroach, smoking a cigarette, with strands of toilet paper dangling from her legs. "Dirty toilets attract the wrong crowd," reads the caption. As Minister Say placed a five-star plaque outside a restroom at a shopping mall, he said, "I am looking forward to experiencing this toilet myself so I can walk out of it feeling happy!"

Future visitors to Singapore are well advised to take the Happy Toilet program seriously. Stiff fines will be imposed on any toilet users who forget to flush.

Barbie (the doll) has a last name: Roberts. Ken's last name is Carson.

HEROIC BIRDS

Look up in the sky! It's a bird, it's a plane...no, it's a bird. But not just any bird—it's Superbird!

JOE TO THE RESCUE!

On October 18, 1943, the British 56th Infantry Division was scheduled to attack the German line at Calvi Vecchia, Italy. U.S. air support was called on to help soften the resistance. But it wasn't needed. The Germans unexpectedly withdrew, and British troops swarmed into the area well ahead of schedule. But when they went to call off the U.S. bombers, they suddenly discovered that their communication systems were out. The bombing raid was imminent—hundreds of lives were at risk. That's when the British summoned G.I. Joe, their faithful carrier pigeon. With a message attached to his leg, he was released and arrived at the air field 20 miles away just as the planes were about to take off.

It's estimated the G.I. Joe saved 1,000 lives that day. In 1946 he was awarded the Dickin Medal, Britain's award for animal gallantry. G.I. Joe retired to the Detroit Zoo until his death in 1961 at the age of 18.

RUPERT TO THE RESCUE!

Lynn Norley had two dogs and a 12-year-old parrot named Rupert. Late one night in February 1998, Norley's Willistown, Pennsylvania, farmhouse caught fire. The dogs either didn't know about the fire or didn't know what to do. But Rupert knew. He screeched loudly until Norley woke up. She managed to get the parrot and the dogs into the second-story bathroom as flames overtook the lower floor. By that time, the smoke had become too much for Rupert and he collapsed in Norley's arms. Assuming he was dead, she placed the bird's body in the shower stall before escaping out the window with the dogs.

The next day, Norley somberly picked through the smoldering wreckage in the hopes of finding Rupert, to give him a proper burial. She found him alright—and he was still breathing! Having survived intense heat, smoke, water, and being buried alive, the heroic bird spent the next month in intensive care and, amazingly, recovered. Said a grateful Norley, "I would not be here to tell this story if it wasn't for Rupert."

CHER AMI TO THE RESCUE!

In the trenches during World War I, 194 soldiers of New York's 77th Infantry Division got separated from the rest of the American forces in Verdun, France. Completely surrounded by enemy troops, the 77th suddenly realized they were being fired at by their own artillery. Their only method of communication with the outside world: three carrier pigeons.

The soldiers attached a message to the leg of the first pigeon: "Our artillery is dropping a barrage on us. For heaven's sake, stop it!" That bird was hit by shrapnel…and so was the second bird they sent. Only one remained—a Black Check Cock carrier pigeon named Cher Ami (French for "dear friend").

Like the others, Cher Ami was hit in midair. But even though his leg was mangled, somehow he kept flying. Then he was hit again, this time through his breast. Still he kept flying. Cher Ami arrived safely with the message barely attached to his dangling leg. Because of the pigeon's perseverance, the 77th was saved. French officials awarded him the Croix de Guerre for his heroic deed.

Sadly, Cher Ami died as a result of his wounds. His body is on display at the War History branch of the Smithsonian.

SONNY TO THE RESCUE!

At his home in Cheddar, England, 58-year-old Richard Stone was peacefully working in his garden when the emergency brake on his van failed, knocking him down and pinning him to the ground. "Help!" he cried, "I'm trapped under my van!" But no one heard him—except Sonny, a parrot living in an adjacent trailer park.

Doing what parrots do, Sonny repeated what he'd heard, squawking, "Help, I'm trapped under my van!" Two people in the trailer park heard the bird, went to investigate, and then faintly heard Stone's voice. They immediately located the trapped man and freed him.

According to the parrot's owner, "Sometimes you won't get a word out of him. It's just lucky Sonny was in a talkative mood."

IF MURPHY WERE A...

BRI member Aaron Allerman sent us these "laws." For more great axioms, check out Arthur Bloch's collection in Murphy's Law.

...LAWYER

Alley's Axiom: Justice always prevails...three times out of seven.

Green's Rule: What the large print giveth, the small print taketh away.

First Law of Negotiation: A negotiation shall be considered successful if all parties walk away feeling screwed.

Power's Principle: If the law is on your side, pound on the law. If the facts are on your side, pound on the facts. If neither is on your side, pound on the table.

Potter's Parking Principle: The person you beat out of a prime parking spot will be the judge in your first case of the day.

Goulden's Law of Jury Watching: If a jury in a criminal trial stays out for more than 24 hours, it is certain to vote not guilty, save in those instances when it votes guilty.

Bloom's Law: The judge's jokes are always funny.

Andrew's Law: Honesty is almost the best policy.

...DOCTOR

Dolman's First Law: The first time you screw up a colonoscopy, your patient will definitely be a lawyer.

First Rule for Interns: Never say, "I'm new at this," to a patient.

The HMO Principle: The necessary procedure will not be allowed.

Edd's Law of Radiology: The colder the X-ray table, the more of the body the patient is required to place on it.

The First Rule for Ob/Gyns: All babies are born between midnight and 5:00 a.m.

Morse's Law of Online Research: Any search for medical information will yield at least one porno site.

Law of Laboratory Work: Hot glass looks exactly the same as cold glass.

Stettner's Law for Surgeons: Never say "oops," while your patient is conscious.

Breezy's Translation: When the doc says, "That's interesting," he really means, "Oops."

Barth's Distinction: "There are two types of people in the world...

MISSING PARTS

*Parts is parts—you can't let a missing finger, leg,
or eye get you down. These folks didn't.*

TYCO BRAHE (1546–1601)
Missing Part: Nose

Known as the father of astronomy, Tyco Brahe compiled the world's first accurate and complete set of astronomical tables. While a student at the university in Rostock, Germany, he and a fellow student, Manderup Parsbjergh, began quarreling over an obscure mathematical point. The argument went on for weeks, until they decided to settle it with a duel…in the dark…with swords! Result: Parsbjergh sliced off a chunk of Brahe's nose. Brahe's vanity wouldn't let the disfigurement stop him from achieving greatness—in public he wore an artificial nose made of gold and silver.

MORDECAI BROWN (1876–1948)
Missing Part: Index finger

As a pitcher for the Chicago Cubs, Brown helped win four championships in the early 1900s. When he was seven his right hand had gotten caught in a corn shredder—his index finger had to be amputated; his thumb and pinkie were permanently impaired. Three weeks later, while chasing a pig, he broke his other two fingers, which never healed properly. With little more than a stub to pitch with, Brown—known as "Three Finger"—learned to throw a sharp curveball and went on to win 239 major-league games. He was elected into the Baseball Hall of Fame in 1949.

HERBERT MARSHALL (1890–1966)
Missing Part: Leg

The British actor lost a leg fighting in World War I. But being an amputee didn't stop him from acting. Marshall spent 50 years as a romantic lead on the stage and on the screen starring opposite such stars as Marlene Dietrich in *Blonde Venus* and Greta Garbo in *The Painted Veil*. Audiences never even knew that he wore an artificial leg—film directors kept his onscreen movements to a minimum to hide it.

JERRY GARCIA (1942–1995)

Missing Part: Finger

He was four years old when it happened: Jerry and his older brother, Tiff, were splitting wood and playing "chicken" with the ax. Jerry mistimed removing his finger from the block, and Tiff accidentally chopped Jerry's finger off. It didn't hold him back, in 1957, at the age of 15, Jerry discovered the guitar and went on to become guitarist and singer for the Grateful Dead.

SARAH BERNHARDT (1844–1923)

Missing Part: Leg

Probably the most famous actress at the turn of the 20th century, Sarah Bernhardt suffered from a festering knee injury and had to have her leg amputated while touring in a production of *Jeanne Dore* in 1915. But this didn't stop her. Fitted with a wooden leg, "the Divine Sarah" continued to tour in plays, acted in movies, and even performed at the front during World War I.

HAROLD LLOYD (1893–1971)

Missing Parts: Thumb and index finger

One of the greatest comedians of the silent movies, Harold Lloyd was posing for a photograph in 1919 when he grabbed a prop—a papier-mâché "bomb"—and lit it with his cigarette. The prop turned out to be a real bomb: it exploded, taking the thumb and index finger from Lloyd's right hand. But he didn't let it ruin his career—he just started wearing gloves. And ultimately, Lloyd's gloves, like his horn-rimmed glasses, became part of his comic persona.

LANA TURNER (1921–1995)

Missing Parts: Eyebrows

For her role as an exotic handmaiden in the 1938 film *The Adventures of Marco Polo*, Turner shaved off her natural eyebrows and replaced them with fake straight, black ones. Her real eyebrows never grew back, so from that point on Lana Turner either painted or glued on fake eyebrows in every film she made.

*   *   *

Q: What was the original name of the Jordanian city Amman?
A: Philadelphia.

HOST WITH THE MOST

The Academy Awards is showbiz's premier event. Almost as important as selecting the nominees is selecting a celebrity host who can make or break the entire evening.

THE WRITE STUFF

The host of the Academy Awards is expected to be perfect. He's supposed to be smooth and gracious, funny but not too irreverent; ready with a witty ad-lib if something goes wrong, and most importantly, properly respectful of the evening's events. And he's supposed to do it all on live television in front of millions of people. It may look easy from the audience, but it takes *a lot* of preparation.

When Steve Martin was asked to host the 2003 Academy Awards, he assembled a team of top-notch comedy writers six months in advance of the event. They met at his home in Los Angeles eight times before the big night to prepare "the greatest opening monologue ever." Martin had a list of nominees, presenters, and stars who might be attending the ceremonies. At each meeting he sat at his laptop while the team of seven jokesmiths tossed out ideas. So who made the team?

• **Dave Barry,** Pulitzer Prize–winning columnist for the *Miami Herald* since 1983. He has written 24 bestselling humor books and is the subject of the CBS TV show *Dave's World.*

• **Bruce Vilanch,** *Hollywood Squares* regular and award-winning writer for the Oscar, Emmy, Tony, and Grammy shows as well as for Bette Midler and Whoopi Goldberg.

• **Rita Rudner,** standup comic and TV host.

• **Dave Boone,** head writer for *Hollywood Squares.* An Academy Award veteran, he also wrote material for Billy Crystal and Whoopi Goldberg.

• **Andy Breckman,** writer for David Letterman and *Saturday Night Live.* He also created the TV show *Monk.*

• **Beth Armogida,** joke writer for Jay Leno and for Drew Carey on *Whose Line Is It Anyway?*

• **Jon Macks,** staff writer for *The Tonight Show with Jay Leno* and an Academy Award veteran.

THE BIG NIGHT

On Oscar night, while Martin stood at the microphone onstage, his comedy advisors were gathered in a small room, just offstage. As he delivered lines like, "A movie star is many things: tall, short, thin, or skinny," they sat in a semi-circle facing a wall of television screens that showed the audience and the stage. Martin would introduce a presenter and then run to join the team for instant feedback and new jokes. When something unusual happened during the presentation, the writers wrote a few funny lines about it and Martin delivered them seconds later. For example, when Sean Connery appeared in a tuxedo accented with a frilly white front, Martin quipped, "So many people here tonight are wearing Armani but Sean is wearing Red Lobster."

Martin's team even handled the most controversial moment of the night with ease. When the outspoken filmmaker Michael Moore accepted his Oscar for *Bowling for Columbine*, Martin hurried to join his writers backstage. As Moore criticized President Bush for his handling of the war in Iraq, drawing cheers and catcalls in equal measure, the backstage writers went to work. From a list of possible jokes, the writers picked one, refined it, and sent Martin back onstage to ease the tension: "Backstage, it's so sweet. The Teamsters are helping Michael Moore into the trunk of his limo."

*   *   *

Will Rogers, Frank Sinatra, Whoopi Goldberg, Jimmy Stewart, Fred Astaire, Jerry Lewis, Robin Williams, Chevy Chase, David Letterman, and even Paul Hogan hosted the Academy Awards. But who hosted the most?

• **Bob Hope** hosted 17 times—the most ever. "Welcome to the Academy Awards, or as they're known at my house, Passover," he said, referring to his failure to win an Oscar.

• **Billy Crystal** hosted 7 times, 1990–1993, 1997–1998, 2000.

• **Johnny Carson** hosted 5 times, 1979–1982, 1984: The first non-movie star to host, he called the ceremony "two hours of sparkling entertainment spread over a four-hour show."

CELEBRITY LAWSUITS

*Here are a few more real-life examples of
unusual legal battles involving celebrities.*

PLAINTIFF: Michael Costanza
DEFENDANT: Jerry Seinfeld
LAWSUIT: In 1998 Costanza filed a $100 million lawsuit
against Seinfeld and the producers of the show *Seinfeld*, TV's
"show about nothing." He claimed that the character George
Costanza, played by Jason Alexander, was actually based on
him. He and Seinfeld had been friends at Queen's College, he
said, and his privacy rights had been violated when his "name,
likeness, and persona" were used to create the neurotic George
without his permission. He and George even had some of the
same jobs, he said. Seinfeld never denied knowing Costanza, but
spokesmen for the show insisted that the character was based on
the show's producer, Larry David, not on Costanza. David called
Costanza, who was "never that close of a friend to the star," a
"liar" and a "flagrant opportunist." (Which actually does sound
kind of like George.)

VERDICT: Michael Costanza lost. In June 1999, Justice Harold
Tompkins wrote, "While a program about nothing can be successful, a lawsuit must have more substance."

PLAINTIFF: Painter James Abbott McNeill Whistler
DEFENDANT: Critic John Ruskin
LAWSUIT: In July 1877, Ruskin, England's most famous art critic,
wrote a vicious attack on Whistler's Impressionist painting *Nocturne
in Black and Gold: The Falling Rocket*. Ruskin was not a fan of the
still-new, non-traditional style of Impressionism and accused
Whistler of trying to sell "unfinished paintings." He went on to
write, "I have seen, and heard, much of Cockney impudence before
now; but never expected to hear a coxcomb [a fool] ask two hundred
guineas for flinging a pot of paint in the public's face." Whistler, an
expatriot American who was already famous in his own right for
paintings such as *Arrangement in Grey and Black* (better known as
Whistler's Mother), sued for libel. In one heated exchange, Ruskin's

lawyer asked, "The labor of two days is that for which you ask two hundred guineas?" Whistler responded, "No. I ask it for the knowledge I have gained in the work of a lifetime." Ruskin himself refused to appear in the courtroom, but his lawyer reported Ruskin's promise to retire from criticism forever if he lost the case.

VERDICT: Ruskin lost the case. He lived the rest of his years in seclusion. But Whistler lost, too: the jury gave him a dubious award—one farthing and no court costs. He had to declare bankruptcy, losing his home and most of his personal property to pay the fees.

PLAINTIFF: The states of Arizona, Arkansas, Connecticut, Florida, Illinois, Michigan, Missouri, North Carolina, Ohio, Pennsylvania, Washington, West Virginia, and Wisconsin, and the District of Columbia

DEFENDANT: Robin Leach

LAWSUIT: In 1999 Leach, former host of the television show *Lifestyles of the Rich and Famous*, appeared in ads hawking vacation packages for three Florida-based travel companies. Residents of various states received letters suggesting they had "won" a vacation to Florida and a cruise to the Bahamas. Anyone who claimed the prize received a video in which Leach promised "world-class" vacations and "an experience you'll never forget." That last claim turned out to be true. "Winners" ended up paying up to $1,100 for their "free" vacation and instead of ritzy beachfront hotels, got roach-infested motels miles from shore. The "cruise" turned out to be an uncomfortable one-day ferry ride; the "Las Vegas entertainment" was a bingo game. Customers complained, and attorneys general across the country filed suit.

VERDICT: The three travel companies paid millions in restitution to their customers. Leach paid, too: Federal Trade Commission rules say a spokesperson must believe that any claims they make are true, and those beliefs must be based on personal experience. Leach agreed to an undisclosed settlement. "Next time Robin Leach puts his name behind a vacation package promising champagne wishes and caviar dreams," said Washington attorney general Christine Gregoire, "he'd better know those promises are true."

Soft rock: The Rock of Gibraltar is mostly grey limestone.

IT'S A WEIRD, WEIRD WORLD

More proof that truth really is stranger than fiction.

CAGEY PROPOSITION

"In Halberstadt, Germany, in September, an organist kicked off a performance of the late, radical composer John Cage's 'Organ 2/ASLSP' (an acronym somehow derived from 'as slow as possible'), which was written for 20 minutes, but thanks to technology and imagination, will be performed over a period lasting 639 years. The first six months will be devoted to creating the organ's first note. The purpose of the performance is to contrast the piece with the frenzied pace of modern society."

—Medford *Mail Tribune*

DON'T FEED THE HUMAN

"Adam Zaretsky knows what it's like to live in a fishbowl: He's on exhibit at the zoo.

"Zaretsky is known as 'Zed, species *Homo sapiens*,' in the 'Work-horse Zoo' exhibit. His home is an 8-by-8-foot glass room he shares with albino frogs, families of mice, microscopic worms and yeast.

"'I'm actually trying to blur the boundary between what is human culture and what is reality,' said 34-year-old San Francisco conceptual artist, Zaretsky, while stretched out on an ambulance gurney that he uses for a bed.

"Julia Reodica, who was Zaretsky's teaching assistant while he served as a visiting professor at San Francisco State University, is the zookeeper. 'As a serious researcher, I am finding Zed temperamental and unpredictable,' observed Reodica, clad in a Boy Scout uniform with long, zip-up black go-go boots. 'When agitated, he throws rubbish against the windows.'"

—*SFGate*

ALE-EMENTARY SCHOOL

"Got beer? Belgian first graders do. A group called Limburg Beer Friends has talked at least two elementary schools into serving

The double popsicle stick was introduced in the Depression...so two people could share it.

low-alcohol lagers and bitters at lunch, and more may follow this fall. Students are lapping up the program, says LBF chair Rony Langenaeken, who's convinced beer is better for kids than sugary soda drinks."

—*Newsweek*

THANK YOU, COME AGAIN

"When an armed robber who took less than $100 from a 7-11 store in St. Peters, Missouri, couldn't get his getaway car started, he returned to the store, handed back the money and told the two clerks it was all just a joke. They agreed to give his vehicle a jump start, not to write down his license plate number and wait about 40 minutes before calling the police. 'We have a friendly town out here,' police Officer David Kuppler noted, indicating the suspect was arrested anyway, 45 minutes later."

—*Wacky News*

BIRD BRAIN

"When David Ashley was charged with raising poultry without a permit, he appeared in court in Seneca Falls, NY, with a rooster tucked under his arm. Village Justice Gordon Tetor ordered the bird removed, but Ashley told the judge the bird was his attorney, explaining it 'was the only legal counsel I could afford.'"

—*Strange Tails*

*   *   *

DO AS WE SAY…NOT AS WE DO

"*Consumer Reports*, the magazine that tests products for safety and reliability, had to recall 15,000 glove compartment organizers that the magazine gave as an incentive to new subscribers. Reason: They hadn't tested the product. The plastic flashlight included in the kit turned out to be prone to overheating and melting, and the tire gauge gave inaccurate readings, which might cause people to inflate their tires improperly. In a letter to its readers the magazine admitted their goof. 'We've learned a valuable lesson,' president Jim Guest told readers."

—*Oops!*

DRIVER SLEEPING

Every year, BRI member Debbie Thornton sends in a list of
real-life bumper stickers. Have you seen the one that says...

The weather is here—
wish you were beautiful

DYSLEXICS ARE TEOPLE POO

Lottery: A tax on people
who can't do math

Friends help you move. Real
friends help you move bodies

It's lonely at the top, but
you eat better

If at first you do succeed, try
not to look astonished

ALL GENERALIZATIONS
ARE FALSE

TIME IS THE BEST TEACHER;
UNFORTUNATELY, IT KILLS ALL
ITS STUDENTS

I majored in liberal arts.
Would you like fries with that?

If we are what we eat, I'm
fast, cheap and easy

Stress is when you wake up
screaming and you realize you
haven't fallen asleep yet

Your proctologist called,
he found your head

If you're psychic,
think "honk"

Vote Jack Kevorkian for
White House physician

A hundred thousand sperm...
and you were the fastest?

Please do not honk—
driver sleeping

Back off! I'm not that kind of car

A woman's place is in the
House—*and the Senate!*

PROUD MEMBER OF PETA:
PEOPLE EATING TASTY ANIMALS

Heart Attacks: *God's revenge*
for eating his animal friends

Okay, who put a "stop payment" on my reality check?

The IRS: We've got what it
takes to take what you've got!

GROW YOUR OWN DOPE—
PLANT A MAN

Some people just don't know
how to drive. I call these
people "everybody but me."

CHAOS. PANIC. DISORDER.
MY WORK HERE IS DONE.

Q: Where does singer and songwriter Stevie Nicks do...

HOW PAPER BECAME MONEY, PART II

For most of history, people felt that gold and silver were "real" money and that paper money was worthless. (If you feel that way, too, please take all the worthless paper money you can find and mail it to Uncle John at the address listed in the back of this book.) Here's how paper money became established in Western civilization.
(Part I of the story is on page 47.)

MY MONEY OR YOUR LIFE
The concept of paper money originated in China as early as 140 B.C. But it wasn't until the late 1200s, when the Italian traveler Marco Polo wrote about it in his memoirs, that the idea was introduced to Europe.

So did paper money catch on in Europe soon after that? Not a chance—in China despots like Kublai Khan were quick to kill anyone who refused to accept the notes. Under that kind of pressure, paper money caught on fast.

In Europe things were different. Sure, there were plenty of European tyrants, but none of them tried to force paper money on their subjects the way Kublai Khan did. Paper notes had to earn their way into the public's confidence, via a very gradual process of evolution. Here's how it happened.

DON'T LEAVE HOME WITHOUT THEM
Many travelers use *traveler's checks* instead of cash. Merchants all over the world accept them just as if they were cash, yet they have no value to thieves because once they're reported stolen, they can't be used. The traveler gets a new book of checks and the thief ends up with nothing.

It turns out there was a way to avoid traveling with cash even before traveler's checks were invented. As far back as the Middle Ages, when people went on business trips they could deposit gold coins or other valuables with a trusted merchant—frequently a jeweler, or *goldsmith*—when they traveled outside of their home town. The traveler carried a note from the goldsmith that stated how much money had been left on deposit and promised to release the gold to anyone who presented the note for payment of a debt, provided that 1) the traveler had signed the note over to the debtor by name, and 2) he had endorsed it with his signature.

SAFE AT HOME

If the goldsmith was well known and trusted, this note was literally as good as gold. If the note was stolen, it didn't matter, because the gold was still safely locked in the goldsmith's vault and would not be released without the owner's signature. These early "promissory notes," as they came to be called, were the forerunners of modern banknotes.

Goldsmiths soon realized that people tended to deposit more money than they withdrew, and that the difference could be lent out temporarily to borrowers who agreed to repay the money with interest. Storing gold and other valuables, lending money, and other services (such as exchanging foreign coins) proved to be so lucrative that by the mid-1600s, some goldsmiths had gotten out of the goldsmithing business altogether, focusing exclusively on financial services. They were the first modern bankers.

MAKING CHANGE

At first each promissory note was unique and read something like, "John Cooper has deposited 20 pounds, 6 shillings, and 10 pence and promises to pay any debts he incurs out of these funds." But by the late 1600s, the volume of transactions had increased over the years and goldsmith bankers found that it was much easier to issue standardized notes in nice round amounts like £100, £50, £20, £10, £5, and £1. So instead of getting one note for exactly 20 pounds, 6 shillings, and 10 pence, John Cooper would get one note for 20 pounds, another for 5 shillings, another for 1 shilling, and would probably have to carry the 10 pence (similar to a dime) in cash.

These standardized "banknotes" were made payable to the bearer and no longer required the traveler to endorse it with his signature. This made banknotes more convenient. But if you wanted the security of a signature, there was another new invention: checks.

PASS IT ON

Standardized banknotes were used as money, but they were still thought of as receipts, having no intrinsic value in themselves. Merchants accepted the notes as payment and then went to the bank, claimed the gold, and brought it home for safekeeping.

But what happened when *this* person wanted to take a trip? He had to gather up his gold and trudge right back to the bank and exchange it for banknotes all over again. Why even bother? As people came to trust the banknotes more and more, they stopped redeeming them for gold. They just traded the banknotes. A single banknote might pass from person to person to person for months or even years before being redeemed for gold.

There would be some more fine-tuning to produce the bills we use today (that story is in *Uncle John's Absolutely Absorbing Bathroom Reader*), but for all intents and purposes...paper currency had arrived.

FOOTNOTE

So you can take paper money down to your local bank or to the U.S. Treasury and redeem it for gold, right?

Wrong. At one time, the U.S. government pegged the value of a dollar to a fixed amount of gold (the gold standard). In 1933, for example, the value of $1 was set at exactly 1/35 of one ounce of gold. But that year the federal government began easing away from the gold standard, in the hope that it might help end the Great Depression (it didn't). The government continued to define the value of the dollar in terms of gold but outlawed the circulation of gold coins. Until 1933 there were six denominations of U.S. gold coins: $1, $2.50 (quarter eagle), $3, $5 (half eagle), $10 (eagle), and $20 (double eagle).

In 1971 the government took another step away from the gold standard when it stopped the free exchange of U.S. gold for foreign-owned U.S. dollars, which was depleting U.S. gold reserves.

Finally, in 1978, Congress removed the dollar from the gold standard entirely. You can still *buy* gold with dollars, but you can't *redeem* dollars for gold. The amount of gold that a single dollar can buy changes all the time, and that's true of all the major currencies of the world. Governments today don't want their economies directly tied to the price of any commodity—including gold.

SAM'S BRAINTEASERS

BRI members are always asking for more of these tricky questions. We aim to please. Think you can figure them out? (Answers on page 499.)

1. Mr. Red, Mr. White, and Mr. Blue met at a coffee shop. One man was wearing a red suit, one a white suit, and the other a blue suit. After a short while, Mr. White exclaimed, "Why, I just noticed that none of us is dressed in the same color as his own last name."

"Really?" remarked the man in the red suit. "So?"

Can you figure out what color suit each man is wearing?

2. What do the following words have in common? (It's really not that difficult if you chip away at them for a while.)

Sheath   Pirate   Ashamed   Brandy

3. Mr. Tidball purchased two clocks from Gordo's Repair Shop and set them at the same time. He soon discovered, however, that one clock was two minutes slow per hour and the other was one minute fast per hour. The next time Tidball looked, one clock was exactly an hour ahead of the other. How long had it been since he last set the clocks?

4. Uncle John's cousin, "Bozo" Newman, was about to board a city bus with his newly purchased, five-foot-long novelty toothbrush, when the bus driver informed him of a city ordinance prohibiting packages more than four feet tall. Bozo only had enough money to take the bus home so he tried returning the toothbrush—but the store wouldn't take returns. Five minutes later, Bozo was on the bus riding home...with the big toothbrush in one piece.

How'd he do it?

5. Uncle John was in the "reading room" when he came across a word puzzle in the daily newspaper. After some active thinking, he solved it. Can you? It read, "Which is the odd word out and why?" Here's the word list:

Brush   Taste   Shampoo   Stench   Flush   Wash   Seat

...Life expectancy for women in the U.S.: In 1900, 48.7 years; in 2000, 76.1 years.

6. What's the closest relation the son of your father's brother's sister-in-law could be to you?

7. A long time ago in a faraway land, there lived a queen called Bubbles and her gorgeous daughter, Princess Porcelain. The princess wished to be married, but Queen Bubbles would not allow it—she never wanted Porcelain to leave the throne room.

So Bubbles devised a scheme to rid the palace of suitors. All a suitor had to do to win Porcelain's hand was to draw a piece of paper from a golden bowl. But there was a catch: there were two pieces of paper in the bowl. One said "My Child," resulting in marriage to the princess, while the other said "The Snakes," which meant the suitor would be thrown into a pit of venomous snakes, never to be seen again. Somehow, the suitors always seemed to end up in the snake pit.

One day a handsome knight named Sir Flushalot came along and Porcelain fell head over heels for him. The princess pulled him aside and whispered, "I think my mother is a cheat. I believe both pieces of paper say 'The Snakes.'" Flushalot assessed the situation and said, "Fear not—I've got a plan." Aware that he cannot expose the queen as a cheater, how does Sir Flushalot win Princess Porcelain's hand in marriage?

*   *   *

ANOTHER LUCKY FIND

The Find: A Victorian masterpiece painting
Where It Was Found: In a Colorado building
The Story: In the 1960s, a man (he refused to release his name to the media) bought a building in Colorado. Inside the building was a painting, signed "Waterhouse," depicting a sultry Cleopatra reclining on a chair. He thought it was "pretty and rather sexy." Nearly 40 years later he heard about a "Waterhouse" being sold for millions of dollars, so he called Christie's and sent a photo. Christie's senior director, Martin Beisly, immediately flew from London to Colorado and confirmed that it was a painting that hadn't been heard of since 1889. "Scholars knew about the picture," he said, "but had no idea where it was and even thought it might have been destroyed." Estimated worth: $900,000.

Toys "R" Us was originally called the "Children's Supermart."

WISE WOMEN

Some thoughtful observations from the stronger sex.

"You can have it all. You just can't have it all at once."
—**Oprah Winfrey**

"When I stand before God at the end of my life, I would hope that I would not have a single bit of talent left and could say, 'I used everything you gave me.'"
—**Erma Bombeck**

"The only time a woman really succeeds in changing a man is when he's a baby."
—**Natalie Wood**

"If you think you can, you can. And if you think you can't, you're right."
—**Mary Kay Ash**

"You may be disappointed if you fail, but you are doomed if you don't try."
—**Beverly Sills**

"I have become my own version of an optimist. If I can't make it through one door, I'll go through another door—or I'll make a door. Something terrific will come no matter what."
—**Joan Rivers**

"If you don't like something, change it. If you can't change it, change your attitude. Don't complain."
—**Maya Angelou**

"You gain strength, courage, and confidence by every experience in which you really stop to look fear in the face."
—**Eleanor Roosevelt**

"The greater part of our happiness or misery depends on our dispositions and not our circumstances."
—**Martha Washington**

"When you get into a tight place and everything goes against you till it seems you could not hold on a minute longer, never give up then—for that is just the place and time that the tide will turn."
—**Harriet Beecher Stowe**

"Difficult times have helped me to understand better than before, how infinitely rich and beautiful life is in every way, and that so many things that one goes worrying about are of no importance whatsoever."
—**Isak Dinesen**

Sheryl Crow's two front teeth are fake—the real ones got knocked out when she tripped onstage.

(B)AD PROMOTIONS

*When a company comes up with a sales promotion, the idea
is to attract potential customers and make a bunch of
money. But sometimes it doesn't work out that way.*

Brilliant Marketing Idea: In 1994 Prudential Securities was trying to improve its image, tarnished by allegations that agents had been lying to customers for years. Their $20 million campaign started with a "straight talk" newspaper ad highlighting the honesty of their agents. A full-page photo of real-life Prudential broker Susan B. Gooding featured the caption, "From where I sit, preserving integrity is not a lost art." Underscoring her integrity, the ad finished with, "One of my clients is my father."

Oops! Gooding's father had been dead since 1991 and, the *Chicago Sun Times* reported, he was never her client. Prudential claimed it was an honest mistake and pulled the ads immediately.

Brilliant Marketing Idea: In January 2002, CNN ran a TV commercial for news anchor Paula Zahn's new show, *American Morning*. In it the announcer says, "Where can you find a morning news anchor who's provocative, super-smart, and oh, yeah, just a little sexy? CNN…Yeah, CNN." And as he says "sexy," the word appears on the screen—and the sound of a zipper opening can be heard.

Oops! CNN was immediately slammed by rival networks for using sex to sell a news broadcast. "It was a major blunder by our promotions department," said Chairman Walter Isaacson. " The spot was pulled after being shown only twice.

Brilliant Marketing Idea: In March 2003, the Hong Kong Tourism Board put their new slogan—"Hong Kong Will Take Your Breath Away"—in ads in several major publications in England.

Oops! In a bizarre coincidence, just as the ad campaign began, Hong Kong was hit by an outbreak of SARS (*Severe Acute Respiratory Syndrome*). The outbreak led to a rapid decline in tourism, severely damaging the economy. "As soon as the outbreak began," said a Tourism Board spokesman, "we realized it would be pretty embarrassing, but it was too late to pull the ads." What was so embarrassing? One of SARS' main symptoms is shortness of breath.

The bestselling tie colors in the U.S.: blue and red.

AERO-NUTS

The first balloonists and aviators were called aeronauts, from the Greek aer, meaning "air," and nautes, meaning "sailor." Judging from the crazy risks some of them took, common sense was not a job requirement.

PILATRE DE ROZIER

Claim to Fame: The first person ever to ascend in a balloon, in 1783.

Other **Claim to Fame:** He tried to combine the two early methods of ballooning: hot air, which used ordinary air heated by an open flame, and hydrogen gas, which is lighter than air but is highly explosive when exposed to fire. (Helium, which is not explosive, was not discovered until 1868.)

When he attempted to float across the English Channel on June 15, 1785, he used a "hybrid" balloon—one compartment filled with air heated by an open flame, the other filled with explosive hydrogen gas.

What Happened: Exactly what you think happened: about 15 minutes into the flight, the flame found the hydrogen and de Rozier's ballooning career ended with a bang as he plunged more than 3,000 feet. De Rozier, the first person to ascend in a balloon, also became the first person to die in one.

MARIE BLANCHARD

Claim to Fame: Ballooning's first female aeronaut and the widow of Jean-Pierre Blanchard, the first person to cross the English Channel by balloon (1784).

Other **Claim to Fame:** She tried to put a spark back into ballooning—literally.

Background: Watching the first aeronauts float into the sky in huge balloons was a thrill in the 1780s. But by the turn of the 19th century, aerial shows weren't as big a deal as they had been just a decade before. Even well-known pioneers like the Blanchards had trouble making a living at it.

Jean-Pierre had a heart attack and fell out of his balloon during a flight over the Netherlands in 1808. Confined to his bed and unable to fly, he was so broke that he suggested his wife drown herself, since he had "nothing to leave her."

Marie Blanchard ignored this advice and kept ballooning. To keep the crowds coming, she began flying at night, so that she could shoot off fireworks in midflight—not a very good idea considering that Mademoiselle Blanchard preferred balloons filled with explosive hydrogen gas.

What Happened: On a flight over Paris on July 7, 1819, the fireworks show got a little bigger than Blanchard had bargained for: one of her rockets ignited the hydrogen, causing her balloon to explode. Blanchard managed to land on the roof of a building, but to the horror of the crowd below, she then slid off the roof to the street, breaking her neck. History's first female aeronaut died just as the first male aeronaut had: in a balloon accident.

IVAN BLAGIN

Claim to Fame: He was an ace Soviet fighter pilot of the 1930s.

Other Claim to Fame: The first aviator to become a dirty word.

Background: In 1934 the Soviet Union scored a propaganda coup when it rolled out the *Maxim Gorky*, then the world's largest airplane. Bigger than a Boeing 747, the *Maxim Gorky* had a movie theater, newspaper office, 16-line telephone exchange, darkroom, laundry, pharmacy, and café.

On some flights the *Maxim Gorky* was accompanied by an ordinary single-engine plane, so that onlookers could compare the two and see just how big the *Maxim Gorky* really was. On May 18, 1935, Ivan Blagin was the pilot flying the smaller craft. He was supposed to fly in tandem with the large plane...but he decided to perform aerobatic stunts instead to impress the crowd below.

What Happened: When Comrade Blagin tried to loop his plane around the *Maxim Gorky*, he miscalculated the distance and slammed into one of its wings, causing both planes to break apart several thousand feet above the ground. Blagin died in the crash, as did all 43 people aboard the *Maxim Gorky*. Soviet officials were so furious with Blagin that they coined a new word—*blaginism*—which means "selfish exhibitionism and lack of proper Socialist discipline."

Charles Lindbergh's first words after his historic flight: "Are there any mechanics here?"

TAWK O' DA TOWN

While looking through the book New Yawk Tawk *by Robert Hendrickson, we were surprised to find out that many words and phrases in the English language were born in the Empire State.*

SENT UP THE RIVER. Slang for "sent to prison." The river is the Hudson and the prison is Sing Sing, which is upriver from New York City.

DEPARTMENT STORE. It didn't invent the concept of one store with different departments, but the first store to actually call itself this was H. H. Heyn's Department Store in 1887.

COCKAMAMIE. Meaning "worthless" or "absurd," this word may come from the inability of early 20th-century kids in Manhattan's Lower East Side to pronounce *decalcomania,* a cheap picture to be transferred onto wood or china (a decal).

FLEA MARKET. It got its name because secondhand items have fleas, right? Guess again. Downtown Manhattan was home to *vallie* (valley) *markets* in Dutch Colonial days. The term was abbreviated to *vlie* (pronounced "flee") *market,* and was eventually anglicized to *flea market.*

COWBOY. Sounds like a word from Wyoming, but it was actually the term given to bands of men who rustled cows in New York in the 1800s.

REUBEN. This grilled sandwich of corned beef, Swiss cheese, sauerkraut, and Russian dressing on rye bread was invented at Reuben's Delicatessen in Manhattan at the turn of the 20th century.

ALMIGHTY DOLLAR. Coined by New Yorker Washington Irving in 1836: "The almighty dollar, that great object of universal devotion throughout the land..."

PUNK ROCK. Attributed to *Punk* magazine editor Legs McNeil, describing the 1970s music scene that started in lower Manhattan.

MULTIMILLIONAIRE. At his death in 1848, New York fur trader John Jacob Astor was worth $20 million (about $80 billion in today's dollars). The term was first applied to him.

RUSH HOUR. First used to describe commuter gridlock on New York streets in 1890.

OUT IN LEFT FIELD. Far from the action. *Right* field might be more fitting, because that's where the fewest baseballs go. But at Yankee Stadium, the seats in left field were far away from the biggest player of the day, *right* fielder Babe Ruth.

PORTERHOUSE STEAK. Named in 1814 for the New York restaurant that popularized it, Martin Morrison's Porterhouse.

YUPPIE. An acronym of "*y*oung *u*rban *p*rofessional." This term comes from New York City in the 1980s. Possibly coined by Jerry Rubin, one of the founders of the 1960s *yippie* movement.

THREEPEAT. Coined in 1993 by New York Knicks coach Pat Riley after the Chicago Bulls won their third straight championship.

PUBLIC RELATIONS. First used by publicity writer Edward Bernays, nephew of Sigmund Freud, for his 1920 wedding announcements in an attempt to make his occupation sound more respectable.

BUNT. A baseball term meaning to hit the ball softly. Most likely a corruption of the word *butt* (as in "butting" the ball with the bat). The first known utterance of *bunt* was in 1872 by a player named Pearce on the Brooklyn Atlantics.

BLAST FROM THE PAST. Made popular by NYC disc jockey Murray the K in the 1960s, referring to old records.

KEEPING UP WITH THE JONESES. Created by New York cartoonist "Pop" Momand in 1913 as the title of a comic strip that showed middle-class people living beyond their means. It was originally going to be called "Keeping Up with the Smiths," but Momand changed it because he thought "Joneses" sounded better.

HEADLINE. The first one appeared on the October 27, 1777, edition of the *New York Gazette*.

SIDEKICK. New York writer O. Henry first recorded the term in 1904. It was street slang for "buddy." Why? Men's side pants pockets—called *sidekicks*—were the most difficult for pickpockets to reach and therefore reliable, like a trusted friend, always at your side.

Technical term for goosebumps: *horripilation.*

TRUE GLUE

It's been used on elephant tusks, racing cars, space shuttles—even human wounds. It's cyanoacrylate, better known as superglue. Here's its story.

ACCIDENTAL INVENTION

Dr. Harry Coover was a researcher working for Kodak Research Labs in 1942. While trying to develop a clear plastic gun sight for use during World War II, he discovered something else: cyanoacrylates. But it was no good for what he needed—it stuck to everything, which created a huge mess. So he set it aside and moved on.

Nine years later Dr. Coover was working at the Tennessee Eastman Chemical Company. This time he was trying to find a tough polymer for jet canopies. While experimenting, he remembered the cyanoacrylate and wondered about its ability to refract light. A fellow researcher named (ironically) Dr. Fred Joyner spread a film of ethyl cyanoacrylate between two prisms of a refractometer. Not only did it not refract light, but it once again left a big sticky mess. And no matter how hard they tried, the two scientists couldn't pry the expensive prisms apart.

Embarrassed, they sheepishly told company execs about the ruined equipment. But instead of ridicule, they received praise—and orders to begin developing the adhesive for commercial use. Eastman Compound #910 hit the market in 1958, but initial sales were low. Why? People didn't believe Eastman's claims about the glue. So to prove its worth, Dr. Coover appeared on the TV quiz show *I've Got a Secret* and lifted host Gary Moore completely off the floor...using only a single drop of the glue.

HOW IT WORKS

Here's how it works: Cyanoacrylate, CA for short, is a highly reactive liquid, and when left to its own devices will quickly solidify. The addition of an acid stabilizer prevents the CA from reacting and keeps it in a liquid state. When the acid stabilizer comes into contact with a catalyst, its stabilizing effect is neutralized. This allows the CA molecules to react with each other, forming long polymer chains. The catalyst for the acid stabilizer is hydroxyl ions, which are conveniently located in every molecule of water. So do you have to mix CA with water? No. Most surfaces already have a tiny bit of water on them. If they don't, there are always minuscule amounts of water available in the air. The water acts like a trigger, allowing the molecular structure of the CA to change. The molecules join up like a long series of popper beads. What was a thin liquid becomes a hard mass of molecular spaghetti noodles, bonding to whatever it contacts.

HELPFUL TIPS FOR USING SUPERGLUE
• Make sure the parts being glued don't move *at all* during the formation of the chains. If so, the chain will break and the glue won't hold.
• A little dab'll do ya. Superglue bonds best when it's used at the rate of one drop per square inch. More than that requires a much longer bonding period, which may result in a weaker bond.
• If you're gluing two flat surfaces together, rough them up with sandpaper first. That'll give the glue more surface area to bond to. But make sure you blow off any dusty residue first.
• Glued your fingers together? Use nail polish remover. Don't have any? Try warm soapy water and a little patience. Your sweat and natural skin oils will soon loosen the bond.

STICKY FACTS
• Superglue is so strong that a single square-inch bond can lift a ton of weight.
• Why doesn't superglue stick to the bottle? Because it needs moisture to set and there is no moisture in the bottle.
• What's the difference between superglue and Krazy Glue? Nothing. Krazy Glue is just one of many brands available. It first went on sale in 1973. Some other brands: SuperBonder, Permabond, Pronto, Black Max, Alpha Ace, and (in Mexico) Kola Loka.
• Cyanoacrylate products are a $325 million-a-year industry. Approximately 90% of U.S. homes have at least one tube.
• During the Vietnam War, tubes of superglue were put in U.S. soldiers' first-aid kits to help seal wounds. Special kinds of superglue are now used in hospitals worldwide, reducing the need for sutures, stitches, and staples. (It doesn't work on deep wounds or on wounds

where the skin does a lot of stretching, such as over joints.)

• Superglue is now used in forensic detection. When investigators open a foil packet of ethyl-gel cyanoacrylate, the fumes settle on skin oils left behind in human fingerprints, turning the invisible smears into visible marks.

STICKY SITUATIONS

• **Lovers use it.** An ex-con who violated his parole glued himself to his girlfriend so the police couldn't arrest him. An Algerian woman tried the same trick with her husband to keep him from being deported. Neither attempt was successful.

• **Pranksters use it.** An Atlantic City man sued a casino after he got stuck to a glue-smeared toilet seat and had to waddle through the casino for help.

• **Veterinarians use it.** A tortoise that cracked its shell falling from a second-floor window was successfully glued back together. Other superglued animals: racing pigeons have had their feathers glued together for better aerodynamics, fish have had their fins reattached, and horses have had their split hooves mended.

• **Protestors use it.** A man protesting tax laws that left people penniless in Bristol, England, took matters into his own hands. After more than 200 attempts to contact the Inland Revenue helpline, he went down to the local tax office armed with a tube of superglue. When they wouldn't help him, he glued his hand to a desk, vowing to stay attached until he got some answers. After finally getting unstuck, he was allowed to voice his views on a local radio station.

• **Fishers use it.** The winner of the "How Krazy Glue Saved the Day Contest" was a woman who fell asleep while fishing in a small rowboat on a Minnesota lake. More than a mile from shore, she was awakened when her feet started getting wet. Frantically, she mopped up the water with an old shirt, but it was still coming in through a small leak in the bottom of the boat. So she took a tube of Krazy Glue out of her tackle box (she used it to make fishing lures), cut a thick piece of leather from her boot, and glued the leather over the leak. "The leak stopped and I kept on fishing," she said. "By the way," she added, "I can't swim—Krazy Glue saved my life!"

Alaska has a sand desert with dunes more than 100 feet high.

FORE!

*Next time you're playing golf, watching a match, or
even driving past a course, be forewarned! Golf balls go
where they're hit, not always where the player wants
them to go. For example, a ball could hit...*

A MOVING VEHICLE

Sean Hutchins regularly drives past San Geronimo Golf
Club in California. His advice to other drivers: Beware—
"The number of golf balls hitting vehicles seems to be on the rise."
His current tally: two have hit his truck; one ball hit his friend's
Chevelle; another hit that same friend's mother's pickup; a fifth
hit the friend's girlfriend's car; and a sixth smacked a California
Highway Patrol car.

A BIRD

Benin, a small nation in Africa, doesn't have a golf course, but
that didn't deter Mathieu Boya. He would routinely practice driving balls in a field adjacent to the Benin Air Base—until one day
in 1987 when his ball struck a gull, which then fell into the open
cockpit of a jet taxiing the runway, which caused the pilot to lose
control, which caused the plane to barrel through the other four
Mirage fighter jets sitting on the tarmac...which wiped out the
entire Benin Air Force.

A FAN'S FOREHEAD

John Yates, 52, realized a dream-come-true when he got to watch
the world's most famous golfer, Tiger Woods, in person at the 2003
Buick Open in Grand Blanc, Michigan. But Yates got more than
he bargained for. Woods's approach shot on the seventh hole went
wild and struck Yates smack-dab on the forehead. After a few
dazed minutes on his back, Yates looked up to see Woods leaning
over him, apologizing profusely. For his trouble, the fan got three
stitches, the errant ball, and an autographed golf glove. Woods got
something out of the deal, too. As Yates recalled: "I helped him
out because my head knocked the ball back toward the hole. He
birdied the hole, I guess. I didn't see it. But it's my most memorable moment in golf."

A popcorn kernel must contain at least 13.5% water to pop.

THE BOTTOM OF THE CUP

As the sun was setting on the seventh hole of the Roehampton Golf Club course in England in 1964, Bill Carey hit a tee shot that landed near the pin, but because it was getting dark, he couldn't see exactly where it rolled to. So Carey and his opponent, Edgar Winter, went to look for it. After an unsuccessful search of the green and the hill below, Carey finally conceded defeat as darkness settled in. But a few minutes later he found the ball in the one place he never thought to look: at the bottom of the cup. Even though Carey had hit a hole-in-one, he never got credit for it...and lost.

QUICKSAND

Bayly MacArthur, playing in a 1931 tournament in Australia, hit a ball into what he thought was a sand trap. It wasn't—it was quicksand. And unfortunately, MacArthur found out the hard way when he stepped into the quicksand to play the ball. It took four other golfers to pull him out.

A SPECTATOR'S BRA

At the 1973 Sea Pines Heritage Classic in South Carolina, Hale Irwin's worst shot of the match (and perhaps his career) hit a woman's chest and lodged in her bra. She was relieved when Irwin decided to forgo the shot, taking a two-stroke penalty instead.

THREE SPECTATORS

In 1971 Vice President Spiro Agnew played in the Pro-Am portion of the Bob Hope Desert Classic. After his first two shots injured *three* members of the crowd, Agnew made the wise choice and became a spectator himself.

AN OPPONENT'S ARM

Why hit someone with a golf ball when you've got a golf *club*? In 1980 at the final round of the Boone Golf Club Championship in North Carolina, Margaret McNeil and Earlena Adams were tied for the lead after 18 holes. They had to play one sudden-death hole to decide the match. At the tee, McNeil was practicing her stroke when she accidentally smacked Adams on the arm with her backswing. Result for Adams: Her arm was broken; she couldn't play the hole. Result for McNeil: She was awarded first place.

A regulation hole in golf is 4.25 inches in diameter, and "no less than 4 inches deep."

REVENGE!

We all have fantasies of getting even with people who annoy us...but we seldom actually go through with them. Here are some examples of what could happen if we did.

REVENGE OF THE PHONE CLERK

Background: In early 2002, New Zealander James Storrie called New Zealand Telecom Corporation to complain that his cell phone had been disconnected. When the representative informed him that the phone had been reported stolen, Storrie insisted that he still had the phone and that he had not reported its theft. The mistake was cleared up, but the representative (identity unknown) was apparently offended by Storrie's attitude.

Revenge Gone Wild! When Storrie received his next phone bill, he found that he'd been charged an extra $140. What for? The explanation was printed right on the bill: "penalty for being an arrogant bastard." N.Z. Telecom apologized profusely, offered Storrie some undisclosed financial compensation, and promised to investigate the vengeful billing.

REVENGE OF THE BAD WAITER

Background: One evening in June 2003, Wayne and Darlene Keller of Corona, California, took their two children to a Sizzler's restaurant. Mrs. Keller requested vegetables with her dinner, instead of potatoes. According to the family, the waiter, Jonathan Voletner, rudely told her that she had to choose between French fries or a baked potato. "When I told him my wife can't eat potatoes," said Mr. Keller, "he brought back a really small salad, practically threw it at her, and told her to go get the dressing herself." After the meal, the Kellers left—and they didn't leave a tip.

Revenge Gone Wild! Voletner had his girlfriend follow the Kellers home to get their address. When he got off work, he, his girlfriend, and his brother went to the Keller home, waited until 1 a.m., and then doused their house, yard, and mailbox with a gallon of maple syrup, smashed eggs, toilet paper, duct tape, and plastic wrap. They might have gotten away with it, but in a state of heightened stupidity, Voletner rang the doorbell. Then he hid in the bushes and waited to see their reaction. Their reaction: They called the police.

Officers found Voletner in the bushes and his co-conspirators in a nearby car. When they presented the suspects to the Kellers, Mrs. Keller said, "Oh my God! It's the waiter from the restaurant!" They were all charged with vandalism, with Voletner receiving an extra charge of child endangerment because his girlfriend was a minor. He was also fired by Sizzler's. "The company doesn't allow this sort of thing," the manager said.

REVENGE OF THE POSTMASTER

Background: On October 17, 2001, 62-year-old James Beal was fired from his job as relief postmaster in Empire, Michigan.

Revenge Gone Wild! The next day, Beal showed up at the post office carrying two five-gallon buckets full of worms, grubs, and porcupine poop. He proceeded to splatter several of his former co-workers with the putrid concoction, completely saturating two of them. He was on his way to his car for another bucket when police arrived. For his bizarre act of revenge, he was charged with four counts of assaulting a federal worker. "I let my anger sort of overrule my judgments," Beal told the court. He was sentenced to 18 months in federal prison.

REVENGE OF THE NON-WITNESS

Background: Jane White was upset that Jehovah's Witnesses had come to her house once a month, every month, for 12 years. At first, she politely told them that she wasn't interested. Finally, after a visit on a Saturday in January 2002, she had had enough.

Revenge Gone Wild! White went to the group's local Kingdom Hall in Peacehaven, England, the following morning, carefully tim-ing her visit for the middle of the Sunday service. She banged on the door loudly, again and again, until someone answered, and then proceeded to offer members of the congregation religious literature that she had brought along. "I tried to hand out free magazines just like the Jehovah's Witnesses hand out," she said. "Nobody seemed to want them, though." She continued her "mission" for 30 minutes until the police showed up and asked her to leave.

REVENGE OF THE SPAM HATERS

Background: In November 2002, *Detroit Free Press* columnist

The *Mayflower* was dismantled by the Pilgrims and turned into a barn.

Mike Wendland wrote a story about a man named Alan Ralsky. Ralsky had become a multimillionaire through marketing spam on the Internet. How much spam? His company sent up to 250 million e-mails a day. The story told readers about Ralsky's new 8,000-square-foot, $740,000 home. The spammer bragged that one entire wing of the house was paid for by a single weight-loss e-mail.

Revenge Gone Wild! A group of spam haters decided to give Ralsky a dose of his own medicine. They posted his home address on hundreds of websites, and Ralsky started getting tons—literally—of junk mail. Then they posted his e-mail address and his phone number, and the mega-junkmailer got inundated with the very thing he had made his millions from—spam. And, no surprise: *He was annoyed!* Ralsky later complained, "They've signed me up for every advertising campaign and mailing list there is. These people are out of their minds! They're harassing me!"

* * *

THE WORLD'S LARGEST...

• Roanoke, Virginia, has the "World's Largest Man-Made Illuminated Star," an 88-foot electric wonder set atop a mountain.

• Artichoke-growing region Castroville, California, proudly trumpets its "World's Largest Artichoke."

• Both Menton, Indiana, and Winlock, Washington, claim their 11-foot egg sculptures are the world's largest.

• The owner of a Magnolia, Arkansas, grill store constructed a working 70-foot "World's Largest Charcoal Grill."

• "The World's Largest Wind Chime" has been removed from Lakeside, California, because locals said it was too loud.

• Though many towns claim they're home to the "World's Largest Peanut," only Ashburn, Georgia, has constructed a towering 10-foot peanut atop a 15-foot brick stack, leaving the lesser peanuts of Pearsall and Floresville, Texas; Durant, Oklahoma; and Dothan, Alabama, behind. Those wishing for an all-peanut day of tourism can see the Ashburn peanut and then check out the nearby big-toothed 13-foot "Jimmy Carter Peanut" of Plains, Georgia.

GO DIRECTLY TO JAIL

Four stories of dumb crooks who saved us all a lot of trouble.

SELF HELP

"A 22-year-old Green Bay man led police on a chase that moved as slowly as 20 mph and ended in the Brown County Jail's parking lot. The man parked his pickup in the jail's lot, smoked a cigarette, got out of the truck, and lay face-down on the ground to be arrested, police said. He told the officers he knew he was drunk and was going to be sent to jail, so he just drove himself there."

—*Milwaukee Journal Sentinel*

SUPPLY-SIDE ECONOMICS

"Sylvain Boucher of Quebec was spotted by prison guards standing between the prison wall and an outer fence. Assuming he was trying to escape, they grabbed him, but soon discovered he was not an inmate...and he was carrying a large amount of illegal drugs. Boucher was trying to break *in*, thinking the prison would be a good market for his drugs. He'll get to find out. Before he had the supply, but no market. Now he has the market, but no supply."

—*Moreland's Bozo of the Day*

IS THIS WHY THEY CALL IT "DOPE"?

"Philomena A. Palestini, 18, of Portland, Maine, walked into Salem District Court to face one criminal charge, but walked out in handcuffs with two. Court Security Officer Ronald Lesperance found a hypodermic needle and two small bags of what police believe is heroin in her purse as she walked through the security checkpoint. 'This doesn't happen very often,' said Lesperance."

—*Eagle Tribune*

THE "IN" CROWD

"A man who tried to break *into* a Rideau correctional center with drugs and tobacco was sentenced to two years in prison yesterday. Shane Walker, 23, was believed to be bringing drugs to a jailed friend last week when he was foiled by corrections workers who heard bolt-cutters snapping the wire fence and apprehended him."

—*The National Post*

Only country in the Middle East without a desert: Lebanon.

MOON SCAM?

Is nothing sacred? Those conspiracy nuts won't leave anything alone. They attack our most sacred institutions. (On the other hand, they could be right.)

MOONSTRUCK

On July 20, 1969, millions of television viewers around the world watched as Neil Armstrong stepped down from a lunar landing module onto the surface of the moon and spoke the now famous words, "That's one small step for man, one giant leap for mankind."

In western Australia a woman named Una Ronald watched. She saw the images of the moon landing in the early hours of the morning. But as the camera showed Armstrong's fellow astronaut Edwin "Buzz" Aldrin demonstrating his moon walk technique, Ronald swears she saw something else. She swears she clearly saw a Coke bottle kicked into the picture from the side. The scene was edited out of later broadcasts, she says.

Was this alleged "blooper" evidence of a giant hoax?

MISSION IMPOSSIBLE

If Una Ronald was the first to suspect the moon landing wasn't quite what it appeared to be, she certainly wasn't the last. And there was a lot more than just the Coke bottle to excite skeptics.

Ten years before Apollo 11 supposedly went to the moon, Bill Kaysing was head of technical publications at Rocketdyne Systems, a division of Boeing that still makes rocket engines for the space program. In his book *We Never Went to the Moon*, Kaysing says that in 1959 Rocketdyne estimated that there was about a 14% chance we could safely send a man to the moon and back. According to Kaysing, there is no way the space program could have advanced enough in the following 10 years to send the three Apollo 11 astronauts to the moon, followed by five more moon landings in the next three years.

NASA experts recently admitted that they currently do not have the capability of sending manned missions to the moon. So how could they have done it more than 30 years ago? Even simulations these days require powerful computers, but the computer onboard the *Columbia* had a capacity smaller than many of today's handheld calculators.

Kaysing and others think they know the answer, and cite a number of anomalies that lead them to conclude that the Apollo missions were faked:

✔ **The Fluttering Flag:** In 1990 a New Jersey man named Ralph Rene was reviewing old footage of the moon landing. As he watched the American flag fluttering in the airless atmosphere of the moon, it suddenly dawned on him: how can there be a breeze if there is no air?

Rene's suspicions led him to research inconsistencies in the Moon landing story, and to publish a book called *NASA Mooned America*. The fluttering flag was just the beginning.

✔ **Phony Photos:** A close look at the thousands of excellent still photos from the moon landings reveal some very odd features. For one thing, they are a little too good. The astronauts seem to be well lit on all sides, regardless of where the sunlight is coming from, almost as if there were some artificial light source.

• Defenders claim that light was reflected from the lunar surface, bouncing back to light the shadow side of the astronauts. Oddly, that same reflective light does not illuminate the dark side of lunar rocks, which are even closer to the ground.

• Shadows seem to fall in different directions and look to be different lengths even for objects of a similar height, such as the two astronauts. This leads some to conclude that there were multiple light sources—possibly some man-made ones.

• Even when everything else is in shadow, the American flag and the words "United States" are always well lit, and sometimes seem to be in a spotlight. Was someone trying to squeeze extra PR value out of fake photos?

✔ **Starlight, Star Bright:** Some skeptics cite the absence of stars in photos of the lunar sky as evidence that they were not taken on the moon. After all, in the dark sky of the moon with no atmosphere, stars should be clearly visible.

• Experts agree—to the naked eye, stars in the sky of the moon *should* be magnificently clear. But, the experts say, *stars* wouldn't show up on film that was set to expose the much brighter lunar surface.

• On the other hand, why were there no pictures taken of the stars in the lunar sky? Surely how the stars look from the moon would have interested many people. Was it because astronomers could spot the fake photos too easily?

✔ **Where's the Dust?** One of the most memorable images NASA released from Apollo 11 was the imprint of Buzz Aldrin's boot in the lunar dust. But the lunar landing module apparently had less of an impact on the moon's surface.

• Moon photos show no visible disturbance from the high-powered thrust engines the *Eagle* landing module used to land, nor is there any dust in the landing pads.

• If the *Eagle* blew away all the dust, as some speculate, how did Aldrin make such a nice footprint?

✔ **Deadly Radiation:** In a recent press conference, a NASA spokesman said that radiation is one of the biggest obstacles to space travel. Wouldn't it have been a problem 30 years ago?

• Two doughnut-shaped rings of charged particles, called the Van Allen Belts, encircle the Earth. To get to the moon, astronauts would have had to pass through the belts, exposing themselves to deadly radiation unless they had a lot more protection than the thin shield the Apollo spacecraft provided.

• Once outside the radiation belts and Earth's protective atmosphere, astronauts would have been exposed to solar radiation. Expert opinions differ as to whether this exposure would have been life-threatening. But inexplicably, *not one* of the astronauts from the seven lunar missions got cancer, a well-known result of overexposure to radiation.

• Even more sensitive to radiation is photographic film. On all those beautiful moon photos there is absolutely no sign of radiation damage. Why not?

✔ **Follow the Bouncing Astronaut:** What about the movie footage showing the astronauts demonstrating the moon's low gravity by bouncing around the surface? Skeptics say that could have easily been faked. In the moon's gravity—a sixth of Earth's—the astronauts should have been able to leap 10 feet in the air. But they didn't.

• In fact, in the movie footage they don't get any farther off the

---

There are more than 90 different scientific theories on how dinosaurs became extinct.

ground than they could on Earth.

• And if it looks like they are moving in slow motion, that is because they are—half speed to be exact. Bill Wood, a scientist who worked for the NASA subcontractor responsible for recording Apollo signals and sending them to NASA headquarters in Houston, explains that the original film footage, shot at 30 frames per second, was transferred to video, which runs at 60 frames per second. If the film of the astronauts walking on the surface of the moon is viewed at regular speed their movements look remarkably normal.

✔ **Moon Rocks:** Besides the photos and film footage, the only physical evidence we have that astronauts actually went to the moon is lunar rocks.

• NASA points to the fact that scientists around the world have examined the rocks brought back by the Apollo missions and have no doubt that they originated on the moon. But the moon isn't the only place to find such rocks.

• In the ice of Antarctica, scientists have found remnants of lunar rocks blasted off the moon by meteoric impacts. Numerous expeditions have explored the continent for rock samples from the moon, Mars, and comets.

• In 1967, two years before the Apollo mission, such a group visited Antarctica, including ex-Nazi rocket scientist Wernher von Braun, by then working for NASA. Why would a rocket scientist be sent to look for rocks? Was he collecting fake evidence?

WHY FAKE IT?

These anomalies in the "information" given to the public about the Apollo moon missions have caused many to question whether we really did send anyone to the moon. But if the moon landings were faked, how was it done, and why?

The why is fairly easy to understand. The 1960s were the height of the Cold War. The Space Race was on, and the Soviet Union had already beat the United States by launching the first satellite to orbit Earth, the first man—and woman—in space, and the first space walk, among other important achievements. The United States was clearly behind. In 1961 President Kennedy issued a challenge: "I believe this nation should commit itself to achieving a goal, before this decade is out, of sending a man to the moon and

---

Mae West never kissed her leading men on screen.

returning him safely to the Earth."

The Apollo program was born, and five months before the end of the decade, NASA displayed pictures of Americans on the moon, proof that we had beat the Russians to the most important prize. We won. Mission accomplished.

But was it accomplished by actually sending men to the moon, or just making it look that way?

A Funny Thing Happened on the Way to the Moon

Investigative journalist Bart Sibrel claims to have found a mislabeled NASA film showing multiple "takes" of a scene shown to the public as part of the "live" broadcast of the Apollo 11 flight. In the footage the astronauts appear to be rehearsing the lines the public heard. Sibrel claims to have spent half a million dollars investigating the moon landings, and produced a video called *A Funny Thing Happened on the Way to the Moon.*

In 2002 Sibrel, backed by a Japanese film crew, confronted Buzz Aldrin outside a Beverly Hills hotel and challenged him to swear on a Bible that he had really gone to the moon. Aldrin responded by punching Sibrel in the face.

And what about those marvelous still photos? Many believe they were staged, perhaps in a secret location in Nevada, or even in a giant geodesic soundstage in Australia. Either way it would have been much easier to manipulate the lighting to get the results shown in the moon landing photos.

Would such a monstrous hoax have been easy to pull off? Certainly not. But to some people it seems more possible—and cheaper—than actually sending someone to the moon and back. Consider these statistics: Of the seven manned missions to the Moon, only Apollo 13 had trouble, which is an 86% success rate. In the years since, 25 unmanned craft have been sent to Mars. Only seven have succeeded—a 28% success rate. Which figure seems more realistic?

JUST WHEN YOU THOUGHT IT WAS SAFE

Before you get too comfortable with the idea that the government created a huge hoax because we couldn't have possibly gone to the moon, keep in mind that there are also people who believe the film *is* fake, but that we actually *did* go to the moon. So why fake it? To cover up what we *really* found there. But that's another story...

LIMERICKS

Limericks have been around since the 1700s. Here are a few of the more "respectable" ones that our BRI readers have sent in.

The one-eyed old painter McNeff
Was color-blind, palsied, and
    deaf;
When he asked to be touted
The critics all shouted:
"This is art, with a capital F!"

A certain young man of great
    gumption,
Among cannibals had the
    presumption
To go—but, alack!
He never came back.
A bona fide case of consumption.

An amoeba named Sam and his
    brother,
Were having a drink with each
    other;
In the midst of their quaffing
They split their sides laughing,
And each of them now is a
    mother.

There once was a fellow named
    Paul
Who went to a masquerade ball
Dressed up like a tree,
But he failed to foresee
His abuse by the dogs in the hall.

A cheerful old bear at the zoo
Could always find something to
    do.
When it bored him, you know,
To walk to and fro,
He reversed it and walked fro
    and to.

There was a faith-healer of Deal
Who said, "Although pain isn't
    real,
If I sit on a pin
And it punctures my skin,
I dislike what I think that I
    feel."

An amorous dentist named Moss,
Fell in love with the charming
    Miss Ross;
But he held in abhorrence
Her given name Florence,
So he called her his dear Dental
    Floss.

A man to whom illness was
    chronic,
When told that he needed a
    tonic,
Said, "Oh, Doctor, dear,
Won't you, please, make it beer?"
"No, no," said the doc, "that's
    Teutonic."

There was a young lady from
    Natchez
Who sat in some briar-wood
    patches.
Now she lies on her face
With an awful grimace
And scratches and scratches and
    scratches.

There was a young poet from
    Crewe,
Whose limericks stopped at line
    two.

Leprosy is the oldest documented infection—first described in Egypt in 1350 B.C.

NOT-SO-WISEGUYS

When people enter the federal government's Witness Protection Program they're supposed to hide, right?

WISEGUY: Henry Hill, a member of New York's Lucchese crime family and participant in the $5.8 million Lufthansa heist from New York's Kennedy Airport in 1978, the largest cash theft in U.S. history

IN THE PROGRAM: The Witness Protection Program relocated him to Redmond, Washington, in 1980, and Hill, who'd changed his name to Martin Lewis, was supposed to keep a low profile and stay out of trouble. He wasn't very good at either—in 1985 he and writer Nicholas Pileggi turned his mob exploits into the bestselling book *Wiseguy*, which became the hit movie *Goodfellas*.

WHAT HAPPENED: When the book became a bestseller, "Martin Lewis" couldn't resist telling friends and neighbors who he really was. Even worse, he reverted to his life of crime. Since 1980 Hill has racked up a string of arrests for crimes ranging from drunk driving to burglary and assault. In 1987 he tried to sell a pound of cocaine to two undercover Drug Enforcement officers, which got him thrown out of the Witness Protection Program for good.

"Henry couldn't go straight," says Deputy Marshal Bud McPherson. "He loved being a wiseguy. He didn't want to be anything else."

WISEGUY: Aladena "Jimmy the Weasel" Fratianno, Mafia hit man and acting head of the Los Angeles mob. When he entered the Witness Protection Program in 1977, Fratianno was the highest-ranking mobster ever to turn informer.

IN THE PROGRAM: Fratianno has another claim to fame: he is also the highest-paid witness in the history of the program. Between 1977 and 1987, he managed to get the feds to pay for his auto insurance, gas, telephone bills, real-estate taxes, monthly checks to his mother-in-law, and his wife's facelift and breast implants.

WHAT HAPPENED: The Justice Department feared the payments made the program look "like a pension fund for aging mobsters," so he was thrown out of the program in 1987. But by that time, Fratianno had already soaked U.S. taxpayers for an estimat-

---

Actors are called *thespians* after Thespis, the Greek founder of theater.

ed $951,326. "He was an expert at manipulating the system," McPherson said. Fratianno died in 1993.

WISEGUY: James Cardinali, a five-time murderer who testified against Gambino crime boss John Gotti at his 1987 murder trial. Gotti, nicknamed the "Teflon Don," beat the rap, but Cardinali still got to enter the Witness Protection Program after serving a reduced sentence for his own crimes. After his release, federal marshals gave him a new identity and relocated him to Oklahoma.

IN THE PROGRAM: Witnesses who get new identities aren't supposed to tell anyone who they really are, and when Cardinali slipped up and told his girlfriend in 1989, the program put him on a bus to Albuquerque, New Mexico, and told him to get lost.

But Cardinali wouldn't leave quietly. When he got to Albuquerque, he made signs that read "Mob Star Witness" and "Marked to Die by the Justice Department." Then, wearing the signs as a sandwich board, he marched back and forth in front of the federal courthouse, telling reporters he would continue his protest until he was let back into the program or murdered by mobsters, whichever came first. "If I get killed," Cardinali told reporters. "I want everybody to see what they do to you."

WHAT HAPPENED: Cardinali flew to Washington D.C. to appear on CNN's *Larry King Live*. But leaving the state violated his parole, so when he got back to New Mexico he was arrested, taken to jail...and released into the custody of the U.S. Marshals Service. Then he vanished. Did he embarrass the Witness Protection Program into letting him back in? The Marshals Service "will neither confirm nor deny" that he did.

WISEGUY: John Patrick Tully, convicted murderer and member of the Campisi crime family of Newark, New Jersey

IN THE PROGRAM: Tully served a reduced sentence for murder and entered the Witness Protection Program in the mid-1970s. By the early 1980s, he was living in Austin, Texas, where, as "Jack Johnson," he worked as a hot dog and fajita vendor. (It was a "nostalgic" choice—years earlier, he'd robbed a bank and used the money to buy a hot dog cart.)

Tully's business thrived, but he had repeated run-ins with the

---

In 1986 a guard in an armored car was killed when $50,000 worth of quarters fell on him.

police and was arrested numerous times for public intoxication and drunk driving. At some point the police figured out who "Mr. Johnson" really was and then, Tully alleges, they started harassing him.

WHAT HAPPENED: Tully fought back by publicly revealing his true identity. He wrapped himself—literally—in the American flag, and, standing on the steps of city hall with his seven-page rap sheet in one hand and a beer in the other, announced his entry in the 1991 race for mayor. His reasons for running: 1) As a reformed criminal he was a better candidate than typical politicians who "get into office and *then* start crooking," and 2) "If the police are going to hit me, they're going to have to hit me in the limelight."

Tully actually won 496 votes…but lost the race.

WISEGUY: Joseph "Joe Dogs" Iannuzzi, bookie, loan shark, and member of New York's Gambino crime family from 1974 to 1982

IN THE PROGRAM: Joe Dogs had a reputation for being an excellent cook—even in the mob. After turning State's evidence in 1982, he supported himself by opening a bagel shop in Florida.

Then in 1993 he wrote *The Mafia Cookbook.* How can someone in the Program promote a book? They can't—witnesses are forbidden from contact with the media, and Joe Dogs had to pass on several offers to appear on TV. But he was a huge fan of David Letterman, so when he was asked to appear on *The Late Show,* he agreed, even though he risked being thrown out of the program. Why would he take the chance? "Dave was my idol," Iannuzzi explained.

WHAT HAPPENED: It finally dawned on somebody at *The Late Show* that bringing a man marked for death by the mob into New York City and putting him on TV with Dave in front of a live studio audience might not be such a good idea. At the last minute, just as Joe Dogs was getting ready to cook Veal Marsala, show staffers told him his segment had been cancelled.

Iannuzzi was furious—according to some accounts he even threatened to "whack" Letterman. And although he never actually went on the show, the U.S. Marshals Service kicked him out of the Witness Protection Program anyway.

"What am I going to do now? Well," he told reporters, "I can always cook."

Duh! A hijacker took over a public bus in Argentina—and insisted on being driven to Cuba.

BEHIND THE HITS

Ever wonder what inspired some of your favorite songs?
Here are a few inside stories about popular tunes.

The Artist: Santana
The Song: "Smooth" (1999)
The Story: One night in 1997, Rob Thomas, lead singer of Matchbox 20, had a dream: he was on the cover of *Rolling Stone* shouting something into the ear of one of his musical heroes, guitar legend Carlos Santana. A month later, Thomas was invited by R&B composer Itaal Shur to contribute a song to Santana's next album. Thomas was thrilled.

They wrote a song (inspired by Thomas's wife, Marisol Maldonado) and sent a rough demo tape to Santana. Thomas recommended English pop star George Michael for the vocals, but Santana liked what he heard on the demo, "I believe it when he sings." So Thomas flew to San Francisco to meet his idol and record the song.

"Smooth" was Santana's first #1 song ever (it was on top for 12 weeks in 1999), was his first to reach the top 10 in 30 years, earned Thomas BMI's Pop Songwriter of the Year award, and won nine Grammies. (Santana made the cover of Rolling Stone in March, 2000...without Thomas.)

The Artist: The Charlie Daniels Band
The Song: "The Devil Went Down to Georgia" (1979)
The Story: Starting his music career in 1959, virtuoso fiddle player Charlie Daniels had enjoyed moderate success as a session musician and songwriter. He was known in music circles but the Charlie Daniels Band couldn't get much radio airplay—he was too country for rock stations, too hard rock for country stations.

In 1979 Daniels decided to write the "ultimate fiddle song." While brainstorming for ideas, he remembered a Stephen Vincent Benet poem he had learned in school called "The Mountain Whippoorwill." In the poem, Hill-Billy Jim enters a fiddlin' contest and then "all hell breaks loose in Georgia."

Daniels modernized the words, but went into the studio with-

Mark Twain invented a Trivial Pursuit–like game called "Mark Twain's Memory-Builder."

out any music. Armed with only a poem about a boy who beats the devil, Daniels and his band did something just as improbable—they created a hit right there on the spot.

The record company knew it, too, and released it as a single. Result: The song was a hit on country *and* rock radio stations, turned Daniels into a star, and was named the Country Music Association's Single of the Year for 1979.

The Artist: Tag Team
The Song: "Whoomp! (There it is)" (1993)
The Story: Cecil "DC, the Brain Supreme" Glenn was a DJ at Atlanta's Magic City nightclub. He dreamed of producing a hit rap record. One night he heard another DJ chanting into the mike, "Whoomp! There it is!" When Glenn saw the nightclub crowd's unified response, he knew that was his hit. So he and his best friend, Steve "Roll'n" Gibson, wrote and recorded a song around the phrase.

The song was a hit at the club, but they couldn't sell it to a major label. So they borrowed $2,500 to press the record themselves and founded a small label called Bellmark Records to distribute it. The song took off immediately, hitting the Billboard Top 10 and has been a staple at sports arenas ever since.

Close Call: Another rap group, 95 South, recorded "Whoot, There It Is" and actually released it a month earlier. So why did Tag Team's song hit the big time and not 95 South's? According to *Rolling Stone*'s Tracy Hopkins, "Tag Team's version had more crossover appeal. 95 South's chorus of 'Tell me where the booty at/Whoot, there it is!' was just too raunchy."

The Artist: Julia Ward Howe
The Song: "Battle Hymn of the Republic" (1862)
The Story: At the onset of the Civil War, Howe was riding through the streets of Washington, D.C., with her husband one warm summer night, watching Union troops prepare for battle. One group of men was sitting outside an inn singing a sad Southern folk song that began "John Brown's body lies amouldering in the grave." Howe couldn't sleep that night. She couldn't get the tune out of her head. So she tried to think about more uplifting words, and out came:

> Mine eyes have seen the glory of the coming of the Lord;
> He is trampling out the vintage where the grapes of wrath are
>   stored...

Inspired, she got out of bed and stayed up all night finishing the lyrics. A few days later, Howe brought the lyrics to her friend James T. Fields, the editor of *Atlantic Monthly*. He featured the song in the magazine, where it caught the eye of President Lincoln. Lincoln loved it so much that he adopted "Battle Hymn of the Republic" as the theme song of the Union army.

Double Irony: "John Brown's Body" was a Southern folk song, but its melody was used to rally the Northern troops. "Dixie," the theme song adopted by Confederate troops, was written by a northerner, Daniel Decatur Emmett, who had never even visited the South.

The Artist: Bob Dylan

The Song: "Like a Rolling Stone" (1965)

The Story: Bob Dylan was fed up with the music business—he was tired of the grueling road schedule, shady promoters, and pressure to keep churning out hit after hit. So in 1965 he hid away in a little cabin in Woodstock, New York, to regroup. He recounted his experience in the book *Bob Dylan: Behind the Shades*.

> I'd literally quit playing and singing, and I found myself writing this song, this story, this long piece of vomit about twenty pages long, and out of it I took "Like a Rolling Stone."...The first two lines, which rhymed "kiddin' you" with "didn't you" just knocked me out.

Dylan was so impressed with the song that he came out of hiding to record it. It was the first single from his seminal album *Highway 61 Revisited* and began the second chapter of his legendary career. Not only was it Dylan's first top 10 hit, peaking at #2, but it was also the first song over six minutes long to reach the Billboard Top 40.

*   *   *

CELEBRITY GOSSIP

O. J. Simpson was originally cast for the title role in the movie *The Terminator* but was ultimately rejected because, according to a studio executive, "People would never have believed a nice guy like O. J. could play the part of a ruthless killer."

Cyndi Lauper's 1984 hit "Girls Just Want to Have Fun" was written by a man.

DIVORCE, PROSPECTOR-STYLE

*When our friend Jeff Cheek dug up this nugget
and asked us to assay its value for bathroom
reading, we said, "Eureka! It's a gold mine!"*

YOU'RE ALL MINE
John Howard was a prospector in Colorado in the 1860s.
When his wife, Mary E. Howard, sued for divorce, John did not contest it. He was unfamiliar with civil law but as a prospector, was well-versed in mining laws. So to make sure that he was completely free of his former wife (and maybe to get a laugh), he sent the Denver City Court of Chancery a "quit-claim" deed to his wife. And he courteously left a blank space for any future husband to fill in his name, if Mary ever remarried.

To the Plaintiff in the above entitled action:

Know all them (and one woman) by these presents, that I, John Howard, of Canon City, of the first part, do hereby give, grant, bargain, convey, and quit-claim, all my right, title and interest in the following (un) real estate, to wit:

The undivided whole of that ancient estate known as Mary Howard (the title of which I acquired by discovery, occupancy, possession and use), situated at present in the town of Denver, Jefferson Territory, together with all the improvements made and erected by me whereon, with all the rents, profits, easements, enjoyments, long suffering and appurtenances thereto in anywise appertaining, unto _____ of the second part, to have and to hold unto the said _____ so long as he can keep her, without recourse upon the grantor or endorser.

In testimony whereof, I have hereunto set my hand, and seal, this, the 24th of January 1861.

Signed, JOHN HOWARD
Signed in the presence of A. Rudd, Clerk of District Court

(No word on whether Mrs. Howard was a gold digger.)

Most toilets flush in E flat; most electric razors buzz in B flat. (English razors buzz in G.)

Q & A: ASK
THE EXPERTS

*More random questions, with answers
from the nation's top trivia experts.*

OH, DO I HAVE A HEADACHE

Q: *How do woodpeckers avoid brain damage after hitting their heads against trees all day?*

A: "The force generated by the woodpecker pecking does not pass through its braincase—it travels along the bird's upper jaw, which connects below the brain and allows shock to dissipate throughout the bird's entire body. Naturally, some of the blow does reverberate back into the cranium, but since the woodpecker's brain surface area is relatively large, the impact is absorbed as a slap, not a punch. And because the avian skull fits tightly around its bird brain—like a bicycle helmet—it prevents internal bruising. Every bit of cushioning helps: According to experts, the acceleration force felt by a common acorn woodpecker measures between 600 and 1,200 g's—enough that its eyeballs would literally pop out on impact if it didn't blink." (From *The Wild File*, by Brad Wetzler)

A MARK OF DE-STINK-SHUN

Q: *Why does sweat leave a yellowish stain?*

A: "The most likely culprits are body secretions called apocrine sweat and sebum, the oily secretion of the sebaceous glands, although deodorants and antiperspirants may also play a role.

"The underarms are rich in apocrine sweat glands, which produce milky secretions. Apocrine sweat contains many chemicals, including the acidic substances that produce underarm odor.

"The sebaceous glands are usually associated with hair follicles. Cells filled with fatty droplets die and burst, providing lubrication for the skin and hair. When the oils are exposed to air, they oxidize, turning yellowish, and if not quickly removed by laundering, they can permanently yellow clothing. Sebaceous glands at the back of the neck cause 'ring around the collar.'" (From *The N.Y. Times Second Book of Science Questions and Answers*, by Claiborne Ray)

Be careful! Every 45 seconds, a house catches fire in the United States.

THE ANSWER IS BLOWIN' IN THE WIND

Q: *Where does wind come from?*

A: "Wind is the movement of a mass of air, caused by differences in pressure in the atmosphere. A wind always flows from a high- to a low-pressure area, trying to equal out the pressure. Picture the air in a balloon, which is at higher pressure than the air outside. Puncture it: the air rushes out, from the high to the low area of pressure.

"Over the equator is a band of low pressure, and over each of the poles is a band of high pressure. There are alternating bands of high and low pressure over the rest of the planet, and they control wind direction. These patterns, and the effect of the Earth spinning on its axis, create winds which blow east and west, not north and south." (From *What Makes the World Go Round?*, by Jinny Johnson)

LOSE YOUR BLUES

Q: *How does bleach get clothes white?*

A: "Most laundry bleaches are oxidizing agents. In the washing machine they release free-roving molecules of sodium hypochlorite or peroxide. The color of a stain or spot is made up of a group of atoms and molecules linked together by a pattern of double and single bonds. The oxidizing agent tears into those bonds, destroying the bond pattern and fading the color or changing it completely to white. The stain is still there, albeit invisible, until detergent and the agitation of the machine lift most of it off.

"Fabric colors are also made up of bonds, so if you add bleach to clothes that aren't colorfast—you'll notice that the colors you liked might also become invisible." (From *More How Do They Do That?*, by Caroline Sutton and Kevin Markey)

USELESS INFORMATION

Q: *Why do our palms sweat when we get nervous?*

A: "Palms sweat very easily—they contain more sweat glands than other parts of the body. The reason may go back to the days when our ancestors climbed trees to escape danger. Fear of the danger activated the sweat glands, making the palms moist, and this moisture provided our ancestors with a better climbing grip. As in the case of goose bumps and body hair, sweaty palms no longer serve the same purpose but are still with us even after millions of years of evolution." (From *Ever Wonder Why?*, by Douglas Smith)

Q: What percent of a dime is silver? A: 0%

CHICKEN NUGGETS

Question: What looks like a chicken, squawks like a chicken, and walks like a chicken? Don't know? Answer: a chicken. (And we thought the chicken was dumb.)

STICKIN' CHICKENS

What do you do when a hen won't lay eggs? Try acupuncture! That's what researchers in Taiwan have been doing to hens who have turned "broody" (which means they would rather hatch an egg than lay another). A needle is inserted between the nostrils of the hen's beak, and left there for two days. Apparently the treatment works—it "cures" the hen of the desire to hatch her eggs.

TV DINNERS

"Battery" (egg-laying) hens get depressed and angry. Who can blame them—they spend their entire lives in tiny cages, where they're expected to lay 300 eggs a year. Researchers in Scotland decided to look for a way to make these hens' lives happier. So did they let the birds roam free? No. Scientists at the Roslin Institute introduced the hens to TV. Now they're addicted. Whenever the television is turned on, they sit, mesmerized. Their favorite viewing: screen-saver images of flying toasters and schools of fish that move slowly across the screen.

SINGING SUPPER

A rural New Zealand woman and her friend were waiting for their dinner to finish cooking when they heard something that sounded like a chicken squawking. They looked around outside, but there wasn't a fowl in sight. They suddenly realized the noise was coming from *inside* the house. They followed the cries into the woman's kitchen. The noise was coming from the oven. When she looked inside, she saw that steam was pouring out of the roasting chicken's neck. The chicken was long dead, but as the steam passed over the bird's intact vocal chords, it caused them to vibrate. The woman and her friend turned off the oven and became vegetarians for the night, having cheese and lettuce sandwiches for dinner.

Rah-rah-rah! In 1898 all cheerleaders were male. Now 3% are.

COMIC RELIEF, TOO

More funny lines from funny people.

"I don't see the point of testing cosmetics on rabbits, because they're already cute."
—**Rich Hall**

"My wife's an earth sign. I'm a water sign. Together we make mud."
—**Henny Youngman**

"When authorities warn you of the sinfulness of sex, there is an important lesson to be learned: Do not have sex with the authorities."
—**Matt Groening**

"How come if you mix flour and water together you get glue? And when you add eggs and sugar, you get a cake? Where does the glue go?"
—**Rita Rudner**

"Contraceptives should be used on every conceivable occasion."
—**Spike Milligan**

"My wife asked for plastic surgery; I cut up her credit cards."
—**Rodney Dangerfield**

"Never moon a werewolf."
—**Mike Binder**

"Mario Andretti has retired from racecar driving. He's getting old. He ran his entire last race with his left blinker on."
—**Jon Stewart**

"I buy books on suicide at bookstores. You can't get them at the library, because people don't return them."
—**Kevin Nealon**

"My mother breast-fed me with powdered milk. It was my first do-it-yourself project."
—**Buzz Nutley**

"I like to leave a message before the beep."
—**Steven Wright**

"Of course we need firearms. You never know when some nut is going to come up to you and say something like, 'You're fired.' You gotta be ready."
—**Dave Attell**

"I wonder if the Buddha was married...his wife would say, 'Are you just going to sit around like that all day?'"
—**Garry Shandling**

HOW TO COOK A PORCUPINE

No kidding—this recipe is real. The next time your dinner party guests ask where you got your recipe for a large rodent with quills, tell them you found it...in the bathroom.

INGREDIENTS:

1 porcupine
1 stalk of celery
1 medium yellow onion, sliced

2 medium carrots, sliced
1/4 tsp. pepper
1 tsp salt
1 bay leaf

COOKING INSTRUCTIONS

1. Find, catch, kill, skin, and *dress* the porcupine. (Dress means clean the animal by removing the guts). Good luck! Watch out for the quills, and be sure to wear gloves—game animals carry *tularemia*, a fever-causing disease that can be spread to humans.

2. Hang the porcupine in a cool, dry place for 48 hours, preferably in your garage or someplace where you won't mind the smell.

3. Place the porcupine in a bath of salted water. Soak in the refrigerator overnight.

4. Bring water and porcupine to a boil. Discard water. Immerse porcupine in fresh, cool water, bring to boil again. Discard water again.

5. Remove meat from porcupine. Chop into small pieces and place in a large pot or dutch oven. Add 3 cups of water or porcupine stock, celery, onions, carrots, pepper, salt, and bay leaf. Simmer until the meat is tender, 2-1/2 hours if the porcupine is young, longer if it is older. Be sure the meat is cooked through—game animals can also harbor the parasitic disease *trichinosis*.

6. Remove bay leaf.

Serves 4-6

Note: In *Uncle John's Ahh-Inspiring Bathroom Reader* we brought you a recipe for shrunken heads. This year, it's porcupines. Who knows what we'll cook up next year?

Hard heads: There are more than 600 stone statues on Easter Island.

BETS YOU CAN'T LOSE

*BRI stalwart Rhys Rounds often challenges us to some friendly
"contests of skill"...and he beats us every time. So for
revenge, we're passing along a few of his secrets.*

I'LL BET... "I can make you say the word 'black.'"
SETUP: Start asking your mark the colors of various objects
in the room, making sure that none of them are black or blue.
After three or four objects, ask "What are the colors of the American flag?"
PAYOFF: When they respond, "Red, white, and blue," you say, "I
win! I told you I could make you say 'blue'!" Nine times out of ten
they'll come back with, "You didn't say *blue*, you said *black*." Then
you say, "Now I really do win!'"

I'LL BET... "I can make you say what I want you to."
SETUP: When the other person agrees to the bet, tell them to
say "multifarious verbiage."
PAYOFF: When they say that they won't or that they don't know
what that means, you've won the bet. Why? To say multifarious
verbiage means to say a variety of words...which they've just done.

I'LL BET... "I can roll the cue ball underneath a cue stick without holding it and without the ball touching the stick."
SETUP: To demonstrate the difficulty, place the cue stick over
the two long side rails of the pool table. Then have the sucker try
to roll the cue ball underneath the stick, which they won't be able
to do—the space between the stick and the tabletop is too small.
PAYOFF: But *you* can do it. Pick up the cue ball, put it on the
floor under the table, and roll it underneath the table so it passes
below the cue stick above. It will never touch the stick.

I'LL BET... "You can't lift my hand off the top of my head."
SETUP: Put your palm on the top of your head and instruct the
person to try to remove it by pushing up on your forearm. It works
best when a smaller person challenges a bigger, stronger person.
PAYOFF: They won't be able to. We're not sure why; it's one of

those freaks of nature (not you, the trick).

I'LL BET... "I can remove this quarter from underneath this napkin without touching the napkin or blowing on it."
SETUP: Put a quarter under a napkin. After you've set up the trick, discreetly put another quarter into your hand. Then put that hand underneath the table, say some magical incantations, and after a moment, reveal that the quarter is magically in your hand!
PAYOFF: The person will most likely go straight for the napkin to prove you wrong. When they remove it, pick up the quarter and you've won the bet.

I'LL BET... "You can't taste the difference between an apple and a raw potato if you close your eyes and plug your nose."
SETUP: The best way to ensure success with this one is to make them try it three times. Just once is a 50/50 guess. Three times puts the odds in your favor.
PAYOFF: It's not really a trick. According to experts, smell and sight are more important in tasting things than most people realize. Without those two senses, the tastebuds don't have enough info to send to the brain.

I'LL BET... "You can't eat eight saltines in 60 seconds."
SETUP: Make sure that you stipulate the person isn't allowed to wash them down with anything—and that they have to eat them one by one.
PAYOFF: Because of the saltiness of the crackers, most people will get "cotton mouth" and not be able to eat more than five or six. Don't wager too much, though, because there is the occasional big mouth that can pull this one off. But at least you've gotten them to make a fool of themselves.

I'LL BET... "I can jump higher than this house."
SETUP: Just jump up in the air six inches or so.
PAYOFF: You've just jumped higher than any house ever could.

Kangaroos can't walk.

THE WORST BUSINESS DECISION IN U.S. HISTORY

*The worst decision in history? A bold claim, especially when
you consider how many bad decisions people make every day
(except Uncle John). Still, have you driven a Daisy lately?
No, and you never will, either. Here's why.*

TILTING AT WINDMILLS

In the early 1880s, a Plymouth, Michigan, watch repairman named Clarence J. Hamilton came up with the idea of making windmills from metal instead of wood. Farmers used windmills to pump water for crop irrigation, and in those days most of them built the windmills themselves. Hamilton thought that if he could design a better, sturdier windmill made from iron and sell it at a low enough price, farmers would line up to buy them. So in 1882 the Plymouth Iron Windmill Company opened for business.

It turns out Hamilton was wrong—farmers in the 1880s were loathe to spend money on anything they could make themselves, even if his iron windmills were better. After six years in business, the Plymouth Iron Windmill Company was still struggling, so Hamilton invented something else that he thought would help boost windmill sales: a toy rifle that used compressed air to shoot industrial ball bearings —"BBs" for short—instead of bullets. It wasn't the first BB gun ever invented, but this one was made of metal, which made it sturdier and a better shot than competing guns, which were made of wood. His idea was to give a free BB gun to every farmer who bought a windmill.

FLOWER POWER

Hamilton showed the air rifle to the company's general manager, Lewis Cass Hough, who shot at the trash can in his office and then went outside and shot an old shingle from 10 feet away. "Boy!" he said. "That's a daisy!" The name stuck…but Hamilton's idea of giving away free BB guns with every windmill didn't— farmers wanted the guns, not the windmills. So the Plymouth Iron Windmill Co. changed its name to the Daisy Manufacturing Co. and started making BB guns full time.

The city of Tsuenchen, China, was designed to resemble a carp when viewed from above.

BB KING

In 1891 Lewis Hough hired his nephew Charles Bennett and made him Daisy's first salesman. Smart move. Thanks to Bennett's hard work, by the turn of the century, Daisy was manufacturing 250,000 air rifles a year.

By 1903 Bennett was president of the company and a pillar of the Plymouth business community. To celebrate his success, that spring he made a trip into nearby Detroit to buy an Oldsmobile, the hottest-selling car in the country.

But before he took his test drive, Bennett happened to stop at a tailor shop to buy a suit, and while there he mentioned he was going to buy a car. A man named Frank Malcomson happened to overhear him, and as Bennett was leaving, Malcomson introduced himself. He explained that his cousin, coal merchant Alex Malcomson, had started his own auto company with the help of a business partner. So far they'd managed to build only one test car, but Malcomson told Bennett that he should really take a ride in his cousin's car before he signed the papers on the Oldsmobile. Bennett agreed to go for a ride that very afternoon.

About an hour later, Alex Malcomson's business partner, a relatively unknown engineer named Henry Ford, pulled up in the test car, which he called the Model A. Bennett hopped in, they went for a drive, and by the time they were through, Bennett had given up his plans to buy an Oldsmobile. The Model A was a better car, he told Ford, and he was willing to wait until it came on the market.

But how long would that take? And how much would it cost? Ford said he wasn't sure and that Alex Malcomson was a better person to ask. So he drove Bennett to Malcomson's office, dropped him off, and then sped off to parts unknown. "He probably had someone else that he was taking for a ride," Bennett reminisced many years later.

RISKY BUSINESS

Would the Model A ever come to market at all? The *car* may have been impressive, but the company behind it, if it could even be called a company, was a mess. Ford & Malcomson, soon to evolve into the Ford Motor Company, was having trouble coming up with the cash it needed to begin production. Henry Ford deserved a lot of the blame: in less than two years he'd wrecked one auto company and gotten himself thrown out of another. He had a bad habit of sneaking off to tinker on race cars when he should have been designing regular cars to sell to the public. And in the process he'd burned through nearly $90,000 of his investors' money—about $1.8 million today—while managing to build only about a dozen cars.

Malcomson was hardly better. He was the largest coal dealer in the area, but he'd built up his business by borrowing huge sums of money from nearly every banker in Detroit. He was so overextended, in fact, that he had to hide his interest in the Ford company so that his bankers wouldn't know what he was up to.

When Ford and Malcomson made the rounds of Detroit's wealthiest investors to raise funds for yet another auto company, few took them seriously. The two men were reduced to cajoling money out of relatives, suppliers, Malcomson's attorneys, his coal company employees, his landlord, and anyone else they could think of…including Charles Bennett.

DEAL OF A LIFETIME

When Bennett went into Malcomson's office to talk about buying a car, Malcomson offered him a chance to buy a stake in the company. A *huge* stake in the company. Reports vary as to exactly how much he was offered, but it was at least 25% and may have been as much as 50%—for as little as $75,000.

A 50% stake would have made Bennett the largest individual shareholder, with Ford, Malcomson, and the others dividing up the other 50%. Bringing Bennett into Ford made a lot of business sense: Associating with such a successful businessman would make the Ford Motor Company seem viable, too, making it easier to attract other investors and to borrow money from bankers no longer willing to lend money to Malcomson alone.

Bennett knew a good product when he saw one, and he wanted in. There was only one thing stopping him—he didn't have $75,000. But the Daisy Manufacturing Company did. So when he got back to Plymouth, Bennett told his business partner Ed Hough (Lewis Hough's son) that he was going to invest some of Daisy's money in a car company.

SLOW DOWN, PARDNER

That was when Daisy's attorneys informed Bennett that the company charter forbade investing its funds in other companies. The reasoning was logical. What would happen if Ford & Malcomson went under like so many other auto companies had? Daisy would lose its investment. And if it merged with the automaker (another idea Bennett was toying with), it might even have to make good on that company's losses. Besides—kids were always going to want BB guns for Christmas. Would anyone still be interested in automobiles five years from now? Maybe cars were just a fad.

"Bennett's fellow directors at Daisy balked at the proposal, on the grounds that there was no reason to diversify from air rifles into something as whimsical as the automobile," writes Douglas Brinkley in *Wheels for the World*.

THANKS, BUT NO THANKS

Bennett tried everything he could think of to get Daisy's directors to agree to invest in the auto company, but nothing worked—and Daisy never did buy in. Instead of getting half of the company, Bennett had to settle for buying a 3.3% stake for $5,000, which was all he could personally afford.

To be fair, there's a good chance that even if Daisy had been willing to buy half of what would soon become the Ford Motor Company, Henry Ford might not have allowed it. Ford was determined to be his own boss, and when the investors in his earlier auto companies tried to assert themselves, he just walked away, leaving them holding the bag. That as much as anything had caused him to fail. It's questionable whether he would have allowed anyone other than himself to own such a huge stake in the new company.

Plus, there was talk that if Daisy got involved with the new company, Bennett might want to give a BB gun away with each car sold, or even worse, that he would insist the new car be called a Daisy. According to Brinkley, Henry Ford "was not about to see his latest creation named after a flower or a gun."

DUMB DECISION #2

Bennett owned 3.3% of Ford, so when the company introduced the Model T in 1908 and grew into the largest auto manufacturer

on Earth, Bennett became stinking rich, right? Wrong. After he
and Malcomson took sides against Henry Ford in a power struggle
(never a good idea) and lost, Bennett sold his Ford shares. That
was in 1907—the year *before* the Model T changed the world.
Bennett got $35,000 for his shares.

GO AHEAD AND CRY
Had Bennett held onto his 3.3% stake in the Ford Motor Company until 1919—for 12 more years—when Henry Ford bought out
the last of the other shareholders and assumed full ownership, he
would have earned $4,750,000 ($47 million today) in dividends.
His stock would have been worth $12.5 million ($123 million
today). Not a bad return on a $5,000 investment.

Had Daisy bought 50% of the company in 1903 (and had
Henry Ford not run the company into the ground, as he had done
with earlier ventures when he wasn't allowed to call the shots),
their half of the Ford Motor Company would have been worth at
least $125 million ($1.24 *billion* today), and possibly as much as
$500 million ($4.95 *billion* today).

"The original investors in the Ford Motor Company had received
the largest return on risk capital in recorded business history,"
Robert Lacey writes in *Ford: The Men and the Machine*. Thanks to
one bad decision, Daisy's investors didn't get a penny of it.

*   *   *

SMART CROOKS (for a change)
How do you make sure the police won't interrupt your burglary?
Fix it so they can't even leave their headquarters. That's what
happened in 2001 in the Dutch town of Stadskanaal. Thieves simply padlocked the front gates of the high fence that surrounds the
police compound, then robbed a nearby electronics store. That set
off a burglar alarm in the police station, but there was nothing
police could do about it—they were all locked in. As the crooks
made off with TVs and camcorders, Stadskanaal cops had to sit
and wait for reinforcements to arrive from the next town. A police
spokesman said, "It's a pity all our officers were at that moment in
the police station. Normally most of them are on patrol." They've
since taken precautions to make certain it never happens again.

URBAN LEGENDS

*Hey—did you hear about the girl who needed to get a tan
in just three days? Urban legends seem to be true...but
are they really? Here are a few we've looked into.*

LEGEND: McDonald's purchases cow eyeballs from a company called "100% Beef," and adds them as filler to Big Mac patties, claiming they are "100% beef patties."

HOW IT SPREAD: By word of mouth, probably for as long as McDonald's has dominated the American fast food industry. In the very first *Bathroom Reader*, we wrote about a similar claim (false) that McDonald's uses worms as ground-beef filler.

THE TRUTH: McDonald's *doesn't* add cow eyeballs to hamburgers or use them as a thickener in its milkshakes (another legend). For one thing, the U.S. Department of Agriculture regulates the usage of the term "100% beef." Theoretically, companies can't use it unless their patties really are what they claim to be. Plus, if you think about it, every cow that ends up as beef consists of hundreds of pounds of meat, while two eyeballs weigh less than a Quarter Pounder. Even if McDonald's had wanted to add cow eyeballs to its beef patties (it doesn't) and such a thing were legal (it isn't), there simply aren't enough of them to taint that much meat.

LEGEND: A sorority girl wants a dark tan for a formal dance that's just a few days away. She goes to a tanning salon, and they tell her she can't stay under the lamps for more than 30 minutes because any more would be unsafe. You can't get a dark tan in 30 minutes, so she spends the next two days traveling to every tanning salon in town, spending 30 minutes in each.

She gets a beautiful tan and looks great at the formal...but the next morning her sorority sisters find her dead in her room with smoke billowing out of her eyes, ears, and mouth. An autopsy reveals that the tanning rays had cooked her body from the inside out, like a burrito in a microwave oven.

HOW IT SPREAD: Like wildfire—the tale first appeared in 1987 and was repeated all over the country. Sometimes the victim is a bride-to-be, sometimes she's a high-school girl getting ready for her prom. And she doesn't always die—sometimes she is permanently blinded or has to have a "fried" arm or leg amputated. It was one of the most popular—and most widely believed—urban legends of the 1980s.

THE TRUTH: The story is not only false, it's also scientifically impossible. Yes, tanning rays are dangerous—overexposure can cause sunburns, skin cancer, cataracts, and other problems. But tanning beds don't cook the human body from the inside out. This story features two traditional urban legend themes: fear of new technology and excessive vanity that is punished by fate.

LIFE IMITATES URBAN LEGEND! In May 1989, two years after the first broiled-girl rumors started, a woman named Patsy Campbell actually did die from burns received after spending just 25 minutes in a tanning bed. Campbell, who had been taking medication that made her skin very sensitive to light, was the first and so far only person ever to receive fatal burns in a tanning bed.

LEGEND: A young couple gets married. The reception is held at the bride's grandmother's house, and they continue a family tradition of playing a game of hide-and-seek. When it's the bride's turn to hide, she disappears. After hours of searching, they still can't find her. They finally call the police to assist in the search…but she is never found.

Years later the bride's sister gets married and despite the tragedy, hide-and-seek is played again. The sister decides to hide in a large steamer trunk in the attic and when she pops it open, she finds the dead body of her long-lost sister—who suffocated when the trunk lid slammed shut and locked her in—still in her wedding gown.

HOW IT SPREAD: Word of mouth…for almost 300 years. In the 1830s, Thomas Haynes Bayly wrote *The Ballad of The Mistletoe Bride*:

> At length an oak chest, that had long lain hid,
> Was found in the castle—they raised the lid,
> A skeleton form lay mouldering there
> In the bridal wreath of that lady fair!
> O, sad was her fate! in sportive jest
> She hid from her lord in the old oak chest.
> It closed with a spring! and, dreadful doom,
> The bride lay clasped in her living tomb!

THE TRUTH: It never happened.

SIMPLE SOLUTIONS

How often have you seen a clever solution to a difficult problem and said, "That's so obvious—I wish I'd thought of that!" Here are some simple, but brilliant, inventions that could change the world.

MONEYMAKER-PLUS

Problem: How can people irrigate crops in impoverished parts of the world? With electric pumps? Nope—electricity is often nonexistent, and where it is available it's too expensive for poor farmers.

Simple Solution: A foot-powered irrigation pump

Explanation: Approtec, a nonprofit company in Nairobi, Kenya, calls it the MoneyMaker-Plus. Working the pedals like a stair-climbing exercise machine, one person can pull water from a stream, a pond, or a well 20 feet deep, send it to sprinklers, and irrigate up to one and a half acres a day. In underdeveloped countries, such a device can be life-changing. As of 2002, Approtec estimates that 24,000 MoneyMaker-Plus pumps were in use, bringing an average of $1,400 a year more to people who previously earned less than $100 a year. The pumps helped create 16,000 new jobs and generate $30 million a year total in profits and wages. They're made from local materials (creating more jobs), they're easily repaired without special tools, they're lightweight for easy transport (25 pounds), and most importantly, they're affordable—they cost only $38.

ANTI–CELL PHONE SANDWICH

Problem: How can people effectively, cheaply—and legally—stop the ringing of cell phones in designated cell phone–free zones?

Simple Solution: Wall panels that jam cell phone signals

Explanation: Electronic jamming of cell phone transmissions is illegal in the United States, but Hideo Oka and fellow engineers at Japan's Iwate University figured out a way around that—they invented a nonelectronic method. The system consists of a layer of magnetic material (they use nickel zinc ferrite) sandwiched between two thin layers of wood. It looks like 3/8-inch wood pan-

---

Only two books in the Bible are named for women: Ruth and Esther.

eling. The nickel-zinc ferrite interferes with the electromagnetic waves that cell phones rely on. That means that theaters or restaurants or homeowners can use it to build "cell-free" zones. Oka believes he can find a way to manufacture the device with recycled materials, which would make it very affordable. Naturally, the cell phone industry isn't happy—observers say a legal battle is looming.

STAR

Problem: Arsenic in drinking water. Scientists say that naturally occurring contamination of groundwater in some developing countries causes as many as 200,000 deaths a year. How can people without access to high-tech filters or water-treatment plants make their water safe to drink?

Simple Solution: STAR, a patented—and remarkably cheap—filtration system

Explanation: In 2001, Xiaoguang Meng and George Korfiatis, scientists at the Stevens Institute of Technology, successfully tested a system that consisted of two buckets, some sand, and a tea-bag-sized packet of iron-based powder. This filter reduces arsenic levels in well water from 650 parts per billion (deadly) to 10ppb, the level recommended by the World Health Organization. Cost per family: $2 a year.

KENYA CERAMIC JIKO (KCJ)

Problem: In Kenya, most families use small metal charcoal-burning stoves—called *jikos*—for cooking. But they're terribly inefficient. And with the cost of wood and wood-based charcoal skyrocketing, how can people afford to cook for their families?

Simple Solution: The highly efficient Kenya Ceramic Jiko stove

Explanation: The KCJ is a small, hourglass-shaped metal stove with a ceramic lining in its top half. It uses up to 50% less fuel—saving the average family more than $60 a year. The manufacturer, KENGO (Kenya Energy and Environment Organization), has held workshops all over the country, demonstrating how the stoves work and even teaching villagers how to set up shops to make them. (Several women's groups make the ceramic linings.) The KCJ burns cleaner, reducing emissions, and costs only $3.

Q: How can you tell when a platypus feels threatened? A: It growls.

WHAT'S THE NUMBER FOR 911?

*Another installment of some of our favorite 911 calls
from Leland Gregory's book,* What's the Number
for 911 Again? *Believe it or not, they're all real.*

Recorded during a power outage.
Dispatcher: "911. Fire or emergency?"
Caller: "My power's out!"
Dispatcher: "Yes, sir, we're aware of that. Do you have an emergency?"
Caller: "No, I don't have a damn emergency. I just want to know if I'm going to be getting a rebate for the length of time I'm without power."
Dispatcher: "Uhhh, no, sir, you won't be charged for the electricity you *didn't* use."
Caller: "Well, that's more like it!"

Dispatcher: "911. What's the address of your emergency?"
Caller: "I need to know what I can do about someone who came into my home and put boogers on my wall."
Dispatcher: "Did you invite this person into your home?"
Caller: "Yes, but I didn't give him permission to put boogers on the walls."

Dispatcher: "911. What's the address of your emergency?"
Citizen: [no response]
Dispatcher: "911. What's the address of your emergency?"
Citizen [tentatively]: "Hello?"
Dispatcher: "Yes, this is 911, can I help you?"
Citizen: "You have the wrong number!"

Dispatcher: "911.What's the address of your emergency?"
Caller: "Can I give you my credit card number over the phone to pay on my warrant?"
Dispatcher: "What's the offense?"
Caller: "Credit card fraud."

Dispatcher: "911."
Caller: "Help! Help! Send the police! I been shot."
Dispatcher: "You said you've been shot?"
Caller: "I been shot!"
Dispatcher: "How many times were you shot?"
Caller: "This is the first time."

Dispatcher: "911. What is your emergency?"

Male Caller: "You have got people working in the school right now. And they've been working all night long violating the noise code over here."

Dispatcher: "Sir, a noise complaint is not an emergency call. You'll have to call on the business line."

Male Caller: "Well how about if I shoot them, would it be an emergency then?"

Dispatcher: "Sure would."

Male Caller: "Alright."

Dispatcher: "911."

Male Caller: "I need a paramedic. Can you send one or do I have to call someone else?"

Dispatcher: "I'll take care of that, sir. Just calm down. What's the problem?"

Male Caller: "I saw a medical special on TV last night about a rare disease, and I think I have all the symptoms. My neighbor thinks I do, too."

Dispatcher: "911."

Female Caller: "I am trapped in my house."

Dispatcher: "Trapped? Is someone holding you there?"

Female Caller: "Someone? No. But there is a frog on the front porch."

Dispatcher: "A frog?"

Female Caller: "Yes, a frog."

Dispatcher: "Okay, but what is preventing you from leaving the house?"

Female Caller: "I told you. There is a frog on the porch and I am afraid of frogs."

Dispatcher: "And you don't have another door to the house?"

Female Caller: "No. There is only one door and I can't get out of the house with the frog sitting there."

Dispatcher: "Why don't you take a broom and sweep the frog off the porch?"

Female Caller: "I can't do that. I told you, I am afraid of frogs. He might get me."

Dispatcher: "Um...I'm not sure I can help you with this."

Dispatcher: "911. What is the location of your emergency?"

Caller: "Yes, I just wanted to let you know that I have some information that will help you to solve many of your cases."

Dispatcher [noting that the call originated from the state hospital]: "Okay, go ahead with that information."

Caller: "I am prepared to meet with the detectives and to reveal the true identity of Cinderella's stepmother."

Dispatcher: [Pause] "Okay."

READING TOMBSTONES

In olden days, families had special symbols carved into gravestones to tell something about their loved ones, to express their grief, or to reflect their belief in eternal life or their faith. So, next time you're strolling through a cemetery, look around—the dead are talking to you.

Anchor: Steadfast hope

Tree trunk: The brevity of life

Birds: The soul

Snake in a circle: Everlasting life in heaven (also called *ouroboros*)

Cherub: Divine wisdom or justice

Broken column: Early death

Cross, anchor, and Bible: Faith, hope, and charity

Cross, crown, and palm: Trials, victory, and reward

Crown: Reward and glory

Dove: Purity, love, the Holy Spirit

Horseshoe: Protection against evil

Gourds: Deliverance from grief

Lamb: Innocence (usually on a child's grave)

Swallow: Motherhood

Hourglass: Time and its swift flight

Arch: Rejoined with partner in heaven.

Ivy: Faithfulness, memory, and undying friendship

Laurel: Victory

Lily: Purity and resurrection

Mermaid: Dualism of Christ—half God, half man

Conch shell: Wisdom

Oak: Strength

Palms: Martyrdom

Shattered urn: Old age

Peacock: Eternal life

Poppy: Eternal sleep

Column: Noble life

Garland: Victory over death

Rooster: Awakening, courage, vigilance

Shell: Birth and resurrection

Six-pointed star: The creator

Weeping willow: Mourning, grief

Triangle: Truth, equality, trinity

Olive branch: Forgiveness

Dolphin: Salvation, bearer of souls across water to heaven

Skeleton: Life's brevity

Broken sword: Life cut short

Crossed swords: Life lost in battle

Heart: Devotion

CHAIR-LEADERS

*Pull up a chair for this one. On page 68 we told you about
giant Paul Bunyan statues. Well, it turns out that
someone's been building them places to sit down.*

CLASH OF THE TITANS

Small towns seem to love being the home of "the World's
Largest" anything. Oversize statues, balls of string, and
other oddities are good for tourism and civic pride. For example:

• Ashburn, Georgia, has been a popular photo op spot ever since
1975, when the "World's Largest Peanut" was erected on I-75.

• Castroville, California, one of the world's top growing centers
for artichokes, is the proud home of a 15-foot-tall artichoke,
which sits next to an artichoke-shaped restaurant.

• Kissimmee, Florida, has a restaurant shaped like an orange
called Orange World.

But what happens when different towns want the same "World's
Largest" claim to fame? The battle over who has the world's
largest chair has been raging for almost a century.

HIGH CHAIRS

In the late 1800s, Gardner, Massachusetts, with 20 furniture factories, was becoming a chair-manufacturing center. In 1905 the town
decided to draw attention to its manufacturing prowess by erecting
a 12-foot Mission-style chair on Elm Street. Postcards and placards
soon proclaimed Gardner to be "Chair City of the World."

A few years later, Thomasville, North Carolina, which called
itself the "Furniture Capital of the World" built its own giant chair,
and at 13-feet, 6-inches, it was just a bit bigger than Gardner's.

Gardner's town fathers were infuriated. Not to be outdone, they
quickly built a 15-foot Mission chair. And just to be sure their
chair would remain the biggest, in 1935 they replaced that one
with a 16-foot Hitchcock chair.

Wartime production needs quelled the giant-chair feud for a few
years, but after steel production bans were lifted in 1948, Thomasville built an 18-foot steel chair on a 12-foot pedestal. To bolster

---

Claxton, Georgia, claims to be the Fruit Cake Capital of the World.

their position, they convinced the nearby town of High Point to build the world's largest chest of drawers.

WE WON'T TAKE THIS SITTING DOWN

Under cover of darkness, furniture makers from Bassett, Virginia, sent a team to North Carolina to measure Thomasville's big chair. The boys from Bassett planned to build their own big chair and wanted to ensure that, at 19 feet tall, it would be big enough to steal Thomasville's thunder.

Various other towns jumped into the fray, too: Bennington, Vermont, built a 19-foot ladderback; Washington, D.C., erected a 19-foot Duncan Phyfe; and Morristown, Tennessee, erected a massive 20-foot green recliner, so large it could seat 10 people across.

Gardner fought back gamely, building a 20-foot, 7-inch chair for the bicentennial celebrations in 1976. But Gardner's chair was eclipsed by a mammoth ladderback built at Pa's Woodshed in Binghamton, New York: 24 feet, 9 inches tall. The monstrous creation (considered an eyesore by some), made it into the 1979 *Guinness Book of World Records*.

THE CHAIR BATTLE MARCHES ON

• A furniture company in Wingdale, New York, used more than a ton and a half of wood to build its 25-foot-tall Fireside Chair.

• A custom furniture maker in Lipan, Texas, erected a 26-foot rocking chair in 2001.

• Anniston, Alabama, has a 33-foot office chair in the vacant lot next to Miller Office Supply. A spiral staircase leads to the seat of the chair, which was constructed from 10 tons of steel.

• Still after a "World's Largest" title, Bassett Furniture built a 20-foot, 3-inch Mission chair. They sent it on tour to Bassett stores across the United States, calling it the "World's Largest Chair," until Anniston, Alabama, publicly refuted their claim. Now they call it the "World's Largest Chair on Tour."

• But the winner in the battle of the giant chairs is Promosedia in the province of Udine, Italy. Equivalent in size to a 7-story building, it was constructed in 1995 to advertise the chair-building region, known as the "Chair Triangle." Their 65-foot chair is indisputably the largest in the world. (So far.)

Pull up a stone: The chair was invented in about 2500 B.C.

THE GREAT BRINKS ROBBERY

It was the perfect crime—so well planned and executed that all the gang members needed to do to was lie low until the heat cooled down. But could they?

IN AND OUT

The year was 1950. It was a cold January in Boston. At around 7 p.m. on the 17th, a green 1949 Ford truck pulled up in front of the Prince Street entrance of the Brinks Armored Car garage. Millions of dollars in cash, checks, and money orders were stored inside the building. Seven men emerged from the back of the Ford and walked swiftly to the front door. Each man wore a Navy peacoat, gloves, rubber-soled shoes, and a chauffeur's cap.

After a series of blinking flashlight signals from a nearby rooftop, one of the men pulled out a key and unlocked the front door. Once inside, each man donned a Captain Marvel Halloween mask and went to work. They walked up the stairs and encountered a second locked door. Another key was produced, and they entered a room where five surprised Brinks employees were counting money. The gang pulled out handguns and quickly subdued the stunned Brinks men. Once their captives were bound and gagged, the masked men began collecting the loot.

With clockwork precision and very little talking, the gang filled their bags with money. Fifteen minutes after their arrival, the robbers—each carrying two full bags—left the building. Six of them got back into the truck and one got into a Ford sedan parked nearby. As they made their getaway, the employees managed to free themselves and call the police. When it was over, $1.2 million in cash and $1.5 million in checks, money orders, and securities were missing. It was the single largest robbery in U.S. history.

URBAN HEROES

The daring crime made front-page news all over the country. And the public was sympathetic with the robbers almost as soon as they heard about it. Their nonviolent methods and their audacity to

take on a company as huge as Brinks made them cult heroes.
Comedians and cartoonists joked about it, mocking the huge security company's apparent lack of security. On his weekly TV variety
show, Ed Sullivan announced that he had some very special guests:
the Brinks robbers themselves. Seven men wearing Captain Marvel
masks walked onstage to thunderous applause. It became more than
a passing fad—the press dubbed it the "Crime of the Century."

COPS...

The Boston police and Brinks were humiliated. How could seven
men so easily walk off with more than $2.7 million? The FBI took
over the case and immediately found some good news: word on
the street was that the caper had been in the works for months,
and informants were naming names. Among the prime suspects:
some of Boston's most notorious petty criminals, such as Anthony
Pino, Joseph McGinnis, Stanley Gusciora, and "Specs" O'Keefe—
all men known for pulling off similar crimes, although nothing
nearly as big. The bad news: they all had alibis. But when a green
Ford truck matching witnesses' descriptions was found in pieces at
a dump near where O'Keefe and Gusciora lived, the investigators
knew they were hot on the trail. They just needed proof.

...AND ROBBERS

The Feds' instincts were correct: O'Keefe and Gusciora *were* two
of the key men behind the Brinks job. But what they didn't know
was that it was Anthony Pino, an illegal alien from Italy, who first
came up with the idea...back in 1947.

Pino had the savvy to do the job, but he couldn't do it alone.
So he'd called a meeting of some members of the Boston underworld and put together a gang. By the time they were ready to go,
there were 11 members: Pino; his associate, liquor store owner
Joseph McGinnis; strong-arms O'Keefe and Gusciora, both experienced criminals with reputations for keeping their cool and handling weapons; Pino's brother-in-law, Vincent Costa, the lookout;
Adolph "Jazz" Maffie; Henry Baker; Michael Vincent Geagan;
Thomas "Sandy" Richardson; James Faherty; and Joseph Banfield.

It would be the heist of a lifetime, and the gang spent the next
two years preparing for it. Pino cased the Brinks building from
nearby rooftops, and was amazed at how lax the security was. Still,

---

Scientists say: The color combination with the most visual impact is black on yellow.

they would take no chances: They broke in after hours on several different occasions and took the lock cylinders from five doors, had keys made to fit them, and returned the cylinders. And while inside, they obtained the Brinks shipment schedules. It took discipline to not steal anything on those smaller break-ins, but they knew the real score would be on the big break-in, planned for a time when the day's receipts were being counted and the vault was open. They were willing to wait.

By December 1949, Costa, the lookout man, could tell exactly how many employees were in the building and what they were doing by observing which lights were on. After about a dozen dress rehearsals, the gang made their move. The job went down without a hitch.

THE LONG GOOD-BYE

The robbery was the easy part. Now each gang member had to keep quiet, not spend money like crazy, and lay low for six long years, after which the statute of limitations would run out. If they could do that, they would all be scot-free…and very rich.

A small portion of the loot was split up among the gang members, but most of it was hidden in various places. O'Keefe and Gusciora put their share ($100,000 each) in the trunk of O'Keefe's car, parked in a garage on Blue Hill Avenue in Boston—with the agreement that the money was not to be touched until 1956.

Even though they were careful to destroy any physical evidence tying them to the crime, they were known criminals and couldn't evade suspicion. Many were picked up and questioned by the FBI. All denied involvement; all provided alibis (though more than a few were shaky); and all of their homes and businesses turned up nothing in searches. Still, investigators knew there was something fishy going on. Their best approach would be to get one of the men to sing; they just had to watch closely and wait for someone to slip up.

SOMEONE SLIPS UP

Less than six months after the Brinks job, O'Keefe and Gusciora were nabbed for robbing an Army-Navy store in Pennsylvania. Police found a pile of cash in the car, but none of it could be tied to the Brinks job. O'Keefe was sentenced to three years in the Bradford County jail; Gusciora was sentenced to five years.

Flying fish "fly" at 40 mph.

O'Keefe wanted to appeal but had no money for legal bills, so he talked Banfield into retrieving his share of the money from the car. It was delivered a few weeks later (minus $2,000). But O'Keefe couldn't keep it behind bars, so he sought out another gang member, the only one left on the outside that he thought he could trust—Jazz Maffie. Bad move: Maffie took O'Keefe's money, disappeared, then reappeared claiming it had been stolen. Then Maffie said he had spent the money on O'Keefe's legal bills. O'Keefe, meanwhile, was stuck in jail and getting angrier.

The Feds worked this angle, trying to create a wedge between O'Keefe and the rest of the gang. They told O'Keefe that the gang had ratted him out for the Brinks job. But O'Keefe stuck to his guns and kept denying any involvement.

THE TENSION MOUNTS

Prior to committing the robbery, the 11 men had agreed that if any one of them "muffed" (acted carelessly), he would be "taken care of" (killed). Sitting in jail, O'Keefe convinced himself that the other members of the gang had "muffed." And he vowed he would get his share of the loot…one way or another.

After he was paroled in the spring of 1954, O'Keefe returned to Boston to ask McGinnis for enough money from the loot to hire a lawyer for his pending burglary charge. But McGinnis wouldn't budge. So O'Keefe kidnapped McGinnis's brother-in-law, Costa, demanding his share as ransom. He only got some of it but still released the hostage. Pino and McGinnis, in the meantime, decided that O'Keefe needed to be "taken care of."

BULLET-PROOF

That June, O'Keefe was driving through Dorchester, Massachusetts, when a car pulled up next to him and sprayed his car with bullets. O'Keefe escaped unharmed. Days later, fellow gang member Henry Baker shot at him, but O'Keefe escaped again. Fearing retribution, Pino brought in a professional hit man named Elmer "Trigger" Burke. When Burke found his target and shot him in the chest and wrist with a machine gun, Specs O'Keefe lived up to his reputation as one of the toughest crooks in the Boston underworld by surviving. By this point, he was extremely angry.

O'Keefe immediately went to the cops and fingered Burke, who was arrested and convicted for attempted murder. But the plan backfired. While he was talking to police, they discovered that O'Keefe was carrying a concealed weapon, a violation of his parole. He was arrested and sentenced to 27 months in prison. Knowing that there was a contract on O'Keefe's life, the FBI stepped up their interrogations. But he still wouldn't confess.

THE HEAT IS ON

Time was starting to run out. It had been more than five years since the crime, and the deadline for the statute of limitations was getting closer and closer. Thousands of hours had gone into identifying the suspects, but the FBI still had no hard evidence. As the case remained in the public eye, each passing day without an arrest was an embarrassment.

Through all of it, the Feds knew that O'Keefe was the key, so they kept chipping away at him. When they informed him that a huge portion of the loot had been recovered, he finally gave in. On January 6, 1956, Specs O'Keefe called a meeting with the Feds and said, "All right, what do you want to know?" It was 11 days before the six-year statute of limitations would take effect.

O'Keefe spelled out every detail to the police—except where the rest of the money was hidden. He had no idea. (Neither did the police—they had exaggerated the loot-recovery story as a ruse to get O'Keefe to talk.)

TRIED AND CONVICTED

Police rounded up all of the remaining members. They were arrested and tried amid a media circus. More than 1,000 prospective jurors had to be excused because they admitted they were sympathetic to the robbers. In the end, a jury found all of them guilty. Each man was sentenced to life in prison. Some died there—others were later released on parole.

For turning state's evidence, O'Keefe was given a reduced sentence. After prison, he changed his name, moved to California, and reportedly worked as Cary Grant's chauffeur.

The Brinks gang stole $2.7 million in cash and securities. The government spent *$29 million* trying to catch them and bring them to justice. But in the end, only 0.2% of the loot—$51,906—was recovered. What happened to the remaining 99.8% is a mystery.

RETURN OF THE MAN FROM C.R.A.P.

More odd acronyms. Submit any complaints to
C.R.A.P.—the Committee to Resist Acronym Proliferation.

GHOST
Stands For: Graffiti Habitual Offenders Suppression Team (*Undercover LAPD cops who bust graffiti artists*)

POETS
Stands For: Piss Off Early, Tomorrow's Saturday (*British slang for "TGIF"*)

SCAM
Stands For: Southern California Auto Mart

CACA
Stands For: Canadian Agricultural Chemicals Association

FIB
Stands For: Fishermen's Information Bureau (*It was this big...really.*)

SAP
Stands For: Society for American Philosophy

EATM
Stands For: Exotic Animal Training Management

SWIFT ANSWER
Stands For: Special Word Indexed Full-Text Alpha-Numeric Storage With Easy Retrieval (*The longest true acronym in English...so far*)

BARRF
Stands For: Bay Area Resource Recovery Facility

NAPS
Stands For: National Alliance of Postal Supervisors

RUIN
Stands For: Regional Urban Information Network

SLUTS
Stands For: School of Librarianship Urban Transportation System

GORK
Stands For: God Only Really Knows (*How doctors refer to patients they can't diagnose*)

WUNY
Stands For: Wait Until Next Year (*Said after a losing season*)

ANIMAL SUPERSTITIONS

Uncle John is so superstitious, he only works on this page when his one-eyed, three-legged dog, "Lucky," is resting at his right foot. (Resting at Uncle John's left foot is bad luck—everybody knows that!)

Bees must be made aware of a death in your family or they will leave the hive and make no more honey. Hang something black upon the hive.

A butterfly inside the home is a sign that a wedding is near.

If you buy a horse and change its name, you will have bad luck.

When it's time to separate a calf from its mother, if you take the calf out of the barn backward the mother will not mourn the loss.

If a rabbit crosses your path from left to right, it is a sign of good luck. From right to left is a sign of bad luck.

If you eat a coyote, you will become a coward.

Feeding mistletoe to the first calf born in the new year brings good luck to the entire herd.

If you see a white cow or a white horse, spit three times or you will suffer bad luck.

Snakes travel in pairs. If you kill one, kill both or the snake that survives will seek revenge.

A bird tapping on the window is an omen of death.

Bats playing in the early evening is a sign of good weather to come. A bat hitting the side of a building is a sign of rain.

Bulls cannot be struck by lightning.

Keeping a chameleon as a pet will ward off evil.

If a cat jumps over a corpse, the corpse will become a vampire.

A black poodle appears on the graves of clergymen who have broken their vows.

If a pregnant woman sees a donkey, her child will grow up well behaved and wise.

If you are bitten by a fox, you will not live longer than seven years.

Las Vegas gets an average of only 4 inches of rainfall annually.

SWEET SUCCESS!

It's hard to get to the top and harder to stay there. Here are some thoughts on the subject from people who should know.

"Success is not the key to happiness. Happiness is the key to success. If you love what you are doing, you will be successful."
—**Albert Schweitzer**

"There is no success without hardship."
—**Sophocles**

"The road to success is always under construction."
—**Lily Tomlin**

"You only have to do a very few things right in your life so long as you don't do too many things wrong."
—**Warren Buffett**

"If A equals success, then the formula is A = X + Y + Z. X is work. Y is play. Z is keep your mouth shut."
—**Albert Einstein**

"I have not failed 700 times. I have not failed once. I have succeeded in proving that those 700 ways will not work."
—**Thomas Edison**

"Losing is simply learning how to win."
—**Ted Turner**

"I don't know the key to success, but the key to failure is trying to please everybody."
—**Bill Cosby**

"It is not the going out of port, but coming back in, that determines the success of a voyage."
—**Henry Ward Beecher**

"Success is relative. It is what we can make of the mess we have made of things."
—**T. S. Eliot**

"Flaming enthusiasm, backed by horse sense and persistence, is the quality that most frequently makes for success."
—**Dale Carnegie**

"I don't measure a man's success by how high he climbs but how high he bounces when he hits bottom."
—**General George S. Patton**

"People of mediocre ability sometimes achieve outstanding success because they don't know when to quit. They succeed because they are determined to."
—**George Allen**

The kid on the Cracker Jack box is named Robert.

THE MAD BOMBER, PT. II

When we left the case of the Mad Bomber (page 110), Dr. James Brussel, the original "profiler," had just released his theories to the press, setting the game afoot. Here's how it played out.

FOUND OUT

The Mad Bomber's response to his case being made public: he took his terror a step further. The bombs kept coming and the letters got more brazen. "F. P." even called Brussel on the telephone and told him to lay off or he would "be sorry." Brussel had him exactly where he wanted him.

The final clue came when police received a letter revealing the date that began the Mad Bomber's misery: September 5, 1931—almost 10 years before the first bomb was found. Brussel immediately ordered a search of Con Ed's personnel files from that era. An office assistant named Alice Kelly found a neatly written letter from a former employee named George Metesky who had promised that Con Edison would pay for their "DASTARDLY DEEDS."

I WILL make THE CON Edison sorry •• I WILL Bring them before the bar of JuSTicE—PUBLIC OPINION will condEMn them — for BewArE I will PLACE MORE bombs under Theatre SEATS IN THE NEar futuRe .

The police traced Metesky to what neighborhood children called the "crazy house" on Fourth Street in Waterbury, Connecticut, just beyond Westchester County, New York. When they arrived, George Metesky was wearing…pajamas. He greeted them warmly and freely admitted to being the Mad Bomber. He even showed them his bomb-making workshop in the garage.

They told him to get dressed for his trip to the station. He returned wearing…a double-breasted suit, buttoned.

DEDUCTIVE REASONING

So how was Dr. Brussel able to provide such an accurate description?

• It was pretty evident that the Mad Bomber was a man. In those days, very few women would have had the knowledge necessary to make bombs. Bomb-making is, moreover, a classic behavior of paranoid males.

• Because 85% of known paranoids had stocky, muscular builds, Brussel added it to the profile. Metesky had a stocky, muscular build.

• Male paranoiacs have difficulty relating to other people, especially women, and usually live with an older, matriarchal-type woman who will "mother" them. Metesky lived with his two older sisters.

• Another clue to Metesky's sexual inadequacy, Brussel claimed, was his lettering. His script was perfect except for the "W"s—instead of connecting "V"s that would have been consistent with the rest of the letters, Metesky connected two "U"s, which Brussel saw as representing women's breasts.

• Brussel concluded that Metesky was between 40 and 50 years old because paranoia takes years to develop, and based on when the first bomb was found, Metesky had to have already been well down the road. Brussel was close—Metesky was 54.

• What led Brussel to believe that Metesky did not live in New York City was his use of the term "Con Edison"—New Yorkers call it "Con Ed."

• Metesky's language identified him as middle European, too. His use of "dastardly deeds," as well as some other phrases, was a sign of someone with Slavic roots. There was a high concentration of Poles in southern Connecticut, and Brussel connected the dots.

• Paranoids believe that the world conspires against them, so Brussel knew that something traumatic must have happened to Metesky. He was right. On September 5, 1931, Metesky was injured in a boiler explosion at a Con Ed plant. He complained of headaches, but doctors could find no sign of injury. After a year of sick pay and medical benefits, Metesky was fired. A failed lawsuit sent him over the edge, and he began plotting his revenge.

One species of moth lives entirely on cow tears.

- Brussel also predicted that the Bomber would have a debilitating heart disease. He was close: Metesky suffered from a tubercular lung.

- How did Brussel know what kind of suit Metesky would be wearing when he was arrested? Simple: Paranoids are neat freaks, as was apparent in his letters and bombs. He would wear nothing less than the most impeccable outfit of the day—a double-breasted suit, buttoned.

AFTERMATH

George Metesky proudly explained everything to the police. In all, he had planted more than 30 bombs, but miraculously, no one was killed. Metesky said that that was never his intention. "F. P.", he explained, stood for "Fair Play."

On April 18, 1957, George Metesky was found mentally unfit to stand trial and was committed to the Matteawan Hospital for the Criminally Insane. In 1973 he was deemed cured and was released. Metesky lived out the remainder of his days in his Waterbury home, where he died in 1994 at the age of 90. Dr. Brussel gained celebrity status for his role in the case; today he's considered the father of modern psychological profiling in criminal investigations.

TRAGIC LEGACY

Although Metesky's bombs never killed anybody, it was more because of strange luck than "Fair Play." (Police called it a "miracle" that his theater bombs—planted inside the seats—never took any lives.) Even worse, Metesky may have helped pave the way for others who were more successful in their terrible exploits. According to investigators, both the "Zodiac Killer," who killed at least six people—some with bombs—in the San Francisco area in the 1970s, and Ted "Unabomber" Kaczynski, who killed three people in the 1980s and 1990s with package bombs, were inspired by George Metesky, New York City's Mad Bomber.

✻   ✻   ✻

"One thing I can't understand is why the newspapers labeled me the Mad Bomber. That was unkind."

—George Metesky

IRONIC, ISN'T IT?

*There's nothing like a good dose of irony to put the
problems of day-to-day life in proper perspective.*

THE ANIMAL KINGDOM

• The crow population of Woodstock, Ontario, grew so
large that residents started complaining to the city council
about the noise. The council's solution: frequent bursts of fireworks to scare the crows away.

• Bill Pettit Jr. of Southampton, New Jersey, recently opened his
335-acre farm to bird hunters. Pettit is a veterinarian.

• While driving through Versailles, New York, Wendy Maines saw
five dogs attacking a cat. She stopped the car, honked the horn,
and scared the dogs away. Then she accidentally ran over the cat.

UP AND AWAY

Hours after Michael Antinori miraculously walked away from a
helicopter crash on June 3, 2002, he climbed into his single-
engine plane and took off. Shortly thereafter, the plane went
down. He died on impact.

SEW TOUGH

At Albion State Prison, a new class is being offered to inmates.
Guards say it has become so popular among the most violent criminals that there is a waiting list to sign up. What's the subject of
the class? Quilting.

LAW AND ORDER

• Chris Axworthy, Saskatchewan's justice minister, was getting
fed up with the car-theft problem in his hometown of Regina so
he called a committee meeting to announce a government crack-
down on car thieves. When he left his home to go to the meeting,
he found that his Chrysler Intrepid had been stolen.

• Two plainclothes German police officers were making their way
through a crowd of protesters to meet up with some uniformed
cops. But the uniforms met them halfway and beat the two with
nightsticks. The bruised officers are suing the department.

Q: What color are Green Cards (U.S. permanent resident I.D.'s)? A: Surprise! They're yellow.

- Love Your Neighbor Corp. of Michigan recently sued Love Thy Neighbor Fund of Florida for trademark infringement.

OCCUPATIONAL HAZARD

Robert Young Pelton wrote a book called *The World's Most Dangerous Places*. In chapter 23 he states that "the most likely place to be kidnapped is Colombia." After the book was released, Pelton traveled to the South American country on a writing assignment for *Adventure* magazine...and was abducted by a paramilitary group. (He was later released.)

ROCK AND ROLE

Some Hawaiians are questioning the decision to cast wrestler/ actor Dwayne "The Rock" Johnson in the lead role for a new movie about Hawaiian king Kamehameha I. What's wrong with that? It turns out The Rock is part Samoan, and historically, Samoans are fierce enemies of the Hawaiians.

LADIES' MAN

Johnny Hamilton gives $400,000 a year to women's shelters, scholarships, and feminist charities in Michigan. He is the owner of a topless bar in Detroit.

LOVE AND MARRIAGE

- A 21-year-old man from Rockville, Maryland, was arrested for peeping into a ladies' restroom stall while he was at the county courthouse. He was there to pick up his new marriage license.

- Anne Jonsson of Stockholm, Sweden, viciously attacked her husband, Lars. She fractured his skull, broke his nose, and gave him various cuts and bruises. What did Lars do to deserve all this? He refused to take her to a rally against domestic violence.

FALSE ADVERTISING

After falling short of its projected profits, *Success* magazine declared bankruptcy in 1999.

*   *   *

"My mother never saw the irony of calling me a son-of-a-bitch."
—**Richard Jeni**

Prior to 1953, the slogan of L&M cigarettes was "just what the doctor ordered."

SORRY (NOT REALLY)

Uncle John once called the BRI researcher who worked on this article
"a big dummy." He now regrets making that remark. Here are
some other insincere apologies the big dummy dug up for us.

BUSH LEAGUE

Who Said It: Presidential candidate George W. Bush

Slip of the Lip: Just before a speech in Illinois during the 2000 campaign, then-Governor Bush leaned over to his running mate, Dick Cheney. "There's Adam Clymer," he said, "major league a**hole from *The New York Times*." Cheney responded, "Big time." Problem: They were speaking near a live microphone. Members of the press heard the slur, and soon most of the world did, too.

Insincere Apology: When questioned about it, Cheney refused to comment. Asked later that day whether he would be apologizing, Governor Bush said, "I regret people heard the comments."

YOU CAN RUN BUT YOU CAN'T HYDE

Who Said It: Alec Baldwin

Slip of the Lip: In 1998 on NBC's *Late Night with Conan O'Brien*, Baldwin was asked about the ongoing impeachment trial of President Clinton. Speaking about one of the leaders of the impeachment movement, Rep. Henry Hyde, Baldwin went on a rant. "If we were in another country we would stone Henry Hyde to death! We would stone him to death!" He added that, "We would stone Henry Hyde to death and we would go to their homes and we'd kill their wives and their children. We would kill their families."

Insincere Apology: Baldwin's publicist denied it was anything more than a big joke. The tirade was just "a parody on the hysteria in this country coming from right-wing fanatics."

SETTING AN EXAMPLE

Who Said It: Reverend Jerry Falwell

Slip of the Lip: On CBS's *60 Minutes* in October 2002, he said, "I think Muhammad was a terrorist," adding, "Jesus set the example for love, as did Moses. Muhammad set an opposite example." Outraged religious leaders around the world demanded an apology.

Emily Warner of Frontier Airlines was the first woman to pilot a commercial jet in 1973.

Insincere Apology: "I sincerely apologize that certain statements of mine were hurtful to the feelings of many Muslims," he said. "I intended no disrespect to any sincere, law-abiding Muslim."

THE DOCTOR IS OUT

Who Said It: Talk show host "Dr. Laura" Schlessinger

Slip of the Lip: She called homosexuals "deviants" and "biological errors" numerous times on her radio show.

Insincere Apology: On March 10, 2000, Schlessinger took out a full-page ad in *Variety*. "Regrettably," it read, "some of the words I've used have hurt some people, and I am sorry for that." Critics questioned the timing of the statement: a *Dr. Laura* TV show was in the works, and the producer, Paramount Pictures, was getting bombarded by e-mails, phone calls, and advertiser boycott threats.

Insincere Apology Retracted: Days later, in the *Boston Herald*, Schlessinger took it back, saying it was "not an apology," it was a "clarification." (Her TV show bombed.)

MARKETING MAGIQ

Who Said It: Los Angeles Lakers basketball star Shaquille O'Neal

Slip of the Lip: Asked in June 2002 about Yao Ming, the NBA's first Chinese player, Shaq replied with a mock-Chinese accent, "Tell Yao Ming 'Ching-chong-yang-wah-ah-so.'" He thought it was so funny, he repeated it in December. When columnist Irwin Tang wrote about it for AsianWeek.com, Asian community groups began protesting and reporters peppered O'Neal with questions.

Insincere Apology #1: "To say I'm a racist against Asians is crazy. I said a joke. It was a 70-30 joke. 70% of the people thought it was funny. 30% didn't. If I hurt anybody's feelings, I apologize."

Insincere Apology #2: Protesters refused to let the issue die. A few days later, O'Neal said, "If I was the first one to do it, and the only one to do it, I could see what they're talking about. But if I offended anybody, I apologize." Asian Americans were still angry.

Insincere Apology #3: Protests grew. After a game against Yao's Houston Rockets in January, O'Neal tried again: "Yao Ming is my brother. The Asian people are my brothers. It was unfortunate that one idiot writer tried to start a racial war over that." He added, "But because of what I said, 500 million people saw this game. You ought to thank me for my marketing skills."

The original Macy's made a total of $11.06 on its first day of business in 1858.

DUMB CROOKS

More proof that crime doesn't pay.

WHERE THERE'S SMOKE...

"A southern California firefighter, who was paid for each fire that he fought, was arrested for starting forest fires after his fellow firemen noticed that he always started warming up the fire engine just before the fires were called in."

—"The Edge," Portland *Oregonian*

THERE'S A CRACK IN HIS ALIBI

"Fred Benevento, 47, a math teacher at Fairfax (Virginia) High School, was arrested during a stakeout conducted by D.C. police, who said they found 13 plastic bags of crack cocaine in his car.

"Benevento, who has been suspended pending the outcome of the trial, pled not guilty to the charge. His defense? He told police that the bags of cocaine found in his car 'came flying through his open window' and that he 'was just looking at them when the police officers arrived.'"

—*Washington Post*

IS THIS THE COMPLAINT DEPARTMENT?

"In South Carolina, a man walked into a local police station, dropped a bag of cocaine on the counter, informed the desk sergeant that it was substandard cut, and asked that the person who sold it to him be arrested immediately."

—*Miami Herald*

COMING CLEAN

"Police officers of the Russian city of Ulyanovsk arrested a 33-year-old who warned them of a bomb that was placed in the bath house (*banya*) on Pushkin Street. The police quickly determined that the telephone terrorist called from the pay phone across the street from the bath house. When questioned, the man confessed his motive: He wanted to see naked people running out of the banya. (It should be mentioned here that it was "Women's Day" at the banya.)"

—*Reuters*

Tailor talk: A bolt of cloth is 120 feet long.

CURE FOR WHAT AILS YE

Uncle John believes that placing this page against your forehead and rubbing vigorously will cure headaches, fever blisters, tennis elbow, planter's warts, swimmer's ear, lazy eye, pinkeye, the evil eye, weak knees, and tired blood. Here are some of Uncle John's other favorite folk remedies:

To cure lung infections, rub onions on your chest.

To ease arthritis pain, carry a peeled potato in your pocket. If that doesn't work, try a pocketful of buckshot... or the ashes from a turtle shell.

For kidney troubles, eat... kidney beans. If that doesn't work, try chewing the bones from a dogfish head.

To cure a cold, rub your feet with grease. If that doesn't work, eat some bear brains.

Fox fat, when warmed and placed in the ear, will cure an earache.

To get rid of a wart, rub the wart with a peeled apple, then feed the apple to a pig.

To treat a burn, rub it with mashed potatoes.

To cure a child of whooping cough, put them on a donkey and lead the donkey in a clockwise circle nine times.

Eating beaver fat will calm your nerves.

Rubbing a fox tongue on your eyes will cure cataracts.

To cure a headache, tie a string around a buzzard's head and wear it around your neck.

Frostbite? Mix cow milk with cow manure and apply it to the affected area.

To fix a limp, rub the bad leg with skunk or wildcat grease.

To stop a nosebleed, pack your nose with cobwebs.

To reduce fever, eat watermelon or chew turnips.

To cure swollen eyes, put crab eyes on the back of your neck.

A piece of deer hoof worn in a ring will cure epilepsy.

If you touch a sleeping person with a frog tongue, they will reveal their secrets to you.

Them's the breaks: No insurance company will underwrite Jackie Chan's productions.

AMERICA'S FIRST REALITY TV SHOW

Survivor and The Real World *may seem innovative, but they owe a huge debt to a show that hasn't aired since 1973, despite being named one of the greatest shows of all time by TV Guide. Here's the story of the show that started it all.*

GET REAL

In 1971 a documentary film producer named Craig Gilbert came up with a novel idea for an educational TV show: film the lives of four American families in four different parts of the country—the West Coast, the Midwest, the South, and the East Coast. A different film crew would be assigned to each family and would film their lives for four straight weeks, from the moment the first person got up until the last person went to bed. Many hours of footage would be filmed, then it would be edited and condensed into four one-hour documentaries, one on each family. The documentaries would be broadcast on PBS.

Television programming was a lot different in those days—for years viewers had been fed a steady diet of decidedly *un*realistic family shows like *Ozzie and Harriet, Father Knows Best, The Waltons,* and *The Brady Bunch.* Gilbert figured viewers might be interested in a new aspect of American family life: reality.

FAMILY SECRETS

For the West Coast family, Gilbert chose the Louds, an upper middle-class family living in Santa Barbara, California—parents Bill and Pat, and their five teenage children: sons Lance, Kevin, and Grant, and daughters Delilah and Michele. "They basically said, 'How would you like to star in the greatest home movie ever made?'" Lance Loud remembered. "We didn't have to do anything, just be our little Southern California hick selves."

Gilbert hired two filmmakers, Susan and Alan Raymond, to film the family. Shortly after production got underway, he decided to dump the four-family concept and focus exclusively on the Louds—for a longer time period. To this day it is unclear whether

Craig Gilbert knew it at the time, but the Louds' marriage was in serious trouble (thanks to Bill's philandering), and their son Lance, who lived in New York, was gay. The Louds had assumed that keeping their family secrets for four weeks wouldn't be that difficult; but now Gilbert was asking them for permission to film for months on end. Could they withstand this invasion of their privacy?

Bill and Pat thought it over…and decided to take a chance. "I thought I might get away with just saying, 'These are my children and my kitchen and my pool and my horses, over and out.'" Pat Loud recalled years later. "What naifs we were!"

OPEN HOUSE

Bill and Pat need not have worried about protecting Lance Loud's privacy—he was completely open about his sexuality, even when the film crew was present. He was the very first openly gay teenager ever shown on American television; for many viewers, he was the first out-of-the-closet homosexual they had ever seen.

As for the Louds' marital problems, they proved both impossible to hide and impossible to repair. As the weeks passed and Pat became more comfortable around the cameras, she began to open up about the problems she was having with Bill. Their marriage continued to deteriorate until finally, a few months into filming, Pat threw Bill out of the house. The Raymonds were there, and they captured it all on film.

12-STEP PROGRAM

By the time the Raymonds wrapped up production, they'd been filming the Louds for seven solid months. They had so much raw footage—more than 300 hours worth—that it took them the better part of two years to edit it down to the 12 one-hour episodes that would air as *An American Family* beginning in January 1973.

One of the reasons the Louds agreed to allow the film crew into their home in the first place was because they didn't think many people would ever see the finished product. This was a documentary, after all, and one being made for educational television at that. PBS wasn't even broadcast in Santa Barbara in 1971 (by 1973, it was); besides, Pat didn't watch much educational television and she didn't think anyone else would, either. "We erroneously believed the series would be a simply interminable home movie that no one in their right mind would watch for more than five minutes," she recalled in 2002. Lance Loud thought of the film as "a very odd, never-to-be-noticed project."

HITTING THE BIG TIME

But when *An American Family* finally hit the airwaves in January 1973, more than 10 million people tuned in, making it one of the most-watched series in PBS history. The viewers were there for episode 2, when Lance's sexuality was revealed; they were there for episode 9, when Pat Loud asked Bill for a divorce; and they stayed glued to their sets until the series came to an end in episode 12.

Overnight, the Louds became one of the most famous families in America. They were on the cover of *Newsweek* (underneath the banner "Broken Family"), they made the national television talk shows, appearing with Dick Cavett, Dinah Shore, Mike Douglas, and Phil Donahue, and their problems were discussed around the water coolers of every workplace in America. Everyone knew who they were.

ROUGH GOING

Today, more than 30 years later, the Louds may be remembered with fond nostalgia, but that wasn't the case in 1973. Many viewers were stunned by what they saw. The Louds were an upper middle-class family, more affluent than most of the viewers who watched them. Like the fictional TV families people were used to seeing on the tube, the Louds seemed to have it all: They lived in a big, beautiful house in sunny Southern California; they had steady, high-paying jobs; they had four cars, five beautiful children, three dogs, two cats, a horse, a swimming pool—seemingly everything that anyone could possibly want. So why weren't they happy? Why couldn't Bill and Pat save their marriage? Why was Lance Loud gay? What on Earth was *wrong* with these people?

Many viewers—not to mention pundits and TV critics—came to see Bill and Pat Loud as unfit parents and their family as the personification of everything that was wrong with American families in the early 1970s. *Newsweek* called the Louds "affluent zombies" and described the series as "a glimpse into the pit." *The New York Times Magazine* called Lance Loud a "flamboyant leech," the "evil flower of the family," and an "emotional dwarf."

That wasn't at all how the Louds had expected to come across. "People were shocked, and we were shocked that they were shocked," Lance Loud remembered.

> We thought people would be on our side and sympathize with a family responding to all the different moods and trends of the times. But they didn't sympathize; they misunderstood, thinking that we were arrogant in our stupidity. They were totally wrong.

NO HOLLYWOOD ENDING
In the end, nearly everyone associated with the film ended up regretting ever getting involved. Bill and Pat accused the Raymonds of distorting their family life, zooming in on problems and controversies at the expense of everything else. "It seemed that the entire series was all about Lance being homosexual and my husband and I divorcing," Pat Loud says. "My other four children and their friends seemed to be of no real interest to the editors."

The Raymonds had their own regrets. Though they did make two more films about the Louds—in 1983 and 2003—they swore off making documentaries about any other family. "It was too brutal," Susan Raymond says. "We made films on policemen, on a prison warden, on a principal of a school—people who are public officials. But we didn't do anything on ordinary people or families. We didn't think they could handle that kind of scrutiny."

FINAL CHAPTER
After the show ended, Lance Loud spent several years as the lead singer of a punk rock band called the Mumps, but though his fame brought the band some notoriety, it also made it harder for them to be taken seriously. The Mumps broke up in 1980 and Lance returned to Southern California, where he worked as a freelance journalist, published in magazines like *The Advocate*, *Interview*, and *Vanity Fair*. He also abused intravenous drugs for nearly 20 years, which caused him to become infected with hepatitis. In 1987 he learned that he was HIV positive.

In late 2001, his health failing, Lance checked into an L.A. hospice and called the Raymonds to see if they would document his relationship with his family during this final phase of his life. They agreed. Why did Lance want to do it? Felled by years of unsafe sex and drug addiction, he'd come to see his life as a cautionary tale. But he also wanted to show viewers that for all the problems the Louds had gone through, 30 years later they still loved each other and were close. "He could have asked for a priest or a minister, but he called for his filmmakers," Susan Raymond says.

Lance Loud died on December 22, 2001 at the age of 50—the same age his father was when *An American Family* premiered in 1973. *Lance Loud! A Death in an American Family* aired on PBS in January 2003.

After the original series ended, Pat Loud moved to New York and became a literary agent. She has since retired and now lives in Los Angeles. Bill Loud remarried in 1976; he is retired and also lives in Los Angeles. Kevin Loud lives with his family in Paradise Valley, Arizona; Grant, Delilah, and Michele Loud and their families all live in Los Angeles.

DUBIOUS ACHIEVERS

Alan and Susan Raymond, credited with filming the first-ever reality TV show, are still making documentaries...but they refuse to watch any of the shows their work has inspired. Anthropologist Margaret Mead predicted that *An American Family* would come to be seen "as important a moment in the history of human thought as the invention of the novel," but judging from the shows that have followed it—*The Real World, Big Brother,* and *The Osbournes* among them—it's a safe bet she was wrong.

"Like Frankenstein's monster, it's a mixed blessing to be considered someone who spawned this reality TV genre," Alan Raymond says. "I think it's a largely superficial, stupid genre of television programming that I don't think as a documentary filmmaker I take much pride in."

*　　*　　*

A Final Note. For all it cost them personally, how much money were the Louds paid for letting a crew film them for seven months? Not much. "The family received no compensation for their participation in the film," Pat Loud says. "The only money we got was a check for $400 to repair the kitchen where the gaffer's tape had pulled the paint off the walls."

MEAD'S CREED

When Margaret Mead died in 1978, she was the most famous anthropologist in the world. Her 44 books and more than 1,000 articles helped shape our understanding of human behavior.

"We are now at a point where we must educate our children in what no one knew yesterday, and prepare our schools for what no one knows yet."

"No matter how many communes anybody invents, the family always creeps back."

"I was brought up to believe that the only thing worth doing was to add to the sum of accurate information in the world."

"Every time we liberate a woman, we liberate a man."

"Always remember that you are absolutely unique. Just like everyone else."

"The solution to adult problems tomorrow depends on large measure upon how our children grow up today."

"What people say, what people do, and what they say they do are entirely different things."

"I learned the value of hard work by working hard."

"Our humanity rests upon a series of learned behaviors, woven together into patterns that are infinitely fragile and never directly inherited."

"One of the oldest human needs is having someone to wonder where you are when you don't come home at night."

"Nobody has ever before asked the nuclear family to live all by itself in a box the way we do. With no relatives, no support, we've put ourselves in an impossible situation."

"Sister is probably the most competitive relationship within the family, but once the sisters are grown, it becomes the strongest relationship."

"Thanks to television, for the first time the young are seeing history made before it is censored by their elders."

"We need to devise a system within which peace will be more rewarding than war."

FAMILIAR PHRASES

Here are more origins of common phrases.

TO BREAK THE ICE

Meaning: To start a conversation

Origin: "Severe winter weather is a major nuisance to operators of boats. Until the development of power equipment, it was frequently necessary to chop ice at the river's edge with hand tools in order to make channels for plying about the river. The boatman had *to break the ice* before he could actually get down to business." (From *Cassell Everyday Phrases*, by Neil Ewart)

TO PULL ONE'S OWN WEIGHT

Meaning: To do one's share or to take responsibility for oneself

Origin: "The term comes from rowing, where a crew member must pull on an oar hard enough to propel his or her own weight. In use literally since the mid-19th century, it began to be used figuratively in the 1890s." (From *Southpaws & Sunday Punches*, by Christine Ammer)

TO KICK THE BUCKET

Meaning: To die

Origin: "There are a number of explanations for the origin of this expression, but the most plausible one has to do with the way some people committed suicide in the past. It was once fairly common for a man bent on killing himself to do so by standing on an upturned bucket, putting a noose around his neck, and then 'kicking the bucket.'" (From *Ever Wonder Why?*, by Douglas B. Smith)

A SHOT HEARD AROUND THE WORLD

Meaning: An act of great importance, which has far-reaching consequences

Origin: "The shot from which this phrase derives wasn't literally heard around the globe, but its repercussions were certainly felt far from Concord, Massachusetts, where it was fired on April 19, 1775. On that day, British troops marched to Concord to seize a cache of weapons they believed were being hidden there by American patriots. A confrontation between Colonial militiamen and the Redcoats took place at Concord Bridge of which the essayist, Ralph Waldo Emerson wrote, 'Here once the embattled farmers stood, And fired the shot heard 'round the world.' The American Revolution had begun. Not only did that first shot have great significance for the Americans and the British, but it had a tremendous impact on the rest of the world as well." (From *Inventing English*, by Dale Corey)

THREE SHEETS TO THE WIND

Meaning: Very drunk

Origin: "The phrase comes from the world of seafaring and the sheets referred to are ropes. The first thing one learns about ropes once aboard ship is that they are never called ropes. They are named according to their particular function: *halyards* (which move or hold things vertically, usually sails), *sheets* (which move or hold things horizontally), and *lines* (which hold things in a static position). The sheets in this case are those ropes that hold the sails in place. If one sheet is loose, the sail will flap in the wind, and the ship's progress will be unsteady. Two sheets loose ('to the wind'), and you have a major problem, and with three sheets to the wind, the ship reels... like a drunken sailor. (*Four sheets to the wind*, by the way, meant 'completely unconscious.')" (From *The Word Detective*, by Evan Morris)

GET OFF YOUR HIGH HORSE

Meaning: Stop being arrogant

Origin: "The 14th-century English religious reformer John Wycliffe once described a royal pageant in which high-ranking personages were mounted on *high horses*, or chargers, and these mounts became symbols of their superiority and arrogance. Mounted knights were certainly superior to foot soldiers, and even in 19th-century armies the cavalry regarded itself superior to the infantry. Ever since, telling someone to *get off their high horse* has meant to stop behaving arrogantly, with or without justification." (From *It's Raining Cats and Dogs*, by Christine Ammer)

Q: What's the official name of India? A: Bharat.

ANTE UP!

Bet you didn't know that poker is a relatively new invention. Think we're bluffing? Read on. (By the way, can you guess Uncle John's favorite poker hand? That's right—the royal flush.)

PLACE YOUR BETS

If anyone tells you they know the true origin of poker, they're not playing with a full deck. People have been betting on cards for more than 1,000 years, about as long as cards have been around—and that makes it hard to trace poker back to any one particular game. For that matter, poker may have descended from several different games which were mixed and matched over centuries to create the game played today. Some likely candidates:

• **Domino Cards,** a game played in China as early as 900 A.D. As the name suggests, these playing cards were marked like dominos, with each card representing the scores thrown by a pair of dice—a one and a six, for example.

• **Tali,** a dice game played in the Roman Empire. In Tali throws of the dice are ranked in much the same way as poker: Three of a kind beat a pair, and high numbers are worth more than low ones.

• **As Nas,** a four-player Persian game that used a deck of 20 cards divided into four different suits. (According to some sources, there was also a five-player, 25-card version.) There were five types of cards in the deck: lions, kings, ladies, soldiers, and dancing girls; when played with a modern deck of cards, aces, kings, queens, jacks, and tens are used instead. Each player is dealt five cards, one at a time, per hand.

• **Primero,** an Italian card game played from the 16th century on. Thanks to the Napoleonic Wars (when soldiers weren't fighting, they liked to sit around and play cards), in the early 19th century, Primero spread across much of Europe and evolved into a number of different regional versions: Brag in England, Pochen in Germany, and Poque in France.

America once issued a 5-cent bill. (Bills worth less than $1 are called "fractional currency.")

BORN ON THE BAYOU

Modern poker is all-American—it evolved from card games that were played in New Orleans in the early 19th century. Exactly how it developed isn't entirely clear, but it's possible that poker came about when the French colonists, already familiar with Poque, learned to play As Nas from Persian sailors visiting the port city. In Poque the only hands that counted were pairs, three of a kind, and four of a kind; but As Nas recognized two pairs and the full house. At some point, card historians speculate, players dumped many of Poque's rules and replaced them with those from *as nas* to make the game more interesting.

The name Poque may have been combined with As (from As Nas) to get *poqas*, which when spoken with a Southern accent sounded like "pokah." Steamboats took pokah up the Mississippi and Ohio rivers to the north, where people pronounced it "poker." From there, poker spread by wagon train and railroad across the continent.

NOT PLAYING WITH A FULL DECK

Have you ever taken notes during a poker game? Hardly anyone ever does—that's one reason why the history of poker is so difficult to trace. Luckily, in 1829 an English actor named Joseph Crowell saw poker being played on a steamboat bound for New Orleans and recorded what he saw, providing a rare glimpse of what poker was like in its earliest form.

Like today, each player was dealt five cards and then placed bets; whoever had the best cards won all the money that was bet. But at that time the deck still had only 20 cards (four suits of aces, kings, queens, jacks, and tens)—it wasn't until the 1840s that the full 52-card deck came into use.

Why were so many cards added? There were two main reasons:
• When the concept of the draw—replacing some of the cards in your hand with new cards taken from the deck—was introduced in the 1840s, a 20-card deck wasn't big enough anymore.
• People who'd been cheated by card sharks playing a crooked game called three-card monte thought a game with 52 cards instead of just 3 would be a lot harder to rig.

The 52-card version of poker (and other games) became so popular that the 20-card deck eventually died out altogether.

WAR GAME

The Civil War was a period of great innovation in poker, thanks to the fact that millions of soldiers learned the game during the war and played it whenever they had a chance. Draw poker became very popular, and a newer variation, *stud-horse* poker (stud poker for short), in which some cards in a hand are dealt face up, and others dealt face down, also became widespread. The straight (five cards of sequential rank, such as 3, 4, 5, 6, and 7) also became a recognized poker hand during the war.

PLAY CONTINUED

When the Civil War ended and the soldiers went home, they brought poker with them, and the innovations continued:

• The wild card was introduced in about 1875.

• Low ball (the *worst* hand, not the best, wins the pot) followed in about 1900.

• Why settle for playing only one type of poker per game? "Dealer's choice" games—in which the dealer gets to pick any version of poker they want for that hand—also became popular at the turn of the century.

YOUR GOVERNMENT AT WORK

Were it not for this period of innovation, poker might have faded into obscurity or disappeared altogether. All forms of gambling fell out of favor in many parts of the country at the turn of the 20th century, and many states passed antigambling laws. These laws naturally applied to poker, too... or did they?

In 1911 California's attorney general had to decide whether poker was a form of gambling and thus should be outlawed. His conclusion: standard poker and stud poker, in which you had to play the cards you were dealt, were purely games of chance. That made them a form of gambling, he reasoned, and that made them illegal. *Draw* poker was another story. Drawing new cards from the deck—or deciding not to—made it a game of skill, and games of skill were not illegal under California law. So draw poker not only survived, it thrived—and today hundreds of different variations of draw poker are played all over the world.

I'LL SEE YOU AND RAISE YOU

Here's a look at some of the most popular forms of poker. How many have you played?

- **Seven-Card Stud.** Two down cards (face down) and one up card (face up) are dealt to each player. They bet, and then four more cards are dealt one at a time—three up and the last one down—and bets are placed after each of these cards is dealt.

- **Razz.** Like Seven-Card Stud, except that the lowest hand wins, not the highest.

- **Texas Hold 'em.** Each player gets two down cards, then they place their bets. Three *common* cards are dealt face up to the center of the table, then the players place their bets again. Two more common cards are dealt, with bets being placed after each one. The best combination of five cards you can make from your two cards and the five on the board constitutes your hand; the highest hand is the winner.

- **Omaha High.** Each player gets *four* down cards; then bets are placed.

- **Omaha High-Low.** The same as Omaha High, except that the high hand and the low hand split the pot (the winnings).

- **Five-Card Stud.** Each player is dealt one down card and one up card, then bets are placed. Each player is dealt a second up card, and bets are placed again. A third and then a fourth up card are dealt to each player, each one followed by a round of betting.

- **Five-Card Draw.** Each player is dealt five cards down. Bets are placed, then each player may discard one or more cards and replace them with new cards from the deck, then bets are placed again.

- **Lowball.** The same as Five-Card Draw, except that the lowest hand, not the highest, wins.

- **Indian Poker.** Each player is dealt one card only, which they are not allowed to see. They hold it up against their forehead—supposedly like an Indian feather—so that everyone else can see it, then bets are placed. High card wins. The idea is that this game is the opposite of all the others—you know what everyone else's cards are, but you don't know your own.

HURRICANES 101

On page 222 we told you how hurricanes
are formed. Here are some more basic facts
about one of nature's deadliest creations.

HOW HURRICANES ARE NAMED
Hurricane names are chosen years in advance. Here's how meteorologists pick them.

In the Atlantic Ocean. Until the 1940s, hurricanes went mostly unnamed. But during WWII long range airplanes began encountering two or more hurricanes in a single flight. So in 1953, to simplify storm tracking, American meteorologists started giving them names—alphabetically to help aviators keep track of whether they were encountering a new storm or one that was dying. As a further refinement, male names were given to hurricanes south of the equator and female names were used for storms north of the equator.

Hurricanes, however, rarely occur in the South Atlantic because the water is too cold for them to form. And because they always move away from the equator, there was no way for a hurricane with a female name to move south and become a him-icane. So, for four decades all the hurricanes that passed over North America had female names. By the 1970s charges of sexism prompted American meteorologists to reconsider the system and in 1979 they began to use male and female names alternatively.

Pacific Politics. The Pacific Ocean is so huge and bordered by so many nations that meteorologists divide it into several regions. How a typhoon (in the Pacific, hurricanes are called "typhoons") is named depends on where it was born.

• **The central Pacific** uses Polynesian names: Akoni, Lo, Oke, Peke, and Walaka.

• **Australia** uses English names, such as Fiona, Vance, Graham, and Harriet.

• **The southwest Indian Ocean** uses names an Indian influence plus a few holdovers from the British Raj: Atang, Boura, Kalunde, and Winston.

• **The northwest Indian Ocean** region doesn't use names—

Father of his country: The name Attila means "little father."

typhoons are numbered.

• **The northeast Pacific** uses names from the Americas: Andres, Carlos, and Kevin.

• **In the northwest Pacific**, there were so many different countries demanding to be included in the naming process that the United Nations had to step in. Names were submitted by Japan, China, Vietnam, Thailand, Malaysia, Cambodia, Micronesia, North and South Korea, the Philippines, and the United States. The current list of 141 names includes: Longwang (a mythological Chinese dragon); Damrey (Cambodian for "elephant"); Kodo ("cloud" in the Marshall Islands); and Higos ("fig" in the Marianas).

HOW HURRICANES ARE RATED

Hurricanes are classed by wind speed: a category 1 has speeds of 74–95 mph; a category 2 has speeds of 96–110 mph; a category 3 has speeds of 111–130 mph; a category 4 has speeds of 131–155 mph; and the rare category 5 storms have speeds of 156 and up.

The highest known sustained wind speed from a cyclone was Typhoon Tip, located in the northwest Pacific Ocean. Tip's sustained surface wind on October 12, 1979, was estimated at 190 mph. In the Atlantic region, Hurricane Camille in 1969 and Hurricane Allen in 1980 registered winds also estimated at 190 mph. But these are only estimates—category 5 winds are so strong that the instruments used for measuring them are often destroyed, leaving scientists to guess at how fast the wind really was.

THE FIRST RECORDED HURRICANE

In 1495, while anchored in Hispaniola, Christopher Columbus noted on his ship's log: "When the storm reached the harbor, it whirled the ships round as they lay at anchor, snapped their cables, and sank three of them with all who were on board."

Does this mean that Europeans had never heard of hurricanes before 1495? Actually, it does. Hurricanes can't reach Europe because the Earth's rotation always sends them west and north. Typhoons don't make it because they would have to cross Asia. The spent remains of Atlantic hurricanes *have* struck Europe (from the Arctic circle) but before modern meteorology, the Europeans just thought they were big rain storms.

THE WAY OF THE HOBO

Have you ever dreamed of hopping on a freight train and living off the land? Trust Uncle John, it's not as glamorous as it sounds. But just in case you do, here's a starter course.

HOBO HIERARCHY

What's the difference between a hobo, a tramp, and a bum?

Hobo: A migratory worker (the most respected of the three). Hoboes are resourceful, self-reliant vagabonds who take on temporary work to earn a few dollars before moving on. Some experts think the word *hobo* comes from *hoe boys*, which is what farmers in the 1880s called their seasonal migrant workers. Others say it's shorthand for the phrase *homeward bound*, used to describe destitute Civil War veterans who took years to work their way home.

Tramp: A migratory nonworker. A tramp simply likes the vagabond life—he's never looking for a job.

Bum: The lowest of the low; a worthless loafer who stays in one place and would rather beg than work for goods or services.

HOBO LINGO

Accommodation car: The caboose of a train

Banjo: A small portable frying pan

Big House: Prison

Bindle stick: A small bundle of belongings tied up in a scarf, handkerchief, or blanket hanging from a walking stick

Bull: A railroad cop (also called a "cinder dick")

Cannonball: A fast train

Chuck a dummy: Pretend to faint

Cover with the moon: Sleep out in the open

Cow crate: A railroad stock car

Crums: Lice (also called "gray backs" and "seam squirrels")

Doggin' it: Traveling by bus

Easy mark: A hobo sign, or "mark," that identifies a person or place where one can get food and a place to stay overnight

---

Food fights? Most arguments in the home take place in the kitchen.

Honey dipping: Working with a shovel in a sewer

Hot: A hobo wanted by the law

Knowledge box: A schoolhouse, where hobos sometimes sleep

Moniker: Nickname

Road kid: A young hobo who apprentices himself to an older hobo in order to learn the ways of the road

Rum dum: A drunkard

Snipes: Other people's cigarette butts (O.P.C.B.); "snipe hunting" is to go looking for butts

Spear biscuits: To look for food in garbage cans

Yegg: The lowest form of hobo—he steals from other hobos

HOBO ROAD SIGNS

Wherever they went, hobos left simple drawings, or "marks," chalked on fence posts, barns, and railroad buildings. These signs were a secret code giving fellow knights of the road helpful tips or warnings.

 "Angel food" found here—you have to sit through a sermon to get it.

 The people who live here are rich (a silk hat and a pile of gold).

 This homeowner has a gun—run!

 Be prepared to defend yourself.

 Beware of the "bone polisher" (a mean dog).

 Townspeople don't want you here—keep moving!

 It's safe to camp here.

Police around here don't like hoboes (handcuffs).

Can you taste them? The secret recipe for Dr Pepper is said to contain 23 fruit flavors.

TOILET TECH

Better living through bathroom technology.

INVASIVE ADVERTISING

Company: Captive View (Britain)

Product: Viewrinal, a "digital display for the washroom"

How It Works: It's actually a urinal with a TV built into it—one that shows nothing but 30-second commercials. As of August 2003, the company had installed 150 Viewrinals in the men's rooms of bars, clubs, and movie theaters all over Britain, serving an audience estimated at 400,000 viewers per month.

So why would any company want to pitch their product *there?* "Viewrinals offer a captive audience to advertisers," the company explains, "and they have the ability to target the elusive 18–30 age group in a trendy environment using cutting-edge technology."

Not to Be Confused With: Picturinal—the urinal billboard that talks. "The motion-activated picture frames are positioned above urinals in soccer stadiums. Once triggered, the frame speaks its message—to its now-captured audience."

RISE TO THE OCCASION

Company: Urilift (Holland)

Product: The Urilift, the world's first telescoping "pop-up" urinal

How It works: The Urilift is intended to address the problem of public urination without being too much of an eyesore. During the day when it's in the closed position and not in use, the Urilift looks like a manhole cover built into the sidewalk. But at night, when the bars are open, all a city worker has to do is walk past the manhole cover with a remote control, and voila! Up out of the ground pops an open-air, *pissoir*-style urinal that's about six feet tall and can accommodate three people at a time. Then in the morning when the bars are closed, drinkers have gone home, and respectable people don't want to look at a public urinal, the Urilift sinks back into the ground and disappears out of sight.

SPIN CYCLE

Company: TheCleanSeat.com (United States)

Product: Universal Clean Seat

How It Works: Picture a toilet seat that is perfectly circular instead of the traditional oval shape. If the Universal Clean Seat is dirty, you just wave your hand over a special sensor. A cleaning tool then pops out of the back of the seat, makes contact with the toilet seat ring and spins it like a phonograph record for 15 seconds, during which time it washes, disinfects, and dries the seat.

THE POT THICKENS

Company: TravelJohn Products, Inc. (United States)

Product: Personal Disposable Urinal Pouch

How It Works: "Our revolutionary patented *Liqsorb* pouch absorbs, deodorizes and disinfects while it solidifies liquids instantly into an odorless, spill-proof gel that won't leak! A specially-designed spill guard prevents back flow, and a unisex adapter makes it perfect for that much needed relief—whether sitting or standing. Reusable until it's full."

OTHER ITEMS

• **Hygen-A-Seat.** Be sure you always have a clean restroom toilet seat when you need one—carry one with you! The Hygen-A-Seat looks just like a standard toilet seat, except that it folds in half and has luggage handles to make it easy to carry. Nonslip pads enable it to adhere safely to all toilet seats. Comes with sanitizing spray and sanitary storage envelopes. The toilet-seat-as-briefcase look isn't for you? They also sell a "stylish shoulder bag for inconspicuous storage of your Hygen-A-Seat."

• **Flush Stopper.** A simple adhesive cover that "blinds" the electric eye of an automatic-flush toilet, so that it won't flush when little kids—who can be too small for the electric eye to "see"—are sitting on the toilet. "Our research shows that nearly 40% of all children develop some degree of stress associated with public restrooms due to a bad experience with an automatic-flush toilet," says inventor Jeffrey Kay.

• **Tilt-A-Roll.** Puts an end to the age-old debate: Should the toilet paper roll over the roll, or under the roll? The Tilt-A-Roll lets you have it both ways: it's a toilet paper holder mounted on a swivel so that if you don't like the way the roll is rolled, spin it 180° and it's just the way you like it.

... scholars compiled an 11,095-volume encyclopedia.

CRÈME *de la* CRUD

Most really bad movies die a quick death in the theaters and then gather dust on video store shelves. But not this one.

R ECIPE FOR DISASTER
• Take two A-list movie stars: Ben Affleck and Jennifer Lopez.

• Add a torrid off-screen love affair that doesn't translate into on-screen chemistry.

• Add a huge dollop of media hype about how great the movie's going to be.

• Mix in a vulgar, inane script.

Stir it all together and you have *Gigli* (pronounced *zheelie*), a movie that rivals *Ishtar* and *Battlefield Earth* for the title of Hollywood's biggest flop. Good news: You don't have to see the picture—you can be entertained just by reading the scathing reviews. Here are some samples.

"Looking for something to praise in *Gigli* is like digging for rhinestones in a dung heap."
—**Northwest Herald**

"Larry and Ricki eventually climb between the sheets in a scene that is insulting to the sexuality of all living creatures, from plankton on up."
—**Boston Globe**

"There is not one iota of dramatic weight to it, and so we just sit, slack-jawed, as *Gigli* unfolds, a cinematic train wreck of distinguished proportions."
—**Entertainment Today**

"If you're going to skip one film this year—make it *Gigli*."
—**Talking Pictures**

"*Gigli* looks like a project that was intended for appreciation by precisely two people in the entire universe: Ben Affleck and Jennifer Lopez. For their sake, I hope they buy a lot of tickets."
—**EFilmCritic.com**

"*Gigli* is a rigli, rigli bad movie."
—**Mercurynews.com**

"This is a film that inspires hatred."
—**FilmThreat.com**

"Fifty minutes into this bomb, one character yells, 'I'm getting tired of this!' In our theater, one audience member yelled back 'Me too!'"
—CrankyCritic.com

"If miscasting was a crime, *Gigli* would be proof of a felony."
—CNN

"The rare movie that never seems to take off, but also never seems to end."
—USA Today

"*Gigli* is so unrelentingly bad that people may want to see it just as a bonding experience; viewers (read: victims) will want to talk and comfort each other afterwards."
—San Francisco Examiner

"Lopez even gives a long, carefully detailed speech about how to not only gouge out someone's eye, but to remove the memory of everything they've ever seen. Which, by the end of the movie, wasn't starting to seem so bad."
—The Star-Ledger

"Test audiences reportedly balked at the film's happy ending and wanted Gigli and Ricki to die bloody deaths. And they say critics are harsh."
—Rolling Stone

"Not helping things is Lopez's Betsy-Wetsy lisp that transforms a line like 'brutal street thug' into 'bruel threet fug.'"
—Film Freak Central

"How on Earth did director Martin Brest envision this film? As *Chasing Amy* meets *Rain Man* meets *Pulp Fiction*? Did anyone think that sounded like a winning combination?"
—Chicago Tribune

"Mr. Affleck and Ms. Lopez's combined fees reportedly ran close to $25 million, and they earn their money by hogging as much screen time as possible and uttering some of the lamest dialogue ever committed to film."
—The New York Times

"*Gigli* is as awkward as the word itself. I suggest you spell *Gigli* backwards so it sounds like 'ill gig.'"
—Critic Doctor

"For two hours, not a single hair moved on Ben's head—not even when every hair in the audience was on end and growing in the direction of the exit's welcoming glow."
—Movie Juice

"It wasn't good, and we got buried."
—Ben Affleck

Ted Danson once appeared in a TV commercial as a package of lemon chiffon pie mix.

"EXTREMISM IN THE DEFENSE OF LIBERTY"

*On page 197 we brought you JFK's 1961 inaugural speech.
Now here's one from the other side. On July 16, 1964, Republican
Senator Barry Goldwater of Arizona made this speech accepting his
party's presidential nomination. The Cuban missile crisis had just
ended and the War in Vietnam was just beginning. In reading the
speech today, it's interesting to see how much of yesterday's politics
turn out to have been of passing importance, how much was of
lasting importance...and how much the world is still the same.*

I N THIS WORLD no party can guarantee anything, but what
we can do and what we shall do is to deserve victory, and victory will be ours. The good Lord raised this mighty republic to
be a home for the brave and to flourish as the land of the free—
not to stagnate in the swampland of collectivism, not to cringe
before the bully of communism.

During [the past] four futile years the current administration
has distorted and lost that faith. It has talked and talked and
talked the words of freedom, but it has failed and failed and failed
in the works of freedom.

Now failures blot the sands of shame at the Bay of Pigs; failures
marked the slow death of freedom in Laos; failures infest the jungles of Vietnam; and failures haunt the houses of our once great
alliances and undermine the greatest bulwark ever erected by free
nations, the NATO community. Failures proclaim lost leadership,
obscure purpose, weakening wills, and the risk of inciting our
sworn enemies to new aggressions and to new excesses.

I NEEDN'T REMIND YOU—but I will—that it's been during
Democratic years that our strength to deter war has been stilled
and even gone into a planned decline. It has been during Democratic years that we have weakly stumbled into conflicts, timidly
refusing to draw our own lines against aggression, deceitfully refusing to tell even our people of our full participation and tragically
letting our finest men die on battlefields unmarked by purpose,

---

The temple of Siva in Madura, India, is adorned with 30 million separate carved idols.

unmarked by pride or the prospect of victory.

Yesterday it was Korea; tonight it is Vietnam. Make no bones of this. Don't try to sweep this under the rug. We are at war in Vietnam. And yet the president, who is the commander in chief of our forces, refuses to say—refuses to say, mind you—whether or not the objective is victory, and his secretary of defense continues to mislead and misinform the American people, and enough of it has gone by.

Now, the Republican cause demands that we brand communism as the principal disturber of peace in the world today. Indeed, we should brand it as the only significant disturber of the peace. And we must make clear that until its goals of conquest are absolutely renounced and its relations with all nations tempered, communism and the governments it now controls are enemies of every man on earth who is or wants to be free.

WE CAN KEEP THE PEACE only if we remain vigilant and strong. Only if we keep our eyes open and keep our guard up can we prevent war. This is a party for free men, not for blind followers and not for conformists. In 1858 Lincoln said of the Republican Party that it was composed of "strange, discordant, and even hostile elements." Yet all of the elements agreed on one paramount objective: to arrest the progress of slavery and place it in the course of ultimate extinction.

Today, as then, the task of preserving and enlarging freedom at home, and of safeguarding it from the forces of tyranny abroad, is enough to challenge all our resources and to require all our strength.

I would remind you that extremism in the defense of liberty is no vice! And let me remind you also that moderation in the pursuit of justice is no virtue!

OUR CAUSE IS TO FREE OUR PEOPLE and light the way for liberty throughout the world. Ours is a very human cause for very humane goals. This party, its good people, and its unquestionable devotion to freedom will not fulfill the purposes of this campaign which we launch here now until our cause has won the day, inspired the world, and shown the way to a tomorrow worthy of all our yesteryears.

POKER LINGO

Ever watched rounders and fish splash the pot until they're down to the felt? If so, you've seen some serious poker players. They have their own language, too. Ante up!

- **All in:** Bet all your chips
- **Down to the felt:** So broke all you see in front of you is the green felt of the poker table
- **Tapioca, or Tap City:** Tapped out; out of money
- **Buy the pot:** Make a bet so large that other players are unlikely to match it
- **Tap:** Bet as much as your opponents have on hand, forcing them to bet everything
- **Catching cards:** On a winning streak
- **Railroad bible:** Deck of cards
- **Toke:** The tip you give to the dealer
- **Splash the pot:** Toss your chips into the pot, instead of just placing them there. It's considered bad form because other players can't see how much you're actually betting
- **Rake:** The house's cut
- **Cowboys:** Kings
- **Ladies:** Queens
- **Rock:** A very conservative player, someone who doesn't take big chances
- **Paint:** A face card

- **Trips:** Three of a kind
- **Berry patch:** A very easy game
- **Underdog:** A weak hand that's likely to lose
- **Rag:** An upfacing card so low in value that it can't affect the outcome of the hand
- **Alligator blood:** A player who keeps his cool under pressure has alligator (cold) blood
- **Wheel:** The best hand in lowball poker—6, 4, 3, 2, A
- **Fish:** A very bad poker player. They're only in the game so that you can beat them out of their money
- **George:** A fish
- **Rounder:** A professional poker player. A rounder makes his living parting fishes and georges from their money
- **Base deal:** Dealing from the bottom of the deck
- **In the hole:** In stud poker, the cards dealt face down, so only you can see them
- **Bullets:** Aces in the hole
- **Big slick:** A king and an ace in the hole
- **Boat:** A full house

Emily Dickinson wrote 1,700 poems. Seven were published in her lifetime.

THE HOLLYWOOD QUIZ

So you think you know movies and celebrities like Uncle John does? Take this quiz and find out. (Answers on page 501.)

1. Actor Jack Lemmon once told this story: "In the early 1970s I received an award, and I had a chauffeur who told me he wanted to be a comedian. He said, 'Mr Lemmon, if I'm successful, I want to be your neighbor in Beverly Hills.'" Who was the chauffeur?

a) Rodney Dangerfield

b) Lemmon's driver Bill Papp. "Kid," Lemmon said. "You're not funny. But if you work for me, at least you'll pay the rent."

c) Jay Leno

d) Dr. Phil (He decided nagging people was easier than comedy.)

2. When Bob Hope died in 2003 at age 100, what did he and his *New York Times* obituary writer Vincent Canby have in common?

a) They were stepbrothers: Hope's dad married Canby's mom.

b) Both men were dead.

c) Their first acting gig: co-stars in the same high school play.

3. Actress Salma Hayek likes which of the following snacks?

a) Half an Oreo and a Tic-Tac. "I don't want to get fat," she says.

b) Stir-fried rabbit over noodles. "It's good!" she insists.

c) Bugs and guacamole on a tortilla. "They're delicious!" she says.

4. What odd event took place after Charlie Chaplin died in 1977?

a) Kidnappers dug up his body and held it for ransom.

b) At the moment of death, his famous derby hat turned to dust.

c) The funeral home "lost" his ashes. They've never been found.

5. "Professor Marvel," a character in the 1939 film *The Wizard of Oz*, wore a coat that the wardrobe department bought at an LA thrift store. Who turned out to be the coat's original owner?

a) Abraham Lincoln

b) Mark Twain

c) L. Frank Baum, author of *The Wonderful Wizard of Oz* (1900).

Per capita, the cities of Winnipeg and Calgary, Canada, drink the most Slurpees in the world.

THIS IS...UJNN

Introducing Uncle John's News Network. We scour the globe looking for the strangest of the strange, the oddest of the odd.

*D**ateline: Brazil*—EAR TODAY, GONE TOMORROW
August 2003—A local man named Valdemar Lopes de Moraes walked into a Monte Claros medical clinic to get treated for an earache. A few hours later he walked out (*slowly*)... with a vasectomy. What happened? When the nurses called another man named *Aldemar* Aparecido Rodrigues for his vasectomy, *Valdemar* thought that he'd been called. "Rodrigues was called by the full name, and yet de Moraes thought it was him," the clinic's manager Vanessa Guimaraes told reporters. "The strangest thing is that he asked no questions when the doctor started preparations in the area which had so little to do with his ear. He later explained that he thought it was an ear inflammation that got down to his testicles."

Dateline: Japan—WE AIN'T LION, THAT STINKS!

August 2003—In an average month, trains operated by the West Japan Railway Company strike and kill ten deer who wander onto railroad tracks. So the railroad decided to test a new kind of deer repellent on the rails—lion poop. Lions are the deer's natural enemy, the thinking went, so the smell of the predator would keep the deer away. In August the railroad scrapped the experiment. Not because it didn't work, but because it worked *too* well—the poop kept the deer away, but it smelled so bad that it kept everything else away too, including local residents. "The track really did stink," says railroad spokesperson Toshihiko Iwata. "We're experimenting with more environmentally friendly methods now."

Dateline: Australia—THAR SHE BLOWS!

August 2003—The Johnson family of Coventry, England, took a 10-day sailing vacation to Australia. But their trip came to a sudden end when a 10-ton, 30-foot-long humpback whale leapt out of the water and onto their 40-foot sailboat, damaging the rigging and pulling down the mast. "There was a hell of a crash as it leapt out of nowhere," 61-year-old Trevor Johnson told reporters. The Johnson's were 10 miles from shore when it happened, and the crash knocked out the ship's radio. Luckily, they had a mobile phone with them and they were able to phone for help. "It's amazing no one was hurt or killed," Johnson says. Cost of chartering the boat for the 10-day trip: $238,000. (No word on whether the Johnsons got a refund.)

Dateline: Texas—EXTRA RETIREMENT INCOME

August 2003—a local man later identified as J.L. Hunter "Red" Rountree walked into a branch of the First American Bank in Abilene, handed a large envelope marked "robbery" to a teller, and told her to fill it with money. Moments later Red sped off in his 1996 Buick Regal with $2,000 in small bills. He didn't get far: A witness took down his license number and called the police. Thirty minutes later police arrested Rountree over and recovered the money. So what makes this story so unusual? Rountree is 91 years old—believed to be the oldest bank robber in U.S. history. The First American job was his third heist in five years. Why rob banks? Red blames a bad experience he had with his own bank. "It forced me into bankruptcy," he says. "I haven't liked banks since."

Dateline: England—CRANIAL CRIMINAL CRUSADER

August 2003—A burglar broke into Richard Morrison's Liverpool apartment and began ransacking it—until he saw a big jar with a human head floating in it. The burglar went straight to the police and told them what he found. Police sped over to the apartment, kicked down the door and discovered that Morrison is an *artist*, not a psycho—the object in the jar was a mask he'd made from strips of bacon. The police apologized for the mix-up and promised to fix the door. Morrison says he's not mad. "It's a pretty macabre piece of work," he admits. The burglar was charged with burglary.

Dateline: Czech Republic—PROUD FISHY

January 2002—In Tabor, a man broke into a pub at 4:00 a.m. to rob it. All was going well until a "Sing-n-Swing" wall-mounted fish with a motion-sensor started belting out Tina Turner's version of "Proud Mary." According to the pub's owner, who lived next door, the plastic fish scared the would-be burglar away.

The U.S. is the only western country with restrictions of marriage between cousins.

COYOTE RINGS THE WRONG BELL

Every year it happens—we're less than 24 hours from going to press and Uncle John runs over to Jay's desk and says, "Flying Flushes! We have to replace a 3-page article...hurry!" So Jay calmly goes to the ol' folk tale bookshelf and finds one he likes.

AGE-OLD ADVERSARIES

In Mexico there are many tales about animals, but most of them are about Hare and Coyote. These two always argue and try to outwit each other; they are rivals in hunting and everything else. But since Coyote is much the stronger, Hare has to match his wits against Coyote's strength.

Now, one day Hare finished a fine meal and lay down under a tree for his siesta. Sometimes he gazed up at the blue sky, and other times he just closed his eyes. Finally, after a while, Hare fell fast asleep.

Coyote came along very, very quietly, looking for Hare, for Coyote was hungry. When he saw Hare sleeping, he approached very slowly and silently, and when he was near, Coyote took a great jump and *plppp!* he landed squarely on top of Hare with all four paws.

SURPRISE!

Hare awoke with a frightened start and saw at once that he was in deep trouble. But he was not afraid.

"Now I have you, Hare!" said Coyote. "You must have had a fine breakfast, for you feel nice and fat. Mmm, what a great meal you will make!"

Hare was thinking fast.

"Yes, I did have a fine meal," he said, "And I don't mind if you eat me, for my flesh is old and dry and I don't have much longer to live anyway. But if you will just be patient and wait a bit, perhaps I can give you something to eat that is much more tender and softer than I am."

Odds that a piece of paper money printed by the U.S. Treasury is a $1 bill: 45%.

"I wouldn't mind having something more tender," replied Coyote, "But I don't see anything better to eat around here. So it will have to be you, Brother Hare, Ha, Ha, Ha!"

Hare did not laugh.

"I know," he said, breathing hard, for Coyote was sitting right on top of him and he was very heavy. "I know you see only me right now, because all the tender, young hares are in school, but that is just a little way from here. They are all there, soft and juicy, and just the right age for eating."

Coyote licked his lips.

FOR WHOM THE BELL TOLLS

"Yeeeessssssss," said Coyote, "I know that these little hares are very soft and juicy. But tell me, where is that school, Brother Hare?"

"Just a little way down the hill. They are waiting for me to ring the bell for them to come out and play. But I can't ring it yet, not until the sun reaches the tops of the trees up on the hill. Then I can ring the bell. See? It's right up here in this tree." And he pointed to a tree under which they were lying and in which there was a big, brown hornets' nest.

"Will those little, plump hares come out when you ring the bell?" asked Coyote.

"They will, indeed, but I have to wait a long time. It's too early now. They must stay there a long time yet."

"Would they come out if you rang the bell now?"

"Sure they would, but I won't ring it now. I must wait for the right time."

"Brother Hare, I'm not really that hungry now anyway, and I promise I won't eat you. You see, I am letting you get up. Why don't you go for a little walk, to stretch and get the stiffness out of your joints? I'll stay and ring the bell for you at the right time, my friend." Coyote got off Hare, and Hare stretched himself slowly.

DON'T BEE CRUEL

"I don't mind running off if you will promise to stay and ring the bell. But please do not forget, Brother Coyote, you must not ring it until the sun reaches the tops of the trees on the hill."

"I won't forget, but you must tell me how to ring the bell."

In Bavaria, beer isn't just an alcoholic drink—it's considered a staple food, like bread or eggs.

"It's very easy—all you have to do is shake the tree very hard. Then they will hear it at the schoolhouse. But shake it violently, so they will be sure to hear it."

"You can be sure I'll shake the tree hard enough, Brother Hare. Now run along!"

Hare was off like a flash. When he was at a safe distance, he shouted, "Be sure to wait for the sun to reach the trees, Brother Coyote."

"I won't forget, Hare. Now please, be on your way!"

Hare ran off, while Coyote watched, licking his lips. No sooner was Hare out of sight than Coyote rushed up the tree and began shaking it with all of his might. He shook it and shook it, but no bell rang. Finally, he threw all of his weight violently against the tree, and *klppp!* down fell the hornets' nest and landed squarely on Coyote's back. Suddenly the air was filled with hornets as they flew out in fury form their nest, stinging Coyote all over his body, from the point of his nose to the tip of his tail. You couldn't see his fur anywhere for all of the hornets.

Coyote ran as fast as he could, howling, but the hornets were after him all the way, stinging him at every step, teaching him a painful lesson for knocking down their nest.

And so greedy Coyote had sharp stings for supper instead of plump, little hares.

*   *   *

COYOTE ADVICE

Coyotes thrive throughout Canada, the United States, and Mexico. And contrary to legend, they are actually very clever. They're also predators. Here are a few tips from the Sierra Club to help protect pets and property:

• If you keep livestock or small animals, confine them in secure pens, especially from dusk to dawn when coyotes are most active.

• Guard dogs and electric fences deter predators.

• Coyotes are attracted to food scraps in garbage. Dispose of trash in a metal can, and secure the lid with a bungee cord or chain.

• It is best not to feed cats and dogs outdoors, but if you have to, do not leave bowls or food scraps outside at night.

Ernest Hemingway's rules for manhood: plant a tree, fight a bull, write a book, have a son.

PLEASED TO MEAT YOU

Uncle John once saw a sign on an electrician's truck that said "Let us fix your shorts." He's been collecting wacky business mottoes like these ever since.

Concrete company: "We dry harder."

Taxidermist: "We really know our stuff."

Podiatrist: "Time wounds all heels."

Butcher: "Let me meat your needs."

Pastry shop: "Get your buns in here."

Septic services: "We're number 1 in the number 2 business."

Dry cleaner: "Drop your pants here."

Towing company: "We don't want an arm and a leg…just your tows!"

Window cleaner: "Your pane is our pleasure."

Restaurant: "Don't stand there and be hungry, come in and get fed up."

Diaper service: "Let us lighten your load."

Funeral home: "Drive carefully, we'll wait."

Chimney sweep: "We kick ash."

Trash service: "Satisfaction guaranteed or double your trash back."

Garden shop: "Our business is growing."

Auto body shop: "May we have the next dents?"

Muffler shop: "No appointment necessary. We'll hear you coming."

Car wash: "We take a bite out of grime."

Massage studio: "It's great to be kneaded."

Sod installation: "We just keep rolling a lawn."

Auto repair: "We meet by accident."

Bakery: "While you sleep, we loaf."

Plumber: "A good flush beats a full house."

Butcher: "Pleased to meat you."

Vacuum cleaners: "Business sucks."

Added together, the world's unused frequent flyer miles equal 42,500 round trips to the sun.

THE DOO-DOO MAN

In our opinion, the ability to take a negative experience and turn it into something positive is a real gift. But what inspired this man could appeal only to bathroom readers.

TRAIL HAZARD

In 1985 Dr. A. Bern Hoff stepped in something unpleasant while hiking in Norway's Jotunheim Mountains. The unpleasant "something" had been deposited right in the middle of the hiking trail and, judging from appearances, only minutes before. Maybe it was his keen eyesight, maybe it was his degree in parasitic pathology, but somehow Dr. Hoff knew right away what he'd stepped in: "people droppings," as he delicately puts it.

It wasn't the first time Hoff had trod on people droppings, either: an avid hiker, he'd had similar experiences atop Africa's Mount Kilimanjaro, Hawaii's Haleakala Crater, and the Grand Canyon in Arizona. He stepped into people's "business" so often that it seemed like every hiking trip was turning into a business trip. As a former official with the Centers for Disease Control, he understood that the problem wasn't just disgusting, it was a serious health hazard. Hoff decided it was time for action.

"I got tired of seeing and smelling this stuff on the trail," he says. "Nobody wanted to deal with it, so I said, 'Hey, I'll do it.' This has got to stop." He formed H.A.D.D.—Hikers Against Doo-Doo.

THE NUMBER TWO PROBLEM

Hoff had stumbled—literally—onto a problem that started growing rapidly in the 1980s and continues today: Record numbers of people are hiking and camping out in the wild. And since most first-timers have never been taught how to properly "do their business" in the backcountry, in many popular outdoor destinations around the country, the results are plain to see, smell…and step in.

To counter this disturbing trend, H.A.D.D. offers a number of different "business plans." It teaches new campers tried-and-true waste-disposal techniques, and serves as an international clearing-house for new waste-disposal ideas.

Nothing to sneeze at: The common flu kills 20,000 people a year.

THE CAN

H.A.D.D. has also designed a cheap, sturdy portable privy called "The Can" that can be made from two ordinary 55-gallon drums. At last count, H.A.D.D. members have set up more than 280 Cans in wilderness areas around the world. The organization hopes to one day mount an expedition to bring The Can to the top of Mount Aconcagua, long known as Argentina's "tallest and most defiled peak," and is raising funds to improve the facilities on Russia's Mount Elbrus, which *Outside* magazine dubbed "the world's nastiest outhouse."

When Hoff founded H.A.D.D. in 1990, it consisted of only himself and his soiled hiking boots. Today the organization boasts more than 10,000 members, with chapters all over the world. "We're tongue-in-cheek, of course, but we are serious about trying to clean up the environment," Hoff says.

BUSINESS SCHOOL

Some tips on how to mind your own business in the wild:

• Pack out what you pack in. Bring several square pieces of paper, a paper bag full of kitty litter, and several zipper-type plastic bags or bags with twist-ties. Do your business onto the paper, then put the paper and your business into one of the plastic bags. Pour in some kitty litter, and seal the bag tightly. Dispose of it properly when you get back to civilization.

• If you do have to bury your business, be sure to do it: 1) at least 200 feet away from the nearest water source, trail, or campsite; 2) in organic soil, not sandy soil; and 3) in a "cat hole" dug at least six inches across and six inches deep. (*Hint:* Bring a small shovel.)

• Don't bury your business under a rock: business needs heat and moisture to decompose properly, and the rock will inhibit both.

• Don't bury it in the snow, either: snow melts... but your business doesn't. When spring comes it will reappear.

• Use toilet paper sparingly if at all; if you do use it, *don't* burn it and *don't* bury it with your business. Keep it in a plastic bag and dispose of it properly at the end of your trip.

• Pee at least 200 feet from the nearest water source, and *don't* pee on green plants—otherwise, when your pee dries, animals will be attracted to the salt.

Q: How many bedrooms are there on the board game Clue? A: None.

ACCORDING TO THE LATEST RESEARCH...

It seems as though every day there's a report on some scientific study with dramatic new information on what we should eat...or how we should act...or who we really are under all the BS. Some are pretty interesting. Did you know, for example, that science says...

NIGHT LIGHTS CAUSE CANCER

Researcher: Dr. Richard Stevens

Subjects: Residents of Beaver Dam, Wisconsin

What He Learned: In 2002, citing several studies of women's cancer rates, Dr. Stevens reported to the World Conference on Breast Cancer in Victoria, British Columbia, that artificial night lighting increases the risk of breast cancer. Extended hours of light, he said—night lights, street lights, and even car headlights—rob a person of valuable hours of darkness and disrupt the body's natural clock. That causes the body to make less melatonin, a hormone produced almost exclusively at night. Melatonin limits the body's estrogen levels, and high levels of the female hormone estrogen are known to increase the risk of getting the disease. He recommended red bulbs in night lights—they're less disruptive to sleep patterns.

THE VATICAN EMITS HAZARDOUS RAYS

Researcher: Paola Michelozzi of the Rome health department

Subjects: People who live near Vatican City

What She Learned: EMFs (electromagnetic field emissions) are produced by electric current. In power lines and large communication antennas, those emissions can be very high—and, some say, dangerous. The Vatican has a huge radio and communications station on the outskirts of Rome, and because the Vatican is an independent country, it's not regulated by Italian law. Dr. Michelozzi's team decided to study the area around the station and the effects of the EMFs. Their finding: The rate of deaths for men due to leukemia was three times higher than the expected rate within a 1.2-mile radius. For children it was double. The Vatican refuses to release any information about their transmissions.

What happens when it eats chocolate? If a cow eats onions, its milk will taste like onions.

BEER STINKS
Researchers: Chemist Malcolm Forbes, University of North Carolina
Subject: Beer
What He Learned: Have you ever opened a bottle beer and noticed that it smells "skunky?" Dr. Forbes studied hops, the ingredient that gives beer much of its taste, and found that after exposure to light, a chemical reaction in the hops molecules results in the production of a compound called a *thiol*. Another place thiols can be found: in a skunk's spray gland. "Of course," says Forbes, a beer connoisseur who was happy to do the study, "the best solution we offer is to drink your beer as fast as possible."

REDHEADED WOMEN ARE MORE SENSITIVE
Researcher: Dr. Edwin Liem, University of Louisville
Subjects: Redheads and brunettes
What He Learned: Anesthesiologists have said it for decades: they have to use more anesthetic to put a redhead "under." Now they have proof. Dr. Liem gave a group of women common anesthetic drugs and monitored their reflex movements in response to being pricked with needles. He found that red-haired women needed 20% more of the drug to numb their pain reflexes completely. Doctors think it may be caused by a genetic glitch in redheads related to melanin, a pigment that affects skin and hair color.

LONDON CABBIES HAVE BIGGER BRAINS
Researchers: Scientists at University College London
Subjects: Taxi drivers
What They Learned: To get a license to drive the traditional black cab in London, drivers have to pass a very rigorous test called "The Knowledge." Those that do are known to be excellent navigators. This study showed something else: after giving 49 drivers MRI brain scans, researchers noticed that the drivers had an enlarged hippocampus—the part of the brain associated with navigation in birds and other animals. And even more amazingly, like a muscle, the more it's used, the larger it grows. Longtime cabbie David Cohen was surprised by the results: "I never noticed part of my brain growing. It makes you wonder what happened to the rest of it."

STRANGE LAWSUITS

Here are more real-life examples of unusual legal battles.

THE PLAINTIFF: Paula Blum, 54-year-old mother
THE DEFENDANT: Ephraim Blum, her son
THE LAWSUIT: After years of trying (and failing) to get alimony payments from her ex-husband, Blum switched tactics—she sued her son. Not for alimony, though: Blum used the Family Law Reform Act, which states that upon reaching adulthood, a child has an obligation to give his parents financial assistance.
THE VERDICT: Incredibly, the court found in her favor, ordering Ephraim to pay his mother $270 a month for life.

THE PLAINTIFF: Gerald Mayo
THE DEFENDANT: Satan and His Staff
THE LAWSUIT: Alleging that Satan had deliberately made his life miserable, placed obstacles in his path, and plotted his doom, Mayo sued the Prince of Darkness in federal court. On what charges? Civil rights violations. Mayo claimed that Satan had "deprived him of his constitutional rights."
THE VERDICT: Case dismissed. The judge expressed doubt over whether the defendant was actually a resident of the judicial district and noted that Mayo hadn't included instructions on how to serve Satan with the necessary papers.

THE PLAINTIFF: Ralph Forbes, of Russellville, Arkansas
THE DEFENDANTS: The National Department of Education, the Russellville School District, the High Priests of Secular Humanism, the Communist Party of the USA, the Church of Satan, the Anti-Christ, and Satan, God of This World System
THE LAWSUIT: In 1986, outraged that schools around Little Rock were sponsoring Halloween celebrations, Forbes—a local pastor and candidate for U.S. senator—decided to sue on behalf of Jesus Christ and children everywhere. Calling Halloween activities "rites of Satan," he was determined to stop them.

The Devil's advocate, attorney John Wesley Hall, Jr., argued that the suit should be dismissed because Forbes had failed to prove that Satan owned property or wrote contracts in Arkansas.

THE VERDICT: Case dismissed.

THE PLAINTIFF: An anonymous 19-year-old man
THE DEFENDANT: The New York City Transit Authority
THE LAWSUIT: The man tried to commit suicide by jumping off a subway platform into the path of an oncoming train. He lost one arm, a leg, and part of his other arm—but not his life. Frustrated with the futile attempt, the man filed suit against the Transit Authority. His claim: "The motorman was negligent in not stopping the train quickly enough."
THE VERDICT: Settled out of court for $650,000. While they were negotiating the settlement, the man tried suicide again, using the same method as before—and once again was unsuccessful. (No word on whether he filed a second lawsuit.)

THE PLAINTIFF: "Josef M.", a 62-year-old German man
THE DEFENDANT: Josef M.'s butcher
THE LAWSUIT: Josef M. sued his butcher for $790...for selling him a loaded bratwurst. He claimed the sausage exploded as he bit into it, and hot fat squirted into his mouth, burning it and the inside of his throat. His major complaint: "I couldn't kiss for four weeks," he said.
THE VERDICT: The court rejected the claim as frivolous.

THE PLAINTIFF: Robert Paul Rice, an inmate
THE DEFENDANT: Utah State Prison
THE LAWSUIT: Rice sued the prison for violating his religious freedom, claiming that he listed "the Vampire Order" as his religion and should have his religious needs provided for. According to the suit, prison officials failed to provide a "vampire diet" (only grains and vegetables—no meat) or a "vampress" with whom he could partake in "the vampiric sacrament." Lawyers for the prison argued that it provides five diets to choose from and "vampire" isn't one of them. And a "vampress?" Sorry, prisons in Utah do not allow conjugal visits.
THE VERDICT: Rice lost. The court ruled that the case "raised questions that are so insubstantial as not to merit consideration."

Foggiest place on the U.S. West Coast: Cape Disappointment, WA (107 days per year).

YOU'VE GOT MAIL!

Like anyone with an e-mail address, the BRI gets a lot of unsolicited mail that seems unbelievable. We looked into claims made by some of them, and here's what we found.

YOU'VE GOT MAIL:

To: Everyone
From: Carefulguy@EarthLink.net
Subject: The potential killers among us

This is a genuine test used by a famous psychologist to test whether you have the mind of a killer: While at the funeral of her mother, a girl met a guy and instantly fell in love with him. A few days later, the girl killed her own sister. Question: What is her motive in killing her sister? Answer: She hoped he would show up at the next funeral. If you answered this correctly, you think like a psychopath.

ORIGIN: This e-mail began circulating in May 2002.

THE TRUTH: It's fake. Even psychologists can't predict whether a person is a psychopath. So how could this one-question quiz?

YOU'VE GOT MAIL:

To: Concerned parents
From: FrigidTess@bottlefed.com
Subject: BAN BREAST-FEEDING NOW

Over 200,000 Americans have signed a petition urging Congress to declare breast-feeding unlawful. This primitive ritual violates babies' civil rights and fosters an incestuous relationship between mother and child. Breast-feeding teaches children illicit sex, resulting in an addiction to promiscuity. The Republican Convention must ban it now. Republicans: Choose a candidate who supports our cause!
Tess Hennessy, Founder-Director
Citizens Against Breast-Feeding

ORIGIN: This e-mail first appeared in the weeks leading up to the Republican National Convention in August 2000.

The Thousand Islands of New York and Ontario actually number about 1,500.

THE TRUTH: It's fake. The e-mail included a phone number that turned out to be the number of Spencer Publications, the publisher of several books on hoaxes...just like this one.

YOU'VE GOT MAIL:

To: Beer lovers everywhere
From: GaryA@Millertime.com
Subject: Free beer for the New Year

We at Miller Brewing would like to make a special New Year's offer to our valued customers: If this e-mail makes it to 2,000,000 people by 12:00 P.M. on New Year's Eve of 1999, we will send each e-mailer a coupon for one free six-pack of any Miller beverage.
Enjoy, and Cheers,
Gary D. Anderson, Chief Marketing Director
Miller Brewing Company, Inc.

ORIGIN: It first appeared just before New Year's Eve 1999.

THE TRUTH: It was a fake, and a pretty obvious one at that—how could Miller ever "card" all 2,000,000 e-mailers to make sure they were old enough to drink their free beer? "*We* are the victims of this online prank," says a company spokesperson.

YOU'VE GOT MAIL:

To: CD owners everywhere
From: Larry@CDRefund.gov
Subject: CD price-fixing settlement—Register now!

Compact disc distributors and retailers settled a lawsuit filed by 41 states, and have agreed to pay out $44 million in refunds to customers who purchased any CDs between 1995 and 2000. If you bought a CD or cassette during this time, all you have to do to claim your share is go to the CD settlement website and register online.

ORIGIN: This e-mail began circulating in September 2002.

THE TRUTH: It's actually *true*—there really was a lawsuit and a $44 million cash settlement. The bad news: The deadline to register was March 5, 2003, so if you didn't sign up, you missed the boat. What'd you miss? Only about $12.60, so don't feel too bad.

DUMB JOCKS?

More verbally challenged sports stars.

"He treats us like men. He lets us wear earrings."
—**Torrin Polk, University of Houston receiver,** *on his coach, John Jenkins*

"Left hand, right hand, it doesn't matter. I'm amphibious."
—**Charles Shackleford, NCSU basketball player**

"[He] called me a 'rapist' and a 'recluse'. I'm not a recluse."
—**Boxer Mike Tyson,** *on writer Wallace Matthews*

"In terms of European athletes she is currently second. A Cuban leads the rankings."
—**Paul Dickenson, BBC commentator**

"We can't win at home. We can't win on the road. I just can't figure out where else to play."
—**Pat Williams, Orlando Magic GM,** *on his team's poor record*

"It's almost like we have ESPN."
—**Magic Johnson,** *on how well he and James Worthy play together*

"Me and George and Billy are two of a kind."
—**N.Y. Yankee Mickey Rivers,** *on his relationship with George Steinbrenner and Billy Martin*

"I told [GM] Roland Hemond to go out and get me a big-name pitcher. He said, 'Dave Wehrmeister's got 11 letters. Is that a big enough name for you?'"
—**Eddie Eichorn, White Sox owner**

"Men, I want you just thinking of one word all season. One word and one word only: Super Bowl."
—**Bill Peterson, football coach**

"I want to rush for 1,000 or 1,500 yards, whichever comes first."
—**George Rogers, New Orleans Saints running back**

"Raise the urinals."
—**Darrel Chaney, Atlanta shortstop,** *on how management could keep the Braves on their toes*

In an average day, Canada imports 822 hockey sticks from Russia.

OOPS!

*More blunders and screwups to make
you feel all smug and superior.*

HAPPY MEAL

Washington, D.C., June 2002—"Benjamin Crevier recently got a personal invitation from U.S. Vice President Dick Cheney to a $2,500-a-plate dinner with President George W. Bush. Ben, who is five years old, wrote back to decline, saying he had only $11.97 in his piggy bank."

—*The North County* (Maryland) *Times*

HOMEWRECKERS

"A wrecking crew that was supposed to demolish an abandoned house accidentally plowed a bulldozer into the headquarters of a group that had tried for months to preserve it. The Dade Heritage Trust had failed to save the 102-year-old home of pioneer doctor James M. Jackson, located next door to the trust's headquarters. But the bulldozer operator made a wrong turn, taking out a porch column, a window and roof tiles of the trust's headquarters. 'What can I say?' said Jesus Ramos, bulldozer operator and owner of Shark Wrecking. 'It was an accident.'"

—**Associated Press**

NOT THAT KIND OF GRASS

"In December 2002, Chicago police got an anonymous tip that a major consignment of illegal drugs was being moved in a truck. When officers stopped the vehicle, they found two small plastic bags with crushed green plants thought to be marijuana. Lab tests found no drugs were present. The 'marijuana' turned out to be hay from a church Nativity scene."

—*The National Post,* Canada

ARMED AND DANGEROUS

"A suspect picked the wrong vehicle to carjack in Hollywood Sunday. Los Angeles police say the suspect took one car, then pulled into a gas station, ditched the vehicle and tried to take a minivan. Big mistake. The minivan was full of judo wrestlers from

Florida International University, who were in town to teach a self-defense class. The wrestlers punched the man in the face and hit him from behind, then held him until police arrived. The suspect was jailed on felony charges."

—*Los Angeles Times*

OFF WITH THEIR HEAD
"Officials at England's York Dungeon Museum of Horrors are looking for the visitor who purchased an authentic human skull in the museum's gift shop. The skull was accidentally placed on a bookshelf while an exhibit was being renovated. Someone apparently mistook the real skull for one of the replica skulls sold in the gift shop...and sold it as a souvenir."

—**Reuters**

EGG ON HIS FACE
"A 30-year-old plumber from Perugia in central Italy came up with a novel way of proposing to his girlfriend: He ordered a chocolate Easter egg with an expensive engagement ring, featuring a huge diamond and three rubies set in gold, placed inside. The young man then presented his beloved with the egg, a traditional Easter gift in that part of Italy. He didn't say anything to the girl, wanting her to open it on her own and experience the surprise of her life. Several days went by with no response from the girl, so he finally asked her if she had enjoyed his present. What he heard left him speechless. The girl explained she did not like dark chocolate, of which the egg was made, so she went to a nearby café and exchanged it for an identical egg made of milk chocolate.

"The two rushed to the café, but learned the egg had already been sold to another customer. No trace of the egg or the ring was ever found."

—*Financial Times*

"OH LORD, WON'T YOU BUY ME A..."
"When a gold Mercedes-Benz sports sedan was delivered by mistake to Ruth Shepard's driveway in Uniondale, New York, in May 2002, she thought it was a surprise Mother's Day present. A short time later, she was arrested for resisting police officers' attempts to get the car back to its rightful owner."

—**Universal Press Syndicate**

GRANNY DUMPING

How do doctors, nurses, and other hospital workers deal with the stress of being exposed to illness and death on a daily basis? They come up with irreverent, occasionally morbid—and very funny—terms for what goes on in the hospital every day.

Blood Suckers: People who take blood samples, e.g., nurses or laboratory technicians

Gassers: Anesthetists

Rear Admiral: Proctologist

AGA: Acute Gravity Attack—the patient fell over

AGMI: Ain't Gonna Make It

Coffin Dodger: A patient the hospital staff thought was going to die, but didn't

Gone Camping: A patient in an oxygen tent

Shotgunning: Ordering lots of tests, in the hope that one of them will identify what is wrong with a patient

GPO: Good For Parts Only

D&D: Divorced and Desperate; someone who isn't sick but comes to the hospital because they need attention

CTD: Circling the drain, or close to death

Rule of Five: If more than five of the patient's orifices have tubes running out of them, they're CTD.

UBI: Unexplained Beer Injury

Pop Drop/Granny Dumping: Checking an elderly relative into an emergency room, just so you can go on vacation without them

ECU: "Eternal Care Unit" (deceased), as in: "He's gone to the ECU."

DBI: Dirt Bag Index—a mathematical formula: the number of a patient's tattoos times the number of missing teeth equals the number of days since they last bathed.

VIP: Very Intoxicated Person

Hand Them a Bible So They Can Study for the Final: They're going to die.

UNIVAC: Unusually Nasty Infection; Vultures Are Circling

Eating In: Feeding by way of an intravenous tube

GTTL: Gone To The Light (deceased)

Silver Bracelet Award: A patient brought in wearing handcuffs

Bathroom fact: The average water temperature for showers in the U.S. is 105°F.

WORD ORIGINS

Ever wonder where words come from?
Here are some more interesting stories.

PANDEMONIUM

Meaning: Wild and noisy disorder or confusion

Origin: "John Milton's word for the capital of Hell in *Paradise Lost* (1667). He wrote it as 'Pandaemonium'—meaning "all demons" in Greek—having no idea that in the 19th century the word would mean 'uproar.' So when, as he also wrote, 'All Hell broke loose,' all the demons in Hell were scattered, marking the disintegration of the infernal city." (From *The Secret Lives of Words*, by Paul West)

COOKIE

Meaning: A small sweet cake, typically round, flat, and crisp

Origin: "The word was borrowed from the Dutch *koekje*, 'little cake,' which is the diminutive of Dutch *koek*, 'cake.' *Cookie* came into American English from the Dutch settlers of New York. It first appears in 1703 in the statement that 'at a funeral, 800 cockies…were furnished.' This early English spelling of the word differs from our modern spelling, but several other spellings also arose, such as *cookey* and *cooky*. The spelling *cookie* may have won out because the word is very common in the plural, spelled *cookies*." (From *Word Mysteries and Histories*, by the Editors of The American Heritage Dictionaries)

DRAB

Meaning: Lacking brightness, dull

Origin: "In the 16th century, *drab* was a word for a kind of cloth, coming into English from French *drap*, 'cloth.' From this, the word came to mean the common color of such cloth, which was its natural undyed color of dull brown or gray. Hence the fairly general meaning 'dull,' whether of an object's color (where it usually is brown or gray still, as 'drab' walls) or in a figurative sense, as a 'drab' day or someone's 'drab' existence." (From *Dunces, Gourmands & Petticoats*, by Adrian Room)

Old softie: Princeton professor John W. Tukey coined the term *software* in 1958.

URANIUM

Meaning: A dense radioactive metal used as a fuel in nuclear reactors

Origin: "In 1781 the brilliant English-German astronomer Sir William Herschel first recognized the seventh planet in our solar system, and named for it Uranus from the Greek god *Ouranos*. Eight years later the German chemist Kloproth discovered element 92, which he named *uranium* in honor of Herschel." (From *Word Origins*, by Wilfred Funk)

NONCHALANT

Meaning: Feeling or appearing casual and relaxed

Origin: "The nonchalant person is cool and indifferent, a literal etymology, since the word is from French *nonchaloir*, meaning 'not heated,' which is derived from Latin *noncalere*, 'not to be hot.' *Calor* is Latin for 'heat,' from which we get *calorie*, the amount of food needed to heat you or energize you." (From *More About Words*, by Margaret S. Ernst)

SALARY

Meaning: A regular payment made by an employer to an employee

Origin: "A salary, during the great days of the Romans, was called a *salarium*, 'salt-money.' The ancients regarded salt as such an essential to good diet (and before refrigeration it was the only chemical that preserved meat) that they made a special allowance in the wages of soldiers to buy *sal* (Latin for 'salt'). With time any stipend came to be called a *salarium*, from which English acquired the word salary." (From *Hue and Cry and Humble Pie*, by Morton S. Freeman)

BLINDFOLD

Meaning: A piece of cloth tied around the head to cover the eyes

Origin: "The name of the folded piece of cloth has only a coincidental resemblance to the way the material is doubled over. *Blindfold* actually comes from the Middle English *blindfeld*, 'to be struck blind.' Walter Tyndale used *blyndfolded* in his English translation of the Bible (1526), and if he was not the first to make the mistake, he was certainly the most influential." (From *Devious Derivations*, by Hugh Rawson)

Q: What woman's body part would ancient Chinese artists never paint? A: The feet.

EH TWO, CANADA?

While rummaging through the trivia vault here at the BRI, we kept coming across a fascinating fact: Of the 175-plus nations in the world, Canada—the 35th most populous country—comes in second in a surprising number of categories.

Canada was the 2nd country to legalize medical marijuana. (*1st: Belgium*)

Canada has the 2nd coldest national capital: Ottawa. (*1st: Ulaanbaatar, Mongolia*)

Canada is the 2nd largest foreign investor in Chile. (*1st: United States*)

Canada has the 2nd highest University enrollment rate in the world. (*1st: United States*)

Canada has the 2nd most tornadoes. (*1st: United States*)

Canada is the 2nd in pork exports. (*1st: Denmark*)

Canada has the 2nd highest amount of gum chewed per capita. (*1st: United States*)

Canada has the 2nd highest broadband Internet access in the world. (*1st: South Korea*)

Canada was the 2nd country to publish a National Atlas. (*1st: Finland*)

Canada has the 2nd highest fresh water use per capita. (*1st: United States*)

Canada has the 2nd highest water quality. (*1st: Finland*)

Canada is the 2nd largest per capita emitter of greenhouse gases. (*1st: United States*)

Canada has the 2nd most biotech companies. (*1st: United States*)

Canada is the 2nd largest exporter of red meat. (*1st: Australia*)

Canada is the 2nd biggest market for U.S. seafood. (*1st: Japan*)

Canada is the 2nd largest foreign investor in Korea. (*1st: United States*)

Canada has the 2nd highest incidence of breast cancer in the world. (*1st: United States*)

Canada is the 2nd most workaholic nation in the world. (*1st: Japan*)

Canada was the 2nd country with triple platinum sales of *Prodigy's* "Fat Of The Land," featuring the single *Smack My Bitch Up.* (*1st: New Zealand*)

Only 20% of the Sahara is covered with sand—the rest is rocky.

Thanksgiving Day in **Canada is the 2nd** Monday in October.

Canada has the 2nd most foreign visitors to Texas. (*1st: Mexico*)

Canada was the 2nd country to establish a Ministry of the Environment. (*1st: France*)

Canada was the 2nd country to require daytime running lights on all new vehicles. (*1st: Norway*)

Canada has the 2nd largest oil reserves in the world. (*1st: Saudi Arabia*)

Canada has the 2nd highest proportion of immigrant population. (*1st: Australia*)

Canada was the 2nd country with a Boy Scout program. (*1st: England*)

Canada has the 2nd most civilian pilots in the world. (*1st: United States*)

Canada has the 2nd highest cable TV access in the world. (*1st: Belgium*)

Canada was the 2nd country in the world to have a nuclear reactor. (*1st: United States*)

Canada was the 2nd country to develop a jet airplane. (*1st: Great Britian*)

Canada is the 2nd largest country in the world. (*1st: Russia*)

ALTHOUGH...

- Canada is **1st** in literacy rate.

- Canada is **1st** in waste generated per person.

- Canada was the **1st** country to mine uranium.

- Canada was the **1st** British colony to gain self-government.

- Canada was the **1st** western country to recognize Ukrainian independence.

- Canada was the **1st** country to conduct a national survey on violence against women.

- Canada was the **1st** country to have a domestic communications satellite.

- **Canada is 1st** in ATM usage.

- **Canada was the 1st** to adopt a national multiculturalism policy.

- **Canada is 1st** in hydropower generation.

- **Canada also has...**

...the highest ocean tides (They're in the Bay of Fundy).

...the longest covered bridge (New Brunswick).

...the longest street (Younge Street, Toronto, at 2,000 miles).

...the largest National Park (Wood Buffalo National Park in Alberta/North West Territories).

No surprise: Canada is the largest importer of American automobiles.

LITTLE THINGS MEAN A LOT

A few more little things that caused big problems.

ANOTHER CONVERSION ERROR

The Mars Climate Orbiter blasted off in December 1998. Ten months later, it suddenly stopped transmitting signals and was presumed lost. An investigation found that the satellite had entered Martian orbit 60 miles too low and was destroyed entering the atmosphere. What caused the error? Lockheed Martin, which operated the satellite for NASA, had been sending maneuvering data to the orbiter in standard English units...unaware that the navigation team had done its calculations in *metric* units. Asked if they knew that NASA used the metric system, a Lockheed spokesman said, "obviously not." Estimated loss: $125 million.

A COMMA

In 1997 the American Asphalt Co. submitted the winning bid ($27 million) for a contract to build and pave the planned Las Vegas Beltway. But one of the losing bidders noticed something— American had mistakenly put a comma where a period was supposed to be, and road signs that were supposed to be priced at $23.80 per square foot were priced at $23,800 instead. This erroneous amount hadn't been added to the final price—the $27 million bid was still correct—but rather than risk a lawsuit, county officials scrapped all the bids and changed the scope of the bid, delaying construction for weeks...and adding $3.1 million in new costs.

A CHIP OF PAINT

On April 24, 1990, NASA launched the $1.5 billion Hubble Space telescope into Earth orbit...only to have it send back blurry images. What happened? A single chip of paint flaked off one of the instruments used to measure the shape of the telescope's huge 94.5-inch main mirror. That distorted some of the measurements and caused the mirror to be shaped slightly too flat. NASA eventually fixed the problem, but it took an extra space shuttle mission to do it and cost them millions of dollars.

Up or down? The Congo is the only river that flows both north and south of the equator.

DISEASES THAT JUST WON'T DIE

Before modern medicine and sanitation, diseases routinely decimated
huge portions of the population. Some of these scourges, such as
smallpox, have been virtually eliminated... but not all of them.

THE PLAGUE. It thrives in unsanitary environments and comes in two main varieties: bubonic and pneumonic. Bubonic plague is transmitted by infected fleas carried by rats. It's 50% to 60% fatal without treatment. Pneumonic plague is even worse—it's spread via airborne droplets and kills nearly 100% of untreated victims.

Over the course of world history, plagues have been responsible for 200 million human deaths and it's still with us. According to the Centers for Disease Control, a dozen Americans get it every year, mostly in southwestern states. It's treatable today, but still deadly: two U.S. citizens died of the disease in 1996.

RICKETS. This condition—caused by a lack of vitamin D— won't kill you. But it weakens your bones to the point where they become deformed. Children who develop rickets can end up with curved spines and bow-shaped legs resembling wishbones.

Rickets was a widespread ailment until the 1920s, when the introduction of vitamin D–fortified milk, along with a greater awareness of nutrition, led to a dramatic decline in cases. Yet the preventable condition still occurs where bad eating habits prevail. In 2001 the CDC identified six cases of rickets among children in Georgia.

LEPROSY. Contrary to popular belief, leprosy does not cause body parts to fall off. It is an infectious disease that kills all feeling in the victim's nerve-endings. Because lepers can't feel pain, their infected parts are easily bruised, battered, and burned, which can result in a loss of digits and limbs.

Leprosy is still common in developing countries. The CDC says there were 738,284 cases of the disease in 2000, largely in India, Nepal, and Myanmar. But Americans still get it, too. According to the CDC, 108 cases of leprosy were identified in the U.S. in 1999.

What are *zoonoses*? Not what you think—they're animal diseases communicable to man.

THE ICE WORM COMETH

*The BRI library has an entire wing for books and
articles on hoaxes. Here are a few classics.*

KLONDIKE ICE WORMS

Background: In 1898 a young journalist named "Stroller" White got a job in Dawson, Alaska, with the *Klondike Nugget*. The terms of his employment were tough: he had to increase sales...or he was out in the cold. Just then, a fierce storm took hold of the area and it gave him an idea. He wrote an article about "ice worms" that had crawled out of a nearby glacier to "bask in the unusual frigidity in such numbers that their chirping was seriously interfering with the sleep of Dawson's inhabitants."

What Happened: Sales of the *Nugget* skyrocketed as people began forming expedition teams to search for the noisy creatures. White got to keep his job and the ice worm story became so popular that bartenders started serving "ice-worm cocktails," in which they added a piece of frozen spaghetti to a customer's drink. Annual ice worm festivals became a local tradition—and are still held today.

Update: For years everyone assumed that ice worms were just a figment of White's imagination, but scientists recently claimed to have found real evidence of the existence of ice worms living inside Alaskan glaciers. No word on whether or not they chirp.

PRINCESS CARABOO

Background: One spring morning in 1817, a strange woman strolled into Almondsbury, England. She was five-foot-two and stunning, wearing a black shawl twisted like a turban around her head. She spoke a language no one could understand and had to use gestures to communicate. In those days a homeless woman roaming the street was usually tossed in the poorhouse, so the stranger was directed to see the Overseer of the Poor. But instead of sending her to the poorhouse, he sent her to stay at the home of Samuel Worrall, the county magistrate.

Days later a Portuguese sailor arrived at the Worrall household claiming to speak Caraboo's bizarre language. He translated as Caraboo revealed her secret past: she was no homeless beggar—

she was a princess from the island of Javasu. Pirates had kidnapped her and carried her across the ocean, but as they sailed through the English Channel, Caraboo jumped ship and swam ashore.

What Happened: The Worralls informed the local press and soon all England knew of Princess Caraboo. And for weeks, Caraboo was treated royally...until her former employer came forward.

A woman named Mrs. Neale had recognized the newspaper description of "Princess Caraboo" as her former servant, Mary Baker, a cobbler's daughter. The giveaway: Baker had often entertained Mrs. Neale's children by speaking a nonsense language. "Caraboo" reluctantly confessed to the fraud she and the "sailor" had perpetrated.

Amazingly, Mrs. Worrall took pity on Caraboo and gave her enough money to sail to Philadelphia. Seven years later she returned to England and made a living selling leeches to the Infirmary Hospital in Bristol.

CROSS-DRESSING KEN

Background: In July 1990, Carina Guillot and her 12-year-old daughter, Jocelyn, were shopping at a Toys "R" Us in Florida. As they strolled up and down the store aisles, they caught a glimpse of a peculiar-looking Ken doll. Sealed inside of a cardboard package was Barbie's friend Ken, dressed in a purple tank top and a polka-dotted skirt with a lace apron. As doll collectors, the Guillots immediately knew this one was out of the ordinary and brought it to the front register for closer inspection. Employees determined that the doll hadn't been tampered with and was indeed a genuine Mattel original. The Guillots purchased it for $8.99.

What Happened: Word of the "cross-dressing Ken" quickly hit the national media circuit. Newspapers wrote about it; TV talk shows talked about it. Collectors made outrageous bids of up to $4,000 for it. But the Guillots wouldn't sell. Instead they kept the doll long enough for the truth to come out of the closet. Finally, a night clerk at the store, Ron Zero, came forward and confessed to the prank. Apparently Zero had dressed Ken up in Barbie's clothes and then carefully resealed the package with white glue. Toys "R" Us fired him four days later.

MORE DIAMOND GEMS

Another collection of fantastic baseball feats. If you like these you can find more in Who Was Traded for Lefty Grove? *by Mike Attiyeh.*

HE WHAT?

In 1960 Stan "The Man" Musial of the St. Louis Cardinals did something almost unheard of in today's world of professional sports. After receiving one of baseball's biggest ever contracts—$100,000 a year—in 1958, Musial had a subpar year in 1959 (he failed to bat above .310 for the first time in his 17-year career). So he demanded—and received—a $20,000 pay cut.

BUSY DAY

Mets center fielder Joel Youngblood showed up at Wrigley Field in Chicago on August 4, 1982, having no idea he was about to make history. In the third inning, he hit a two-run single off the Cubs' Ferguson Jenkins. The following inning, he was told that he'd been traded to the Montreal Expos—and that they were waiting for him. So he packed his stuff and caught a plane to Philadelphia. He joined the Expos' lineup late in the game and singled off Phillies ace Steve Carlton. Youngblood made the record books for being on two different teams, batting against two future Hall of Famers, and getting hits off both of them...all on the same day.

BET ON PETE

He may have had a gambling problem off the field, but on the field, Pete Rose was a gambler's best friend. Rose has the distinction of being on the winning side in more games than any other player in baseball history: 2,011 games.

IN LIKE A LION, OUT LIKE A LAMB

When most fans hear the words "Red Sox" and the date "1986," only one thing comes to mind: the infamous ball that went through Bill Buckner's legs, which cost them game 6 of the World Series, which the "cursed" Red Sox then lost in game 7. But the Red Sox season started on a positive note. For the only time in major-league history, Dwight Evans hit the very first pitch of the baseball season over the fence for a home run.

Full moon? We see a man in the moon; other cultures see a woman, an ape, or a rabbit.

FROM A TO Z

Hank Aaron holds arguably the game's most coveted record: 755 career home runs. He comes in first in another category as well: alphabetically. Of the more than 15,000 players in the history of the game, Aaron's name comes first. (In case you were wondering, Dutch Zwilling of the 1910 Chicago White Sox comes last.)

HE COULDN'T KETCH UP

Joe DiMaggio's 56-game hitting streak in 1941 is another one of professional sport's most revered records. But it fell one hit short of landing "Joltin' Joe" a $10,000 sports endorsement. The Heinz Ketchup company was all set to pay DiMaggio to endorse their Heinz 57 Sauce...if the streak went to 57 games. But on July 17, 1941, thanks to stellar plays by Cleveland Indians third baseman Ken Keltner, DiMaggio went 0 for 3, so the streak ended at 56 games. One Heinz exec was quoted as saying, "I'll be damned if I'm going to change the name to Heinz 56 Sauce!"

KEEPING HIS EYES ON THE BALL

Ted Williams's biggest goal in life was to have people say, "There goes Ted Williams, the greatest hitter who ever lived." Knowing that eyesight was every bit as important to hitting as strength and speed, "Terrible Ted" went to great lengths to protect his peepers. He never read in a moving vehicle, and never chewed gum because it "made his pupils move up and down."

RECORD COLLECTOR

So who holds the record for the most records in baseball? Nolan Ryan. Arguably the game's best hurler, Ryan pitched in the big leagues from 1966 to 1993. When he retired, he owned or shared more than 40 American League and National League records.

*　　*　　*

"Managing a team is like holding a dove in your hand. Squeeze too hard and you kill it, not hard enough and it flies away."
—**Tommy Lasorda,**
manager, Los Angeles Dodgers

Literature quiz: What are Dr. Jeckyll's and Mr. Hyde's first names? A. Henry and Edward.

A PIG IN PINK TIGHTS

We invited our legion of BRI members to enter our original limerick contest.
Their humor and creativity bowled us over. Here are the winners.

HONORABLE MENTIONS

I used to hate having to go,
I was so very bored, you know.
But when I got the *Reader*,
My visits got sweeter,
Now I'm hoping my "business" is
slow.
    —Charlie Lopez

There once was a pig in pink tights.
He wanted his name up in lights,
So he held up his nose
and danced on his toes
'Til the farmer made bacon one
night.
    —Martin Slate

I'm known for my sparkling wit.
So when I need a trivial tidbit
It doesn't take long
'Cause I've got Uncle John
I just couldn't make doo without it!
    —Jonathan Gewirtz

A wicked young woman from Yop
Thought TP should roll from
the top.
It tore her marriage asunder
(Hubby rolled his from *under*).
At least that's what she said to the
cop.
    —Warren Blair

Find in these lines what I see
And then you'll understand me
Can't find it yet?
Too early to fret
Stop reading across. Read vertically.
    —Paul Ferro

I sob, I weep, I shed a tear.
No one can help—my fate is clear.
Although I must grieve
I just cannot leave;
For the paper's gone. I'm stuck in
here.
    —Carolyn Wright

There once was a cow who said,
"Moo.
I really don't have much to do.
I stand here all day,
And chew on some hay,
And then chew it again when I'm
through."
    —Carolyn Martinez

Said his wife, "It's addictive, I've
heard,
But to take quite this long is absurd.
He's been locked in the john,
Since before August one,
And now it's November the third."
    —Philip Lynch

AND THE WINNER IS...

i never did two good in scool
i always apeered such a fool
so i bought a p.c.
just for spellcheck, you see
but i can't turn it on. oh how crule!
    —Danielle Garvey

The closest black hole, known as V4641 Sgr, is 1,600 light years from Earth.

A LOT TO LOSE

*Overweight, but tired of dieting? More and more celebrities—
and regular folks—are opting to forgo dieting and exercise
in favor of a shortcut way to lose weight: surgery. (Would
Uncle John ever have weight-loss surgery? Fat chance.)*

SHARON OSBOURNE
Top Weight: 225 pounds
Last Splurge: All the chocolate she could eat

Big Loser: The wife of heavy-metal star Ozzy Osbourne was used
to her husband being in the spotlight, but when she became a star
of MTV's reality show *The Osbournes*, the spotlight suddenly
focused on her. She became more conscious about her looks than
ever before, especially her weight. As it crept up over 200 pounds,
Osbourne, a confessed chocoholic, decided to turn to a type of
weight-loss surgery called vertical banded gastroplasty (VGB).

The surgeon implants a silicone band around the top part of
the stomach, reducing the pocket of the stomach and, in turn,
restricting the amount of food a person can eat before feeling full.
Osbourne says if she hadn't had the operation she'd weigh "500
pounds and be in a wheelchair." Today she weighs about 130
pounds.

AL ROKER
Top Weight: 320 pounds
Last Splurge: Multiple steaks, onion rings, Häagen-Dazs ice
cream, Krispy Kreme donuts

Big Loser: The weatherman on NBC's *Today Show* said, "At a
certain point I started eating and I never stopped." Roker was a
guy who ate Quarter-Pounders in pairs and donuts by the dozen.
He tried diets and exercise programs, but couldn't stick with them.
Each time he lost weight, he'd eventually gain it back, along with
an extra 10 pounds. When he tipped the scales at 320 pounds,
"Fat Albert," as the kids called him in his elementary school years,
decided to take drastic action.

Roker turned to surgery to reduce his stomach from the size of a
football to the size of a chicken egg. But Roker was embarrassed to

---

Ninety percent of the wildlife species on the island of Madagascar are found nowhere else.

admit he was getting the surgery: what if it didn't work? He told everyone he was having his gallbladder removed, but what he really had was a procedure commonly called stomach stapling.

Roux-en-Y Gastric Bypass is the official name for this procedure, after the Swiss surgeon who invented it, Dr. Cesar Roux. The stomach is separated into two parts with titanium staples. The upper part forms a small pouch. The lower stomach and first portion of the small intestine (duodenum) are bypassed by cutting the small intestine and connecting the lower section (jejunum) to the upper stomach. Food then passes directly into the jejunum. The tiny new stomach can only hold 5 to 10 bites of food at a time.

The operation worked. Roker went from eating 3,000 calories per day to 1,300. He's lost 100 pounds and so far has experienced no downside to the surgery.

There *is* a side effect, however, called "Dumping Syndrome" that affects many patients who make the mistake of continuing the habit of eating foods too high in fat or sugar. The stomach contents move too quickly through the small intestine, resulting in such symptoms as nausea, weakness, sweating, and faintness. But as long as Roker sticks with a healthy food plan, this won't happen to him.

Follow-up: By the way, despite the "embarrassment," Roker had his operation filmed…just in case there might be a story in it. Surprise: there was. Roker finally fessed up and *Dateline NBC* devoted an entire show to his adventures in weight loss.

CARNIE WILSON

Top Weight: 300+ pounds

Last Meal: Avocado spring rolls, pasta with cream sauce, and cheesecake

Big Loser: Wilson, daughter of Brian Wilson of Beach Boys fame, always struggled with her weight. Even when she was a member of the platinum-selling pop group Wilson Phillips, she fought the battle of the bulge. When taping the group's music videos, Wilson says she was asked to stand behind potted plants or pillars. When the group broke up in 1993, Carnie's weight ballooned to more than 300 pounds. Her blood pressure shot up, her cholesterol was high, she was short of breath—and she was only 31 years old.

Wilson knew she had to do something about her weight, once and for all. On August 10, 1999, she had her stomach stapled. And

---

Japan has more than 13 million golfers, but only 1,200 golf courses.

in an incredible display of show-biz exhibitionism, she had the surgery in front of 250,000 people who logged on to the Internet to watch. (If you missed it live, videotapes are available for sale.)

Follow-up: For Wilson, surgery meant losing 150 pounds and going from a size 28 to a size 8. Of course, when you lose a lot of weight, you end up with a lot of loose skin. So three years later, Wilson turned to cosmetic surgery, including a tummy tuck that left her seven pounds lighter with a repositioned belly button, a breast lift, liposuction on her torso and hips, and the removal of half a pound of skin from under each armpit. To show how successful the surgeries were, Wilson posed for *Playboy* magazine in 2002.

OTHER FAMOUS "LOSERS"

• Anne Rice, bestselling author (*Interview with the Vampire*). She weighed 254 pounds before gastric bypass surgery. She's lost 44.

• Roseanne, actress and comedian. She weighed 240 pounds before having a gastric bypass. She's lost 80 pounds so far.

• Ann Wilson, lead singer of the rock group Heart, had gastric band surgery and has gone from 245 pounds to 185.

• John Popper from the band Blues Traveler lost 200 pounds.

• Jennifer Holliday, heavyweight singer from the Broadway musical *Dreamgirls*, went from 400 to 135 pounds.

THE SKINNY ON WEIGHT-LOSS SURGERY

Interested in weight-loss surgery? Here are a few facts that celebrity tell-alls don't tell you:

• It's not for anyone who's just a few pounds too heavy—you must be morbidly obese (at least 100 pounds overweight)

• Cost of surgery: upwards of $30,000 (including hospital costs)

• Cost of follow-up cosmetic surgery: about $20,000

• Possible risks of surgery include respiratory problems, infections, bleeding, bowel obstruction, leakage of the bowel connections, and obstruction of the stomach outlet.

• More risks: Decreasing the amount of food you eat also means decreasing the amount of protein, vitamins, and minerals you get. Combine that with rapid weight loss, and some people end up with a double whammy of hair and muscle loss.

BACK IN THE SADDLE

Peggy Thompson and Saeko Usukawa have put together a collection of great lines from Westerns called Tall in the Saddle. *Some samples:*

"Boys who play with guns have to be ready to die like men."
—**Joan Crawford,**
Johnny Guitar **(1954)**

"A horse is a man's slave, but treat 'em like a slave and you're not a man. Remember that."
—**James Cagney,** *Tribute to a Bad Man* **(1956)**

"Honey, you were smelling bad enough to gag a dog on a gut wagon."
—*The Ballad of Cable Hogue* **(1970)**

"I'd like to make a dress for her. Half tar, half feathers."
—*Destry Rides Again* **(1939)**

"There are two kinds of people in this world: those with pistols, and those who dig. You dig."
—**Clint Eastwood,** *The Good, the Bad and the Ugly* **(1966)**

Eleanor Parker: "The women always look beautiful when they get married, and the men always look scared."
William Holden: "They both get over it."
—*Escape from Fort Bravo* **(1953)**

"I like grumpy old cusses. Hope I live long enough to be one."
—**John Wayne,**
Tall in the Saddle **(1944)**

Parson: "I sure hope this town has some pretty girls in it."
Yellowleg: "You get this far out in the brush, they're all pretty."
—*The Deadly Companions* **(1961)**

"Faith can move mountains. But it can't beat a faster draw."
—*El Dorado* **(1967)**

"I almost got married once myself. It was all set until her family came West in a covered wagon. If you'd've seen her family, you'd know why the wagon was covered."
—*Gun Fury* **(1953)**

"Don't spill that liquor, son. It eats right through the bar."
—**Walter Brennan,**
The Westerner **(1940)**

Spencer Tracy: "I'll only be here twenty-four hours."
Conductor: "In a place like this, that could be a lifetime."
—*Bad Day at Black Rock* **(1955)**

...By the year 2000 A.D., the world population was more than 6 billion.

NEWS CORRECTIONS

Uncle John was thumbing through his local newspaper when he noticed the "Corrections" box. It turned out to be one of the most entertaining sections of the paper.

"The 'Greek Special' is a huge 18-inch pizza, and not a huge 18-inch penis, as described in an ad. Blondie's Pizza would like to apologize for any confusion Friday's ad may have caused."
—*The Daily Californian*

"In last week's *Democrat*, some words were transposed through a typesetting error. The paragraph that began 'Occasionally circus elephants spent ninety-five percent of their lives chained by two legs…' should have read 'A majority of circus elephants…' while the paragraph that began 'A majority of circus elephants go mad…' should have read 'Occasionally circus elephants…'"
—**Coös County *Democrat***

"In our story on London Hosts, it was stated that the 'Pub 80' concept probably appealed more to the younger drinker or those looking for bad food. This should, of course, be 'bar food'. We apologize for any embarrassment caused."
—*Morning Advertiser*

"A book review…quoted a passage from the book incorrectly. It says, 'Your goal should be to help your daughter become a sexually healthy adult'—not 'a sexually active, healthy adult.'"
—*The New York Times*

"The following corrects errors in the July 17 geographical agent and broker listing: *International*: Aberdeen is in Scotland, not Saudi Arabia; Antwerp is in Belgium, not Barbados; Belfast is in Northern Ireland, not Nigeria; Cardiff is in Wales, not Vietnam; Helsinki is in Finland, not Fiji; Moscow is in Russia, not Qatar."
—***Business Insurance***

"Due to a typographical error in last week's issue, the words 'Con-Men' appeared on the border of an Ashley & Nephews advertisement. 'Con-Men' was the headline of a story that was not used because of lack of space and is absolutely nothing to do and is in no way connected with Ashley & Nephews."
—*The Enfield Independent*

"Just to keep the record straight, it was the famous Whistler's Mother, not Hitler's, that was exhibited at the recent meeting of the Pleasantville Methodists. There is nothing to be gained in trying to explain how the error occurred."
—*Titusville (Pa.) Herald*

"Tuesday's edition called a charge residents pay for 911 service a 'surge' charge. It is, of course, a sir charge."
—**Carlsbad *Current-Argus***

"An article about Ivana Trump and her spending habits misstated the number of bras she buys. It is two dozen black, two dozen beige, and two dozen white, not two thousand of each."
—*The New York Times*

"In our issue of November 30 we reported that the Lubavitch Foundation in Glasgow held a 'dinner and ball' to celebrate its tenth anniversary. This was incorrect. A spokesman explained: 'The Lubavitch movement does not have balls.'"
—*Jewish Chronicle*

"Sunday's Lifestyle story about Buddhism should have stated that Siddartha Gautama grew up in Northern India, not Indiana."
—*Bloomington Herald-Times*

"The following typo appeared in our last bulletin: 'Lunch will be gin at 12:15 p.m.' Please correct to read '12 noon.'"
—**California Bar Association newsletter**

"I would like to point out that what I did in fact write was that the council forced piped TV 'on us' not 'up us' as printed in the *County Times* on October 25. T. A. Wilkinson"
—*County Times & Express*

"November is a heavy publishing month for all newspapers and with large issues misprints inevitably increase. Note, however, that there are 5 000 characters in every full column of type. Even if there are five misprints a column that is only an error of 0,1 percent. We are working constantly on the problem, aiming to keep problem, aiming to keep
—Editor"
—*The Johannesburg Star*

*   *   *

"Newspapers are unable to discriminate between a bicycle accident and the collapse of civilization."   —**George Bernard Shaw**

Light conversation: In Saudi Arabia, there are solar-powered pay phones in the desert.

THE BUGS AND THE BEES

*We sometimes wonder about insects creeping and crawling
in the garage or out in the garden. What do they do all
day? It turns out that even with six or eight legs,
they still have a one-track mind.*

CHEAPSKATE FLIES

The mating ritual of a type of flies called *Hilara*, commonly known as "dance flies," involves gift-giving. The male catches a small insect, wraps it in silk, and then presents it—along with a wing-waving mating dance—to his potential mate. When she accepts it, he mounts her while she's busy eating the gift. But some dance flies are too lazy to even catch the bug. In one species, the male offers the female what *looks* like a gift-wrapped insect. While she unwraps it, he mates with her, trying to complete the act before she discovers there's no bug in the bag.

TRICKY ORCHIDS

The female tiphiid wasp can't fly. So she climbs to the top of a tall plant and releases her pheromones into the air. The male flies by, grabs her, and flies away. Mating takes place in midair.

One type of orchid has made an interesting adaptation: its flower looks just like a female tiphiid. Not only that, its scent is almost identical to her pheromones. The unsuspecting male wasp grabs the flower and tries to take off with it; in the struggle, he brushes against the pollen before becoming frustrated and flying away. He goes on to the next orchid and goes through the same routine, thus pollinating the orchids.

HUNGRY SPIDERS

The female black widow spider is genetically programmed to control the black widow population in her neighborhood, based on available food supply. Here's how she does it: A male approaches her web, sits on the edge, and bobs his abdomen, causing the web to vibrate. If she's not in the mood, she won't respond. If she is willing to mate, she'll send out an answering pattern of vibrations calling him toward her. But if she's hungry, she'll send the male the *exact same* mating response. And when he gets close enough...she eats him.

CARD-PLAYING SUPERSTITIONS

Over the centuries, card players have come up with all sorts of strange superstitions to help them win—and elaborate explanations for why they're losing. (Ignoring, of course, the possibility that they're just bad card players.)

GOOD LUCK

• Blow on the cards or spit on them, preferably when no one is looking. (Remember to wipe up any excess spit, so no one knows you've fouled them.)

• Wear an article of dirty clothing when you play cards, especially when you play poker. The dirt helps keep evil at bay.

• Stick a pin in your lapel, or in a friend's lapel.

• There's one lucky card in each deck. If you can figure out which card it is, touch it with your index finger before the game begins.

• If you're sitting at a table made of wood, choose a seat that lets you lay your cards with the grain instead of against it.

• Whenever you're on a losing streak, tilt your chair up on its forelegs and twist it three times. This works best if you twist following the path of the sun—i.e., from east to west.

• If twisting doesn't help, rotate the chair so the back faces the table, then sit astride it so that you're facing the seat back.

• If you're sitting astride your chair and still losing, try sitting on a handkerchief, or walk clockwise three times around the table. (If you still lose, switch to a new deck of cards or consider taking up dominos.)

• If you see a hunchback on the way to your game, that's good luck. Don't touch the hump—just seeing the hunchback is all it takes.

BAD LUCK

• Don't sing or whistle during a card game. It's unlucky (not to mention annoying).

• Don't pick up any of your cards until all the cards have been

---

The brain can record about 86 million bits of information each day.

dealt, and when you do pick them up, use your right hand.

• Never, ever let someone hover over you and look at your cards, unless that person never plays cards. If they never play cards, then standing over you may actually bring you luck. People who bring you luck are known as "mascots."

• Don't sit with your legs crossed. You're literally crossing out your luck.

• Never play cards in a room with a dog in it.

• Never let anyone place their foot on the rung of your chair. On the other hand, if you want to give bad luck to someone who's beating you, put your foot on the rung of *their* chair.

• Never play cards with a cross-eyed man or woman. (This superstition dates back to the days when people thought that cross-eyed people could see the cards of the people sitting next to them.)

• Never play *any* gambling game in a room where there's a woman present, unless the woman is playing, too. If you're a woman, the same rule applies with men.

MORE BAD LUCK

• Never play cards on a bare table. (Bring felt or a tablecloth, preferably green, with you…just in case.)

• Don't lend money during a card game. Don't borrow it, either.

• If you are dealt a steady succession of black cards, it means that you or someone in your family will die soon.

• Pilots, coal miners, soldiers, fishermen, and sailors should never carry playing cards on their persons. If they do and bad luck occurs—a storm or an enemy attack, for example—throw the cards as far away from you as you can. They're bringing you bad luck.

LUCKY AND UNLUCKY CARDS

• The four of clubs is "the devil's bedstead." Discard it unless you absolutely need it. If you're dealt the four of clubs in the first hand of the game, throw down the cards and leave the game—you'll have nothing but bad luck.

• Dropping any card on the floor is bad luck, but dropping one of the black aces is worst of all. If you drop a black ace, leave the game immediately. Nobody recovers from luck that bad.

Half of the genes in a banana are the same as in a human.

I ♥ THE '80s!

Power Ties? Just say no? Baby on Board? Just do it.

1985

- New Coke flops; Coca-Cola reintroduces "classic" Coke
- Reagan meets Gorbachev in first U.S./Soviet summit
- Pete Rose breaks Ty Cobb's record of 4,191 base hits
- Live Aid concert held in New York and London simultaneously
- #1 movie: *Back to the Future*
- *Calvin and Hobbes* comic strip premiers
- A *Yugo* costs $3,990

1986

- Space shuttle *Challenger* explodes
- Russian space station *Mir* launched
- Martin Luther King Day becomes U.S. holiday
- Soviet nuclear plant Chernobyl has major meltdown
- 20-year-old Mike Tyson becomes youngest heavyweight champ ever
- Album of the Year: Paul Simon's *Graceland*
- On TV: *Miami Vice Cheers, Family Ties*

1987

- Televangelist Jim Bakker resigns after sex scandal with secretary Jessica Hahn
- Best Director: Oliver Stone, *Platoon*
- Oct. 17, Black Monday—Stock Market crashes
- #1 single: George Michael's "Faith"
- Van Gogh's painting "Sunflowers" sells for $39 million
- British humanitarian Terry Waite kidnapped in Lebanon
- Yugoslavian baby declared Earth's five billionth inhabitant

1988

- George H. W. Bush elected 41st U.S. president (defeats Michael Dukakis)
- After eight years of fighting, Soviet army begins withdrawal from Afghanistan
- Oliver North indicted for his role in Iran-Contra scandal
- Pan Am 103 crashes in Lockerbie, Scotland
- #1 film: *Rain Man*
- *Uncle John's Bathroom Reader* debuts

1989

- Iranian Ayatollah Khomeini issues *fatwa* (death sentence) on *Satanic Verses* author Salman Rushdie
- Time, Inc. and Warner Communications announce plans to merge
- Oil tanker Exxon *Valdez* crashes, causing worst oil spill in U.S. history
- Chinese troops squash pro-democracy demonstrators in Tiananmen Square
- Sega *Genesis* released
- Berlin Wall falls
- #1 movie: *Batman*
- Top TV show: *The Cosby Show*

'80s quiz: In 1987 for the first time live models advertised what on TV? A: Bras (Playtex).

UNCLE JOHN'S STALL OF SHAME

*Don't abuse your bathroom privileges...or you may
wind up in Uncle John's "Stall of Shame."*

Honoree: Joseph Carl Jones, Jr., an alleged burglar

Dubious Achievement: Landing in the can after a trip to the can.

True Story: On the morning of February 7, 2003, Janie Sidener of Mineral Wells, Texas, arrived to open the store where she worked. She should have been the first one in the building that morning, but shortly after she entered she noticed something unusual, so she looked around. That's when she saw Joseph Carl Jones, fast asleep on a bed that the store had for sale. "Apparently he needed to take a break," said police spokesperson Mike McAllister.

Sidener quietly called her employer, who called the police. They woke the burglar, arrested him, and hauled him off to the slammer. So what was it that alerted Sidener to the fact that something was amiss? Before his nap, Jones had used the bathroom...and hadn't flushed.

Adding Insult to Injury! The store Jones had picked to rob was owned by the wife of the district attorney.

Honoree: Jon Carl Petersen, 41, head of the Iowa office of the U.S. Bureau of Alcohol, Tobacco and Firearms (ATF)

Dubious Achievement: Wrecking his own career with alcohol, toilet paper, and firearms (ATPF).

True Story: During Homecoming Week 2002, a pickup truck full of Indianola high school sophomores decided to TP some houses in town, an unofficial Homecoming tradition for many years. Too bad they chose the street where Petersen lived. And too bad Petersen had been drinking.

When he saw the kids throwing toilet paper in his yard, he jumped in his patrol vehicle and chased them with lights flashing and sirens blaring. When they finally stopped, he ordered the sophomores out of their truck and held them at gunpoint until police arrived...and arrested *him*. A sobriety test showed that Petersen had a blood alcohol level of 0.22%, twice the legal limit. He was charged with drunk driving, 10 counts of assault with a weapon, and two counts of simple assault. If convicted on all counts, he faces up to 20 years in prison and a $50,000 fine.

"He deserves what he gets," said one of the kids involved. "It's kind of stupid that he's an Alcohol, Tobacco and Firearms agent, and he was doing two of the things he's trying to prevent."

Honoree: Catherine Tarver, the mother of an accused murderer
Dubious Achievement: Using a public restroom to influence the outcome of a trial.
True Story: In May 2003, Judge Walter McMillan ordered that Tarver be barred from Georgia's Washington County Courthouse. Reason: A courthouse employee saw Tarver cracking open eggs and sprinkling chicken feathers, chicken blood, and what has been described as "voodoo powder" in the restroom. So Judge McMillan imposed a ban, telling her, "If I find any more eggs in this courthouse, you will face criminal charges."

Sheriff Thomas Smith speculates that Tarver was trying to influence the outcome of the trial. "I think it's a curse against the prosecution," he told reporters. "There's been four incidents of it in the courthouse bathroom where brown eggs have been busted. It always happened on the day of Brandon Tarver's hearings."

Tarver denies using voodoo. "I don't even know what that is," she claims.

Honoree: Dr. Michael Warren, a South Carolina dermatologist
Dubious Achievement: Turning his bathroom into an ICU—a peekaboo ICU.
True Story: When the staff restroom went out of order in 2002, Dr. Warren cheerfully allowed female employees to use his private restroom. But when months went by without Dr. Warren making an attempt to get the restroom fixed, his staff became suspicious. That's when they found a hidden camera in the doctor's bathroom. Dr. Warren admits that he installed the camera but claims that he did so "as a security measure, after cash and checks were stolen from his office." (No word on what a thief would steal from the doctor's bathroom.)

In how many Agatha Christie mysteries did "the butler do it?" None.

WORLD-CLASS LOSERS

Everyone makes mistakes. Some are just better at it than others.

PAPER WEIGHT
   In 1965 an aspiring English publisher named Lionel Burleigh announced he was starting a newspaper called the *Commonwealth Sentinel*, which he promised would be "Britain's most fearless newspaper." Burleigh did everything it took to make the paper a success—he promoted it on billboards, sold advertising space, wrote articles, and printed up 50,000 copies of the first issue so that there would be plenty to go around. Burleigh remembered every detail, except for one very important thing: distribution.

In fact, he had forgotten it completely until he received a phone call from the police informing him that all 50,000 copies had been deposited on the sidewalk in front of the hotel where he was staying. They were blocking the entrance. Could he please come and remove them?

Britain's "most fearless paper" folded after just one day. "To my knowledge, we only sold one copy," Burleigh remembered years later. "I still have the shilling in my drawer."

A LOAD OF BULL
In 1958 the town of Lindsay, Ontario, organized the country's first-ever bullfight. There aren't many bullfighting bulls in Canada, and even fewer matadors, so they had to bring in both from Mexico. But the bulls brought ticks with them, and ticks from other parts of the world aren't allowed into Canada. The bulls had to be quarantined for a week. By the time they got out, the matadors had returned to Mexico. Result: no bullfight.

HORSE SENSE
Horatio Bottomley (great name) was a convicted fraud artist and ex-member of the English parliament. In 1914 he figured out what he thought was a foolproof way to rig a horse race: He bought all six horses in the race, hired his own jockeys to race them, and told them in which order he wanted them to cross the finish line. Then he bet a fortune on the horses he'd picked to win, and also

---

The sun's diameter is 109.12 times the diameter of the Earth.

placed bets on the order of finish. Everything went according to plan...until a thick fog rolled in over the track in the middle of the race. It was so thick that the jockeys couldn't see each other well enough to cross the finish line in the proper order. And Bottomley lost every bet he placed.

MORE LOSERS

Not to be outdone by civilians, the "military intelligence" personnel of past war machines have had their day in the doghouse as well.

Brits in the Pits. In the early 1940s, the English military came up with what they thought would be a simple but powerful antitank weapon: a four-and-a-half-pound hand grenade covered with sticky adhesive that would help it stick to the sides of tanks. The grenade was withdrawn from service a short time later. Reason: It stuck a little too well...to the soldier who was trying to throw it. It was so sticky, in fact, that the only practical way to put it to use was to run up to the tank and stick the grenade on manually— which was practically a suicide mission because the bomb's short fuse gave its user less than five seconds to get away.

Peru's Blues. As part of its Air Force Week celebrations in 1975, the Peruvian military decided to show off the might of its newest fighter planes. Fourteen derelict fishing boats were towed a short distance out to sea to serve as targets. After the crowds had gathered along the coast, a squadron of 30 fighters swooped down and attacked the boats with bombs and machine-gun fire for 15 minutes. They didn't sink a single boat.

France's Chance. In 1870 the French military made preparations to use its own new machine gun, called the *mitrailleuse*, in the imminent war against Prussia. Machine guns were new at the time and the government wanted to keep the technology a secret. So it distributed the guns to military units...without instructions for how to use them; the instructions weren't sent until *after* the war had begun. But by then it was too late—France lost.

*   *   *

"Whoever said, 'It's not whether you win or lose that counts,' probably lost."

—Martina Navritilova

There is one slot machine in Las Vegas for every eight inhabitants.

EVERYDAY OBJECTS

They once were miracle inventions—now they're so common we throw them in a junk drawer. Here are the stories behind three items that make life just a little bit easier.

SAFETY PIN

In 1849 a New York inventor named Walter Hunt had a problem: he was too broke to pay an employee the $15 he owed him. But the employee gave him an out—he'd forgive the $15 debt if he could have the rights to whatever Hunt could invent from a single piece of wire.

Hunt was a prolific inventor—he'd designed a fire engine warning gong, a stove that burned hard coal, and even an early sewing machine (which he decided not to market because he didn't want to put seamstresses out of work). But for all his skill, he seemed unable to profit from any of his inventions.

Hunt had no money, so he had no choice—he accepted the employee's challenge. After three hours of twisting an eight-inch piece of brass wire, Hunt had created the world's first safety pin. It had a clasp at one end, a point on the other, and a coil in the middle to act as a spring and keep the point tucked into the clasp.

So did Hunt hand over his "dress pin," as he called it, to the employee? No—he reneged on the deal and patented the safety pin himself. Then he sold the rights to his new invention for $400 (about $5,000 today), from which he paid his draftsman the $15, keeping the rest. Millions of safety pins have been made and sold since then, but Hunt never made another cent on his invention.

CAN OPENER

Strange but true: the metal can was invented a full 50 years before the first practical can opener.

Peter Durand, the English merchant who developed the "tin cannister" in 1810, had figured out a way to preserve foods *in* cans, but he neglected to come up with a way to get the food *out*. Early cans carried instructions advising users to cut around the top with a chisel and hammer. British soldiers didn't carry chisels—they had to open their canned rations with bayonets or pocket knives, and, in desperation, sometimes shot them open with their rifles.

In 1858 a man named Ezra Warner came up with a can opener that looked like a bent bayonet, with a large, curved blade that could be driven into the rim of a can and forced around the perimeter to cut off the top. It was unwieldy and dangerous; but grocery stores that sold canned food had to buy them so they could open cans as a service to customers. The customers would then leave the store carrying the opened cans. Not surprisingly, it wasn't a big hit.

Then in 1861 the Civil War broke out, creating a sudden and urgent need for food that could accompany soldiers into battle without spoiling. Union soldiers were issued canned rations...and Warner's bayonet-style can openers. Canned food became so popular with soldiers that after the war, more and more canned goods appeared on market shelves. But people still needed an easier way to open the cans.

Connecticut inventor William Lyman had the answer, and in 1870 patented his "cutting wheel" can opener, a crank-operated gadget that held a circular metal wheel that could cut through can tops. And since then not much has changed. In 1925 the Star Can Company of San Francisco added a serrated wheel to hold the can and rotate it against the cutting wheel. The electric can opener was introduced in 1931. But amazingly, even the most modern versions of the can opener still look and work pretty much like the one Lyman invented...more than 130 years ago.

DRINKING STRAW

Marvin Stone liked mint juleps. Back in the 1880s, every day after putting in his time manufacturing paper cigarette holders in his Washington, D.C., factory, Stone would stop by the same tavern and order a mint julep—a concoction of bourbon, mint, sugar, and water, served over ice. Keeping the drink chilled was important (warm mint juleps tend to lose some of their minty tang), so mint julep fans would avoid touching the glass with their warm hands. Instead, they sipped the drink through a natural hollow piece of wheat straw.

Stone didn't like the grassy taste the wheat straw imparted to his favorite drink. He also didn't like the way the straw would get dusty and start to crack as it was used repeatedly. There had to be a better way. One day, as he watched his cigarette holders being wound out of paper, he had an inspiration. Why not make an artificial straw by winding thin strips of paper around a cylinder?

He made a prototype in 1888, winding a continuous strip of paper around a pencil and fastening it with dabs of glue. It worked. Stone made several drinking straws for his own use and asked his favorite bartender to stash them behind the counter. When other customers noticed Stone's invention, they wanted their own, so Stone decided to mass-produce it.

Lemonade was a popular drink in the late 19th century, and Stone reasoned that people might like using straws for lemonade as well as for mint juleps. He fashioned an eight-and-a-half-inch paper straw out of wax-coated manila paper (to resist sogginess) and set the diameter just wide enough to allow lemon seeds to pass through without clogging the straws. By 1890 the Stone Cigarette Holder Factory was producing more drinking straws than cigarette holders.

Most straws today are made of plastic, not paper. But the winding technique Stone invented lives on: most cardboard tubes (like the one at the center of a toilet paper roll) are still made in the same way that Stone wound his first straw. Straws themselves have undergone an evolution: there are straws of colored plastic, with flexible shapes, loop-the-loops, and even flavored straws. But they still do the same basic job: getting liquid into your mouth, fast and cold.

*   *   *

INSPECTOR GADGET?

Have you ever been snooping with your binoculars, only to have your arms get tired just when you're sure something really important is about to happen? If so, U.S. Patent #5,131,093—the *Bino Cap*—may be just the invention for you. It's a foldable, lightweight combination binoculars/baseball cap. Just put it on and snoop away; your arms are free to take notes, stir your coffee, or record observations into your voice-activated digital recorder. (Despite the fact that it's been patented, no word on whether the device is actually available yet.)

Radar was used for the first time in the battle of Britain in 1940.

EATIN' THE TIN SANDWICH

The history of the harmonica will take you to China, Africa, Europe, the Mississippi Delta, and beyond...

BLOWING IN THE WIND

When musicians like Bob Dylan and John Lennon became famous in the 1960s, they did it with a little help from the harmonica. And they gave the harmonica a boost, too. Sales of the tiny instrument skyrocketed when folksingers and rock musicians brought it back into the limelight. But it wasn't the first time the "harp" became a sensation.

From the 1920s until the 1940s, the harmonica was one of the most popular instruments in the country. The biggest blues, jazz, country, and hillbilly bands—and even theater companies—had harmonica players as part of their acts. Harmonica classes became a regular part of curriculums in many public schools. By the 1930s, the German company M. Hohner, the biggest maker of harmonicas worldwide, was selling over 25 million a year.

Where did the easy-to-carry instrument originate? That's a very old story.

THE SOUND OF OLD SHENG-HAI

Most musicologists agree that the earliest predecessor to the harmonica was developed in China between 3,000 and 5,000 years ago. It was a three-foot-long instrument made of bamboo pipes called the *sheng*, which means "sublime voice." Although neither the sheng nor its ancient sisters, the *naw*, the *yu*, and the *ho*, looked anything like a harmonica, they all had one important feature in common: free reeds.

A reed is a thin strip of cane, wood, plastic, or metal that vibrates when air passes over it. A "free reed" instrument, like the accordion or harmonica, produces sound from a reed vibrating inside a chamber—the vibrating reed produces a single note and doesn't touch anything else.

"Fixed reed" instruments, like the clarinet and the saxophone,

---

use a reed that vibrates against some other part of the instrument. On the clarinet or sax, it's the mouthpiece, which is attached to a tube with holes in it. Cover the holes and you change the pitch.

The *sheng* had multiple free reeds set inside bamboo tubes, which allowed chords (multiple notes that sound good together) to be played. For thousands of years, *sheng* and similar instruments were played all over China and Southeast Asia.

FREEING THE PITCH

Fixed-reed instruments had been played in Europe for centuries (and some say that even those were introduced from Asia), but free-reeds had not. In 1776 French Jesuit missionary Pierre Amiot sent several *shengs* from China to Paris—and people who heard them loved them. Within a few years European instrument makers were building their own free reed devices, making instruments such as the harmonium and the reed organ.

In 1821, a 16-year-old named Christian Friedrich Ludwig Buschmann was experimenting with different ways to combine pitch pipes in order to create a new instrument. He soldered together 15 pipes of different pitches, similar to the *sheng* and, without knowing it, made the next big step toward the modern harmonica.

THE INS AND OUTS

Buschmann's harmonica, known as the *aura*, was an immediate hit, and soon other instrument makers began experimenting with the design. In 1825 a man named Richter (his first name is unknown) came up with the idea of a 10-hole, 20-note configuration, one row of reeds activated by inhaling, the other by exhaling.

Richter arranged the notes with the common person in mind: no matter where the mouth is placed, it would always play notes that were in harmony—that sounded good—together, whether inhaling or exhaling. That's why the instrument is called a "harmony-ca"—it's always in harmony. Richter's three-octave model has been changed little since. (Pretty impressive when you consider that a grand piano has an eight-octave range, but weighs about 1,000 pounds—4,000 times as much as a harmonica.)

Franklin Delano Roosevelt once owned a Christmas tree farm.

HARMONIC CONVERGENCE

In 1857 Matthias Hohner, a clockmaker from Trössingen, Germany, visited a harmonica maker in Vienna, Austria, and decided to make his own instruments. He started making them in his kitchen with the help of his family and sold 650 harmonicas the first year. In 1862 relatives in the United States urged him to export some of the instruments. He did, and by 1887 was producing more than a million harmonicas a year, with sales across Europe and the United States.

BLEND IT LIKE HOHNER

One of the things that helped make the harmonica so successful was its musical flexibility. It could play romping *Biergarten* music, plaintive European folk songs, and even complex classical music. And it was small and inexpensive, so even poor people could afford one. By the late 1800s, African Americans in the southeast, who had their own musical traditions developed over thousands of years, were inventing a new kind of music: the blues. And the "harp" would be part of it. The trademark "bending" of the notes—using air direction and pressure to slide between notes—would become the trademark sound of the blues. The popularity of the music would soon influence other new styles of American music—jug band, Dixieland, jazz, and swing—and would help carry the harmonica to even greater popularity.

THE GOLDEN YEARS

The 1920s began the first golden age for the harmonica. Two new technologies were sweeping the country: radio and recording. That meant that people could become national stars relatively quickly—and so could the instruments they played: Vernon Dalhart's 1925 recording "Wreck of the Old 97," with Dalhart singing and playing harmonica, became country music's first million-seller.

By the end of the 1920s, hundreds of artists were making recordings and many of them featured the harmonica. And it wasn't just for accompaniment: all-harmonica bands became hot tickets. Then, in the late 1930s, a musical virtuoso named Larry Adler gave it another boost: Adler played classical and jazz—as a harmonica soloist. How popular was he? From the 1940s until he died in 2001, he regularly played with the biggest stars of the day:

Jack Benny, George Gershwin, Billie Holiday and later, Sting and Elton John.

ELECTRIFIED

The harmonica went into decline in the 1950s, but bluesmen like Little Walter, Howlin' Wolf, and Sonny Boy Williamson kept it alive, creating a modern blues-harp sound that would be carried on by James Cotton and Charlie Musselwhite. By the 1960s, the harmonica was back, thanks first to the folk music craze and then to Beatlemania.

Since then, harmonica players like Stevie Wonder, John Mayall, Huey Lewis, Delbert McClinton, Magic Dick (J. Geils Band), Neil Young, Bruce Springsteen, Charlie McCoy, Mickey Rafael (Willie Nelson's band), and John Popper (Blues Traveler) continue to show the world what one little instrument can do.

HARMONICA TRIVIA

• Nicknames for the harmonica: the *Harp*, the *Tin Sandwich* (Cowboy dialect), the *Mississippi Saxophone* (Blues lingo), and the *Mouth Organ* (from the German *mundharmonika* or *mundorgan*).

• Presidents Lincoln, Wilson, Coolidge, and Reagan were all harp players of varying ability. Lincoln reportedly wrote a letter to Hohner, telling how he enjoyed playing the harmonica to relax.

• The best-selling record of 1947 was "Peg O' My Heart" by a harmonica trio called The *Harmonicats*. After the *Harmonicats'* success, the musicians union decided to classify the harmonica as an instrument. Before that they called it a toy.

• On December 16, 1965, astronaut Wally Schirra played *Jingle Bells* on the harmonica—from Gemini Six, at an altitude of 160 miles above Earth.

• In 1986 the M. Hohner Company sold their one billionth harmonica.

• Currently, the most expensive harmonica in the Hohner catalog is a "Chord 48" (the size of a baseball bat, with hundreds of reeds). Cost: $1,500.

• More expensive, but not in the catalog: the solid gold, gem-encrusted model that Hohner presented to Pope Pius XI in the 1930s.

Benjamin Franklin once wrote an essay on the possibility of waterskiing.

Q & A: ASK THE EXPERTS

*More random questions, with answers
from the nation's top trivia experts.*

A BALANCED DIET

Q: *What do mosquitoes eat when people or other warm-blooded animals aren't around?*

A: "Your first mistake is assuming that all mosquitoes bite people or other warm-blooded animals. Fact is, a large number of the world's roughly 2,000 mosquito species prefer birds, while others dine on cold-blooded critters, such as frogs. Your second mistake (a common one) is assuming that blood is a mosquito's food source. Actually, they eat good old-fashioned carbohydrates, found in fruits, grasses, and the nectar of flowers. So why do mosquitoes bite animals? Females need the protein and amino acids found in blood in order to form their eggs. Males have no need for blood, so they don't bite people." (From *The Wild File*, by Brad Wetzler)

PAYING WITH THE BAND

Q: *How do the magnetic strips on credit cards work?*

A: "The magnetic strips on the backs of credit cards consist of tiny particles of iron-based ferric oxide. A coating of these particles is bonded to a thin plastic base. They can be magnetized in a northern or southern direction, corresponding to the ones and zeros of binary computer programming. The tape that holds the magnetized particles is similar to cassette recording tape.

"Like recording tape, the magnetic strip will have tracks, but the tracks don't play music—they contain information such as a valid card number, expiration date, credit limit, and whether that limit has been reached." (From *Popular Science* magazine)

THE OUTER LIMITS

Q: *Does the fourth spatial dimension really exist?*

A: "That depends on what you mean by 'space.' There are only three dimensions to our everyday, commonsense kind of 'space,'

Marine turtles rid their bodies of excess salt by weeping.

the 'space' we can perceive and move in. But physicists have developed persuasive theories using an extra *six* spatial dimensions. These higher dimensions are curled up into tiny circles, or similar closed surfaces. This curling up of dimensions is like our observing, say, a piece of string from a distance and seeing it as a line, then moving closer and observing that it actually has an extra, circular dimension. If we could observe any point (say a subatomic particle) at a large enough magnification, we would similarly see that it is not a point, but has further dimensions in unexplored directions." (From *The Best Ever Queries*, by Joseph Harker)

THE VISION THING

Q: *How do antifogging treatments for mirrors and eyeglasses work?*

A: "They force the tiny droplets of water that make up fog to merge into a transparent sheet. An antifogging agent is sprayed on as liquid, and when it dries, it forms a clear film. Normally, water beads up, but with the film, the beads run together. The water is still there, but you can see through it. Such agents are called *surfactants*—chemicals that lower the surface tension of the liquid with which they are in contact, in this case water.

"A low-cost emergency substitute is potato juice. In research on land mine removal, potato juice was tested for use in poor countries to keep blast-protection visors from fogging up. It performed as well as some brand-name products." (From *The N.Y. Times Second Book of Science Questions and Answers*, by Claiborne Ray)

MAKES CENTS

Q: *Why do dimes, quarters, and half-dollars have notched edges, while pennies and nickels do not?*

A: "The U.S. Mint began putting notches on gold and silver coins to discourage people from shaving small quantities of the precious metals off the edges. At one point the shaving problem was so bad that merchants refused to accept coins without weighing them to determine their true value. Notching corrected the problem since any attempt to shave a notched coin could be easily detected.

"Dimes, quarters, and half-dollars are notched because they contain silver. There is no need to notch pennies and nickels— the metals they contain are not valuable enough to make shaving worth the effort." (From *Ever Wonder Why?*, by Douglas Smith)

Tough to swallow: Tibetans drink a tea made of salted rancid yak butter.

DEATH ON THE MISSISSIPPI

Few people know about the Sultana, *despite the fact
that it suffered the worst maritime disaster in U.S.
history. For some reason, it is almost completely
ignored by history books. Here's the tragic story.*

HEADING HOME

The Civil War was finally over. It was April 1865, General Robert E. Lee had surrendered; Abraham Lincoln had been shot; and Confederate president Jefferson Davis had been captured. After four years of bloodshed, the war-torn nation was ready to start the process of healing and rebuilding. The first order of business was to get the weary troops home.

Captured Union soldiers were being released from Confederate prison camps. Thousands amassed along the Mississippi River seeking passage on one of the many steamships making their way upriver to the north.

One such riverboat was the *Sultana*, a state-of-the-art side-wheeler that had been built for transporting cotton. But now her cargo was people. By law, she was allowed to carry 376 passengers and a crew of 85, and the ship's captain and owner, J. C. Mason, had a reputation as a careful river pilot. But in the end, the money he stood to make from the Union government for transporting extra troops was too tempting to pass up: $5 for each enlisted man and $10 per officer.

A SETUP FOR DISASTER

The *Sultana* left New Orleans on April 21 carrying a small number of passengers, about 100, and headed north. Each time she stopped, though, the ship took on more troops. The men who boarded were weak, tired, and homesick. After spending months or even years in brutal prison camps, the only thing they wanted to do was get back to their families.

On April 24, the *Sultana* made her regular stop in Vicksburg, Mississippi, to take on more passengers. Captain Mason docked

---

A soda can can hold 90 pounds per square inch of pressure... 3 times as much as a car tire.

the ship to find thousands of soldiers waiting there. Under normal circumstances, the ship would have made a brief stop, allowed the prescribed number of passengers to board, and then departed. But one of the ship's three main steam boilers had sprung a leak and needed to be repaired.

First of all, Captain Mason made the decision to have a piece of metal welded over the leak to reinforce it (which took less than a day) instead of having the boiler replaced (which would have taken three days). While the boiler was being repaired, the waiting soldiers did everything they could to muscle their way onto the ship. Bribes were paid, and more and more men packed on. When the repairs were completed, Mason was eager to get underway, so he broke another rule. He let all of the passengers get onboard before their names were logged in. Result: The ship was overloaded and no one on shore had a complete or accurate copy of the passenger list.

When an Army officer raised his concerns, Mason assured him that the *Sultana* was a competent vessel that could more than carry the load. "Take good care of those men," the officer told him. "They are deserving of it."

THE MIGHTY MISS

Four years of war had been hard on the series of levees and dikes that control the flow of the Mississippi River. The spring of 1865 saw heavy rains, which, combined with winter snowmelt, caused the river to rise to flood stage. By April it was several miles wide and the icy current was much stronger than usual.

But the *Sultana* was solid and Captain Mason an able river man. As the ship trudged slowly upriver, she made a few more scheduled stops, picking up even more men at each one. The huddled passengers filled every bit of space on the 260-foot-long vessel—the bottom hull, the lower decks, the cabins, the pilothouse, and the hurricane deck on top. Yet even though the soldiers were tired and packed in like sardines, their spirits were high. They sang songs, told war stories, and shared their plans for when they finally got home…unaware of the disaster to come.

On the cool night of April 26, 1865, the *Sultana* disembarked from Memphis around midnight, carrying an estimated 2,300 people—six times its capacity. There were only two lifeboats and 76 life preservers onboard.

HELL AND HIGH WATER

At around 2 a.m., the overloaded *Sultana* had made it nine miles north of Memphis when her weakened boiler could take no more. It exploded. The other two boilers went in quick succession.

The tremendous blast split the ship in two. Burning-hot coals shot out like bullets. The horrified passengers were jarred awake, some sent hurtling through the air into the icy water, others scalded by the tremendous blast of steam. Still others were trapped on the lower decks to either suffocate, burn, or drown. The men on the top decks had a choice—albeit a dismal one: stay and face the spreading flames or try to swim to shore, more than a mile away in either direction.

One survivor remembered, "The men who were afraid to take to the water could be seen clinging to the sides of the bow of the boat until they were singed off like flies." Others who had waited too long on the hurricane deck were crushed when the two large smokestacks collapsed on them. Others slid down into the hottest part of the fire when the burning deck gave way.

Shrieks and screams pierced the night, as did the crackling of flames and the booms of small explosions. But loudest of all was the hissing sound as sections of the flaming steamboat sank into the water. Another survivor described it like this:

> The whole heavens seemed to be lighted up by the conflagration. Hundreds of my comrades were fastened down by the timbers of the decks and had to burn while the water seemed to be one solid mass of human beings struggling with the waves.

What was left of the *Sultana* drifted downstream until finally banking on a small island in the middle of the Mississippi River. The ship's broken, burning body then slowly disappeared into the dark water.

DAWN OF THE DEAD

As first light rose on the river, the devastation was overwhelming. Hundreds upon hundreds of bodies were floating down the Mississippi. Dotted between the corpses were dazed survivors floating on makeshift rafts of driftwood and ship parts. Some sang marching songs to keep their spirits up. Others just floated silently among the carnage.

All the way to Memphis, men—alive and dead—were washing

...got to land on the surface and walk around. (Or did they? See page 278.)

up onshore. Barges and other steamships were dispatched for search and rescue. At least 500 men were treated at Memphis hospitals; 200 of them died there. Because the passenger list went down with the ship, no one knows for sure how many lives were lost that night, but most estimates put the number around 1,700—including Captain Mason.

INTO THE DUSTBIN OF HISTORY

So why is the *Sultana* disaster such an unknown part of U.S. history? Mostly because of timing. After the bloodiest war in U.S. history, the nation was largely desensitized to death. What was another 1,700 in the wake of hundreds of thousands of casualties? The newspapers were full of articles about the end of the war, a new presidency, and a nation rebuilding. On the day before the disaster, the last Confederate army had surrendered and John Wilkes Booth had been captured. The story of the sinking of the *Sultana* was relegated to the back pages.

Another reason for the minimal coverage was that it was an embarrassing story. A lot of people—from the ship's captain to the army officers in charge of boarding—had failed miserably at their jobs. The Army was not anxious to publicize such a horrible dereliction of duty.

But the fact remains that the explosion and sinking of the *Sultana* was—and still is—the worst maritime disaster in U.S. history. Her bow is still lying on the muddy bottom of the Mississippi River as a sad memorial to the men who never made it home.

*　　*　　*

REAL-LIFE COURT TRANSQUIPS

Q: So, you were unconscious, and they pulled you from the bucket. What happened then?

A: Mr. Stewart gave me artificial insemination, you know, mouth-to-mouth.

Plaintiff's Attorney: Why do you think your home developed cracks in the walls?

Defendant's Attorney: Objection! The witness has no expertise in this area, there is an obvious lack of foundation.

"I had a lazy eye as a kid and it gradually spread to my whole body." —Tom Cotter

NOW THEY TELL US

*The "experts" told us one thing...and
then a new set of experts comes along.*

USDA FOOD PYRAMID

They Used to Say: A healthy diet includes lots of bread
and cereal, plenty of dairy products, red meat, and very
little fat. That's what the USDA—with the grateful support of the
farming industry—had recommended since the 1950s, packaging
it into a triangle-shaped "Food Guide Pyramid" in 1992.

Now They Tell Us: The Food Pyramid is unhealthy, will make
you fat, and puts you at greater risk for heart disease. Leading
nutritionists slammed the guidelines in 2001. "The food pyramid
is tremendously flawed," said Dr. Walter C. Willett of Harvard. "It
says all fats are bad; all complex carbohydrates are good; all protein sources offer the same nutrition, and dairy should be eaten in
high amounts. None of this is accurate." A new guide is scheduled
to be released in 2005.

BRAIN CELLS

They Used to Say: You can't grow new brain cells.

Now They Tell Us: Oh yes you can. Researchers at Princeton
University did an extensive study and proved in 1999 that many
areas of the brain do indeed grow new brain cells, or neurons,
throughout an adult's life. "The assumption has been for over a
hundred years that there are no new neurons added," said psychologist Charles G. Gross, a co-leader of the study. "We have shown
they are added, and to the regions of the brain involved in the
highest cognitive function."

SIPPY CUPS

They Used to Say: The sippy cup is a healthy way to wean a
child from a bottle. Doctors have been recommending them for 50
years.

Now They Tell Us: According to childhood development
experts, sippy cups make it harder for kids to learn the complicat-
ed action of drinking from a glass. That, in turn, slows the devel-

---

Tennessee Williams was born in Mississippi.

opment of articulate speech. And because children often sip milk, juice, or other sugary drinks over several hours, sippy cups can promote tooth decay.

Subject: Daily sleep requirements
They Used to Say: You need at least eight hours of sleep a day.
Now They Tell Us: Sleeping eight hours a day might be fatal. The University of California did a six-year study in which they monitored such factors as the lifestyle, health, and sleep patterns of 1.1 million people. They found that subjects who slept eight hours a day were 12% more likely to have died during that six-year period than people who slept seven hours a day. People who slept nine hours were 23% more likely.

Subject: Iron
They Used to Say: Iron-rich foods are good for you.
Now They Tell Us: Drop that can of spinach, Popeye! One study at the University of Washington in 2003 suggested that people with a diet high in iron were 1.7 times more likely to get Parkinson's disease than those with a low-iron diet. Sources of iron: red meat and poultry. And, if it's combined with manganese, the risk goes up to 1.9 times more likely. Sources of iron and manganese: spinach, beans, nuts, and grains. But you'd have to eat an awful lot of these to overdo it. The researchers said that more study was needed before they could recommend any dietary changes.

Subject: Planets
They Used to Say: There are nine planets in our solar system.
Now They Tell Us: You're spaced out—there's only eight. Seventy years after it was first classified, the Hayden Planetarium in New York City, one of the nation's leading astronomical centers, removed Pluto from its list of planets in 2001. They said it's far too small—smaller than our moon—and is probably just a big lump of ice. The announcement drew much criticism from traditional astronomers, but officials at the center say they're just being defensive. "There is no scientific insight to be gained by counting planets," said Neil de Grasse Tyson, director of the planetarium. "Eight or nine, the numbers don't matter."

In 2002 the average driver spent 62 hours stopped in traffic. L.A. drivers spent 136.

SO LONG, NEIGHBOR

One thing that nearly all Americans born after 1965 have in common is that they grew up watching Mr. Rogers. He was one of the true pioneers of children's television. We haven't written much about him before, and when he passed away in 2003 we decided it was time we did.

HOME FOR THE HOLIDAYS

In 1951 a college senior named Fred McFeely Rogers finished school in Florida and went home to stay with his parents in Latrobe, Pennsylvania. He wasn't exactly sure what he wanted to do with his life. For a while he wanted to be a diplomat; then he decided to become a Presbyterian minister. He'd already made plans to enroll in a seminary after college, but as soon as he arrived home he changed his mind again.

Why? Because while he was away at school, his parents had bought their first TV set. Television was still very new in the early 1950s, and not many people had them yet. When Rogers got home he watched it for the very first time. He was fascinated by the new medium but also disturbed by some of the things he saw. One thing in particular offended him very deeply. It was "horrible," as he put it, so horrible that it altered the course of his life.

What was it that bothered him so much? "I saw people throwing pies in each other's faces," Rogers remembered. "Such demeaning behavior."

KID STUFF

You (and Uncle John) may like it when clowns throw pies and slap each other in the face, but Fred Rogers was appalled. He thought TV could have a lot more to offer than pie fights and other silliness, if only someone would try. "I thought, 'I'd really like to try my hand at that, and see what I could do,'" Rogers recalled. So he moved to New York and got a job at NBC, working first as an associate producer and later as a director.

Then in 1953, he learned about a new experimental TV station being created in Pittsburgh. Called WQED, it was the country's first community-sponsored "public television" station. WQED

The squiggle over the 'n' in mañana is called a 'tilde.'

wasn't even on the air yet, and there was no guarantee that an educational TV station that depended on donations from viewers to pay for programming would ever succeed. No matter—Rogers quit his secure job at NBC, moved to Pittsburgh with his wife, Joanne, and joined the station.

"I thought, 'What a wonderful institution to nourish people,'" Rogers recalled. "My friends thought I was nuts."

LOW-INCOME NEIGHBORHOOD

When Rogers arrived at WQED in 1953, the station had just four employees and only two of them, Rogers and a secretary named Josie Carey, were interested in children's programming. The two created their own hour-long show called *The Children's Corner* and paid for all of the staging, props, and scenery (mostly pictures painted on paper backdrops), out of their own meager $75-a-week salaries.

Because *The Children's Corner* had to be done on the cheap, Rogers and Carey decided that much of the show would have to revolve around showing educational films that they obtained for free. Rogers was in charge of hustling up the free films and playing the organ off camera during the broadcast; Carey would host the show, sing, and introduce the films.

LUCKY BREAK

That was how *The Children's Corner* was *supposed* to work, but the plan fell apart about two minutes into their very first broadcast. The problem wasn't that Rogers couldn't scrounge up any free films, it was that the films he *did* manage to get were so old and brittle that they were prone to breaking when played. Sure enough, on the first day of the show, on WQED's first day on the air, the first film broke.

Remember, this was before the invention of videotape, when television shows were broadcast live—so when the film broke, the entire show came to a screeching halt. *On the air.* In the broadcast industry this is known as "dead air"—the TV cameras are still on, and the folks at home are still watching, but there's nothing happening onscreen. Nothing at all.

PAPER TIGER

At that moment Rogers happened to be standing behind a paper backdrop that had been painted to look like a clock. He quickly looked around and spotted "Daniel," a striped tiger puppet that the station's general manager, Dorothy Daniel, had given him the night before as a party favor at the station's launch party.

"When the first film broke, I just poked the puppet through the paper," Rogers remembered years later, "and it happened to be a clock where I poked him through. And he just said, 'It's 5:02 and Columbus discovered America in 1492.' And that was the first thing I ever said on the air. Necessity was the mother of that invention, because it hadn't been planned."

The puppet worked and the old films didn't, so *The Children's Corner* became an educational puppet show. Daniel Striped Tiger, who lives in a clock, remained a fixture on Rogers's shows for the rest of his broadcast career. Numerous other characters, including King Friday XIII, Lady Elaine Fairchilde, and X the Owl all made their debut on *The Children's Corner*.

NEIGHBORHOOD WATCH

The Children's Corner stayed on the air for seven years; then in 1963 Rogers accepted an offer from the Canadian Broadcasting Corporation to host a 15-minute show called *Misterogers*, the first show in which he actually appeared on camera. (That year he also became an ordained Presbyterian minister.)

By 1965 *Misterogers* was airing in Canada and in the eastern United States, but it had the same problem that *The Children's Corner* had—not enough money. *Misterogers* ran out of funds and was slated for cancellation...until parents found out: when they learned the show was going off the air, they raised such a stink that the Sears Roebuck Foundation and National Educational Television (now known as the Public Broadcasting Service, or PBS), kicked in $150,000 apiece to keep the show on the air.

Lengthened to a full half hour and renamed *Mister Rogers' Neighborhood*, the show was first broadcast nationwide on February 19, 1968.

INNER CHILD

Very early in his broadcasting career, Rogers drew up a list of things he wanted to encourage in the children who watched his show. Some of the items on that list: self-esteem, self-control,

---

And it floats! When filled, the oil tanker *Jahre Viking* weighs 1.13 billion pounds.

imagination, creativity, curiosity, appreciation of diversity, cooperation, tolerance for waiting, and persistence. *How* Rogers encouraged these things in his young viewers was heavily influenced by his own childhood experiences:

• **His grandfather.** Many of the most memorable things Rogers said to children were inspired by things his own grandfather, Fred Brooks McFeely, said to him. "I think it was when I was leaving one time to go home after our time together that my grandfather said to me, 'You know, you made this day a really special day. Just by being yourself. There's only one person in the world like you. And I happen to like you just the way you are,' " Rogers remembered. "That just went right into my heart. And it never budged." (Rogers named Mr. McFeely, the show's Speedy Delivery messenger character, after his grandfather.)

• **The neighborhood of make-believe.** Fred Rogers was a sickly kid who came down with just about every childhood disease imaginable from chicken pox to scarlet fever. He spent a lot of time in bed, quarantined on doctors' orders. To amuse himself, he played with puppets and invented imaginary worlds for them to live in. "I'm sure that was the beginning of a much later neighborhood of make-believe," Rogers said.

• **Explanations.** Like most children, when Rogers was very little, he was frightened by unfamiliar things—being alone, starting school, getting a haircut, visiting a doctor's office, etc. "I liked to be told about things before I had to do them," he remembered, so explaining new and unfamiliar things became a central part of the show. (On one episode he even brought on actress Margaret Hamilton, who played the Wicked Witch of the West in *The Wizard of Oz*, to explain that she was just pretending and that kids didn't need to be afraid.)

• **Sweaters.** Rogers got most of his sweaters from his mother, who knitted him a new one every year for Christmas. He wore them all on his show.

• **Sneakers.** Those date back to his days on *The Children's Corner*—"I had to run across the studio floor to get from the puppet set to the organ," Rogers explained. "I didn't want to make a lot of noise by running around in ordinary shoes."

GOODBYE, NEIGHBOR

Rogers taped nearly 900 episodes of Mr. *Rogers' Neighborhood* over its more than 30 years on the air. They're still broadcast by more than 300 public television stations around the United States as well as in Canada, the Philippines, Guam, and other countries around the world. Videotapes of the show are used to teach English to non-native speakers (singer Ricky Martin credits Mr. Rogers with teaching him to speak English).

Rogers retired from producing new episodes of the show in December 2000, and the last new episode aired in August 2001. He came out of retirement briefly in 2002 to record public service announcements advising parents on how to help children deal with the anniversary of the September 11 attacks. He made his last public appearance on January 1, 2003, when he served as Grand Marshal of the Tournament of Roses Parade and tossed the coin for the Rose Bowl Game. Mr. Rogers passed away from stomach cancer two months later.

THOUGHTS FROM MR. ROGERS

• "The world is not always a kind place. That's something children learn for themselves, whether we want them to or not, but it's something they really need our help to understand."

• "Anything we can do to help foster the intellect and spirit and emotional growth of our fellow human beings, that is our job. Those of us who have this particular vision must continue against all odds."

• "People don't come up to me to talk about the weather. I've even had a child come up to me and not even say hello, but instead say right out, 'Mr. Rogers, my grandmother's in the hospital.'"

• "So many people have grown up with the 'Neighborhood,' I'm just their dad coming along. You know, it's really fun to go through life with this face."

One of the most common things people who met Mr. Rogers say about him is that he was the very same person off camera that he was on camera. And yet to the cynical, that seemed hard to believe. Was Fred Rogers really the person he appeared to be on TV...or was he too good to be true? Turn the page to find out.

The French Poodle isn't French and the Great Dane isn't Danish. They're both from Germany.

NEIGHBORHOOD GOSSIP

Like a lot of celebrities, Mr. Rogers was the subject of some preposterous rumors over the years. Here are three of the strangest.

MYSTERY: Why did Mr. Rogers always cover his arms?
URBAN LEGEND: He was a sniper in Vietnam. He wore long-sleeved shirts, sweaters, and jackets to cover up the many tattoos he got while serving in the military.
THE TRUTH: Rogers was born in 1928, which makes him too old to have served in Vietnam. He never served in any other war, either; he began his career in television right after he graduated from college in the early 1950s. So why did he always wear long sleeves? Dressing somewhat formally was a technique he used to establish himself as an authority figure to the children who watched the show.

MYSTERY: *Mr. Rogers' Neighborhood* is a kids' show. So how come kids almost never appeared on the show?
URBAN LEGEND: Rogers was once convicted of abusing children and instead of jail, was sentenced to community service. Appearing on the show for more than three decades was how he served out his sentence. As a convicted child abuser, Rogers wasn't allowed to be alone with kids—even on the TV show.
THE TRUTH: Rogers got his start in broadcasting in the early 1950s, before the invention of videotape. Shows had to be broadcast live, which is why kids seldom appeared on *any* kids' shows back then—they are too unpredictable for live TV.

MYSTERY: How did Mr. Rogers really feel about kids?
URBAN LEGEND: After more than three decades of hosting a children's show, Mr. Rogers showed how he *really* felt about children on his very last show: he gave kids the finger on TV.
THE TRUTH: There is such a picture floating around on the Internet, but it's a fake—somebody doctored a real picture to make it look like Rogers was flipping the bird. It never happened. Anyway, by the end of his career new episodes were taped months in advance of broadcast, and such an image would never have been allowed to air.

Number of holes in a Ritz cracker: 7—six in a hexagon shape, and one in the center.

WORD ORIGINS

*Ever wonder where certain words came from? Here
are the interesting stories behind some of them.*

M ONEY
Meaning: Currency; a medium of exchange in the form of coins and banknotes

Origin: "Hera, queen of the Greek gods, kept her name out of the vulgate [common speech] until she moved to Rome and became Juno. As Juno Moneta (Juno the Monitress), she presided over a Roman temple where gold was coined. Moneta became the eponym of money, and Moneta's temple a mint." (From *Thou Improper, Thou Uncommon Noun*, by Willard Espy)

PADDY WAGON

Meaning: A police van

Origin: "A carryover from the days when Irish immigrants were low men on the social totem pole and hence fair game when a roundup of miscreants was needed to create favorable publicity for the law enforcers. Paddy was a common nickname for Irishmen." (From *Dictionary of Word Origins*, by William and Mary Morris)

EROTIC

Meaning: Relating to sexual desire or excitement

Origin: "*Eros* was the god of love, and the fairest of the gods in the Greek pantheon. But he was vain and spoiled and for sport shot his love-poisoned arrows into the hearts of men and gods. At his festival, the *erotia*, married couples of the day were supposed to patch up their differences and end all quarrels. From the Greek name *Eros* comes the word *erotic*, meaning 'full of sexual desire,' or 'morbidly amorous.'" (From *Word Origins*, by Wilfred Funk)

JUGGERNAUT

Meaning: An overwhelming force that crushes anything in its path

Origin: "The word comes from Hindi; its origin lies in *Jagganath*, a Hindu god, the Lord of the World. The city of Puri in eastern India is the site of an annual festival in his honor at which the

---

New Zealanders eat the most butter annually—about 20 lbs. per person.

image of the god is carried on a gigantic wheeled vehicle 45 feet high, drawn through the streets by pilgrims. It was said (mostly inaccurately) that fanatical followers would throw themselves under the wheels." (From *Merriam-Webster's Dictionary of Allusions*, by Elizabeth Webber and Mike Feinsilber)

COCKTAIL

Meaning: An alcoholic drink consisting of spirits mixed with other ingredients

Origin: "One idea is that it came from cockfighting. A cock's courage was fired up by slipping him a mixture of stale beer, gin, herbs, and flour, which was called *cock-ale*. More likely, the term was coined by Antoine Peychaud, a New Orleans restaurateur. During the 1800s, Antoine made drinks mixed from a number of different liquors. He served the wicked brew in little egg cups called *coquetier* in French. Wanting to give his drinks a special name, he simply Americanized the French word by changing it to cocktail." (From *Straight from the Horse's Mouth*, by Teri Degler)

PHONY

Meaning: A fraudulent person or thing

Origin: "Newspaperman H. L. Mencken suggested that a maker of fake jewelry named Forney is the origin of this word, but few experts agree with him. The majority opinion is that *phony* is an alteration of *fawney*, British slang for a worthless ring. The word probably comes from the *fawney rig*, a con game in which a worthless ring is planted, and when someone 'finds' it he is persuaded by a 'bystander' that he should pay the bystander for his share in the find." (From *Word and Phrase Origins*, by Robert Hendrickson)

POOPED

Meaning: Exhausted

Origin: "Englishmen headed for the New World found that violent waves did the most damage when they crashed against the stern (rear end), or *poop* of a vessel. Any ship that came out of a long bout with nature was said to be badly 'pooped.' Sailors who described the splintered stern of a ship often confessed that they felt as pooped as their vessel looked. Landsmen borrowed the sea-going expression and put it to use." (From *Why You Say It*, by Webb Garrison)

Pound for pound, a hummingbird consumes the caloric equivalent 228 milkshakes per day.

PETER'S PRINCIPLES

*The Canadian-born writer and educator, Lawrence J. Peter,
became famous when his book* The Peter Principle *was
published in 1969. The Principle: "Every employee rises
to his level of incompetence." He has more to say, too.*

"A man convinced against his will is not convinced."

"Competence, like truth, beauty, and contact lenses, is in the eye of the beholder."

"Equal opportunity means everyone will have a fair chance at being incompetent."

"The red light is always longer than the green light."

"Democracy is a process by which people are free to choose the man who will get the blame."

"Fortune knocks but once, but misfortune has much more patience."

"Against logic there is no armor like ignorance."

"Speak when you are angry and you'll make the best speech you'll ever regret."

"Television has changed the American child from an irresistible force into an immovable object."

"Originality is the fine art of remembering what you hear but forgetting where you heard it."

"The man who says he is willing to meet you halfway is usually a poor judge of distance."

"There are two kinds of failures: those who thought and never did, and those who did and never thought."

"The man with a clear conscience probably has a poor memory."

"Expert: a man who makes three correct guesses consecutively."

"The trouble with resisting temptation is that you may not get another chance."

"An ounce of image is worth a pound of performance."

"A pessimist is someone who looks both ways before crossing a one-way street."

"Despite the cost of living, it's still popular."

EXILE ON EASY STREET

It's a perennial news story: some dictator somewhere is oppressing his people, plundering his country's treasury, and defying international law. Then suddenly he's out of power. You assume he's in jail, but he's probably living in the lap of luxury.

DICTATOR: Augusto Pinochet, Chile

REIGN OF TERROR: Pinochet came to power in a CIA-assisted coup in 1973. During his rule, tens of thousands of Chileans were tortured, killed, or "disappeared." Pinochet relinquished power amid growing opposition in 1990 but remained the commander-in-chief until 1998, when he became "senator-for-life."

WHERE'D HE GO? While visiting England in 1998, Pinochet was arrested by British authorities on charges of torture and genocide. During his house-arrest, he lived at Wentworth, an exclusive estate outside of London. Estimated cost: $10,000 a month. After a long legal battle, a British court ruled that he was too sick to stand trial.

Pinochet went back to Chile, where he was arrested again, with more than 200 charges against him. In 2002 the Chilean Supreme Court ruled him unfit for trial and all charges were dropped. During his house-arrest in Chile, he got the same royal treatment he had in England: he lived on a baronial estate overlooking the Pacific Ocean.

DICTATOR: Alfredo Stroessner, Paraguay

REIGN OF TERROR: He took over Paraguay in a military coup in 1954 and ruled for more than 35 years. (He was "reelected" eight times.) Stroessner was a participant in Operation Condor, a police action that tortured, disappeared, or executed hundreds of thousands of people in South America. And he helped turn Paraguay into a haven for Nazi war criminals.

WHERE'D HE GO? Stroessner was overthrown in 1989 and fled to neighboring Brazil, where he still lives a quiet, comfortable life.

DICTATORS: Ferdinand and Imelda Marcos, Philippines

REIGN OF TERROR: Ferdinand Marcos was elected President of the Philippines in 1966. Under the Philippine constitution, he would have had to leave office in 1973—so he declared martial law and scrapped the constitution. Having taken absolute control of the country, Marcos ordered numerous tortures and executions. And he stole more than $5 billion. When he was overthrown in 1986, the 1,220 pairs of shoes found in wife Imelda's closet infuriated the poverty-stricken nation and became an international symbol of greed.

WHERE'D THEY GO? To Hawaii. Ferdinand died in 1989, but with billions hidden in Swiss banks, Imelda has continued to live in luxury. (She was reported to have over 3,000 new pairs of shoes by the mid-1990s.) The Philippine government recovered $2 billion of the stolen funds, but Mrs. Marcos is still doing alright—in February 2003, she was seen shopping for diamonds in Italy.

DICTATOR: Mengistu Haile Mariam, Ethiopia

REIGN OF TERROR: Mengistu overthrew Emperor Haile Selassie in 1974 and turned to the Soviets for help in starting a Marxist regime. During the two-year campaign dubbed "the Red Terror," tens of thousands of "enemies of the revolution" were murdered. When families came to claim the bodies, they had to pay for the bullets that killed their loved ones before they could take them. After the fall of the Soviet Union in 1989, Mengistu lost support and was finally overthrown in 1991.

WHERE'D HE GO? He fled to Zimbabwe as a "guest" of President Robert Mugabe, where he still lives in a heavily guarded, luxurious mansion. Though he's formally charged with "crimes against humanity" in Ethiopia, Zimbabwe refuses to extradite him.

DICTATOR: Jean-Claude "Baby Doc" Duvalier, Haiti

REIGN OF TERROR: At the age of 19, he succeeded his father, "Papa Doc," as president-for-life. During his 15-year reign, tens of thousands of Haitians were tortured and killed. As Haiti turned into one of the world's poorest nations, Baby Doc stole an estimated $500 million.

WHERE'D HE GO? Although never officially granted asylum, Duvalier moved to France in 1986, taking the stolen money with him. He lived in a villa in the hills above Cannes, drove a Ferrari, and owned two apartments in Paris and a chateau.

PARTIAL PAYBACK: According to news reports, Duvalier went broke. How? He lost everything in his divorce from his wife, Michelle Duvalier, in the mid-1990s.

Two out of three adults in the U.S. will need glasses at some point in their life.

THE LADY OF THE LINES

*If you've ever heard of the Nazca lines, you have this woman
to thank for preserving them for posterity. And if you've ever
doubted that one person can make a difference, think again...*

HELP WANTED
In 1932 a 29-year-old German woman named Maria
Reiche answered a newspaper ad and landed a job in
Peru, tutoring the sons of the German consul. After that, she
bounced from job to job and eventually found work translating
documents for an archaeologist named Julio Tello.

One day she happened to overhear a conversation between
Tello and another archaeologist, Toribio Mejia. Mejia described
some mysterious lines he'd seen in a patch of desert about 250
miles south of the capital city of Lima, near the small town of
Nazca. He tried to interest Tello in the lines, but Tello dismissed
them as unimportant. Reiche wasn't so sure. She decided to go to
Nazca and have a look for herself.

MYSTERIOUS LINES

Gazing out across the desert floor, Reiche was amazed by what she
saw: More than 1,000 lines crisscrossing 200 square miles of desert,
some as narrow as footpaths, others more than 15 feet wide. Many
ran almost perfectly straight for miles across the desert, deviating
as little as four yards in a mile.

The lines were made by early Nazca people, etched into the
desert floor between 200 B.C. and 700 A.D. They had created the
lines by removing darkened surface fragments (known as "desert
varnish") to reveal the much lighter stone underneath.

But why?

WAITING FOR SUNDOWN

An American archaeologist and historian named Paul Kosok had
a theory. At first he thought the lines might be irrigation ditches,
but they weren't large enough or deep enough to transport water.
Then he started to wonder if they might have some kind of astronomical significance. So, on June 21, 1941, the southern hemi-

Dressed to kill: During the French Revolution, a woman named...

sphere's winter solstice, he went out into the desert and waited for the sun to set.

Sure enough, when the sun set, it did so at a point on the horizon that was intersected by one of the Nazca lines. The line seemed to serve as an astronomical marker, telling the Nazca people that the first day of winter had arrived.

BIG BIRD

Kosok had also observed that while most of the Nazca lines were straight, some were curvy. But it wasn't until he plotted one on a piece of paper, then looked down to see that he'd drawn the outline of a giant bird, that he realized that some of the lines were *drawings*. The drawings were so large that they could not be made out by anyone looking at them from the ground.

With the discovery of the solstice line and the giant bird, Kosok became convinced that the Nazca lines were an enormous astronomical calendar, or, as he put it, "the world's largest astronomy book," with each line carefully laid out to correspond to something in the heavens above. Maybe, he speculated, the giant bird represented a constellation in the night sky. He offered Reiche a job helping him survey the lines so that he could prove his theory.

LIFELONG PASSION

She took the job, and after a few months of tramping across the desert each day with little more than a canteen of water and a pencil and paper to record her observations, she found what she was looking for: a line that intersected with the sun on the southern hemisphere's summer solstice, December 21. That was all it took—Reiche was convinced that Kosok's theory was correct. And she would spend the rest of her life trying to prove it.

At first Reiche could afford to visit the Nazca lines only occasionally, and because she was German she was not allowed to work at the site at all during World War II. By 1946, however, she was living in Peru year-round and spending nearly all of her waking hours in the desert trying to unlock the secret of the lines. When Kosok left Peru in 1948, she continued without him.

Studying the lines wasn't as simple as it sounds. In those days, many of them were so obscured by dirt, sand, and centuries of new desert varnish that it was barely possible to find them. That they were distinguishable at all was thanks only to the fact that they were etched a few inches into the desert floor.

CLEAN SWEEP

Reiche decided to "clean" the lines so that they could be more easily seen. First she tried using a rake. When that didn't work, she switched to a broom. It's estimated that over the next 50 years, she swept out as many as 1,000 of the lines by herself, carefully mapping the location of each one as she went along, and returning to the same lines at different times of day and in all lights to be certain that she was following their true courses.

In the process Reiche discovered—and *uncovered*—as many as 30 drawings similar to the giant bird that Kosok had found, including numerous birds, two lizards, four fish, a monkey, a whale, a pair of human hands, and a man with an owl-like head. The scope of her work is astonishing: When you look at an aerial photograph of the Nazca lines—any photograph of any of the lines or ground drawings—there's a good chance that Reiche swept those lines herself. Mile after mile after mile of them, using only one tool—an ordinary household broom.

LOST IN SPACE

Just as Reiche was almost single-handedly responsible for restoring the Nazca lines, she was also the first to bring them to public attention. Her 1949 book *Mystery on the Desert* helped to generate worldwide interest in the lines.

But what really put them on the map was a 1968 book written by a Swiss hotelier named Erich Von Daniken. His book *Chariots of the Gods* proposed that some of the lines were landing strips for alien spacecraft. According to Von Daniken's theory, aliens created the human race by breeding with primates, then returned to outer space. The early humans then etched the drawings into the desert floor, hoping to attract the aliens back to Earth.

JOIN THE CROWD

Chariots of the Gods was an international bestseller, and its success prompted other people to write books of their own with more theories about the origin of the lines. One speculated the lines were ancient jogging tracks; another claimed they were launch sites for

Nazcan hot-air balloonists. These books turned the Nazca lines into a New Age pop culture phenomenon, helping to attract tens of thousands of tourists to the site each year.

As a result, the Nazca lines began to suffer from overexposure—more and more tourists went out into the desert on foot, on dirt bikes, and in dune buggies, doing untold damage to the lines in the process.

Reiche did what she could to protect them. For years she lived in a small house out in the desert so that she could watch over the lines herself, and she used the profits from her writing and lecturing to pay security guards to patrol the desert. By the end of her life she was crippled by Parkinson's disease, but she continued to study the lines and was known to chase intruders away in her wheelchair. By the time of her death in 1998 at the age of 95, she was nearly deaf and almost completely blind. Not that it really mattered to her—"I can see every line," she said, "every drawing, in my mind."

FINAL IRONY

Though Reiche devoted most of her life to proving that the Nazca lines are a giant astronomical calendar, that theory has been largely discarded. Researchers now believe that while a few of the lines may indeed point to astronomical phenomena such as the summer and winter solstices (with more than 1,000 lines running across the desert floor in all directions, even *that* may be a coincidence), most of the lines are processional footpaths linking various sacred sites in the desert. The ground drawings, they believe, are artwork the Nazcans made for their gods.

*   *   *

FOSSIL FUELS

When locomotives were first used in Egypt in the 19th century, wood and coal were scarce. So what did they use for fuel? The one thing they had plenty of: human mummies—millions of them.

MORE SIMPLE SOLUTIONS

*On page 305 we told you about some simple inventions
that are changing the world. Here are a few more.*

HIPPO WATER ROLLER

Problem: In South Africa, more than 15 million people have to carry water from wells or rivers to their homes—sometimes as far as six miles away. It's traditionally carried by balancing five-gallon buckets on top of the head, requiring many trips and often leading to neck and back injuries. How can people get water from one place to another without breaking their backs doing it?

Simple Solution: A big plastic drum with handles

Explanation: It looks like a lawn roller. Fill the large, barrel-shaped drum with water, screw on the lid, lay it on its side, attach the handles, and then just push or pull it home—the barrel becomes a wheel. It holds 20 gallons of water, which weighs 200 pounds. But the design makes the weight feel like 22 pounds, so even kids and the elderly can handle it. And it's made of UV-stabilized polyethylene, durable enough to ride over roots, rocks, and even broken glass. Cost: about $60. (The manufacturer, Imvubu Projects of Johannesburg, has donated thousands of the rollers to water-needy communities.)

XTRABIKE

Problem: Bicycles are an extremely popular mode of transportation in developing nations—often it's the only mode. But carrying a lot of weight on a bicycle can be difficult, if not impossible, and dangerous. How can people carry goods and other large loads on their bikes?

Simple Solution: The Xtrabike, a heavy-duty bike rack

Explanation: Working in Nicaragua and Kenya, a company from Berkeley, California, called XAccess designed a steel-frame extension for the back wheels of a bicycle, with fold-down racks that turn it into a hauler of water, kids, or any other cargo. The design carries the weight low to the ground, so it still rides and turns normally, and an average person can comfortably haul as much as a

200-pound load. (Try doing that on a bike rack.) It costs about
$50, which is a lot for many people, but XAccess has a solution
for that, too. "Can't afford an Xtrabike?" they ask on their website.
"We'll teach you how to make one."

BAYGEN FREEPLAY RADIO

Problem: Many Africans can't get vital information about health-
care because they lack basic communication devices such as TVs
and radios. In many areas there's no electricity, and the cost of one
set of batteries could be an entire month's salary. How can people
get the information they need?

Simple Solution: A wind-up radio

Explanation: Englishman Trevor Baylis learned about the problem
in 1993 while watching a documentary on the spread of AIDS in
Africa. Working with Andy Davis, who helped design the first
Sony Walkman, by 1995 he had invented the BayGen Freeplay, a
spring-driven radio. By 1997 tens of thousands had been sold—
cheaply—in developing countries all over the planet. Wind the
crank, and a specially designed coil spring powers a small genera-
tor, which in turn powers the receiver. How well does it work?
Turn the crank for 30 seconds and you can listen to AM, FM, or
shortwave stations for more than 30 minutes. And the spring can
take 10,000 windings before it wears out. The BayGen has won
endorsements from Prince Charles, Nelson Mandela, and the
International Red Cross.

FOLDABLE FAMILY PANEL COOK KIT

Problem: In many developing countries it is increasingly difficult
to obtain fuel—mostly wood or coal—for cooking. How can people cook without fuel?

Simple Solution: A solar-powered oven

Explanation: Roger Bernard and Barbara Kerr of Solar Cookers
International (SCI) developed such an oven, and the best part is
that anybody can make one. For decades they have been doing
workshops for families in impoverished villages, providing the materials and know-how to make solar ovens. The materials: some cardboard, aluminum foil, glue, and a plastic bag (an oven cooking bag
works best). The oven really works, too. Even on partly sunny days,
it will reach 300°F. Meat, beans, rice, vegetables, breads, and other

---

First pilot ever to fly a loop-the-loop: Lincoln Beachy, on Nov. 18, 1913 (San Diego).

foods can be cooked without using any fuel. It takes longer than conventional ovens (although for many dishes and on sunny days it doesn't), but the benefits outweigh this drawback. Another plus: Put the food in the solar oven, go about your day, and come back later—the solar cooker won't burn your food, it will just keep it hot.

ADAPTIVE EYECARE

Problem: In 2002 the World Health Organization estimated that one billion people around the world who needed eyeglasses could not get them. In the African nation of Ghana alone, there were only 50 opticians for a population of 20 million. Poor eyesight means difficulties in reading, education, and employment. Without enough doctors, how can people get the glasses they need?

Simple Solution: Universal, adjustable eyeglasses

Explanation: In 1996 Oxford professor Dr. Joshua Silver started Adaptive Eyecare. After years of research, he had invented glasses with lenses that were filled with a clear silicon oil. A small pump on the frame changes the amount of oil in the lenses, thus altering their curvature. (The pump is removed after the adjustment.) That means that as a person's sight deteriorates over time, they don't have to go find an optician—they simply turn a knob until their vision is in focus, and voilà! A new pair of glasses! And each lens can be adjusted separately. The glasses are universal, since anyone can adjust them to their own eyes, which keeps manufacturing costs down. The glasses are sold to nonprofit groups and governments around the world, keeping with Dr. Silver's goal of improving the vision of the world's poorest people.

* * *

WEIRD TALES OF THE STAGE

The Bluebird is a classic play about two children who go searching for the Bluebird of Happiness. A designer at a midwestern theater thought it would be a great idea to have *real* bluebirds fly around the theater at the end of the play. So he sprayed pigeons with blue paint and put them in little cages hanging above the audience. Apparently no one ever considered what the paint, combined with the heat from the lights, might do to the birds. On opening night, the cages were opened at the end of the show...showering a horrified audience with hundreds of dead "bluebirds."

The Chinese were the first to use a decimal system, in the sixth century B.C.

FOUNDING (*hic!*) FATHERS

*Before they were (hic) alcoholic beverages, (hic) they were
people (hic) who made alcoholic beverages (hic).*

JOHN WALKER

Background: In 1820, at age 15, Walker started working in his father's grocery, wine, and spirit store in Kilmarnock, Scotland. Unhappy with the inconsistencies in the barrels of whiskey, he set out to refine the process. Walker soon became known throughout Scotland for his technique of blending single malt whiskies.

Famous Name: Walker's son Alexander joined him in 1856 and began marketing Walker's Kilmarnock Whisky in England and Australia, and later in the United States. In 1908 the company name was changed as a tribute to its founder, Johnnie Walker.

DON FACUNDO BACARDI MASSÓ

Background: Born in Spain, Don Facundo emigrated to Cuba around 1830. There he discovered rum—a harsh "firewater" popular among pirates. A cultured man, Don Facundo made it his goal to create a smoother version that could be served in fine restaurants.

Famous Name: It took more than 30 years of experimenting with every step of the manufacturing process, but in 1862, Don Facundo perfected it and introduced Bacardi Rum. The family still runs the business today using the same secret technique created by Don Facundo 140 years ago.

JASPER NEWTON DANIEL

Background: He was born in Tennessee in 1850, the youngest of 13 children, and ran away when he was only six years old. Little Jasper ended up living with a neighbor named Dan Call and earned his keep by helping him make moonshine whiskey. In 1863 Call sold his still to Jasper, who was then only 13.

Famous Name: Known as Jack, Jasper Daniel had a knack for making—and selling—whiskey, and distributed it to both sides during the Civil War. He used his war profits to build a real distillery.

A slight man at 5'2" and 120 pounds, Daniel relied on his personality as much as the quality of his whiskey to make sales. He always wore a mustache and goatee, a planter's hat, and a knee-length frock coat. He never appeared in public without his "costume." When postwar liquor laws changed, Daniel was the first man to register a distillery in the United States, which he called Jack Daniel Distillery No. 1.

JOSÉ ANTONIO DE CUERVO

Background: Sent by the king of Spain, in 1758 José de Cuervo traveled to a small town in central Mexico. There he began cultivating the agave plant, which for thousands of years had been fermented by the indigenous peoples into a beverage known as *mezcal*. De Cuervo produced a more refined version of the liquor, which took on the name of the town in which it was made...Tequila.

Famous Name: His descendants have been producing it ever since, and have become one of Mexico's richest and most respected families. But it wasn't until the turn of the 20th century that Cuervo-produced tequila began to carry the name José Cuervo.

PETER SMIRNOFF

Background: Peter Smirnoff's first batch of vodka came out of his still in 1864. Over the next 15 years, he became famous throughout Russia and in 1886 was named the royal distiller of Czar Alexander III. By 1900 Smirnoff was producing a million bottles of vodka per day.

Famous Name: One of Smirnoff's suppliers, Rudolph Kunett, fled Russia when the czar was overthrown and purchased the rights to sell Smirnoff vodka in the United States. The only problem: no one bought it—the vodka had a reputation as a harsh liquor that led to a bad hangover. Kunett finally gave up and sold his Connecticut distillery to G. F Hublein and Company in 1939. Part of the deal included the last 2,000 bottles of vodka. But they had no vodka corks left, so company president John Martin decided to put whiskey corks on them instead. That changed everything. In the South, a salesman sampled it, loved it, and came up with a new slogan: "Smirnoff's White Whiskey. No Taste. No Smell." It sold out. Why? Fewer people were drinking straight liquor in those days—they wanted something that could be mixed. So Martin resumed the vodka production, advertising it as a mixer. Today it's the bestselling liquor in the United States.

THE CAT'S MEOW

We've done a lot of quote pages about dogs in past Bathroom Readers. *Now, it's time for cats to have their day.*

"After scolding one's cat, one looks into its face and is seized by the ugly suspicion that it understood every word. And has filed it for reference."
—**Charlotte Gray**

"If a cat spoke, it would say things like, 'Hey, I don't see the problem here.'"
—**Roy Blount, Jr.**

"If cats could talk, they wouldn't."
—**Nan Porter**

"I have studied many philosophers and many cats. The wisdom of cats is infinitely superior."
—**Hippolyte Taine**

"Dogs come when they're called. Cats take a message and get back to you later."
—**Mary Bly**

"Cats keep their cool, no matter what. Even when they do things like fall or lose their balance, they'll walk away with an attitude that seems to say, 'I meant to do that.'"
—**Michael Jordan**

"Whether they be the musician cats in my band or the real cats of the world, they all got style."
—**Ray Charles**

"If cats seem distant and aloof it is because this is not their native planet—they are here just to visit and dominate."
—**Hank Roll**

"To bathe a cat takes brute force, perseverance, courage of conviction—and a cat. The last ingredient is usually the hardest to come by."
—**Stephen Baker**

"In order to keep a true perspective of one's importance, everyone should have a dog that will worship him and a cat that will ignore him."
—**Dereke Bruce**

"You may own a cat, but cannot govern one."
—**Kate Sanborn**

"The smallest feline is a masterpiece."
—**Leonardo da Vinci**

Scaredy cat? Charles Lindbergh carried a Felix the Cat doll with him on his famous flight.

BRAINTEASERS

Uncle John emerged from "the brainroom" giving these puzzles three thumbs up—one thumb for being fun, one thumb for being challenging, and one thumb for "I just learned something." (We still can't figure out where he got the extra thumb.) Answers on page 498.

1. You're sitting on a bus. The kid next to you has a helium-filled balloon. She lets go of the balloon and it ends up against the ceiling, just about in the center of the bus. The driver suddenly hits the gas pedal and the bus lurches forward, throwing you back into your seat. What does the balloon do?

      a) It moves backward. **b)** It moves forward.
      c) It stays where it is.

2. How can you make the following equation correct without changing it:

$$8 + 8 = 91$$

3. You place an empty glass on one side of a balance scale and a one-pound weight on the other side. Then you fill the glass with water until the two sides are perfectly balanced. Now you put your finger down into the water without touching the glass. It makes the water level in the glass rise, but it doesn't overflow. What happens to the scale?

      a) The glass side goes up. **b)** The glass side goes down.
      c) It holds still.

4. You're sitting in a boat in a swimming pool. You have a large anchor in the boat. You drop the anchor into the water, and, of course, it sinks immediately. What happens to the water level in the pool?

      a) It goes up. **b)** It goes down. **c)** It stays the same.

5. Try to solve this in your head: Take 1,000 and add 40 to it. Now add another 1,000. Now add 30. And another 1,000. Now add 20. Now add another 1,000. Now add 10. What's the total?

Ask Virginia Woolf: Three percent of all English surnames are derived from animal names.

THE BIGGER THEY ARE...

*Sometimes making big business decisions means
making big blunders, as these folks found out.*

BAD APPLE

In 1988 Apple Computers hired a small computer company from Virginia called Quantum Computer Services to develop an online service for their customers. It was to be called AppleLink Personal Edition and was set to come out in 1989. But before Quantum could launch the service, Apple changed their minds and terminated their contract. Bad idea. Quantum had negotiated in their contract that if Apple let them go, they got to keep the technology. They launched the service themselves in late 1989, with a new name...America Online.

STAR WARS: THE PUBLISHER'S MENACE

British book publisher Dorling Kindersley saw sales of its *Star Wars* books rise dramatically after the release of the movie *The Phantom Menace* in 1999. Elated company execs quickly ordered a huge printing for the Christmas sales season—and sold a whopping 3 million copies. The only problem—they had printed 13 million copies. Loss: $22.4 million. In January 2000, the already debt-plagued company admitted the mistake and CEO James Middlehurst resigned. In March, the once-prosperous worldwide publisher was sold to media giant Pearson. (*Note:* Ten million books would make a stack more than 150 miles high.)

A TOBACCO COMPANY TELLS THE TRUTH!

In 2001 tobacco giant Philip Morris did a study of the effects of cigarette smoking for the leaders of the Czech Republic. The report they issued touted the "positive effects" that smoking has for government. It shortens people's lives, they said, which means lower costs for pensions, housing, and health care for the elderly. The details of the report were supposed to be private, but somehow the press got hold of them and made them public. Result: A major public relations blow to a company that had just spent $100 million to boost its image. Philip Morris issued an apology to the Czech people and then canceled plans to make similar reports in four other nations.

On average, babies born in May are 7 ounces heavier than those born in other months.

A FINE ROMANCE (OR TWO)

In 1991 Random House editor Joni Evans thought she could cash in on the fame of TV's *Dynasty* star Joan Collins and offered her a $4 million contract—with a $1.3 million advance—to write two romance novels. (Collins's sister, Jackie, is a bestselling novelist.) Collins turned in manuscripts for *The Ruling Passion* and *Hell Hath No Fury*, but Evans thought they were terrible and wouldn't publish them. Random House sued Collins but couldn't get the advance money back. As if giving a huge advance to an unproven writer wasn't a big enough blunder, Evans missed a clause put in the contract stipulating that Collins would be paid whether or not her manuscripts were published. Result: Collins ended up with $2.6 million of Random House's cash for two books that never went to press.

IT'S NOT OK

Before she joined Random House (see item above), Evans was a senior editor at the publishing house William Morrow, where she committed another blunder in an otherwise successful career. When Morrow was approached about the paperback rights of a certain new author, she advised her boss against it, sure that the book would never sell. The price for the rights at the time was $10,000…three months later, the rights went for $675,000. The book was the groundbreaking self-help title *I'm OK, You're OK*. It went to #4 on the *New York Times* Best Seller list in 1970 and has sold over 15 million copies since…most of them paperbacks.

LISTEN CAREFULLY

In November 2001, the privately owned Japanese company Dentsu, the world's fourth largest advertising agency, decided to go public. They had the Wall Street firm UBS Warburg handle their initial public offering, and instructed the brokers to sell 16 shares at 610,000 yen ($4,925) each. But the brokers mistakenly listed 610,000 shares at 16 yen (about 13¢) each. Before they discovered the error, 65,000 of the shares had been sold. Warburg had to buy them all back on the open market. The exact amount of Warburg's loss was undisclosed, but it was estimated to be as high as $100 million.

WINGING IT

Anyone who's ever boarded an airplane has probably wondered how a 400-ton hunk of metal could possibly cruise through the air. Is it magic? No, it's physics! Here's a simplified explanation for all you porcelain pilots.

HOW ABOUT A LIFT?

The force that makes it possible for airplanes to fly is called *lift*. Lift is provided by the wings of an airplane. But how do the wings generate lift? There are two characteristics that help them get the plane off the ground:

1. The "Angle of Attack"

• If you've ever stuck your hand out of the window of a moving car, you already understand how the "angle of attack" works. If you tilt your hand so that the front edge of your hand is pointing upward, the air strikes the bottom surface of your hand and pushes it higher in the air.

• Changing the tilt of your hand so that the front edge is pointing downward has the opposite effect: the air strikes the top of your hand and pushes it down. By tilting the front edge your hand up and down, you can "fly" your hand up and down however you want. If this is difficult to understand, try it the next time you're in a car.

• If you look closely at the wings on an airplane, you'll notice that they're tilted. The front edge—known as the *leading edge*—is slightly higher than the *trailing edge*. Aircraft manufacturers do this so that when the airplane is moving through the air, more air strikes the bottom surface of the wing than the top, pushing the wing upward and helping the plane to fly.

2. The Shape

If you were to look at a cross-section of an airplane wing, it would look something like this:

There are 132 Hawaiian islands.

The wing is shaped this way in order to take advantage of something called *Bernoulli's principle*. Understanding the "angle of attack" is pretty easy, but Bernoulli's principle is a little trickier:

• In 1738 Daniel Bernoulli, a Swiss mathematician, observed that when the velocity of a fluid increases, the pressure of that fluid decreases.

• You may not think of air as a fluid, but technically it is. So when air speed increases, air pressure decreases.

• Wings are shaped in such a way that the air that passes over the top surface of the wing moves faster than the air that passes underneath the bottom surface.

• That means that the air pressure underneath the wing is higher than the air pressure above it. This difference in pressure causes the air underneath the wing to literally *press* the wing upward in the air.

• Lift is measured the same way that weight is. If your airplane weighs 1,000 pounds, that means the wings have to generate more than 1,000 pounds of lift for the plane to leave the ground.

STRAIGHT TALK

So how does the shape of a wing make the air passing over it move faster than the air moving underneath it? Well, as we all know, the shortest distance between two points is a straight line. And that's the secret:

• The bottom surface of the wing is relatively flat and straight, but the top is curved. An air molecule passing underneath the wing travels a fairly straight path, which means it travels a shorter distance than an air molecule that passes over the top of the wing. But since it does it in the same amount of time, it's actually moving at a slower rate than the molecule above the wing.

• This is where Bernoulli's principle comes in: since the air passing over the top of the wing is traveling faster than the air traveling underneath the wing, the air pressure above the wing is lower than the air pressure underneath the wing. This difference in air pressure causes the wing to rise in the air, and the plane to be able to fly.

FREE WITH PURCHASE

*These days almost every retailer has some kind of loyalty program—
frequent flyer miles, grocery store club cards, even low-tech
cardboard punchcards at the local sandwich shop. But 100
years ago it all started...with trading stamps.*

A REDEEMING IDEA

Back in 1896, a silverware salesman named Thomas Sperry was making his regular rounds of the stores in Milwaukee when he noticed that one store was having success with a unique program. They were rewarding purchases with coupons, redeemable for store goods. That gave Sperry an idea: why not give out coupons that weren't tied to merchandise from a particular store, but were redeemable anywhere in the country?

With backing from local businessman Shelly Hutchinson, he started the Sperry and Hutchinson Company, and began selling trading stamps. Here's how it worked:

• S&H sold stamps (they looked like small postage stamps, each with a red S&H insignia on a green background) to retailers.

• Retailers gave them to customers as a bonus for purchases, 10 stamps for each dollar spent.

• Customers collected the stamps in special S&H books until they had enough to trade back to Sperry and Hutchinson in exchange for merchandise like tea sets or cookware.

• Retailers who participated in the program hoped that customers would feel like they were getting something for free, which would entice them to continue to shop loyally at their stores.

• At first only a few stores across the country offered the stamps, but over the next 50 years, through economic recessions, the Roaring Twenties, the Great Depression, and two world wars, S&H's popularity grew steadily.

POSTWAR FAD

Interest in trading stamps peaked in the 1950s. Why? More people lived in urban areas with more grocery stores to choose from. Bread, milk, and corn flakes are the same in every supermarket, so rival

---

Call a cab: According to statistics, yellow cars and bright blue cars are the safest to drive.

stores started looking for a way to set themselves apart from the competition. One way was by offering trading stamps.

Collecting trading stamps seemed like a fun way to get great stuff without raiding the household budget. So, with their books full of stamps, postwar consumers got televisions, blenders, transistor radios, and the most popular item, toasters.

Trading stamps became so popular that gas stations, drugstores, and dry cleaners got in on the act, too. By 1964 S&H was printing three times as many stamps as the U.S. Post Office. At the industry's peak in 1969, more than 80% of U.S. households were collecting stamps, and more than 100,000 stores were offering the most popular kind, Green Stamps. The S&H redemption catalog had the largest print run of any publication in the United States.

A WORLD OF STAMPS

Green Stamps were the best known, but there were many other brands of trading stamps in the 1960s. If you shopped at Piggly Wiggly's, for instance, you'd get Greenbax, at A&P you'd get Plaid Stamps, at Kroger you'd get Top Value Stamps, and so on.

Stamps came in a rainbow of colors, too: Orange, Yellow, Red, Pink, Blue Chip, K&S Red, Triple-S Blue, Plaid, Gold Bond, Merchant Green, and World Green, to name a few. And they appeared under a dizzying variety of names: Top Value, Mor-Valu, Shur-Valu, King Korn, Regal, Big Bonus, Double Thrift, Buckeye, Buccaneer, Two Guys, Eagle, Gift House, Double "M", Frontier, Quality, Big "W," and many more.

The stamps had an actual cash value—if you brought in 1,000 stamps, S&H would cheerfully hand you $1.67. But no one cared about the stamps' cash value when catalogs offered tempting merchandise like clock radios and Corningware. What else could you get for your stamps? Fur coats, purebred pets, European vacations, even life insurance policies. King Korn got a lot of publicity in 1969 by offering a work by classic 20th-century American painter Thomas Hart Benton for 1,975 books.

In fact, publicity-hungry trading-stamp companies—always looking for a way to get a leg up over their many competitors—were willing to negotiate with collectors to provide just about anything equal to the cash value of the collected stamps. Some of the more unusual items:

Mr. Mom: Male Malaysian fruit bats can produce milk.

- An eight-passenger Cessna airplane (paid for with Gold Bond stamps by a church congregation)
- A pair of gorillas (paid for with 5.4 million Green Stamps by an Erie, Pennsylvania, school who wanted to supply their local zoo)
- A donkey for an overseas church missionary
- An elephant (also intended for a local zoo)
- School buses, ambulances, and fire trucks

TAKING A LICKING

Eventually, trading stamps became victims of their own popularity. So many stores were giving them away that there was no longer any reason to shop loyally at one store.

The rampant inflation of the 1970s didn't help, either. Businesses that gave trading stamps were perceived as charging higher prices. The 1973 oil embargo and gas shortage killed the program at gas stations, too, since consumers would shop at the gas station with the lowest price, not the station that gave Green Stamps.

But trading stamps didn't die out completely. S&H had $1 billion in annual revenue in 1981 when the company was sold and continued limping along for the next 18 years. By 1999 fewer than 100 stores offered Green Stamps. That's when Walter Beinecke, the great-grandson of founder Thomas Sperry, bought back S&H.

IF YOU CAN'T LICK 'EM...

Under Beinecke's influence, S&H Green Stamps have been recast for the digital age—they're now Greenpoints, with bar-coded cards customers swipe at the registers of participating stores. (Don't worry, the company still redeems the old gummed stickers.)

Greenpoints offers 10 points for every dollar spent, just like it did in the 1960s. But goods are now valued accordingly. The leather wallet that cost one book of Green Stamps (1,200) now costs 9,600 Greenpoints. Four towels that could be bought with 1,200 Green Stamps cost 14,400 Greenpoints today. Camcorders go for 200,000.

The prizes consumers want have changed, too. People no longer want to redeem their points for towels or hair dryers—they're more interested in digital cameras, movie tickets, gift certificates (for Burger King, Blockbuster, and Pizza Hut), and Greenpoints' most popular redemption item, the George Foreman Grill (40,800). And if you have 13,800 Greenpoints, you can still get a toaster.

How does this make you feel? There are 10 inkblots on the standard Rorschach test.

FOOD SUPERSTITIONS

What can you do with food besides eat it? Drive evil spirits away, of course! People actually used to believe in these bizarre rituals.

Bake your cakes while the sun is rising, and do not throw away the eggshells until the baking is done.

Tossing coffee grounds under steps leading to the kitchen will rid the home of ants.

If you don't spit out the seeds while eating a grape, the seeds will give you appendicitis.

Hold a buttercup under someone's chin. If it casts a yellow shadow, that person loves to eat butter.

The sound of thunder will turn milk sour.

Hammer a peg or nail into a fruit tree that bears no fruit, and soon you will have some.

Tipping over a slice of cake on a plate while serving a guest is a sign of bad luck.

If you want your cabbages to flourish, plant them on St. Patrick's Day.

Two yolks in an Easter egg is a good omen—you will be rich someday.

If you spot bubbles in a cup of coffee, try to spoon them up and eat them before they burst. If you succeed, you will receive money from an unexpected source.

It's bad luck to gather blackberries after October 11.

If you love someone and want them to love you, give them an orange.

Onions mixed with ant eggs will cure deafness.

Eating the last piece of bread on a plate is bad luck—it will cause a bachelor to marry, or an unmarried woman to stay unmarried.

Rum poured on the head cures baldness.

Bananas must be broken apart—never cut with a knife. Cutting brings bad luck.

Eating peaches gives you wisdom.

If you grow too much lettuce in your garden, your wife will never conceive children.

There are 24 flowers on every Oreo cookie.

KING OF CANADA

*If politicians were awarded points for weirdness, there'd be
plenty of competition... but this guy would win.*

BLAND MASTER

William Lyon Mackenzie King was Canada's longest-serving
prime minister, leading Canada through most of the Great
Depression and all of World War II.

Born in 1874 in Kitchener, Ontario, King studied law and economics at the University of Toronto and Chicago University.
Inspired to go into government service by his mother's tales of his
grandfather, the rebel William Lyon Mackenzie, King became an
astute politician and leader who made many lasting contributions
to Canadian history.

In public he was an average-looking man who favored black
suits with starched white collars. According to *Canada: A People's
History*, King was "dull, reliable and largely friendless." When
talking to the press or in Parliament, King was deliberately vague
and opaque.

"It was hard to pin him down, to use his own words against
him...because his speeches were masterpieces of ambiguity," writes
Canadian historian Pierre Berton. To the public he was a master
politician and a symbol of stability.

But the public didn't know about his private life.

BEHIND CLOSED DOORS

In those days, a politician's private life really was private. Good
thing for King, because behind his neutral facade, he was a first-
class eccentric.

King never married, and in fact, seemed terrified of all
women—except his mother. No woman, notes Berton, "could
hope to compare for beauty, compassion, selflessness, purity of soul
with his mother, who haunted his dreams... guiding his destinies,
consoling him in his darker moments and leaving precious little
time or space for a rival."

Isabel King continued to control her son even after her death.
Long after she passed away, King held séances and regularly chat-

ted with his mother's "spirit" about matters of state.

He liked to speak with other deceased figures as well. "He spent a lot of time communicating with departed relatives and the famous dead," states *Canada: A People's History*. "In 1934, he returned from Europe, having made friends with Leonardo da Vinci, a member of the de'Medici family, Louis Pasteur, and Philip the Apostle." He also contacted Prime Minister Wilfrid Laurier, British prime minister William Gladstone, Saint Luke, Saint John, Robert Louis Stevenson, and his grandfather.

BAD RAP
King owned a crystal ball, but that's not how he contacted the spirit world. He had a special séance table through which spirits "spoke" to him by rapping out messages that he alone could decipher. Unfortunately, the messages weren't always accurate.

On September 2, 1939—one day after Nazi Germany invaded Poland to start World War II—King held a séance in which his dead father told him Hitler had been assassinated. The prime minister was greatly disappointed when he discovered this wasn't true.

King vastly underestimated the dangers posed by fascist leaders such as Hitler and Mussolini. After visiting Nazi Germany in the 1930s, King decided that Hitler was okay because he allegedly shared certain personality traits with the Canadian P.M. "I am convinced Hitler is a spiritualist," King wrote. "His devotion to his mother—that Mother's spirit is, I am certain, his guide."

King also dabbled in numerology and the reading of tea leaves, and held lengthy policy chats with his dog, an Irish terrier named Pat, to whom he liked to outline issues of national importance. (It's unclear what advice, if any, Pat offered in return.) He reportedly made decisions on national issues based on the position of the hands of the clock, as a vote was being taken in Parliament.

CAN'T KEEP A SECRET
How do we know so much about King's private life today? He kept extensive diaries. He left explicit instructions that after his death for his butler to burn the diaries. But instead of burning them, the butler read them. Now they reside in Canada's National Archives.

What's the only food that provides calories with no nutrition? Sugar.

CHAN THE MAN

As a kid, Uncle John spent many Saturday afternoons glued to the tube watching corny old B-movies featuring the white-suited Chinese detective, Charlie Chan. Though considered politically incorrect today, they're still on TV...and they're still corny.

THE MAN BEHIND CHAN

Charlie Chan has cast a portly shadow across the world of detective fiction since his creation in 1925. The wise and charming Oriental sleuth was the brainchild of a novelist and playwright from Warren, Ohio, named Earl Derr Biggers. Biggers got the idea for the character while on a visit to Honolulu in 1919, where he happened to read an article about real-life Chinese detective Chang Apana.

Charlie Chan debuted as a minor character in Bigger's novel *House Without a Key*, which was serialized for the *Saturday Evening Post* magazine and then turned into a silent movie in 1926. Readers loved Chan, so Biggers immediately wrote another story, this one with the Chinese detective in the lead. Then, for the next five years, Biggers wrote a new Charlie Chan novel every year.

CAN UNDERSTAND CHAN GRAND PLAN

Biggers died in 1933, but his character lived on. Forty-five Charlie Chan films were produced by Twentieth Century Fox and then Monogram Studios during the 1930s and 1940s. The plots all followed the same formula: Charlie Chan, the world famous detective, would stumble upon a murder case in some exotic place like Paris, Cairo, or Monte Carlo. One or two of his sons—identified in chronological order as "Number One Son" and "Number Two Son"—would offer "Pop" their help. For the rest of the movie, these young detective wannabes would get in the way until Chan solved the case in spite of them. And along the way, he would offer numerous pearls of pithy Chinese wisdom.

ONE CHAN, MANY MAN

Six different actors played the Chinese detective on-screen, but amazingly, none of them were Chinese. Warner Oland, probably

---

Chinese fishermen train otters to herd fish into their nets.

the best-known and most popular, was Swedish. But Oland's heritage included some Mongolian blood, which is possibly what allowed him to pass for Asian on the screen when he added a moustache and goatee. In real life, Oland often spoke in stilted speech and referred to himself as "Humble Father," which gave some people the impression that he actually thought he *was* Charlie Chan.

After making 16 Chan films, Warner Oland died in 1938, but once again, Chan was too popular (and valuable) to die. Sidney Toler took his place, doing 22 more movies.

When Toler died in 1947, Roland Winters became Chan. Of all the Chans, Winters was the worst cast—he had a large nose and blonde hair. He tried to look Chinese by squinting and always insisted on being shot from the front so audiences wouldn't see his Caucasian profile. If he needed to speak to anyone at his side, he simply moved his eyes to the right or left. Winters made the last Chan film in the series, *The Sky Dragon*, in 1949.

MORE CHAN, MANY FAN

The franchise extended to radio, too. Walter Connolly and Ed Begley, both Caucasians, played Charlie Chan on a show sponsored by Esso. The radio show ran from 1932 until 1948.

On television, *The New Adventures of Charlie Chan* premiered in 1957 and lasted less than a year. In the lead role was J. Carroll Naish, another Caucasian. In 1971 a made-for-TV movie, *Happiness Is a Warm Clue*, starred Ross Martin (he was Caucasian, too).

The last Charlie Chan movie, a parody called *The Curse of the Dragon Queen*, was made in 1981. It starred (non-Asian) Peter Ustinov as the detective. While in production, Chinese-American groups protested the film and several Asian-American extras were added to the cast.

EPILOGUE

More than 75 years after his first appearance, Charlie Chan lives on. Biggers's novels have never gone out of print, and more than 40 of his movies regularly play on cable television. As Chan says, "Impossible to miss someone who will always be in heart."

CHANISMS

For a fictional detective, Charlie Chan was pretty wise.

"If you want wild bird to sing do not put him in cage."

"Owner of face cannot always see nose."

"Hasty conclusion like gunpowder—easy to explode."

"Grain of sand in eye may hide mountain."

"You talk like rooster, who thinks sun come up just to hear him crow."

"If strength were all, tiger would not fear scorpion."

"Questions are keys to door of truth."

"Only foolish man waste words when argument is lost."

"Man who flirt with dynamite sometime fly with angels."

"Every Maybe has wife called Maybe-Not."

"When money talks, few are deaf."

"Cannot believe piece of carved stone contain evil until dropped on foot."

"Trouble, like first love, teach many lessons."

"Advice after mistake is like medicine after dead man's funeral."

"Waiting for tomorrow—waste of today."

"When friend asks, friend gives."

"Every man must wear out at least one pair of fool's shoes."

"When doing good deed, remember kind-hearted elephant who tried to help hen hatch chicks."

"Cat who tries to catch two mice at one time goes without supper."

"Good idea not to accept gold medal until race is won."

"Man who seek trouble never find it far off."

"Humbly suggest not to judge wine by barrel it is in."

"Words cannot cook rice."

"Cannot tell where path lead until reach end of road."

JUMPING FOR JOY

The origin of the trampoline is just the kind of story we love at the BRI: one man's dream and persistence creates something that millions of people have benefited from.

SKIN-SPIRATION

As a typical teenage boy in Cedar Rapids, Iowa, in the 1920s, George Nissen loved the circus. He was most fascinated with the acrobats—the way they would gracefully fall into the large nets from the high wire, sometimes doing amazing tricks and twists as they bounced. Nissen also loved vaudeville acts. One of the gags he liked best was the springboard. A man would be pushed off the stage into the orchestra pit, only to "magically" bounce back up onto the stage. He wanted to do that! When Nissen read in a high school textbook that Eskimos sometimes stretched walrus skins between stakes in the ground and then bounced up and down on them just for fun, that did it—he decided to make his own "jumping table."

Still in high school, Nissen started his project in 1926. He scavenged materials from the local dump and tinkered away in his garage...for 10 years. In that time he had become a world-class tumbler, winning the National Championship three times in a row, from 1935 to 1937. It was around this same time that Nissen was putting the final touches on his new invention. With the assistance of a local gymnastics coach named Larry Griswold, Nissen used rails from a bed, some strips of inner tube, tightly wound rope, and canvas to build his first jumping table. He called it the trampoline, from the Spanish word *trampolín*, which means "springboard." They took it to the local YMCA, where Nissen worked as an instructor to test-market it. The kids loved it—they stood in long lines for a chance to jump on the new contraption.

BOUNCING BACK

The trampoline became so popular in Cedar Rapids that Nissen began mass-producing them in 1938. One problem: no one bought them. Why? Nissen believed that even though the trampoline intrigued them, people saw it as something only for circus performers. So he strapped a trampoline to the top of his car and took off cross-country, giving exhibitions anywhere a crowd was gathered—schools, fairs, playgrounds, and sporting events.

Taking a lesson from Barnum (see page 23), Nissen taught a kangaroo to jump on a trampoline. He trained it using dried apricots as treats and quickly learned that the best way to avoid getting kicked was to "hold hands" with the kangaroo's front paws. A photograph of man and beast high in the air was printed in newspapers all over the country—exactly the publicity Nissen wanted. It brought the crowds out, and sure enough, sales improved.

Then when World War II started, Nissen convinced the Army that trampolines could train pilots not only to achieve better balance, but also to be less fearful of being upside down. And jumping on a trampoline was great for physical conditioning. The military agreed; thousands of cadets learned to jump on trampolines.

IT'S A FAD!

Still, even after the war, trampolines were mostly found at gymnasiums, primarily used by athletes. Then, in the late 1950s, a new fad emerged: trampoline centers. Here's what *Life* magazine said about it in May 1960:

> All across the nation the jumping business is jumping, and a device called the trampoline, once a tool of tumblers, has overnight become a popular plaything. Matrons trying to reduce, executives trying to relax and kids trying to outdo each other are plunking down 40¢ for a half hour of public bouncing at trampoline centers which are spreading the way miniature golf courses spread several decades ago.

And trampolining wasn't just for the average person. Nissen boasted that "Vice President Richard Nixon, Yul Brynner, the Rockefellers, and King Farouk" were all avid jumpers as well.

But while Nissen must have been happy that his invention was finally catching on, he was very critical of the trampoline centers. Profiteers, he said, were just buying the trampolines and allowing patrons to jump unsupervised. Many of the jumpers were either inept or intoxicated. After a few high-profile injuries (a beauty queen lost her teeth and a high school football star was paralyzed), the centers started folding. Nissen tried opening his own properly supervised centers, called Jumpin' Jiminy. But it was too late—the injuries had given trampolines a bad name.

Kangaroos can cover a distance of 30 feet with one jump.

IT'S A SPORT!

When Nissen saw the interest in trampolines start to dwindle, he understood why. "You have to have programs," he said. "I bounce too, but if I didn't have something new to do on a trampoline, I would lose interest."

So he set his sights on turning trampolining into a sport. First he tried "Spaceball," a combination of jumping and volleyball, but that turned out to be too dangerous. He also tried combining trampolining and running by putting little bounce pads at either end of a track, but that didn't catch on, either.

Then Nissen met a Swiss economist in California named Kurt Baechler, who also happened to be a gymnast. Together they combined trampolining with gymnastics, creating the sport Nissen was looking for. They organized the Nissen Cup trampoline competition, formed the International Trampoline Federation, and financed the first trampolining World Championships in the Royal Albert Hall in London. As the trampoline center fad gave way to hula hoops and pinball arcades, the sport of trampolining started taking off.

Today, trampolines can be found in backyards worldwide. And the Nissen company is still a major manufacturer of gymnastics equipment and trampolines. George Nissen holds 35 patents on sports and fitness equipment (including the seat cushion that protects your bottom from rock-hard bleacher seats). At 83 years old Nissen won California's Senior Fitness Award. And he finally achieved his goal of having competitive trampolining—the idea he came up with when he was 19 years old—recognized as a real sport. It became an Olympic event in 2000.

TRAMPOLINE FACTS

• Jeff Schwartz of Illinois bounced on a trampoline for 266 hours, 9 minutes in 1981, setting a world record. He was allowed breaks for eating, sleeping, and going to the bathroom.

• Another world record was set on July 24, 1999, when a team of 20 people in West York, United Kingdom, did 29,503 somersaults in exactly five hours using two standard trampolines. That averages out to 1,500 somersaults per person.

• The U.S. Consumer Product Safety Commission reported that there were 83,212 trampoline-related injuries in 1996, up from only 19,000 in 1976.

THE GLASS ARMONICA

Benjamin Franklin invented bifocals, the lightning rod, an odometer,
the Franklin stove, swim fins, and street lights. He also invented
the glass armonica. (Doesn't everybody know that?)

SINGING WINEGLASSES

It's a classic party trick: Wet your finger and rub it around the rim of a wineglass. What you'll hear is a very pure musical note. Add some wine, and the pitch gets higher; remove some, and the pitch gets lower.

The singing wineglass trick has been around for hundreds of years. It's mentioned in Persian documents from the 1300s. There's a European reference to tuned water glasses dating from 1492. And Galileo wrote about the phenomenon in his book *Two New Sciences*, published in 1638. But it was Benjamin Franklin in the 1700s who turned the trick into a musical instrument.

Between the years 1757 and 1766, Franklin spent most of his time in Europe as an agent for the American colonies and often attended musical concerts. One evening in 1761, while listening to virtuoso Richard Puckridge perform on the "singing glasses," Franklin was struck with the beauty of the sound. He immediately set about inventing his own glass musical instrument.

BEN INVENTS IT

Franklin worked with London glassblower Charles James to create a special set of glass bowls that did not need to be filled with water to make different musical notes because each was tuned to its own pitch. Painted different colors to represent each note of the scale, the bowls were nested inside each other and looked like a stack of goblets lying on their sides. An iron rod ran through them to a wheel, which was turned by a foot pedal. To create musical sounds, the player would touch the spinning glasses with moistened fingers. By the end of the year, Franklin had completed his invention and using the Italian word for harmony, he named it the *armonica*. He wrote,

> The advantages of this instrument are that its tones are incomparably sweet beyond those of any other; that they may be swelled and softened by stronger or weaker pressures of the fin-

ger, and continued at any length; and that the instrument, being once well tuned, never again wants tuning.

PLEASANT UNDER GLASS

The armonica was an overnight success. Franklin received orders for the instrument from customers in Paris, Versailles, Prague, and Turin. Marie Antoinette took lessons on it. The world's greatest composers, including Mozart, Beethoven, Donizetti, Richard Strauss, and Saint-Saëns, wrote music for it. Thomas Jefferson called it "the greatest present offered to the musical world in this century."

Because of its angelic tones, many people believed the glass armonica had healing powers. Franklin agreed: he used it to heal the "melancholia" of Princess Izabela Czartoryska of Poland in 1772. Dr. Franz Mesmer, the father of hypnotism, used the armonica to calm his patients during his magnetic séances. By 1790 more than 5,000 armonicas had been sold, making it the most celebrated musical instrument of the 18th century.

Then, just as quickly as it began, the musical fad ended.

SHATTERED

Disturbing tales began to circulate about the harmful effects of the glass armonica. Virtuoso player Marion Davies had become extremely ill. Her health and nerves were said to have been ruined by her armonica playing. Other performers were beginning to complain of nervousness, numbness in their hands, muscle spasms, and dizziness. Even some listeners became ill.

In 1798 the German musicologist Friedrich Rochlitz wrote in the *Allgemeine Musikalische Zeitung,*

> The armonica excessively stimulates the nerves, plunges the player into a nagging depression and hence into a dark and melancholy mood that it is an apt method for slow self-annihilation. If you are suffering from any nervous disorder, you should not play it; if you are not yet ill you should not play it; if you are feeling melancholy you should not play it.

Then in 1808, Marianne Kirchgessner, a blind concert artist who had inspired Mozart to write for the armonica, died at the age of 39. Her death was said to be a result of "deterioration of her nerves caused by the vibrations of the armonica."

Many believed the strange nerve disorders were caused by lead poisoning coming from the lead in the glass and in the paint. Others believed that the high-pitched harmonies, having mystical powers, invoked the spirits of the dead and drove listeners insane.

Nothing was ever proven against the glass armonica, but it didn't matter—people became so frightened of the instrument that few people would play one and few would even listen to one being played. By 1820 the armonica was all but forgotten.

THE GLASS IS BACK

The glass armonica made a comeback in 1984, thanks to the efforts of master glassblower and musician Gerhard Finkenbeiner of Boston. The German-born Finkenbeiner first thought of making a glass instrument in 1956. After many years of experimenting, he finally re-created Franklin's armonica, using only lead-free quartz crystal for the glass. Some of the rims have gold baked into them to identify the pitches. (The ones with the gold bands are like the "black keys" on a piano. The "white keys" are clear. The gold bands—and they're real gold—are on the inside of the cups, so the player doesn't actually touch them.) Today, G. Finkenbeiner Inc. in Waltham, Massachusetts, continues to produce the beautiful singing glass armonica.

WARNING
(posted in J. C. Muller's armonica manual of 1788)

If you have been upset by harmful novels, false friends, or perhaps a deceiving girl, then abstain from playing the armonica—it will only upset you even more. There are people of this kind—of both sexes—who must be advised not to study the instrument, in order that their state of mind should not be aggravated.

---

*   *   *

MUSICAL IRONY

The song "When Irish Eyes Are Smiling" was written by a German named George Graff...who never went to Ireland in his life.

Farting contests were held in ancient Japan. Prizes were awarded for loudness and duration.

THE RISE AND FALL OF THE WHIGS

Andrew Jackson was one of the founders of the modern Democratic party (see page 153). But in a sense, he is the founder of two political parties: the Democrats, who loved him, and the Whigs, who hated him.

JACKSON IN OFFICE

Andrew Jackson, a.k.a. "Old Hickory," was probably the most popular man in the United States when he won the presidency in 1828. And when he left office in 1836, he was still considered the champion of the common man—if for no other reason than he angered (and impoverished) a lot of wealthy and powerful people during his two terms.

For starters, Jackson instituted a policy of filling federal government jobs by firing supporters of former president John Quincy Adams and replacing them with his own. And although he ran on an anti-corruption platform, his appointees were, as Jackson biographer Robert Remini puts it, "generally wretched." One of the worst was Samuel Swartwout, a Jackson crony who was appointed to the job of collector of customs in New York. In this position, Swartwout oversaw the collection of more cash than any other government official, about $15 million a year. Swartwout absconded to Europe with more than $1.2 million of it, "more money than all the felons in the Adams administration put together," Remini writes. Adjusting for inflation, Swartwout is *still* the worst embezzler in the history of the federal government.

Jackson also managed to alienate many of his fellow Southerners. In 1832 South Carolina passed a law banning exorbitant federal tariffs, and even considered seceding from the union. That prompted Jackson to threaten to personally lead an army into the state, put down the rebellion and hang the ringleaders himself. The crisis was eventually resolved when Congress lowered the tariffs, but by then Jackson had lost a lot of support in the South.

THE BANK WAR

But what galvanized Old Hickory's opposition more than anything else was what he did to the American banking system.

Charles Dickens's original phrase for Scrooge was "Bah Christmas," not "Bah Humbug."

Like Thomas Jefferson before him, Jackson hated banks, believing them to be corrupt institutions that enriched the wealthy and well-connected. He especially hated the Second Bank of the United States. He hated it all the more when the bank and its director, Nicholas Biddle, sided with presidential candidate Henry Clay in the election of 1832 and even offered to lend money to pro-Clay newspapers to attack Jackson.

Big mistake—Jackson was furious that the bank would try to influence the outcome of the election. "The bank is trying to kill me," he complained, "but I will kill *it*."

FROM SECOND TO NONE

When Jackson won reelection against Clay in a landslide in 1832, he set out to make good on his word. He ordered the Secretary of the Treasury to pay government expenditures out of the Treasury's Second Bank accounts, while making any deposits to state banks. (Critics called them Jackson's "pet" banks.) In less than three months, the federal government's deposits to the Second Bank dwindled to almost nothing.

Biddle was determined to save his bank and believed that the best way to do it was by *maximizing* the economic damage from Jackson's measures. He drastically cut back on lending, prompting banks all across the country to follow suit; the financial panic that resulted sent the country into a recession.

Businesses in every major American city failed, throwing thousands out of work. Yet somehow, the plan backfired—Jackson's popularity actually increased, and his image grew as the protector of the common person against the greed of aristocrats and bankers. In the end, Jackson got what he wanted: the Second Bank finally collapsed in 1841.

BACKLASH

But the Bank War crystallized the political opposition to Jackson. Robert Remini writes in *The Life of Andrew Jackson*:

> The pressures of the Bank War and Jackson's imperial presidency finally brought a new party into being.... National Republicans, bank men, nullifiers, high-tariff advocates, friends of internal improvements, states' righters, and—most particularly—all those who abominated Jackson or his reforms slowly converged into a new political

---

Because of the rotation of the Earth, an object can be thrown farther if it's thrown west.

coalition that quite appropriately assumed the name "Whig."

The word *whig*, a Scottish-Gaelic term that was first applied to horse thieves, later became the name for anti-royalists in the American Revolution. Now it would be used by the opponents of the executive tyranny of the man some called King Andrew I.

WHAT GOES UP...

Had Jackson limited his economic meddling, perhaps the Panic of 1833–34 would have run its course without the Whigs emerging as a major political force. But he didn't.

By January 1835, he had managed to pay down the entire U.S. national debt ($60 million), and the federal government was collecting more revenues than it was spending. Jackson returned some of the surplus to the states, most of whom promptly spent it. Then, anticipating similar federal windfalls in the years to come, many states began borrowing against these future funds and spending that, too. In addition, Jackson's "pet" banks were now bulging with federal deposits, which allowed them to print and issue paper currency backed by federal monies. (In the 1830s, banks printed their own currency.) The country was soon awash with cash. Result: disaster.

The influx of so much capital into the economy led to huge inflation and soaring real-estate prices, creating a speculative economic bubble that burst in 1836 after bad weather led to crop failures in many parts of the country.

...MUST COME DOWN

As the U.S. economy began to teeter, foreign creditors started demanding payment in gold and silver out of a fear that American paper currency was losing its value. Jackson decided it would be good for the federal government to return to "sound money," too. On July 11, 1836, he ordered that all future payments for the sale of public lands (a major source of government income in the 1830s) be made in precious metals. Bank notes were no longer acceptable for these transactions, so they began to lose their value.

More bad news: A financial crisis rocked England, then the world's financial capital and a major buyer of American cotton, the country's largest export. The slump in the U.S. cotton market in turn caused the failure of hundreds of other related businesses.

"By the time Jackson finally retired in 1837, America was in the early stages of its biggest financial crisis to date," Paul Johnson writes in *A History of the American People*. "Far from getting back to 'sound money,' Jackson had paralyzed the system completely."

Jackson's heir apparent, Martin Van Buren, managed to squeak into office in the 1836 election, partly because the economic crisis was just beginning and nobody knew how bad it would be. But the 1840 election would be another story.

The recession deepened into a full-blown depression that dragged on for five long years, wiping out more than 600 banks and shuttering most of the factories in the East. Thousands of people lost their jobs, and food riots broke out in cities all over the nation.

Van Buren never had the popularity that Jackson enjoyed, and the depression ruined his chances for reelection.

WHIGS TRIUMPHANT

In 1840 the Whigs borrowed heavily from the Jackson-Van Buren formula for victory. They put a war hero at the top of the ticket: General William Henry Harrison, who had defeated the Shawnee Indians at the Battle of Tippecanoe 30 years earlier. They staged "monster" rallies all over the country. And when a Democratic writer made the mistake of claiming that Harrison would just as soon "spend the rest of his days in a log cabin with a barrel of cider," he gave the Whigs a perfect campaign theme that they could use to distinguish their man from a sharp-dressing New York dandy like President Van Buren. Harrison rallies became "Log Cabin and Hard Cyder" rallies: supporters built log cabins at every campaign event and served copious amounts of hard cider to the crowds.

Van Buren, vilified by the Whigs as an effete elitist who drank wine from "coolers of silver," seemed a sissy by comparison. On election day, he carried only 7 states to Harrison's 19, and lost in the electoral college, 60 votes to Harrison's 234.

The Whigs also won their first majorities in both houses of Congress, and in 1840 there were Whig governors in 20 of the 26 United States—not bad for a party that was barely seven years old.

WINNING THE BATTLE

The Whigs seemed to be on the brink of becoming permanently

established as the second major party alongside the Democrats. But then their luck ran out.

• Sixty-seven-year-old Harrison delivered his inaugural address outdoors in the snow without wearing a hat, gloves, or overcoat. He spoke for more than an hour and a half (the longest inaugural speech in American history), contracted pneumonia, and died a month after taking office (the shortest presidency in American history).

• Vice President John Tyler, a former Democrat who joined the Whigs after falling out with Andrew Jackson, became president. But he was still a Democrat at heart, and he vetoed a number of pieces of Whig legislation, prompting all but one member of his cabinet to resign and splitting the Whig party in two. The Whig congressional caucus wrote Tyler out of the party.

• In 1844 the Whigs, still bitterly divided, lost the White House to Democrat James Knox Polk. In 1848 the Whigs repeated their 1840 strategy by putting a war hero at the top of the ticket—General Zachary Taylor, hero of the Mexican War—and won the White House. But on July 4, 1850, history repeated itself when President Taylor consumed large quantities of raw fruit, cabbages, and cucumbers, washed it all down with iced water…and then died from acute gastroenteritis five days later, a little more than a year into his first term as president.

WHIGGING OUT

The Whig party was also divided over the issue of slavery. President Taylor himself had contributed to the split: as a plantation owner with more than 300 slaves, he so alienated anti-slavery Whigs in the north that many of them split off to form the Free Soil Party.

When Taylor died, Vice President Millard Fillmore (also a Whig) became president. He added to the controversy by signing the Fugitive Slave Law of 1850, which required the government to assist in the capture and return of runaway slaves to their owners, even in the anti-slavery states of the North. (Though Fillmore was personally opposed to slavery, he feared that ending it would lead to civil war, so he signed the law to cool the secessionist passions of the South.)

Historians generally credit such actions with postponing the

Civil War for 10 years, but they doomed Fillmore's chances for reelection and contributed to the destruction of the Whig Party. By 1848 Fillmore's hedging on slavery had cost the party support in the North; at the same time, the presence of anti-slavery politicians at the top of the party killed its support in the South. "Cotton Whigs," as the party's pro-slavery Southern faction was called, defected to the states-rights appeal of the Democratic Party. And by 1854, most anti-slavery "Conscience Whigs" had defected to a new party founded for the purpose of opposing slavery: the Republicans.

To read about the rise of the Republican Party, turn to page 483.

* * *

AN "OBSCURE" TALE

One morning, a valgus hobberdehoy was cornobbled by a very old leptorrhinian calcographer. "You twiddlepoopy liripoop!" faffled the hobberdehoy, "You've given me a wem that smells of bodewash!"

"So sorry," belched the saprostomous calcographer. "I was unaware that my jumentous mundungus was cornobbling you."

"Whatever, you spodogenous whipjack! Now I must go to my xystus and run my balbriggan galligaskin through my chirogymnasts to get this wem out!"

The calcographer felt like a dasypygal pismire. "I have lost my toxophily," he said sadly.

"Wait a second," faffled the hobberdehoy. "Did you say toxiphily? You remind me of my toxophillic atmatertera. You have the same anisognathous mouth as she."

"Does she go by the name Esmerelda?" asked the calcographer.

"Why yes, yes she does. She was brideloped by a calcographer many moons ago."

And then they looked at each other.

"Bob?"

"Jim?"

And then Bob and his great great great grandfather Jim went happily to Bob's xystus to de-wem his ballbriggan galligaskin.

(What are we saying? Turn to page 227 to find out.)

A species of fern has the most chromosomes of all living things: 630 pairs.

WHO KILLED JIMI HENDRIX?

*Jimi Hendrix had an astounding influence on pop culture.
Yet few people of the 1960s were truly shocked when the
musician died in 1970—he had a reputation for living hard
and fast. Most people assumed he just burned out like a
shooting star. But did he? Or was there more to it?*

DEATH, DRUGS, AND ROCK 'N' ROLL

Hours before Jimi Hendrix died, he was working on a song entitled "The Story of Life." The last lines:

*The story of life is quicker than the wink of an eye.
The story of love is hello and goodbye,
Until we meet again.*

Perhaps no rock musician is more emblematic of the psychedelic 1960s than Hendrix. The flamboyant guitarist became famous not only for such onstage antics as lighting his guitar on fire, but also for the blistering performances that earned him recognition as a musical genius. Although only five albums were released during his lifetime, he was—and is—considered one of the greatest rock guitarists ever.

OVER-EXPERIENCED

James Marshall Hendrix died in the squalid flat of a German girlfriend in London on September 18, 1970, after a long night of drinking and partying. After indulging in a smorgasbord of drugs and alcohol, he and his girlfriend returned to her apartment in the early hours of the morning where, according to the girlfriend, they both took some barbiturate pills to help them sleep.

A normal dose of the downers would have been just half a pill. The girlfriend claimed she took one pill. After Hendrix's death, an autopsy showed he had swallowed nine—18 times the recommended dosage. The autopsy also revealed "massive" quantities of red wine not only in his stomach, but also in his lungs. The quantity and combination of substances might well have been fatal if he hadn't first suffocated on the wine and his own vomit.

Egyptians used urine tests to diagnose pregnancy as early as the 14th century.

There is little mystery as to *what* killed Jimi Hendrix. The question is: *How* did it happen? Was it suicide, an accident…or murder? Ever since Hendrix's death, there have been those who believe there may have been more to the story than just another rock star done in by wretched excess. For some, things don't quite add up.

FATAL MISTAKE OR FOUL PLAY?

Friends of Hendrix rule out suicide. According to them, Hendrix believed the soul of a person who committed suicide would never rest. In spite of his many personal and professional problems, he would never take his own life.

Was it an accident? Hendrix was known for being able to take greater quantities of drugs than anyone else in his circle. He may have mistaken the potent barbiturates for regular sleeping pills and grabbed his usual handful. On the other hand, as experienced a drug-taker as Hendrix was, he was unlikely to make that kind of mistake. Besides, it was common knowledge that drinking alcohol with downers is asking for serious trouble.

But the quantity of wine found inside him, and around him on the bed where he died, raises an intriguing question: Did he drink that much or was it poured down his throat by someone else? How did so much get into his lungs? Oddly, the autopsy showed a relatively low blood-alcohol level in his body, leading some to speculate that Hendrix drowned in the wine before much of it was absorbed into his system.

But who would want Jimi Hendrix dead? It may be impossible to know now, more than 30 years after his death, but here are some compelling possibilities:

✔ **The Girlfriend.** According to the girlfriend, Monika Dannemann, she woke up the morning of the 18th, saw that Hendrix was sleeping normally, and went out for cigarettes. When she returned she saw that Hendrix had been sick and was having trouble breathing. She tried to wake him, and when she couldn't she began to panic and called musician Eric Burdon, with whom they had partied the night before. After first hanging up on her, Burdon called back and insisted Dannemann call an ambulance. Dannemann later told the press that Hendrix was alive when the ambulance arrived a few minutes later, about 11:30 a.m., and that she rode with him to the hospital. According to Dannemann, Hendrix was propped upright on the trip and suffocated on the way.

The ambulance attendants tell a different story. According to author James Rotondi, the two men arrived at the apartment to find it empty... except for Hendrix lying in a mess on the bed, already dead. They say they went through the motions of trying to revive Hendrix because that was standard procedure, but to no avail. They wrapped up the body, carried it to the ambulance, and drove to the hospital; Hendrix was pronounced dead on arrival. The autopsy cautiously concludes that the exact cause and time of death are unknown, but evidence points to a time of death much earlier—possibly several hours before the ambulance arrived.

Was Monika Dannemann trying to cover up something? If so, what and why? The world may never know—she committed suicide in 1996.

✔ **The Government.** Rock music has long been associated with rebellion, revolution, and social change, ideas that appeal to youthful fans but are a cause for concern for "the Establishment." It is well known that during the J. Edgar Hoover era, and perhaps even more recently, the FBI kept dossiers not only on political activists, but on actors, authors, and a wide variety of other potential "threats" as well. It is not surprising that influential musicians such as Jimi Hendrix would draw the interest of the U.S. government—but there may be more to it than that.

In his book *The Covert War Against Rock*, author Alex Constantine says Hendrix's FBI file, released in 1979 to a student newspaper in Santa Barbara, reveals that Hendrix was on a list of "subversives" to be placed in detainment camps in the event of national emergency. Hendrix was an icon of not only rock 'n' roll rebellion, but the Black Power and antiwar movements of the 1960s. Did U.S. intelligence agencies consider Hendrix not only subversive, but dangerous?

There are some conspiracy theorists who believe that Hendrix and other musicians, including Jim Morrison of The Doors, ex-Beatle John Lennon, and more recently, rappers Tupac Shakur and The Notorious B.I.G.—all of whom died under suspicious circumstances—may have been eliminated by the government. It would be remarkably easy to make the deaths look like accidents or murders committed by crazy fans—these musicians lived life close to the edge, anyway. Paranoid fantasy? Or could there be some truth to these fears?

✔ **The Mob.** Government agents may not have been the only ones with an eye on Hendrix. Organized crime figures were involved with the music industry long before Hendrix was. To the Mob, the industry wasn't about music—it was about money and drugs. And there was plenty of both around Hendrix.

According to Constantine, Hendrix was muscled by the Mob after declining an invitation to play at the Salvation, a New York night club controlled by the Gambino crime family. Hendrix had been a regular at the club, but after the proprietor was murdered following an attempt to break free of Mob control, Hendrix evidently felt uncomfortable playing there. Shortly thereafter, Constantine says, a stranger approached Hendrix on the street and, while chatting, pulled out a .38 pistol and casually hit a target 25 feet away. Hendrix got the message and decided to play the club after all.

Another time, Hendrix was kidnapped from the Salvation by some thugs claiming to be part of the Mafia, Constantine claims. They took him to a Manhattan apartment and told him to call his manager, Michael Jeffery, and relay a demand to transfer his contract to the Mob…or else. Hendrix was rescued from the thugs by men sent by Jeffery, but later told people he thought Jeffery had arranged the whole thing.

So Hendrix may have had good reason not to trust his manager…

✔ **The Manager.** Those seeking to tie together the loose ends of government agencies, the Mob, and enormous amounts of money need look no further than Michael Jeffery. Jeffery served in British Intelligence in the 1950s and years later boasted of underworld connections. As Hendrix's manager, Jeffery had control of millions of dollars earned by Hendrix, much of which was diverted by Jeffery to offshore bank accounts.

Hendrix became increasingly aware that Jeffery was cheating him, and just before his death made arrangements to cancel his management contract. The manager understandably could have been upset at the prospect of losing such a lucrative client—but why kill Hendrix? The answer could lie in the rumor that Jeffery had taken out a million-dollar life insurance policy on the star. Additionally, Jeffery could have made much more from the dozens of Hendrix albums released after the musician's death. (There were many hours of unreleased music.)

Whatever involvement the former intelligence agent may have had in Hendrix's death would have had to have been indirect; he was vacationing in Spain when Hendrix died. To some, Jeffery was further implicated when he himself died under unusual circumstances less than three years later, in a plane crash.

FLY ON

A number of times in the weeks before his death the 27-year-old Hendrix asked friends, "Do you think I will live to be 28?" Did he have a premonition of what was coming? Friends say he was becoming increasingly paranoid...and perhaps with good reason. We may never know the truth about the death of Jimi Hendrix, but we do know that his life, as he wrote in his final song, was indeed "quicker than the wink of an eye."

*   *   *

A TALE OF TWO CHORDS

In July 2003, hard-rock band Metallica announced that they were suing the Canadian band Unfaith over their use of the guitar chords E and F. "We're not saying we own those two chords individually, that would be ridiculous," Metallica's Lars Ulrich was reported to have said. "We're just saying that in that specific order, people have grown to associate E and F with our music."

Unfaith's lead singer, Erik Ashley, responded, "I thought it was a prank at first. Now I'm not sure what to think." Actually, he knew exactly what to think. Why? Because he created the prank.

But that didn't stop the media from running with the story without contacting the parties involved. ABC talk show host Jimmy Kimmel reported it, as did MSNBC's Jeannette Walls.

So why did Ashley do it? "To gauge just how willing America was to buy a story as extraordinary—as outlandish—as Metallica claiming ownership of a two-chord progression." He added, "If this week was any indication, America is all too willing to believe it."

But after all of Metallica's well-publicized attempts to sue on-line music downloaders, was it really that hard to believe? Said one anonymous chat room attendant: "I'm not sure what's worse—that the story is a fake, or that it was actually conceivable that Metallica would do that."

THIS OLD (OUT)HOUSE

In all our years writing Bathroom Readers, *this is one of the strangest hobbies we've ever heard of. We're never going to look at a bottle collection the same way again.*

TALKING TRASH

Try to imagine a world with no garbage collection—no garbage man to come and empty your trash cans, and no city or county dump to haul your old stuff to. What would you do with everything you have to throw away?

It wasn't so long ago that nearly everyone in America was faced with this problem. In the 19th century, few if any communities had trash collection, and not many had dumps, either. People were on their own. If trash was edible, they might feed it to animals or compost it for use in the garden. If it was flammable, they burned it. If they didn't know what else to do with it, they threw it in the backyard. "People had really messy yards," says archaeologist Liz Abel. "What they couldn't burn in the cookstove, they threw out back."

But if the item was small enough, oftentimes they went out to the outhouse and dropped it down the hole.

THE FINAL FRONTIER

The people who tossed things into their privies probably assumed that what they disposed of would never see the light of day again. They were wrong. A growing number of antique collectors and amateur history buffs have made it their hobby to dig this stuff up. In the process they've uncovered clues about the daily lives led by people in the 19th century.

"It's amazing what you can tell about someone who lived more than a hundred years ago by what they threw in their outhouse," says Jeff Kantoff, a New York lumber salesman who digs up Brooklyn outhouses in his spare time. "You can tell how many people were in the family, did they have kids, were the kids boys or girls, did they have money, what were their ailments."

Such outhouse excavators—or "privy diggers," as they prefer to be called—insist that as disgusting as it may sound to the uniniti-

---

ated, outhouse digging is really not that bad. Decades of organic activity have converted all that old poop into compost indistinguishable from ordinary dirt. "There is no stink whatsoever," says John Ozoga, a Michigan geologist and privy-digging enthusiast.

THE HOLE TRUTH

Privy digging dates back to the late 1950s, when antique bottle collecting began to take off as a hobby. Bottles are one of the most common items found in outhouses, not necessarily because people liked to drink soda, mineral water, or beer while they answered nature's call, but probably because tossing bottles down the privy was safer than having glass strewn all over the backyard.

And there's much more to find than just bottles. Privy diggers have found coins, clay pipes, pottery, silverware, ice skates, toys, shoes, pistols, billiard balls, false teeth, squirrel bones (people used to eat squirrels), and even Model T parts. In coastal areas it's also common to find oyster shells—*lots* of oyster shells—and not just because people liked to eat oysters. "Oyster shells were an early form of toilet paper," says Kantoff. "I don't know how they were used. I don't want to know."

Thanks to low oxygen levels, many items found in privies are in surprisingly good shape. Apples more than 150 years old still retain their color, and leather goods like shoes and saddlebags (yes, saddle bags) look like they were thrown away yesterday.

LOCATION, LOCATION, LOCATION

The hardest thing about excavating an old outhouse is knowing where to dig. The outhouses themselves have long since been torn down, and the holes, or "vaults," underneath them have been covered over with dirt and forgotten, with few visible clues indicating where they are.

One way of finding likely places to dig is by consulting old fire insurance maps to see if they show outhouse locations. Another trick is to put yourself in the shoes of the home owner—if you had to place an outhouse on your property, where would you put it? They were usually far enough away from the main house to control odors, but not so far as to be inconvenient. In areas with harsh winters, the outhouse is likely to have been closer to the main house, so that people didn't have to trudge through snow to use the facilities. On city lots, the outhouse is likely to be right up against the back property line, frequently in a corner.

PROBING QUESTIONS

Once privy diggers have identified likely areas to dig, they probe these locations, poking a seven-foot-long steel rod into the ground to see if they can detect the presence of a privy vault. What are they searching for? Any area that feels noticeably different from the surrounding ground. A "crunchy" layer could be glass bottles, fireplace ash (commonly dumped into outhouses), or household garbage, indicating the presence of a privy vault. In undisturbed dirt it's difficult to push the probe more than two or three feet into the ground, so if there's a spot in the yard that probes deeper than that, it may well be "the vault."

PRIVY DIGGING DOS AND DON'TS

1. Pick an outhouse that's on private property. Privies on public land may be protected by historical preservation laws, so don't go digging up the backyard of the governor's mansion. When Tim Clements dug up a privy on the grounds of the University of Nebraska in 2001, he was arrested and charged with trespassing and theft. Private property is usually exempt from preservation laws.

2. Ask before you dig. Getting permission to dig in someone's backyard may be easier than you think—just offer to share the artifacts you find. "A lot of homeowners will agree so that they can have something that came from their house," says Illinois privy digger David Beeler.

3. Keep digging. When a privy vault became full, it was common to seal it up by filling the last few feet of the hole with dirt and garbage. There may well be plenty of interesting stuff in this "garbage layer," but most of the artifacts are likely to have sunk all the way to the bottom. So keep going.

4. Check the sides and corners. When an outhouse is in use, material "mounds up in the center," just below where people sat, says privy digger Peter Bleed. "Things tend to roll off to the sides."

5. But wait, there's more! When one privy vault filled up, a new one was dug—frequently right next to the old one. So if you find one privy vault, don't stop! Look for more nearby.

THE OUTHOUSE DETECTIVES

It's amazing what you can learn about people who lived more than a century ago just by studying the junk they disposed of in their outhouses. Still don't believe us? Read on to find out what these privies reveal.

MAGNUM P.U.

As we told you in the previous article (page 463), "privy diggers" are hobbyists who dig up old outhouses to collect the bottles and other objects that people tossed down there more than 100 years ago. These objects may be interesting in their own right, but they also shed light on the daily lives of the people who dropped them there. Some outhouse clues are subtler than others. See if you can figure out what these outhouse discoveries may reveal about their original owners.

DISCOVERY: A child's doll, recovered completely intact

MYSTERY: Most items that are disposed of in an outhouse have clearly been thrown away—they were garbage. It's unlikely that a 19th-century family would have thrown away even an unbroken doll. And yet it's not unusual to find perfectly intact dolls at the bottom of an outhouse. What are they doing down there?

THEORY: They ended up there by accident. "Lots of times, I think, little girls went to the bathroom and accidentally dropped their doll down there," says Michigan privy digger John Ozoga. "Dad wouldn't go get it."

DISCOVERY: A wide variety of items recovered from a "two-holer" (an outhouse with two holes to sit on instead of just one)

MYSTERY: Underneath one of the holes were perfume bottles, pieces of china, and containers of Ruby Foam tooth powder. Underneath the other hole: "I just found beer bottles piled up," Ozoga says. Why the difference?

THEORY: Two-holers, like modern public restrooms, were segregated according to sex. One side—in this case the side with the perfume bottles, china, and tooth powder—was for females; and the side with all the beer bottles was for males. Such a find may also provide insight into the family's attitude toward alcohol consumption: the outhouse was the only place where the men could enjoy a beer in peace.

DISCOVERY: Three bottles of Wilkerson's Teething Syrup, recovered from an outhouse in St. Charles, Missouri. (Teething syrup was used to help relieve a baby's teething pain.)

MYSTERY: What's remarkable about these bottles, privy diggers say, is that they are *never* found alone. "If you see one bottle in a privy hole, you'll see a lot of them," says privy digger David Beeler. Why?

THEORY: The syrup's active ingredient is opium, which is highly addictive. Babies who were given the syrup soon got hooked on the stuff, which meant that "parents had to keep on buying it to keep them from crying," Beeler explains.

DISCOVERY: Bottles, tin cans, and other brand-name items recovered from a 19th-century outhouse on Franklin Street in downtown Annapolis, Maryland. In the 19th century, that area was part of the African-American community.

MYSTERY: A surprisingly high percentage of the items recovered were national brands instead of local products. These findings correspond to other excavations of outhouses in the area, which suggests that African Americans used more national brands and fewer local brands than did white communities. Why?

THEORY: Anthropology professor Mark P. Leone, who directed the excavation, speculates that African Americans preferred national brands because the prices were set at the national level instead of by neighborhood grocers. By purchasing these brands, "they could avoid racism at the local grocery store, where shopkeepers might inflate prices or sell them substandard goods," he explains.

DISCOVERY: A "multitude" of Lydia Pinkham brand patent-medicine bottles, plus an entire set of gold-trimmed china dishes

MYSTERY: These items were recovered from an outhouse behind the 19th-century home of a wealthy Michigan family that was

---

Cold-blooded fact: It takes 35–60 minks to make a single coat.

excavated by John Ozoga in the 1990s. The bottles were clustered in a single layer, and the china dishes were found right on top of them. Why?

THEORY: The wife had fallen ill at a young age and died. Ozoga speculates that she was treated with the patent medicine. When she died, the family emptied the house of her belongings—including the entire set of china, which they threw down the hole in the outhouse—to avoid catching whatever it was that killed her.

* * *

WORDPLAY

How confusing is English to learn? Try on these sentences for size.

1. We have to **polish** the **Polish** furniture.

2. How can he **lead** if he can't get the **lead** out?

3. A skilled farmer sure can **produce** a lot of **produce**.

4. The dump was so full it had to **refuse refuse**.

5. The soldier decided to **desert** his **dessert** in the **desert**.

6. No time like the **present** to **present** the **present**.

7. A small-mouthed **bass** was painted on the big **bass** drum.

8. The white **dove dove** down into Dover.

9. I spent all of last **evening evening** out the pile.

10. That poor **invalid**, his insurance is **invalid**.

11. The bandage was **wound** around the **wound**.

12. They were much too **close** to the door to **close** it.

13. That buck sure **does** some odd things around the **does**.

14. The absent-minded **sewer** fell down into the **sewer**.

15. You **sow**! You'll reap what you **sow**!

16. The **wind** was way too strong to **wind** the sail.

17. After a **number** of injections, my jaw finally got **number**.

18. If you don't **object** to the **object**, I would like to **subject** the **subject** to a series of subjective objectives.

Worldwide, Christmas has been celebrated on 135 different days of the year.

INTREPID: MASTER SPY

Ever heard of William Stephenson? He was an inventor, industrialist, and the father of modern espionage. And if it hadn't been for him, the Germans might have won World War II. Here's the story of one of the most important—and least-known—men of the 20th century.

INTERNATIONAL MAN OF MYSTERY

Although he's not a household name, historians call William Stephenson the "single most important man in the war to defeat Hitler's Third Reich."

But he was reclusive. Never one to seek the public eye, Stephenson preferred to remain behind the scenes and let others take the glory. For this reason, many of the details of his life remain shrouded, and history books tend to contradict each other about his role. The following are factual (probably), agreed-upon (mostly) accounts of his life and work.

Early years. On January 11, 1896, William Samuel Clouston Stanger (changed to Stephenson a few years later) was born in the bleak prairie town of Winnipeg, Manitoba. From an early age, it was apparent to all around him that he was no ordinary child. He taught himself Morse code, commercial cryptography (the system of sending coded telegrams), and demonstrated a photographic memory. Stephenson's school principal described him as a boy with a "strong sense of duty and high powers of concentration."

THE FIRST WORLD WAR

In August 1914, following the outbreak of World War I, that sense of duty prompted him to enlist with the Royal Canadian Engineers, who shipped him off to France. There, Stephenson was injured in a gas attack, and sent to England as an invalid labeled "disabled for life." But within a year he recovered and, although unfit to return to the trenches, he was equally unwilling to settle for a desk job.

So Stephenson joined the Royal Flying Corps, returned to France, and became one of World War I's most decorated fighter pilots, shooting down 26 enemy planes.

In 1918 Sergeant Stephenson's luck seemingly ran out when he

Better bring a map: There are 412 doors in the White House.

was accidentally shot down by his own side in hostile territory. He was captured and sent to Holzminden Camp in Germany. But instead of letting imprisonment break him, the opportunistic young man turned it into a business venture: he stole items from the guards and traded them to other POWs in return for favors.

One of the items Stephenson lifted was a hand-held can opener. After determining that it had only been patented in Germany, Austria, and Turkey, he escaped from the prison camp—with the can opener—and by 1919 was back home in Winnipeg, where he patented the can opener, calling it Kleen Kut. The twin-handled, clamp-style manual can opener is still in use today.

In 1922 he invented a device that improved the way photographs were sent over telephone lines (this device would later lead to the invention of television). Stephenson patented the wireless photography process and became a millionaire before he was 30.

THE MAKING OF A SPY

Although he never planned to work in military intelligence, all of Stephenson's experiences pushed him in that direction. While teaching math and science at the University of Manitoba in the early 1920s, he was approached by a top-ranking British officer and invited to head up a team of cryptanalysts—people who analyze codes. Stephenson immediately left for England.

During his 19-year stay, he became friends with many powerful and influential people, including the authors George Bernard Shaw and H. G. Wells, the nabob of Bhopal, the Aga Khan, and actress Greta Garbo. But Stephenson's most important friendship was with Winston Churchill, a Conservative member of Parliament who was not in the good graces of the ruling Labour Party. Churchill and Stephenson shared an interest in technology and espionage; and both feared the rise of Nazi Germany.

CHATTING WITH THE ENEMY

Stephenson's first dealings with the Nazis came in 1934 when an aircraft built by a company in which Stephenson was an investor, General Aircraft, won the King's Cup air race, the premier flying event of the 1930s. The plane caught the attention of some German military officials, who started a dialogue with Stephenson. To the Germans, Stephenson was nothing more than a rich private citizen (he owned a cement company, a steel manufacturing plant, a movie studio, and real estate). But Stephenson took the opportunity to listen in on the Nazis.

What he learned terrified him: the Germans, with Chancellor Adolf Hitler in charge, were building military aircraft at an alarming rate—positioning themselves for something big... really big. Stephenson reported his findings to Churchill, who in turn reported them to British prime minister Neville Chamberlain. The warnings were ignored at first, but when Stephenson's claims were later verified, England began to prepare for war. Those reports also put Churchill back in the favor of Parliament, paving the way for his historic reign as prime minister.

And always forward-thinking, Stephenson made a bold recommendation, one that would have changed history but was rejected by the British foreign secretary, Lord Halifax. He proposed that British agents assassinate Hitler while they still had the chance. Halifax didn't see what Stephenson saw—he preferred to take a diplomatic approach.

THE SECOND WORLD WAR

As predicted, Germany invaded Poland in 1939. Churchill was elected prime minister the following year, and one of his first acts was to appoint Stephenson station chief for the British Secret Service (SIS) in New York City. Why New York? Because in 1940, that's where Stephenson saw the greatest need. Britain's ambassador had reported that 9 out of every 10 Americans were determined to keep the United States out of the war. The Britons needed the Americans, so Stephenson used covert tactics to change their minds.

• He furnished the media with news bulletins and prepared scripts that spoke of Hitler's brutality.

• He worked to break up the American isolationist groups that had been growing in numbers since the first world war. One such group, led by Senator Gerald Nye, held a rally in Boston in September 1941. Thousands of pamphlets created by Stephenson's organization were handed out, accusing Nye of being a German sympathizer.

• After a speech by another isolationist, Congressman Hamilton Fish, Fish received a card that said, "Der Führer thanks you for your loyalty," and was secretly photographed while holding it. The photographs were then handed out to his supporters.

- An isolationist rally was to be held at Madison Square Garden, but Stephenson printed up hundreds of phony tickets with the wrong date to ensure a low turnout.

INTREPID AND CAMP X

If all that didn't change the Americans' minds, the invasion of Pearl Harbor in December 1941 surely did. With war declared, both Churchill and President Franklin Roosevelt knew that solid intelligence would be key to winning the war. To that end, they assigned Stephenson the job that he had unknowingly been preparing for his entire life: spy trainer.

Under the code name "Intrepid" and the cover "Passport Control Officer," Stephenson ran Camp X, a secret facility somewhere near Toronto, Ontario. Camp X was a top-secret training ground where operatives were taught unconventional warfare techniques: how to kill with their bare hands; make lethal weapons out of household items; and blow up industrial installations. Others were trained in lock picking, safe blowing, infiltration, explosives, listening devices, and Stephenson's favorite, codes and ciphers.

Once their training was complete, agents were flown into occupied Europe on "moon planes" (plywood aircraft painted dull black to be nearly invisible at night), to conduct sabotage and spy operations. It was a perilous assignment—many agents did not return alive. But they were able to perform some of the war's most crucial covert missions, including the murder of Reinhard Heydrich, the brutal German commander who ruled Czechoslovakia.

ENIGMA

But nothing Stephenson did was more important to the Allied war effort than his assistance in cracking the "Enigma" code, Germany's primary method of transmitting secret messages. An Enigma machine looked like an ordinary typewriter; an operator would type a message, then an internal set of rotors would translate the message into code. This code would be transmitted to another operator, who would use a corresponding Enigma machine to decipher it. Because the Nazis believed that Enigma was impossible to crack, they made widespread use of it, and Stephenson saw this reliance as their greatest weakness. Crack Enigma and the Germans would be

---

According to experts, many dinosaurs lived to be 100 years old.

helpless. When Polish agents stole an Enigma machine from a German convoy, they sent it straight to Intrepid at Camp X.

ENTER CYNTHIA

Stephenson teamed up with Elizabeth Thorpe, a beautiful agent who went by the code name "Cynthia." To crack Enigma, they needed to intercept a coded message and then see that same message after it came out of an Enigma machine. So Stephenson instructed Thorpe to seduce some high-ranking diplomats who had received messages. Through a combination of guile and feminine prowess, Thorpe acquired a set of codebooks from her unsuspecting lovers. These codebooks unlocked the secrets of Enigma and helped turn the war against Germany in favor of the Allies.

Stephenson and his agents had many other covert successes during the war, including rescuing Niels Bohr, a leading atomic researcher in German-occupied Denmark. Had the Germans gotten to Bohr, they may have had the A-bomb first. But thanks to the rescue, Bohr was able to work on the Manhattan Project and help the United States build the weapon that would end the war.

INTREPID'S LEGACY

For his efforts, Stephenson received a knighthood from the British and the Presidential Medal of Merit from the Americans (the first non-American to be given one). Ironically, he did not receive recognition from his native Canada until Prime Minister Joe Clark presented him with the Companion of the Order of Canada in 1980. Sir William died in Bermuda in 1989 at 93 years old, outside of the public eye, just the way he liked it.

But Intrepid's legacy goes even deeper. An aide to the chief of British Naval Intelligence during World War II, a young man named Ian Fleming, had the opportunity to observe Intrepid in action and was very taken with him. After the war, they became friends. While both were living in Jamaica, Stephenson would recount spy tales to his friend. That's when Fleming started writing a book about a spy called James Bond. Many of Agent 007's characteristics—his suaveness, brilliance, and slight cockiness— were lifted straight from Stephenson. In fact, Fleming described his secret agent as a "highly romanticized version of the true spy— and Bill Stephenson was the real thing."

According to criminal law: Only 3 people are necessary for a disturbance to be called a riot.

BIRTH OF THE HELICOPTER

It can fly almost anywhere in almost any kind of weather. It can hover like a bee or speed as fast as a falcon. But it took more than 2,000 years to figure out how to make it work.

A MARVELOUS TOY

The desire to fly has inspired inventors for thousands of years. Most of them designed winged aircraft that imitated the flight of birds. But a few put their energies into creating a vertical flying machine, known today as the helicopter.

The Chinese invented one around 400 B.C. It was just a stick with feathers tied to one end like a bouquet, but when the stick was spun quickly between the hands and let go, it flew up in the air. This ancient toy is the first known example of a vertical flying machine.

So where did the Chinese get the idea for their toy? Most likely from watching seeds of the maple tree flutter to the ground. The maple seed has a single leaf attached to it, which acts as a rotating wing. When the seed drops off the tree, the wind spins the leaf like a propeller, thus carrying the seed far from the tree.

INTO THE AIR, JUNIOR BIRD MEN

About 2,000 years later, in 1754, Mikhail Lomonosov of Russia launched a large, spring-powered model resembling the Chinese toy. It was reported to have "flown freely and to a high altitude." More importantly, it proved that vertical flight was truly possible. All that was needed was the right engine.

Englishman Horatio Phillips thought the steam engine might be the solution. In 1840 he built the first vertical flight machine to be powered by an engine. His model aircraft weighed in at 10 kilograms (22 pounds) but it was still a toy. He discovered that the steam engine was much too heavy to be used in a full-scale machine.

Ponton d'Amecourt of France also made some steam-powered models in the 1860s but he's remembered more for the name he gave his machines than the machines themselves. He combined the Greek word *heliko* (spiral) with *pteron* (wing) to create the word *hélicoptère*.

Travel trivia: The Duchess of Windsor took 186 trunks and 83 suitcases on her honeymoon.

GENTLEMEN, START YOUR ENGINES

When the combustion engine hit the scene in the late 1800s, piloted vertical flight became possible. The breakthrough year was 1907. In Douai, France, brothers Charles and Louis Breguet built the first helicopter to lift a person up in the air. They only got a few inches off the ground, but they were flying!

That same year another Frenchman, Paul Cornu, flew his version of the helicopter to a height of almost six feet. His double-rotored craft looked like a pair of room fans mounted horizontally at each end of a giant bicycle, with a lawnmower-sized engine behind the seat. The craft was so unstable that it had to be tethered with sticks, held by men on the ground.

SPIN DOCTORS

Torque. They had the right engine, but there were new obstacles. One was the problem of *torque*. That's the tendency of the spinning rotor to make the body of the aircraft turn in the opposite direction. Early choppers would spin up and around like insane tops. But a Russian engineer named Boris Yuriev came up with the solution in 1911. He suggested adding a vertical tail rotor off the rear of the fuselage to counter the unwanted spinning. He built one in 1912, and it worked, sort of: it didn't spin—but it didn't fly either—it lacked a powerful enough engine. Though it would need refining, Yuriev had solved the problem of torque.

Dissymetrical lift. When a helicopter is moving forward, one side of the rotating blades is advancing into the wind, and the other side is going backwards, away from the wind. The advancing side creates more lift, which caused the early helicopters to flip over during forward flight.

Spaniard Juan de la Cierva solved this problem. He was working on a helicopter-airplane hybrid called an autogyro when he came up with the concept of the "articulated blade." This blade was attached to the rotor with a flexible hinge. Called "flapping," this allowed the advancing blade to lift slightly, decreasing lift on one side, thus balancing the opposing forces. And it worked. He made his first successful flight in 1923. Ironically, the technology would be used for helicopters, and the autogyro never "took off."

At the same time great advances were being made on the *swashplate*, another very important piece of the puzzle. The swashplate

---

According to Middle Eastern tradition, the original forbidden fruit was...a banana.

was a system of adjustable rods and plates that allowed the pilot to control the angle of the blades—both simultaneously and individually. Simultaneous adjustment, called *collective control*, makes the chopper go up or down. Individual adjustment, called *cyclic control*, makes the helicopter go forward, backward, right or left. Now to put all the pieces together.

GOING THE DISTANCE

Using all the up-to-date technology, in 1924 Etienne Oehmichen became the first man to fly a helicopter and actually control it. The Frenchman flew his homemade helicopter just over half a mile. It took 7 minutes, 40 seconds to make the flight. Average speed: 4.9 mph.

Corradino d'Ascanio of Italy set helicopter world records for altitude and flight duration in 1930. He got his chopper up to 57 feet and stayed aloft for 8 minutes, 45 seconds. Six years later, a German Focke-Wulf Fw-61 was flown to an altitude of 11,243 feet and a distance of 143 miles at a speed of 76 mph, making it the world's first fully practical helicopter.

But it was visionary aircraft designer Igor Sikorsky who was most responsible for getting the helicopter accepted as a full-fledged aircraft. He perfected the design of the helicopter that we know today, with its main rotor and single–tail rotor configuration. He called it the R4, and in 1941 it became the first helicopter to be put into mass production. Later models saw heavy service in the Pacific during WWII. By war's end, the helicopter had won over all skeptics and taken its legitimate place in the aviation community.

MOST VERSATILE FLYING MACHINE

Today there are more than 40,000 helicopters in use around the world. No modern military is without them—they do everything from minesweeping to troop transport to antitank missions. Civilian applications of the helicopter are even broader. They are used for police surveillance and traffic news, and work as super taxis for the wealthy. Choppers rescue sailors from sinking ships, pluck lost hikers from the wilderness, and put out forest fires. It's estimated that since their widespread introduction in the 1940s, helicopters have helped save more than a million lives.

A female black bear can weigh 300 pounds...but her babies weigh only half a pound at birth.

CHOPPER FACTOIDS

- Three things a helicopter can do that a plane can't:
  1. Fly backward
  2. Rotate as it moves through the air
  3. Hover motionless

- It takes both hands and both feet to fly a helicopter, which makes it much more complex than flying a plane.

- The helicopter pilot has to think in three dimensions. In addition to cyclic control (forward, backward, left, and right), and collective control (up and down, and engine speed), there is rotational control (spinning in either direction on the axis).

- In 1956 Bell Aircraft Corporation introduced the HU-1. The "Huey" became the best-known symbol of the U.S. military during the Vietnam War.

- The first U.S. president to fly in a helicopter: Dwight D. Eisenhower, in 1957.

- In 1969 the Russian Mi-12 became the largest helicopter ever flown. It could lift a payload of 105,000 kilograms (231,485 pounds).

- In 1982 a Bell 206 completed the first solo crossing of the Atlantic by a helicopter.

- In 1483 Leonardo da Vinci made drawings of a fanciful craft he called a *helical air screw,* but it never got off the drawing board. His concept of "compressing" the air was similar to that used by today's helicopters. However, when a prototype was built recently at the Science Museum of London, it didn't work.

*   *   *

REAL-LIFE COURT TRANSQUIP

Prosecutor: Did he pick the dog up by the ears?

Witness: No.

Prosecutor: What was he doing with the dog's ears?

Witness: Picking them up in the air.

Prosecutor: Where was the dog at this time?

Witness: Attached to the ears.

South Florida is the only place on Earth where crocodiles and alligators coexist in the wild.

THE FRENCH FOREIGN LEGION

Generations of kids—including Uncle John—dreamed of running away to join the Foreign Legion. In its day, it was probably the second most popular runaway destination (after the circus). It's been the subject of countless books, films, and TV shows, too. Here's a look at its history.

ATTRACTING FREE RADICALS

In July 1830, revolution broke out in France and after just three days of unrest the unpopular King Charles X was overthrown and the new "Citizen King," Louis Philippe, was installed in his place. The historic event inspired revolutionaries all over Europe—free thinkers and libertarians who felt stifled by their own monarchical governments. And these admirers began to pour into France by the tens of thousands.

However flattered Louis Philippe may have been by the attention, he wasn't happy with the idea of so many foreign radicals coming into the country. The revolution of 1830 was France's second in just 41 years, and Louis Philippe didn't feel like trying for a third.

The situation in France was made even more unstable by the fact that much of the French military was in North Africa. For more than 200 years, pirates operating out of the port city of Algiers had been disrupting shipping in the Mediterranean. In 1830 the French army captured the city, which ended the piracy. But France intended to colonize the entire region, so the army was staying...indefinitely.

A CREATIVE SOLUTION

Louis Philippe devised a plan: In 1831 he created the Foreign Legion, hoping to solve both problems with one stroke. By drafting foreign-born males between the ages of 18 and 40 and sending them off to fight in North Africa, the king would clear France of foreigners and strengthen his forces in North Africa at the same time. And there was a bonus: The plan reduced the political cost of the colonial wars, because the Legion's casualties would be foreigners, not French.

"So what if 100,000 rifles fire in Africa?" Louis Philippe is reported to have said. "Europe does not hear them."

NOM DE GUERRE

What would become one of the most famous features of serving in the Foreign Legion—*anonymat,* or serving under a false identity—came about because French officials cared more about getting the rabble out of the country than it did about confirming their identities. Even if they had wanted to verify the names people gave upon enlistment, there was no real means of doing so. So the Legion just enlisted people under whatever names they gave—even when people gave their true names, they were assumed to be false.

Over time the practice of enlisting under a false name became institutionalized, not to mention one of the Foreign Legion's strongest selling points: people with shady pasts could join up and begin their lives anew.

NOBODY'S PERFECT

Getting foreign "undesirables" into the military and out of France turned out to be relatively easy. Shaping them into an effective fighting force was another matter.

More than thirty legionnaires deserted on the very first day in Algeria; the next day, the soldiers of one unit got drunk and attacked their commanding officers. Some legionnaires sold their pants and other parts of their uniform to buy alcohol, then returned to their units half naked and drunk. General René Savary, commander of the French forces in Algeria, insisted that the Legion be split into small groups and stationed in separate locations, fearing that "it would take only one drunken binge to touch off an insurrection."

Part of the problem was that officials back in France were so eager to clear the streets of foreigners that they sent *all* of them off to Algeria, even the sick and the insane. But the larger problem was that the French army did not take the Legion seriously as a fighting force. Legionnaires were given the worst and most dangerous jobs, such as draining mosquito-infested marshes, so that French casualties would be kept to a minimum.

Result: between 1831 and 1835, more than 3,200 legionnaires in

Algeria—about one out of every four—were killed or incapacitated by dysentery, typhoid, pneumonia, malaria, cholera, and other terrible diseases. That's in addition to those who died in battle.

GONE TO SPAIN

Then in 1835, Spain asked for French help in putting down a military rebellion of their own. Louis Philippe didn't really want to help, but as an ally of Spain he was obliged to do something. His thoughts soon turned to the legionnaires—he could send *them*. This led to another crafty plan: rather than *lend* the Foreign Legion to Spain (which meant that he might one day have to take it back), he *gave* it to Spain, severing all of its ties to the French army in the process.

Now the Legion was the property of Spain, which meant that if the legionnaires were defeated, Spain, not France, would lose face. Plus, France wouldn't have to go to the trouble and expense of withdrawing the troops when the battle was over. The Legion was now Spain's problem, and it treated the legionnaires even worse than France had. Worn down by hunger, neglect, disease, desertion, and a string of military defeats (plus the fact that when legionnaires finished their term of service, they were free to go home), over the next several years the Foreign Legion dwindled away to almost nothing.

THE FOREIGN LEGION, PART DEUX

That might well have been the end the Foreign Legion experiment, were it not for two factors: 1) Foreigners were still streaming into France, and 2) Louis Philippe still wanted to get rid of them. So on December 16, 1835, even as the original Foreign Legion was still limping along in Spain, the Citizen King created a *nouvelle légion* and started all over again. "The experiment," military historian Douglas Porch writes in *The Foreign Legion*, "gained a new lease on life almost as soon as it was abandoned."

The first waves of new recruits were handed over to Spain to reinforce the old Legion; then in late 1836, Louis Philippe started diverting them back to Algeria, which France had formally annexed two years earlier and was still trying to pacify.

This Legion was as unruly and unreliable as the first. In 1842 the governor-general of Algeria, General Thomas Bugeaud, complained to the minister of war, Marshal Nicolas Soult:

...the Foreign Legion will never offer a force upon which we can count....They fight badly; they march badly, they desert often. They try whenever the opportunity presents itself to sell the enemy their arms, their munitions, and their uniforms, and equipment....There is not one general officer who does not prefer to march with two of our good battalions than with five of the Foreign Legion....I seriously believe that we should cease to have such soldiers in Africa.

And yet somehow the Foreign Legion not only survived, but over the next few decades evolved into one of the most respected and feared fighting forces in Europe. How did that happen?

TURNING LEMONS INTO LEMONADE

As it turns out, the fact that the soldiers in the Foreign Legion were considered expendable by the folks back home in France proved to be instrumental in turning the Legion's fortunes around.

These "disposable" soldiers were frequently the first men sent into battle and the last withdrawn; in the process, the survivors gained more fighting experience and skill than soldiers in other French military units. They also earned a reputation for incredible toughness.

Because the Foreign Legion saw so much action, it became a magnet for the most ambitious officers in the French army. These officers wanted adventure and also hoped that by leading units in combat while other officers sat at home, they would rise more quickly through the ranks.

MOMENT OF TRUTH

Just how much the Foreign Legion changed over the years became evident during fighting in Mexico on April 30, 1863, when three officers and 62 legionnaires near the village of Camerón found themselves surrounded by more than 2,000 enemy soldiers.

The Legion had been sent to Mexico by French Emperor Napoleon III (Napoleon Bonaparte's nephew) with the ambition of setting up Archduke Maximilian of Austria as Emperor and turning the country into a French colony. (Napoleon III failed at both: Maximilian was overthrown and shot in 1867, and Mexico never did become a French colony.)

Cameron was the Foreign Legion's finest hour. Outnumbered by

Wal-Mart is the world's largest private employer. (They had over 1.2 million employees in 2002.)

more than 30 to 1, did the Legionnaires desert? Did they sell their pants and spend the money on booze? No—the 65 men took shelter in a hacienda and held off the Mexican army for nearly twelve hours, fighting until only five Legionnaires were left standing, each with only one bullet left to shoot.

Did they surrender then? No—after each man fired his last bullet, they charged the enemy with their bayonets. The fight didn't end until only three of the men were still alive, and then only when the Mexican commander agreed to let them keep their weapons and to provide medical treatment for a wounded lieutenant. More than 500 Mexican soldiers are believed to have died in the battle.

"Is this all that is left?" an astonished Mexican colonel asked when the last three were led from the hacienda. "These are not men. They are demons."

THE FOREIGN LEGION TODAY

Since its founding, the Legion has been sent all over the world, fighting in every war that involved France. They've been sent to fight in a lot of losing causes, too, yet in spite of this—or maybe *because* of it—the Legion has retained its reputation as one of the toughest fighting forces in the world.

As the number of French possessions around the globe has dwindled in modern times, so has the size of the Foreign Legion, down from more than 36,000 troops in the 1960s to around 8,000 today. What do legionnaires do? France still has a few overseas possessions here and there, including French Guiana in South America and French Polynesia in the South Pacific, and it still has military ties to some former colonies that are now independent. The Legion is sent to these areas when needed, or to hot spots around the world—Bosnia, Somalia, Rwanda, and even Iraq during the first Gulf War—whenever France participates in United Nations peacekeeping efforts.

The Legion has proven very effective in this role. The United Nations has even debated creating a similar force of rapid-reaction troops, so that it doesn't have to rely on member nations to contribute their troops when needed. Who knows? Maybe someday soon if you decide you need a fresh start in life, you'll have *two* legions to run to instead of just one.

Every year in the U.S., 7 tons of gold are used to make class rings.

JOIN THE PARTY: THE REPUBLICANS

We've already told you where the Democrats came from (see page 153). Now here's the background of the Republican Party. In a nutshell, its story is the story of the country's growing resistance to slavery, which culminated in the Civil War. (For the previous chapter on the Whigs, see page 452.)

THE GREAT DIVIDE

By the time that Zachary Taylor, a Whig, was elected president in 1848, the country was deeply divided on the issue of slavery. Slavery was the backbone of the Southern economy, and the South was convinced that the only way to preserve it was to extend it into new western territories as they were admitted to the Union. The North was just as determined to confine its evils to those states where it was already entrenched. Nobody knew how to abolish slavery entirely without starting a civil war.

FROM BAD TO WORSE

President Taylor's election only served to make matters worse. For starters, he was a plantation owner with more than 300 slaves, so even though he'd kept a low profile on the issue of slavery during the election, it was clear where he stood.

The idea of having a pro-slavery Whig president was more than many anti-slavery Whigs could take. Rather than support Taylor in the election, these "Conscience Whigs," as they became known, split off from the party and joined with the "Barnburners," an anti-slavery faction of New York Democrats. Together, they then merged with a third abolitionist party called the "Liberty Party" to form the "Free Soil Party." The Free Soil candidate for president was former president Martin Van Buren.

Taylor managed to win, anyway, thanks in large part to slavery supporters who hoped his administration would be strongly pro-slavery.

They were wrong. When California applied for admission to the Union as a free state, Taylor agreed and asked Congress to

---

In an average day, 3,000 Americans take up smoking. Most of them are kids under 18.

admit it immediately. But that created a problem: admitting California as a free state would upset the even balance of free and slave states, putting the free states in the majority.

DRAWING THE LINE

If California were admitted as a free state, it would also upset the tradition set by the Missouri Compromise of 1820, banning slavery in the new territories north of latitude 36°30', but permitting it below that line. (Missouri is above the line, but the compromise allowed it to enter the Union as a slave state.) Technically this rule only applied to territories that were part of the Louisiana Purchase, and California wasn't part of the Louisiana Purchase.

But Southerners wanted the line to apply anyway, which would have made slavery legal in southern California. They were furious when President Taylor supported the admission of the entire territory as a free state. When these so-called "diehard" Southerners threatened to secede because of it, Taylor, a retired Army general, responded by promising to personally lead the Army against any state that tried to secede.

WAR POSTPONED

California's admission never led to civil war, of course, if for no other reason than that Taylor died from indigestion barely a year into his presidency. His successor, Vice President Millard Fillmore (also a Whig), was willing to compromise. With Fillmore's encouragement, Senator Henry Clay of Kentucky pushed through Congress the Compromise of 1850, consisting of five measures:

1. A new Fugitive Slave Law got the federal government more directly involved in the capture and return of slaves who escaped into free states.

2. Buying and selling slaves was abolished within the city limits of Washington, D.C. (People in D.C. could still *own* slaves, they just couldn't buy or sell them there.)

3. California was admitted as a free state, ending the equal balance of slave and free states in the Union.

4. The territory east of California was divided into the Utah and New Mexico territories, with their final status as free or slave territories intentionally left vague. It was

still possible that either Utah or New Mexico or both might choose to become slave states, and meanwhile, both slaveholders and opponents of slavery were free to settle in these territories.

5. The border between Texas (a slave state) and Mexico was formalized.

ONE STEP FORWARD, TWO STEPS BACK

The Compromise of 1850 was intended to cool passions between the North and the South, and it worked...for a while. But as time passed, two of the five provisions in the compromise made things even worse than they already were.

The Fugitive Slave Act compelled federal marshals to assist in capturing slaves even if they opposed slavery. The marshals faced fines of up to $1,000—a lot of money in the 1850s—if they failed to do so. If a slave escaped while in their custody, *they* were liable for the full value of the slave. And for the first time, anyone who assisted a slave trying to escape could be fined and even jailed for up to six months. Fugitive slaves were denied a trial by jury and were not allowed to testify on their own behalf.

The Fugitive Slave Act was supposed to help Southern slave owners, but what it really did was turn many Northerners even more vehemently against slavery.

SQUATTER SOVEREIGNTY

But what really inflamed passions was the unresolved status of the Utah and New Mexico territories, and the admission of California as a free state on the grounds that that was what Californians wanted. Letting citizens of a territory organize themselves as they saw fit sounds reasonable enough, but "popular sovereignty," as its supporters called it (opponents called it "squatter sovereignty"), proved to be very problematic.

Popular sovereignty undermined an important premise of the Missouri Compromise, which was that *Congress*, not the people, had the power to ban slavery in the territories. If California, New Mexico, and Utah could decide for themselves, didn't that mean that *all* new territories would have that right?

THE KANSAS-NEBRASKA ACT

Tensions escalated dramatically in 1854, when Senator Stephen A. Douglas of Illinois introduced legislation opening much of what was then known as "Indian Territory" to white settlement, which had previously been banned from the region.

Called the Kansas-Nebraska Act, the legislation carved two new territories—Kansas and Nebraska—from land previously used to relocate Native American tribes that had been forcibly moved from their ancestral lands east of the Mississippi River.

Both Kansas and Nebraska were part of the Louisiana Purchase. Both were entirely above the latitude 36°30' line, and according to the Missouri Compromise that meant that slavery was outlawed. But Douglas was determined to apply the principle of popular sovereignty to the new territories, giving settlers the right to decide the slavery question for themselves.

Douglas wasn't motivated by a desire to expand slavery—he wanted to get a northern transcontinental railroad built from Chicago (in his home state) to the Pacific. Running the tracks through Nebraska made the most sense, but to do that he needed to set up a new territory, and to do *that* he needed the support of the South. They weren't about to let another free territory evolve into another free state, so Douglas appeased them by applying the principle of popular sovereignty.

THEM'S FIGHTIN' WORDS

Initially Douglas had only wanted to organize one territory—Nebraska. But Southerners had insisted on two, so Douglas proposed organizing both Nebraska and Kansas, applying the principle of popular sovereignty to both. Even that wasn't enough: Southerners in Congress wanted the language of the bill to specifically repeal the Missouri Compromise.

Douglas resisted at first, but then he and the Southerners, all Democrats, agreed to let President Franklin Pierce, also a Democrat, decide. Pierce sided with the South.

The Kansas-Nebraska Act infuriated Northerners, who for more than 30 years had viewed the 36°30' line as sacred. The act "took us by surprise," an Illinois Whig named Abraham Lincoln wrote later. "We were thunderstruck and stunned." But Douglas rammed the bill through both houses of Congress and in May 1854, Presi-

---

Theodore Roosevelt was the most prolific presidential author, having written 40 books.

dent Pierce signed it into law.

What followed in the Kansas Territory was four years of violent turmoil, as both sides of the slavery issue rushed settlers into Kansas to try to claim the territory for their side. On May 21, 1856, pro-slavery raiders sacked the town of Lawrence; three days later, a Connecticut abolitionist named John Brown retaliated and attacked some pro-slavery supporters at Pottawatomie Creek, killing five. By the end of the year more than 200 people had been killed in this mini civil war.

THE PARTY'S OVER

There were several other casualties of the Kansas-Nebraska Act. President Pierce was one of them—he became so hated that the Democrats didn't even bother to nominate him for a second term. He just served out the rest of his first term and then went home.

The Whig Party was another casualty. Already damaged by the fight over the Compromise of 1850, it collapsed completely when anti-slavery Conscience Whigs bolted the party. By the end of 1854, the party—literally—was over.

So where did the Conscience Whigs go? Many of them joined with other anti-slavery elements to form a brand-new party that made its priority the opposition to slavery in new territories. Drawing its inspiration from the Jeffersonian Republicans, the party named itself the "Republican Party."

THE ELECTION OF 1856

One other thing destroyed by the Kansas-Nebraska Act was Stephen A. Douglas's bid for the presidency in 1856. The struggle over his act had generated so much controversy that the Democrats passed on his candidacy and instead nominated former Secretary of State James Buchanan. What made Buchanan such an attractive candidate? According to historian David Herbert Donald, he "had the inestimable blessing of having been out of the country, as minister of Great Britain, during the controversy over the Kansas-Nebraska Act."

The Republicans nominated former California senator John C. Fremont as their candidate. Buchanan won, but Fremont made an impressive showing, winning 11 states.

Buzz, hiss, and *meow* are examples of *onomatopoeia*—words that mimic sounds.

GREAT SCOTT

Just two days after Buchanan was inaugurated as president, the Supreme Court handed down its infamous Dred Scott decision. Years earlier, Scott, a slave, had been taken by his owner, a U.S. Army surgeon, to live in Illinois and the Wisconsin Territory, both of which outlawed slavery. Scott sued for his freedom, arguing that living where slavery was banned had made him a free man.

The Supreme Court disagreed, finding that as a Negro, Scott was not an American citizen to begin with and thus had no right to sue in federal court. And even if he did, the chief justice argued, *any* laws excluding slavery from U.S. territories were unconstitutional, because they violated the Fifth Amendment by depriving slave owners of their property without due process of law. "The right of property in a slave," he wrote, "is distinctly and expressly affirmed in the Constitution."

Suddenly, it seemed as if every state in the Union might become a slave state.

THE FREEPORT FUMBLE

For many Americans the Dred Scott decision was the final straw. It seemed impossible that the North and the South could remain together as a country much longer. Even Abraham Lincoln observed (in a debate with Stephen A. Douglas the following year): "This government cannot endure permanently half slave and half free."

Lincoln was challenging Douglas for his seat in the U.S. Senate, and it was during the second of their seven debates that Douglas ruined his last chance to win the presidency. In Freeport, Illinois, on August 27, 1858, Lincoln challenged Douglas to reconcile popular sovereignty with the Dred Scott decision: If anti-slavery laws were unconstitutional, how were anti-slavery settlers supposed to ban slavery?

Douglas replied that if settlers refused to legislate a local "slave code" (local regulations that protected the rights of slave owners), slave owners would not bring their slaves into the territory because their property rights were not guaranteed.

Douglas's "Freeport Doctrine," as it became known, did little to appease Northerners and it cost him nearly all of his support in the South. He still managed to win the 1860 Democratic nomination for president, but Southern Democrats were so angry with him that, rather than support him, they split off from the party and nominated their own candidate, John C. Breckinridge.

AND THE WINNER IS...

Abraham Lincoln, who'd just lost the race for Senate, became the Republican nominee for president. The Republican Party was barely six years old, but slavery was such a powerful issue—and Douglas's "Freeport Doctrine" such a huge blunder—that Douglas and Breckinridge split the Democratic vote...and Lincoln, a brand-new Republican, won.

But "it was ominous," David Herbert Donald writes, "that Lincoln had received *not a single vote* in 10 of the Southern states."

Lincoln was elected president on November 6, 1860; barely a month later, South Carolina seceded from the Union, and by the time Lincoln was sworn into office on March 4, 1861, Mississippi, Florida, Alabama, Georgia, Louisiana, and Texas had also seceded. The first shots of the Civil War were just five weeks away.

With the secession of the Southern states (and all of the Southern Democrats), the Republican Party was left in full control of the federal government. As the Civil War dragged on year after year, it seemed that Lincoln's reelection was doomed and that General George McClellan, a Northern Democrat running as a peace candidate, would defeat him. But the tide of the war eventually turned in the North's favor, and in 1864 Lincoln was reelected with 55% of the popular vote. The Civil War finally ended on April 9, 1865; Lincoln was assassinated five days later.

THE RISE OF THE REPUBLICANS

Victory in the Civil War ushered in an era of Republican domination that lasted until the Great Depression of the early 1930s: of the 18 presidential elections held between 1860 and 1932, the Republicans won 14.

Born in an era of terrible crisis that threatened to destroy the Union, the Republican Party managed to save the Union and, in the process, established itself in very short order as one of the great political parties in American history.

That's how America's major political parties, the Democratic and the Republican, began. A lot has changed in the last 100 years...but that's another story. Stay tuned.

SGT. PEPPERS LONELY HEARTS CLUB BAND

"It was twenty years ago today" begins a record album that was released in 1967 and will still be celebrated many years from now. It wasn't actually the first pop concept record, its songs aren't necessarily the Beatles' best, and its supposed theme really isn't one...so why do people consider it one of the greatest albums ever made?

BACKGROUND

Fans may debate whether *Sgt. Peppers* is the best album the Beatles made, but no group, the Beatles included, ever made a more revolutionary one.

As great an achievement as *Sgt. Peppers* was, it wasn't produced in a vacuum. In the years leading up to its release, forces much broader than the Beatles themselves had been setting the stage for an industry-changing album to happen.

In fact, the artistic creativity released by the era's cultural and political turbulence was reaching boundary-busting proportions in 1966, the year that work on *Sgt. Peppers* began. Nowhere was that better reflected than in popular music. Bob Dylan's *Blonde on Blonde*, the Who's *A Quick One*, the Beach Boys' *Smile*, the Mothers of Invention's *Freak Out*, and the Rolling Stone's *Aftermath* all broke important new ground in pop music that year.

WHATEVER YOU CAN DO, I CAN DO BETTER

These landmark releases—and others of similar quality—pushed the Beatles to even greater creative heights than they'd already achieved. No musician or band in that period could stay on top by mimicking earlier successes. With each new record, pop groups in both England and America sought to up the creative ante. It wasn't just a game—it was commercial survival.

In this competitive environment, the Beatles and the Beach Boys viewed each other as the primary challengers and tried to outdo the other with each new album. The Beach Boys released *Pet Sounds* in May 1966 as their answer to the Beatles' 1965 masterpiece *Rubber Soul* (itself spurred by the music of Bob Dylan). *Pet*

Bird brains: Male cardinals take 3 times as long as females to learn a new song.

Sounds' clever songwriting and complex arrangements stunned the Beatles. Paul McCartney called it "the album of all time." But a new contender for that title was already in the can: the Beatles' *Revolver*. The new Beatles album had been completed a few weeks before *Pet Sounds'* release. It hit the record stores in August. And it was just the Beatles' opening shot across the Beach Boys' bow.

BEATLE EVOLUTION

Although cultural forces laid the groundwork for *Sgt. Peppers*, tensions and changes within the band also played a major role. As they entered the studio in November 1966 to begin recording their new album, the four group members were conflicted: exhausted and bitter on the one hand, restless to reinvent themselves on the other.

Their exhaustion came from a brutal touring schedule arranged by their manager, Brian Epstein. They were also enraged at Epstein for not protecting them from rough treatment by police in the cities they were playing. And they were frustrated artistically—the new directions they'd taken on *Revolver* couldn't be reproduced live, which forced them to fulfill their touring contracts by playing in an earlier style that, in their minds, they'd moved beyond. But that didn't matter to their live audiences, especially their female fans, who screamed too loud to hear the music anyway.

Epstein was able (barely) to hold the Beatles together by promising to end the touring. The wild enthusiasm with which fans and critics greeted *Revolver* helped prepare them for the next phase of their careers. As producer George Martin said, the Beatles "all but owned the music business at that time." The size of their audience, their almost universal critical acclaim, and their unprecedented commercial success gave them the power to do whatever they wanted in the studio. They were ready to do something great.

RECORDING THE ALBUM

Despite its legend as one of pop music's greatest "concept" albums, the making of *Sgt. Peppers* was hardly a carefully thought-out affair. Instead, the album came together in a serendipitous, almost haphazard fashion. Two of the best songs written for the new album never even appeared on it: "Strawberry Fields" and "Penny Lane."

The album had been intended to have an autobiographical

theme that would reflect the band's early lives in Liverpool. Those plans had to be trashed when manager Epstein informed the group that they were overdue for a single. So they reluctantly decided, with producer Martin's pushing, to release "Strawberry Fields" and "Penny Lane" as a single with two "A" sides. It disqualified the songs from the new album, because in England songs appearing on the singles chart couldn't also appear on an album released in the same year. The change left only one finished track, Paul's "When I'm Sixty-Four," for the album project. Martin later called the decision to yank the songs "the biggest mistake of my professional life," but it cleared the way for the record that *Sgt. Peppers* would eventually become.

THE SONGS

Side 1

• **"Sgt. Peppers Lonely Hearts Club Band."** Not only was this theme not the original concept, but the title song wasn't even written until the album was half completed. Paul, who wrote the song, came up with the idea of basing the album on the notion that the Pepper band was real. He then suggested to Martin that he use studio effects to weave all the material together around that theme. (John didn't object to Paul taking control of the project. LSD had blurred the edges of his personality, leaving him content—and maybe grateful—to let someone else take charge.)

The Sgt. Pepper persona did something else for the band: it let them step outside themselves. "One of the problems of success was that people had begun to expect so much from them," writes Steve Turner in *A Hard Day's Write*. "As Beatles they had become self-conscious, but as the Lonely Hearts Club Band they had no expectations to live up to."

• **"With a Little Help from My Friends."** Paul and John "wanted to do a Ringo type of song," remembers journalist Hunter Davies, who witnessed them writing it. "That was what they thought was missing on the album so far." Keeping with the theme of the alternate band, Ringo sang under the guise of "Billy Shears." As with some of the other songs, "Little Help" has been accused of promoting drug use. But Paul maintains that the line "I get high with a little help from my friends" means "high" in the spiritual sense.

• **"Lucy in the Sky with Diamonds."** Despite rumors to the contrary that persist to this day, it has nothing to do with LSD. The title, George Martin writes, refers to a drawing that John's then-young son Julian had brought home from school. It depicted a little girl hovering in a black sky, surrounded by stars. Julian explained, "It's Lucy, in the sky, with diamonds." (Lucy O'Donnel was his best friend in school at the time.) The song's imagery—tangerine trees, marmalade skies, and cellophane flowers—was mostly inspired by Lewis Carrol's *Through the Looking Glass*. "Surrealism to me is reality," said John. "Psychedelic vision is reality to me and always was."

• **"Getting Better."** On a 1964 tour, Ringo got sick and session drummer Jimmy Nichol subbed for five nights. After each concert, Paul and John would ask Nichol what he thought of his performance. Each time Nichol would reply, "It's getting better." They loved the phrase and laughed every time they thought of it. A real Lennon-McCartney song—Paul put down the optimistic foundation of the song: "It's getting better all the time." And John added his cynicism: "Can't get much worse."

• **"Fixing a Hole."** Yet another song believed to have been about drugs. (The "hole" was a heroin fix.) But Paul had just bought an old farmhouse, fixed it up, and penned a song about it. "If you're a junky sitting in a room and fixing a hole then that's what it will mean to you," he said. "But when I wrote it I meant if there's a crack, or the room is uncolourful, then I'll paint it."

• **"She's Leaving Home."** Paul read a news article about a 17-year-old girl named Melanie Coe who ran away from home and was inspired to write a song about her plight. McCartney was anxious to record the song soon after he finished it and called up George Martin to request an immediate orchestral score. Martin wasn't available that day because he was doing a session with another artist, Cilla Black. Impatient, McCartney went out and hired Mike Leander to do the job. He then brought in the score to record the next day. It was the only score that Martin didn't write for the Beatles in all his time working with them.

• **"Being for the Benefit of Mr. Kite."** The song is based on an 1843 circus poster that John owned. "I had all the words staring me straight in the face one day when I was looking for a song," he said. The swirling organ sounds that helped create the circus atmosphere weren't created by a professional organists but rather Martin and Lennon, who masked their inadequacies on the instrument with studio tricks, including doubling the tape speed of certain parts and slowing down others. For some bits, Martin cut the master tape up, threw the pieces on the floor, and put them randomly back together.

Side 2:

• **"Within You Without You."** George's first Beatles song about his newfound fascination with Indian mysticism, as well as his first song performed on the sitar. None of the other Beatles were present when "WYWY" was recorded.

• **"When I'm Sixty-Four."** The tune is based on a pre-WWII-style pop melody written by Paul. In their first phase as an English club band, the Beatles used to play the melody as a timekiller when a club's PA system crashed during their set.

• **"Lovely Rita."** A real meter maid named Meta claimed she was the inspiration because she once booked one "P. McCartney" for 10 shillings. When Paul saw the ticket, he told her he liked her name and asked if he could write a song about it. True? Paul says he can't remember (but he admits it makes a nice story).

• **"Good Morning, Good Morning."** John wrote this as a poke at McCartney's irony-deficient song "Good Day Sunshine" on *Revolver*. The sly humor that fills the song turns darker on the fadeout sequence—in the series of farmyard sounds, each animal that appears is a predator of the one heard before it.

• **"A Day in the Life."** Although the album's finale is generally thought of as a John Lennon song, it was a true Lennon-McCartney collaboration, unlike many of the songs credited to both men. John had found inspiration reading the morning paper: "One story was about the Guinness heir who killed himself in a car. On the next page was a story about four thousand potholes in the streets of Blackburn, Lancashire, that needed to be filled." John wrote a dreamy melody around the stories, but he needed a middle section for the song and asked Paul if he had anything he could use. McCartney wrote the "Woke up, got out of bed…" portion, a song-within-a-song, that created an appropriately abrupt transition from the dreamy opening section. The two worked together over a period of a month with George Martin to record it.

After the two parts were recorded, they decided to fill the gap

between them with a "dark, tumultuous orchestra crescendo."
George Martin tells the story:

> At the beginning of the twenty-four bars, [I wrote] the lowest pos-
> sible note for each of the 41 instruments in the orchestra. At the
> end of the twenty-four bars, I wrote the highest note. Then I put a
> squiggly line right through all twenty-four bars.

Other than that, how the orchestra got from low to high was up to
them...provided they finished on the final E chord in unison.

THE ALBUM COVER

Midway through the recording sessions, the Beatles knew they
were making a landmark record, and they wanted a cover to
match. But the most famous album jacket in the history of rock
almost never happened.

Besides the Fab Four, the cover featured life-size portraits of cultural icons the Beatles admired, as well as—for a lark—many they
didn't. The images ran the gamut from Bob Dylan to Frank Sinatra, Marlene Dietrich to Marilyn Monroe, W. C. Fields to Sonny
Liston. John wanted to add Jesus and Hitler to the mix, but Jesus
was scrapped because of the controversy John had created the year
before when he compared the Beatles' popularity to Christianity.
And Hitler was vetoed by the rest of the group.

The record company protested that the collage was a costly
logistical nightmare, because permissions would have to be
obtained from everyone pictured, and in the case of those who
were dead, from their estates. But the band insisted—the Beatles
knew they had created an unprecedented record and wanted a
cover to match. A frustrated EMI handled the details, which
involved sending hundreds of letters all over the world.

IMMEDIATE IMPACT

Sgt. Peppers Lonely Hearts Club Band made its informal public
debut from a window ledge outside the London flat of singer
"Mama" Cass Elliot. The Beatles and assistant Neil Aspinall drove
to Elliot's place at daybreak, dragged the speakers of her high-powered sound system out onto the ledge, put a tape of the album on,
and cranked the volume all the way up. According to Aspinall, not
one of the neighbors complained. In fact, several poked their heads
out of their windows and smiled their approval. Everyone recog-

nized whose music it was and were thrilled to be awakened by it.

For other musicians, though—especially ambitious ones—the music was a different kind of wake-up call. The Beach Boys' creative genius, Brian Wilson, was already showing signs of mental strain from trying to compete with *Revolver*. *Sgt. Peppers* may have added to Wilson's prodigious drug use, which just about finished him off— he soon entered a psychotic swoon that wouldn't end for decades. Another of the era's most admired songwriters, John Sebastian of the Lovin' Spoonful, recalls that *Sgt. Peppers* was "like throwing down a hat in the center of a ring…it seemed like an insurmountable task to come up with anything even in the same ballpark."

The group's nonmusician fans, of course, had no such reservations. The album was celebrated in Europe and America as if it signaled the dawning of world peace. All over the United States, rock and pop radio stations played nothing but *Sgt. Peppers* tracks for days—everything else seemed beside the point. It was endlessly written about in the press and dominated conversation, even among people not ordinarily fascinated with pop culture.

WHY IT MATTERED

Sgt. Peppers is remembered by many as pop music's first concept album, but that is neither accurate nor the core of its greatness. According to many pop experts, the first true concept album in pop music was Frank Sinatra's *In the Wee Small Hours*, released in 1955. By the standard of the Sinatra album, in fact, *Sgt. Peppers* barely even qualifies as a concept record. Yes, the song "Sgt. Peppers Lonely Hearts Club Band" and its reprise sandwich the rest of the album (except for "A Day in the Life") between them. But the other songs barely relate to that theme.

Nor is *Sgt. Peppers* even the first significant concept album in rock. Music critics variously award that title to either 1966's *Freak Out* by the Mothers of Invention or The Who's *The Who Sell Out*, which preceded *Sgt. Peppers* in 1967.

Is it the quality of its songs, then, that makes *Sgt. Peppers* a landmark album? For sheer song-by-song excellence, many Beatle fans and music experts rate *Rubber Soul*, *Revolver*, *Let It Be*, *Abbey Road*, and *The White Album* higher.

TIMING IS EVERYTHING

So what was all the *Sgt. Peppers* fuss about? For one thing, no pop group before then had so perfectly expressed the tenor of its times. It all seemed to come together on that one album—from the era's spiritual quests to its social protests to its irreverent humor. Before then, no album had ever been more famous than the songs it employed. The year 1967 was also the zenith of 1960s optimism, and *Sgt. Peppers*, which was released in May, helped spread the word and inaugurate the "Summer of Love."

Just as importantly, no one had ever employed studio effects, electronic accents, and orchestral arrangements the way the Beatles did on this album. They revolutionized the way studio records would be made ever afterward. Many bands had access to the same recording equipment, but in the Beatles' and Martin's hands, the recording studio became its own musical instrument, and the studio album was transformed into a work of art utterly distinct from music that could be played onstage. If the Beatles and Martin could be turned loose in a studio today, they might well turn out something that would make even *Sgt. Peppers* pale in comparison. But nearly four decades have passed since the Lonely Hearts Club Band first hit the airwaves, and no other record has ever equalled its impact—or advanced popular music as far.

*   *   *

DOUGH-BITUARY

Veteran Pillsbury spokesman, Pop N. Fresh, died yesterday of a severe yeast infection. He was 71. Fresh was buried in a lightly greased coffin. Many celebrities turned out to pay their respects, including Mrs. Butterworth, Hungry Jack, the California Raisins, Betty Crocker, and the Hostess Twinkies. The grave was piled high with flours, as long-time friend Aunt Jemima delivered the eulogy, describing Fresh as a man who never knew how much he was kneaded. Fresh rose quickly in show business though his later life was filled with turnovers. He was not considered a very smart cookie, wasting much of his dough on half-baked schemes. Even as a crusty old man, he was considered a roll model for millions. Fresh is survived by his wife. They have two children and one in the oven. He is also survived by his elderly father, Pop Tart. The funeral was held at 3:50 for about 20 minutes.

Q: What was the true identity of Batman's nemesis, "The Penguin"? A: Oswald Cobblepot.

ANSWER PAGES

THE SOPRANOS QUIZ
(Answers for page 159)

1. c)   2. d)   3. d)

4. b) As a young man, Sirico was arrested 28 times and served a total of seven years in prison, including a 20-month stint for felony weapons possession in 1971. According to court transcripts, Sirico made the threatening statements to the owner of the discotheque. (So was Sirico also a stick-up artist in those days? "Let's just say I made a few withdrawals," he says.)

5. c) Don't confuse it with goombah, which means "godfather" or "dear male friend."

6. a) Like a lot of native New Yorkers, Imperioli never learned how to drive. So when one of the scripts called for him to drive, he ran out and got his learner's permit. Not that it did much good: "During one take Jimmy [Gandolfini] and I were backing up from having just finished beating someone up, and I veered off and hit a tree, smashing the Lexus I was driving," he says.

7. b)

BRAINTEASERS
(Answers for page 432)

1. b) It moves forward. When the van moves forward, the *heavier* air moves to the back of the van. The helium balloon is *lighter than air*, so it is pushed forward. Give it a try!

2. Turn it upside down. It becomes 16 = 8 + 8.

3. b) The glass side goes down. Just because you're not pushing down on the cup doesn't mean you're not pushing down. How much are you pushing down? An amount equal to the weight of the water that your finger displaces.

4. b) It goes down. When the anchor is in the boat, its weight is pulling the boat down causing an equivalent weight of water to be displaced in the pool. Example: If the anchor weighs 10 pounds, it displaces 10 pounds of water. But when you drop the anchor into the pool, it displaces only an equivalent *volume* of water, not an equivalent weight. If the anchor is one quart in volume, then it will only displace one quart of water, which is less than 10 pounds of water.

5. Did you say 5,000? Sorry, that is incorrect. The correct answer is 4,100. (Read the question again…slowly and carefully.)

SAM'S BRAINTEASERS
(Answers for page 261)

1. Mr. Red is wearing white, Mr. White is wearing blue, and Mr. Blue is wearing red.

2. By continuously removing one letter from either the beginning or the end of each word, you create new words, until you are left with a single letter.

> Sheath, heath, heat, eat, at, *a*
> Pirate, irate, rate, ate, at, *a*
> Ashamed, shamed, shame, sham, ham, am, *a*
> Brandy, brand, bran, ran, an, *a*

3. Twenty hours later, the faster clock was ahead by one hour. With every passing hour, the quicker clock gained three minutes on the slower one. (3 min. per hr. x 20 hrs. = 60 min., or 1 hr.)

4. Bozo asked the store manager for a box that was four feet by three feet, which has a diagonal measurement of…five feet.

5. *Stench* is the odd word out because all of the other words can be used as both nouns and verbs. Stench can only be used as a noun.

6. You or your brother.

7. When Sir Flushalot pulled a slip of paper from the bowl, he read it, exclaimed, "I've won!" and then quickly ate the paper. The remaining piece of paper said "The Snakes," and the queen's trickery was never revealed.

NAME THAT COUNTRY
(Answers for page 75)

SAVED: El Salvador
El Salvador is Spanish for "The Saviour." The Spanish conquered

the Pipil, claimed the land, and gave it a new name in 1524.

NOTHING TO IT: Namibia

THE NAMELESS NAME: Australia
Pre-18th-century maps show a large land mass labeled *Terra Australis Incognita*, Latin for "The Unknown Southern Land." Geographers had never seen the land, but insisted that without it, the Earth would be lopsided.

OVER THERE WHERE THE SUN COMES UP: Japan
In China, *jih* means "sun," *pun* means "east," and since the sun rises in the east, *jih pun* means "sunrise." Referring to the islands east of China, it means "land of the rising sun." *Japan* derived from the Malaysian version of the Chinese name: *Japang*.

GRECIAN FORMULA: Great Britain
Pythaes sailed around this island around 300 B.C., naming it *Pretanic*, after the Pritani, or the Prits. *Pritani* is believed to be a Celtic word meaning "people with designs," because the Pritani were extensively tattooed. When the Anglo-Saxons attacked in the 400s, many Britons fled to the European continent and settled what became known as *Brittany*. To differentiate it from this "lesser" Britain, the island was thereafter called *Great Britain*.

A BIT OBTUSE?: England
After the Roman rule of Britain ended in 406 A.D., it became a battleground for many invaders. The most prominent were the Germanic tribes the Angles and the Saxons. The Angles came from a fishhook-shaped region in northern Germany called Angul (believed to be the origin of the word *angle*—to fish).

WHY DON'T THEY SPEAK GERMAN?: France
The Franks were a Germanic tribe that settled along the Rhine River in Germany during the third and fourth centuries. (Frankfurt is named after them.) They would go on to conquer nearly all of northern Europe, eventually settling in what is now France.

OVERCOATIA: Gabon
In the 15th century, Portuguese traders were the first Europeans to visit this land in Africa. They thought the Como River's estuary was shaped like a traditional hooded overcoat from their country called a *gabao*, so that's what they called it—which became *Gabon*.

HOLLYWOOD QUIZ
(Answers for page 352)

1. c) Jay Leno. "As a matter of fact, now he does live on the same street I do," Lemmon added.

2. b) It's common for newspapers to write the obituaries of elderly celebrities in advance, so that when they die the obituary is ready to go on a moment's notice. Canby had already written the obituary when he died in October 2000 at the age of 76.

3. c) "In Mexico certain insects are a delicacy," she says. "We have the crickets, and then the ants' eggs, and then we have these worms. You fry them and put them in a tortilla. And you add guacamole, otherwise they are slippery and fall off the tortilla."

4. a) Barely two months after Chaplin's death, kidnappers dug up his coffin and demanded a $600,000 ransom from the Chaplin family. While the family haggled the kidnappers down to $250,000, police traced the calls and arrested the kidnappers. Chaplin's body was recovered and re-buried…this time sealed in concrete.

5. c) "For Professor Marvel's coat, they wanted grandeur gone to seed," publicist Mary Mayer recounted years later. "So the wardrobe department went down to an old second-hand store on Main Street and bought a whole rack of coats. Frank Morgan (who played Professor Marvel and the Wizard) chose one at random." He wore it in the film, and on one hot day he turned out a pocket and saw the name "L. Frank Baum." How'd that happen? It was a complete coincidence. (Baum's widow and his tailor both identified the coat as authentic.)

*　　*　　*

BUT I'M NOT A ZOMBIE!

In Johannesburg, South Africa, in 1993 Sipho William Mdletshe was severely injured in a traffic accident and was declared dead… but he wasn't. Mdletshe, 24, spent two days interred in a metal box in a mortuary until his cries eventually convinced mortuary workers something was wrong. They opened the box and found him still alive, but it was too late—Mdletshe's life was ruined. His fiancée believed him to be a zombie who came back from the dead to haunt her…and refused to see him ever again.

…coat and two horses were shot from under him.

Uncle John's "Classic" Bathroom Readers

Here's a list of some of our most popular
Uncle John's Bathroom Reader *titles.*

Uncle John's **Ahh-Inspiring** Bathroom Reader
Copyright © 2002. 522 pages. $16.95

Uncle John's **Supremely Satisfying** Bathroom Reader
Copyright © 2001. 522 pages, $16.95

Uncle John's **All-Purpose Extra Strength** Bathroom Reader
Copyright © 2000. 504 pages, $16.95

Uncle John's **Absolutely Absorbing** Bathroom Reader
Copyright © 1999. 522 pages, $16.95

Uncle John's **Great Big** Bathroom Reader
Copyright © 1998. 468 pages, $16.95

Uncle John's **Giant 10th Anniversary** Bathroom Reader
Copyright © 1997. 504 pages, $16.95

Uncle John's **Ultimate** Bathroom Reader
Copyright © 1996. $12.95

The **Best of** Uncle John's Bathroom Reader
Our favorite articles from BRs #1 – 7.
Copyright © 1995. 522 pages, $16.95

Uncle John's **Legendary Lost** Bathroom Reader
BRs #5, #6, & #7 bound together in one big book
Copyright © 1999. 684 pages, $18.95

****

Uncle John's Bathroom Reader **For Kids Only**
Copyright © 2002. $12.95

Uncle John's **Electrifying** Bathroom Reader For Kids Only
Copyright © 2003. $12.95

To Order

Contact:
Bathroom Readers' Press
P.O. Box 1117
Ashland, OR 97520
Phone: 541-488-4642
Fax: 541-482-6159
BRorders@mind.net
www.bathroomreader.com

Shipping & Handling rates:
• 1 book: $3.50
• 2 – 3 books: $4.50
• 4 – 5 books: $5.50
• 5 + books: $1.00/book

Priority Shipping also
available.
We accept checks &
credit card orders.
Order on-line or via fax,
mail, email, or call us.

• Wholesale Distributors •
Publishers Group West (U.S.):
800-788-3123
Raincoast Books (Canada):
800-663-5714

THE LAST PAGE

FELLOW BATHROOM READERS:
The fight for good bathroom reading should never be taken loosely—we must do our duty and sit firmly for what we believe in, even while the rest of the world is taking pot shots at us.

We'll be brief: now that we've proven we're not simply a flush-in-the-pan, we invite you to take the plunge: Sit Down and Be Counted! Become a member of the Bathroom Readers' Institute. Send a self-addressed, stamped, business-sized envelope to: BRI, PO Box 1117, Ashland, Oregon 97520. You'll receive your free membership card, receive discounts when ordering directly through the BRI, and earn a permanent spot on the BRI honor roll!

If you like reading our books...
VISIT THE BRI'S WEBSITE!
www.bathroomreader.com

- Visit "The Throne Room"—a great place to read!
- Receive our irregular newsletters via email
- Submit your own articles and ideas
- Order additional *Bathroom Readers*
- Become a BRI member
  Go with the Flow...

Well, we're out of space, and when you've gotta go, you've gotta go. Tanks for all your support. Hope to hear from you soon. Meanwhile, remember:

Keep on flushin'!